LBJ'S 1968

The year 1968 was unprecedented in terms of upheaval on numerous scales: political, military, economic, social, cultural. In the United States, perhaps no one was more undone by the events of 1968 than President Lyndon Baines Johnson. Kyle Longley leads his readers on a behind-the-scenes tour of what Johnson characterized as the "year of a continuous nightmare." Longley explores how LBJ perceived the most significant events of 1968, including the Vietnam War, the assassinations of Martin Luther King, Jr. and Robert Kennedy, and the violent Democratic National Convention in Chicago. His responses to the crises were sometimes effective but often tragic, and LBJ's refusal to seek reelection underscores his recognition of the challenges facing the country in 1968. As much a biography of a single year as it is of LBJ, *LBJ's 1968* vividly captures the tumult that dominated the headlines on local and global levels.

Kyle Longley is Snell Family Dean's Distinguished Professor of History and Political Science at Arizona State University. He is the author of numerous books, including *In the Eagle's Shadow: The United States and Latin America, Senator Albert Gore, Sr.*, and *The Morenci Marines: A Tale of a Small Town and the Vietnam War.*

LBJ'S 1968

Power, Politics, and the Presidency in America's Year of Upheaval

Kyle Longley

Arizona State University

CAMBRIDGE
UNIVERSITY PRESS

CAMBRIDGE
UNIVERSITY PRESS

University Printing House, Cambridge CB2 8BS, United Kingdom

One Liberty Plaza, 20th Floor, New York, NY 10006, USA

477 Williamstown Road, Port Melbourne, VIC 3207, Australia

314–321, 3rd Floor, Plot 3, Splendor Forum, Jasola District Centre, New Delhi – 110025, India

79 Anson Road, #06–04/06, Singapore 079906

Cambridge University Press is part of the University of Cambridge.

It furthers the University's mission by disseminating knowledge in the pursuit of education, learning, and research at the highest international levels of excellence.

www.cambridge.org
Information on this title: www.cambridge.org/9781107193031
DOI: 10.1017/9781108140379

First published 2018

Printed in the United States of America by Sheridan Books, Inc.

A catalogue record for this publication is available from the British Library.

Library of Congress Cataloging-in-Publication Data
Names: Longley, Kyle, author.
Title: LBJ's 1968 : power, politics, and the presidency in America's year of upheaval / Kyle Longley, Arizona State University.
Description: Cambridge ; New York, NY : Cambridge University Press, 2017. | Includes bibliographical references and index.
Identifiers: LCCN 2017049388 | ISBN 9781107193031 (hardback : alk. paper)
Subjects: LCSH: Johnson, Lyndon B. (Lyndon Baines), 1908-1973. | United States–Politics and government–1963-1969. | Presidents–United States–Election–1968. | Presidents–United States–Biography
Classification: LCC E847 .L63 2017 | DDC 973.923092–dc23 LC record available at https://lccn.loc.gov/2017049388

ISBN 978-1-107-19303-1 Hardback

To my great friends, Bob Brigham and Laura Belmonte

Contents

List of Figures   *page* ix

Preface and Acknowledgments   xi

Introduction 1

1 A Nation on the Brink: The State of the Union Address,
   January 1968 10

2 Those Dirty Bastards, Are They Trying to Embarrass Us?
   The *Pueblo* Incident, January–December 1968 32

3 Tet: A Very Near Thing, January–March 1968 55

4 As a Result, I Will Not Seek Reelection: The March 31,
   1968 Speech 84

5 The Days the Earth Stood Still: The Assassination of
   Martin Luther King, Jr., April 1968 105

6 He Hated Him, but He Loved Him: The Assassination
   of Robert Kennedy, June 1968 137

7 The Big Stumble: The Fortas Affair,
   June–October 1968 160

8 The Tanks Are Rolling: Czechoslovakia Crushed,
   August 1968 185

9 The Perfect Disaster: The Democratic National
   Convention, August 1968 205

10 Is This Treason?: The October Surprise that Wasn't,
   October–November 1968 232

11 The Last Dance, January 1969 256

Conclusion 274

Glossary of Participants   283
Notes   287
Bibliography   333
Index   347

List of Figures

1 While preparing the State of the Union Address at the ranch in
Stonewall, the president took time out to sing with his dog, Yuki,
and entertain his grandson, Patrick Lyndon Nugent 15
2 On February 9, President Johnson, Secretary of State Dean Rusk,
and Secretary of Defense Robert McNamara gathered in the
Cabinet Room to discuss major issues, including the *Pueblo* seizure 48
3 During the tense discussions over the Tet Offensive at National
Security Council meeting in February 1968, President Johnson
and Secretary of Defense McNamara show the strain of dealing
with the crisis in Vietnam 61
4 After giving his speech to the nation on March 31, 1968
announcing his decision not to seek reelection, the president and
his daughter, Luci, watch the playback of the address 102
5 On the day of the assassination of Martin Luther King, Jr., Secretary
of Defense Clifford and a staffer react to the news of the death of
the civil rights leader 109
6 President Johnson stands with Clarence Mitchell after the signing
of the 1968 Civil Rights Act on April 11, 1968 134
7 Johnson and Justice Abe Fortas meet in the Cabinet Room in late
July 1968 to discuss the ongoing battle over his nomination to
Chief Justice of the Supreme Court 176
8 Johnson and his family join him in the bedroom to watch the
Democratic National Convention on television on August 28 229
9 President Johnson and Richard Nixon share an elevator ride in
the White House soon after the presidential election of 1968 251

LIST OF FIGURES

10 President Johnson and the first lady as they prepare for a formal
   event just after the presidential election in 1968 257
11 President Johnson walks with Lady Bird while holding his grandson
   Lyn, as they greet well-wishers at Bergstrom Air Base in Austin on
   Inauguration Day, 1969 271

Preface and Acknowledgments

This project grew out of spending a lot of time in Austin, Texas, starting when I was a young boy, as we often traveled there for sporting events. Over the years, I continued visiting Austin and Central Texas. At one point, we lived in Comfort, Texas, only a short distance away from Stonewall, Texas, where I remember often traveling by the ranch of President Lyndon Johnson on our way to Austin or surrounding towns such as Dripping Springs, where my father took football teams to play.

As I grew older, I began appreciating the history of the region, including that of a place strongly shaped by Johnson. Everywhere I turned, his legacy shone. It was on the streets, waterways (including Lake LBJ), and education, with a significant number of schools honoring him. In addition, the LBJ Library towered above the University of Texas, and the Lady Bird Wildflower Center provided a welcome refuge from urban life. Everywhere in Central Texas, LBJ's shadow loomed large, whether people understood it or not.

Ultimately, my youthful interest in LBJ intersected with my research, including a biography of Senator Albert Gore, Sr., who in many ways paralleled Johnson's rise to power. The Tennessean was raised in a small town and overcame many obstacles to rise to the Senate, just like LBJ. Johnson often appears in Gore's story, both as an antagonist and a protagonist.

Then, I spent a number of years writing two books on the experiences of combat soldiers in Vietnam. Johnson's name became synonymous with the Vietnam War and the suffering of the country and its servicemen in the quagmire that developed. Often, the soldiers criticized their commander-in-chief, who took them deep into the conflict without a solution of how to win or extricate the United States from the morass. At one point, I even reviewed the letters the president sent to the families of the young men from the small town of Morenci, Arizona, who died in the war.

As Johnson kept reappearing in my work, I also became increasingly interested in the anniversaries of the Johnson presidency, ranging from the assassination of John Kennedy to the signing of the Civil Rights Act of 1964, the Gulf of Tonkin Resolution, and the Watts Riots. Often his legacy appears in the news due to the rapid rate of change implemented by Johnson in the environment, health care, civil rights, and government economic programs during his presidency. This ultimately brought me to the idea of looking at Johnson's most trying year of 1968, when the wheels appeared to be coming off in the United States and the world. It has been a rapid whirlwind of a project, but one that I have thoroughly enjoyed researching and writing.

There are many people to thank for assisting me. George Herring, my doctoral advisor and a dean of the historians of the Vietnam War and US foreign relations, read many of the chapters in the book and provided excellent editorial advice. He remains the single most important intellectual influence in my life as well as a good friend who never anticipated the frequent phone calls and correspondence years after he sent me out into the academic world. Along with his wonderful wife, Dottie, he continues to provide significant guidance and support in all of my endeavors.

Others have devoted their time and expertise to this project. Mitch Lerner, Clay Risen, Greg Daddis, and Ken Hughes took time out of their busy schedules to review chapters, providing wonderful comments and helping me tighten the presentation. Others who lived the history, including Larry Temple, Tom Johnson, Jim Jones, and Joseph Califano, read individual chapters and provided feedback from a personal viewpoint of someone involved in policymaking. Their support was invaluable.

I also have been blessed with being a member of a wonderful community of scholars, especially in the field of US foreign relations and some colleagues in the History Department at Arizona State. I would add pages to the book if I thanked them personally, but they know who they are as we have shared many meals and drinks around Tempe and at conferences, where we discussed various projects including this one. Their research and writing also has expanded my limits of learning, helping me better understand the world and the role of the United States in it. I am blessed to have such an amazing group of scholars with whom to work, as well as a good group of students that includes wonderful undergraduates, Chiara Hommel and Kaycee Miller, who provided research support for the project.

Others have been very helpful along the way, including people working at numerous archives throughout the country. In particular, the amazing people at the Lyndon B. Johnson Library assisted me with gathering materials and have been advocates for this project, especially the outstanding archivists Allen Fisher and Brian McNerney. They spent countless hours helping me search for research materials and always updated me on potential finds. We enjoyed a number of wonderful meals together as they shared their expertise way beyond the normal hours of library operations. I also must acknowledge the wonderful Margaret Harman, who helped me track down the photographs for the book. I am happy that my next book will also be on LBJ, which will allow me to continue to work with the best people in the business.

I also want to thank a series of friends whom I have made over the past decade as I worked in the President's Enrichment Program (PEP) at Arizona State University. Again, there are too many names to mention, but they know how much I value their insights and support and the enjoyment that they bring to me in a special classroom, where they make me feel like a youngster in the room. The times spent in and out of the classroom are among the greatest benefits of being a professor.

Finally, I also owe special thanks to Dick and Alice "Dinky" Snell, who have buttressed my work with a generous fund with which to do research and attend conferences. For more than a decade they have been there for me, both as benefactors and friends. I thank them for being such good supporters, and this book has benefited significantly from their patronage.

Finally, I have many family and friends to thank for their encouragement and assistance along the way, including my parents, Joe and Chan, who have nurtured me over the past fifty-four years. They supported my passion for history, and my father especially provided me a great role model of what an educator should and could be. He also remains the toughest editor I have, but proudly brags about the work I do.

The same goes for two of my best friends; Dwayne Goetzel and his wife Dawn have been wonderful comrades, always providing someone to listen and provide words of encouragement as well as remind me of my Texas roots.

Of all my friends and family, the closest person to me remains my wife, Maria. The daughter of an academic, she knew the drill when we married. She has carried a heavy burden during the endless hours of my disappearances to research and write, including long trips to the archives and conferences. She also endured my constant talking about LBJ and provided encouragement during the times when roadblocks sometimes developed. She does all of this while working a job helping homeless families in the East Valley. Often people ask how I am so productive, and I respond that it is largely because of her.

Maria also provided coverage for me, as I had to take time away from my two sons, Sean who is seventeen and Drew who is twelve. Both are the truest pleasures of my life, and they have watched me sit at the computer working away for hours. But they also drew me away from work to be their coach in track and football, helping me destress and get out of the office and into the beautiful sunshine of Arizona.

One of the greatest joys over the past year or so has been Sean often asking me questions about the 1960s, Vietnam War, civil rights, and other topics that he learned about in his world and American history classes. He is a remarkably smart and gifted child who inspires his father to better explain to him and others the importance of understanding our common history.

Along with Sean, Drew proved my best distraction from the work. He is one of the most loveable kids in the world, who could easily pull me away to play, now even teaching me about lacrosse and how to use the stick. In the end, this was a group project, with Maria providing the emotional support and the boys the needed diversions away from very heavy topics. I truly love them.

In addition, I want to recognize the role of the people at Cambridge University Press. I have been blessed along the way with many excellent editors, but none surpass the excellence of Debbie Gershenowitz. She was in many ways as passionate about my project as I was, always maintaining her own special interest in the 1960s dating back to her days in doctoral studies. Both as an editor and a comrade, she remains someone who has pushed me to produce the best manuscript possible.

I also need to thank the production staff, led by Kristina Deusch, which put in many hours in copyediting, gathering and editing photos, and many other tasks. Others, including Sindhujaa Ayyappan, Joshua Penney, Kevin Hughes, and Robert Swanson, also made substantial contributions to the project. The Press has been very supportive of this book, and I truly appreciate it.

In conclusion, I want to highlight that I dedicate this book to two of my best friends in the world: Bob Brigham and Laura Belmonte.

Bob and his wonderful wife, Monica, remain friends I very much look forward to seeing when I can. We started graduate school at the University of Kentucky in the late 1980s. Bob and I were inseparable, despite being the strange mix of a Bostonian and a West Texan. We enjoyed taking classes together and team teaching, but especially playing softball and basketball against the faculty. Even when he went to Vassar and I to Arizona State, we remained close, even taking family vacations together. To this day, we spend most of our time at conferences together, always living up the good ole days while lamenting our teenagers and paying for college.

On the other hand, Laura is my sister from another mother. We have been friends for years now, and I have greatly enjoyed the time spent with Laura and her wonderful partner, Susie, at their home in Tulsa and at other events. We share a love of teaching and the students as well as research interests, but also a sense of justice in the world. She remains my sounding board for many of the challenges of the academic world, including being an administrator. However, what I most enjoy are our long walks and bike rides at conferences as we catch up on the world and plot the future. Her coming into my life has been such a blessing, and I look forward to many years together.

Introduction

I n mid-December 1967, a new year appeared on the horizon. Many Americans, including President Lyndon Johnson, hoped for a better year with fewer riots and antiwar protests as well as a possible breakthrough to end the quagmire in Vietnam. However, none anticipated society worsening, but it did. Little could have prepared Americans for what would happen as the nightmare year of 1968 loomed, which would test the country and world, including the leader of the most powerful nation on earth.

As many prepared for Christmas and New Year celebrations, at 11:35 a.m. on December 17, 1967, President Johnson called his personal pilot, Air Force Brigadier General James Cross, after learning about the drowning death of Australian Prime Minister Harold Holt.

"Cross," the president said, "we may want to go to Australia tomorrow. You better get my big plane out and make sure it's ready to go."

The experienced pilot panicked, admitting his "heart rate shot up" as the intercontinental version of the Boeing 707 lay in pieces at a hangar at JFK Airport in New York.

"Mr. President," Cross replied, "you'll recall, sir, that I sent you a note two weeks ago that the big plane is in the Lockheed Air Service contract facility in New York and it won't be ready for forty-five days."

Immediately, Johnson responded: "Well, go up there, get it fixed and get it back down here. We plan to leave tomorrow."

Cross protested vigorously and the president finally agreed to take one of the backup 707s, although he complained: "Now, I don't like those planes. They don't have good sound-proofing and I don't like the seats and they don't have a bed in them like I'm used to."

Then, he added, "you Air Force people always seem to be able to find some way to make me feel uncomfortable."[1]

Two days later, the plane lifted off for the long trip across the Pacific, first stopping in Hawaii and Pago Pago, American Samoa, before landing in Canberra. While honoring his faithful ally, Johnson spent significant time meeting with President Nguyen Van Thieu of South Vietnam and President Park Chung-hee of South Korea, whose nearly 50,000 troops in Vietnam constituted the largest non-US and Army of the Republic of Vietnam (ARVN) forces.

After attending the funeral, Air Force One headed to a US F-105 fighter/bomber base in Thailand before landing at the large base at Cam Ranh Bay, South Vietnam. Thousands of US servicemen greeted the president, who handed out medals to soldiers, some removed from the jungles for the ceremony.

He gave a short speech to selected officers highlighting an enemy hoping to outlast the Americans and break their will, "but we're not going to yield. And we're not going to shimmy."[2] Then, Johnson told the large group of assembled troops that America "had come from the valleys and the depths of despondency to the heights and the cliffs, where we know now that the enemy can never win."[3]

Then, once more, he jumped on the plane for a long ride first to Karachi, Pakistan, to meet Prime Minister Ayub Khan before jetting to Rome to talk with Pope Paul VI, a consultation facilitated by his former aide, Jack Valenti.

On arriving, Johnson outlined his views on the war, to which the pope emphasized: "We must declare our position to the world as friends of peace and foes of war." But, quickly he added: "Could I be an intermediary for you and say what I know to be true, that the U.S. truly wants peace?"

The response pleased the president, who hoped the pope might influence President Thieu, a Catholic, to move toward negotiations. He talked about how people in Texas liked to have stickers on their Fords, "Made in Texas by Texans." "I would like a slogan in Saigon that says, 'Peace in South Vietnam made by the Vietnamese,'" Johnson remarked.

They ultimately agreed to a joint statement about their discussion. The pope objected to a line "we will never surrender South Vietnam to aggression or attack," afraid it would appear he endorsed the war. The president struck it and left pleased with the outcome. He immediately boarded the plane for the final leg home, reaching the ranch on Christmas Eve.

In less than five days, the president flew more than 28,210 miles and spent 59 ½ hours in the sky and a total of 112 hours away from the White House.

Lady Bird Johnson observed when he arrived home on December 24, "Lyndon was riding high ... he hoped by his presence in Vietnam to give evidence of his special feeling as Commander-in-Chief for those troops, and he had made one further effort toward peace by meeting with the Pope."[4]

But, while feeling good about the trip, the president and his family had experienced a tough year in 1967. In many cases, Vietnam lay at the heart of most problems plaguing the administration. Across the country, people marched in the streets and some picketed outside the White House chanting: "Hey, Hey, LBJ, how many children did you kill today?"

Nothing frustrated Johnson more than Vietnam. Early on, he lamented, "I feel like a hitchhiker on a Texas highway in the middle of a hailstorm; I can't run, I can't hide, and I can't make it go away."[5]

People around him recognized the toll it extracted. Undersecretary of State Nicholas Katzenbach lamented, "Vietnam, Vietnam, Vietnam – It got in the way of everything."[6] Jack Valenti stressed "it was the Vietnam War that cut the arteries of the LBJ Administration."[7]

Even those outside his inner circle recognized the strain. Senator George McGovern (D-SD) left a dinner party at the White House in late 1967 and described LBJ as "a tortured and confused man – literally tortured by the mess he has gotten into in Vietnam. He is restless, almost like a caged animal."[8]

But, he would not retreat, and it caused horrific outbursts. In a private meeting, reporters pestered Johnson to explain the US involvement in Vietnam. A shocked US Ambassador to the United Nations, Arthur Goldberg, watched as "LBJ unzipped his fly, drew out his substantial organ, and declared, 'This is why!'"[9]

Vietnam alienated important sectors of society and widened the chasm between Johnson and his chief political rival, Robert Kennedy.

Journalist William White wrote in December 1966: "President Johnson has had to bear a frightful burden in the unremitting hostility of the Kennedy cult and its common attitude that the man in the White House is not simply a constitutional successor to another man slain in memorable tragedy but only a crude usurper."[10]

It was a mutual contempt. LBJ often used the term "that boy" that became according to one reporter, "Johnson's unloving *nom de guerre* for Robert F. Kennedy."[11] The White House kept files on Bobby's public appearances, including speeches, press releases, and television shows going back to 1964.[12]

The war also led to a significant break between Johnson and Martin Luther King, Jr., who increasingly denounced the war by 1967. Since the Voting Rights Act in 1965, Johnson and King had sought new dragons to slay in the struggle for civil rights, but neither achieved much success as King shifted to economic issues and Johnson focused on fair housing.

However, the summer of 1967 exposed continuing frustrations with unfulfilled expectations after the major civil rights victories. In July, race riots broke out in Newark and Detroit. In the Motor City, police raided an African American club, which provoked a confrontation that led to rioting and looting. Governor George Romney ordered in the National Guard, which one journalist characterized as a "ragged, jittery, hair-triggered lot," in which one soldier emphasized: "I'm gonna shoot anything that moves and is black."[13]

The police and guard proved incapable of stopping (or even containing) the violence. Finally, President Johnson dispatched federal troops, lamenting: "Well, I guess it is just a matter of minutes before federal troops start shooting women and children." For three days, troops patrolled at bayonet point. In the aftermath, forty-three people lay dead, with more than 2,000 injured, 4,000 in police custody, and millions of dollars of damage.[14]

Throughout, the president and his advisors endured criticisms from both parties. The Republican Coordinating Committee stated "widespread rioting and violent civil righters have grown to a national crisis since the present Administration took office." Some Democrats agreed, including his old mentor Richard Russell of Georgia, who charged that Johnson's War on Poverty stoked the flames.[15]

Vietnam and race relations, along with crime, dominated the president's agenda in 1967, but many other challenges existed in the balance of payments, rising deficits, and foreign relations during the perplexing year. It was an extremely difficult year.

But nothing, absolutely nothing, could have prepared Johnson and his countrymen for what lay on the horizon as the New Year rang in only a week after he returned from his round-the-world trip.

LBJ ultimately underscored about 1968: "I recall vividly the frustration and genuine anguish I experienced so often during the final year of my administration. I sometimes felt that I was living in a continuous nightmare."[16]

Many around the president concurred, including Secretary of Defense Clark Clifford. He remembered that his long-time secretary, Mary Weiler, told him: "That was a year that lasted five years. I thought it was going to kill you." Clifford acknowledged: "It was the most difficult year of my life, a year of partial success and ultimate frustration."[17]

Many others recognized 1968 and the challenges. A few months into the year, journalist Richard Rovere wrote in *Atlantic Monthly*: "Never in our history has the individual seemed as wretched and despairing as he is today; and seldom have free men anywhere felt so thwarted and powerless in their relations to government democratically chosen ... Never have disaffection, alienation, and frustration been more widespread."[18]

The polls supported Rovere's portrayal. By December 1968, one found that 28 percent of Americans were "substantially alienated" from the mainstream.[19] Such numbers led pollster George Gallup to conclude in, "all the time we've been operating, thirty-two years now, I've never known a time like this – when people are so disillusioned and cynical."[20]

By the end of the year, the country appeared in disarray, worn out by constant crises. While some found hope in the election of Richard Nixon, most people gladly ushered 1968 out at 11:59 p.m. on December 31. Few years in American history would be so tumultuous and disorienting and few that experienced it wanted it replicated, including the president.

This book reviews a series of crises and challenges in 1968 primarily through the eyes of Lyndon Johnson, one of the most powerful persons on earth. There have been excellent works written on the nightmare year by others, including journalist Jules Witcover and historian David Farber, but they cover a large swath of the year from many perspectives.[21] This work instead extensively focuses on one individual whose position provides particular insights into the turbulent year.

In a way, the book is also a microbiography of Lyndon Johnson, focusing on one critical year as opposed to a lifetime. There are excellent biographies by historians including Randall Woods, Robert Caro, and Robert Dallek on the president.[22] However, they cover many years and sometimes cannot give more than a little attention to his crisis management skills covered in detail in this book, like the Czech Intervention or Chennault Affair.

Finally, at the other extreme are specialized books by authors such as Mitch Lerner and Clay Risen that dive deeply into individual subjects covered in this monograph, such as the *Pueblo* Affair or the turmoil following the assassination of Martin Luther King, Jr.[23] In these accounts, President Johnson often disappears for long periods of time as the authors focus on other actors and contexts.

Ultimately, this book looks at 1968 through the eyes of Johnson and those closest to him, especially Lady Bird and the president's staff and cabinet to show how he managed the ghastly year. The coverage is not comprehensive, as it only touches tangentially on other important events such as the Poor People's March, but it establishes the patterns of how President Johnson dealt with the many challenges that arose that year.

The opening introductory chapters of this book move from the January 1968 State of the Union through the historic March 31 speech when Johnson announced his decision not to seek reelection. In between, it highlights the global challenges of the seizure of the intelligence ship *Pueblo* by the North Koreans and subsequent hostage crisis that plagued LBJ throughout the year. It also focuses on the First Tet Offensive and its aftermath (late January–March 1968), diving deeply into how Vietnam fundamentally shaped his world and led to his isolation and frustration that culminated in his stunning speech on March 1968.

The second part, on the tragedies of the political violence of the year, looks at the challenges of dealing with the assassinations of MLK and RFK in April and June. For many, the death of the two icons, both of whom by that point had contentious relationships with LBJ, caused much disillusionment with the Great Society and America. It also highlighted the obstacles that remained to building off the successes of 1964 and 1965 regarding civil rights. The deaths opened old wounds and created new ones for a country already reeling from widespread protests regarding Vietnam.

The third section focuses on limits of presidential power in 1968 by looking at the Warsaw Pact invasion of Czechoslovakia in August that highlighted how the only weapons readily available to Johnson were rhetorical, not substantive. The nomination of Abe Fortas as Chief Justice and Homer Thornberry to the Supreme Court further underscored the diminution of LBJ's powers over Congress since the heady days of early in his presidency when he rammed through landmark legislation. The Chicago Democratic Convention also demonstrated how his power within his party had declined precipitously since 1964, something caused by his unending intransigence on Vietnam and unwillingness to surrender control of the party.

Finally, the book's concluding section traces the period of the presidential election through the transition of power in January 1969. In many ways, the Chennault Affair highlighted many elements of Johnson's personality in dealing with his own vice president, Hubert Humphrey, and the Republican nominee Richard Nixon. It, along with his last day in office, shows just how tired he appeared of the political battles and his desire to retreat into private life after an exhausting five years. By the end of 1968, Johnson, like much of the country, wanted to simply push a restart button, but conditions prevented it.

What emerge from the narrative are several trends regarding Johnson in the turbulent year of 1968. A series of crises dominated the year, and if one was keeping score in the most general senses, LBJ handled them very well. In fact, his closest domestic advisor, Joe Califano, stressed Johnson encountered challenges that would have made other presidents wilt under the pressure.[24]

Many around Johnson recognized an underlying strength in being able to remain calm under pressure. Lady Bird often said so. For example, while flying on Air Force One to the capitol from Dallas on November 22, 1963, reporter Liz Carpenter sat in his seat and thanked God that "someone is in charge." Lady Bird approached her and told her, "Lyndon's a good man to have in an emergency."[25]

7

Johnson showed a skill at managing the crisis with patience and restraint when it would have been easy to overreact to the provocations of foreign countries or domestic rioters. He took time to weigh all the scenarios and to make decisions that limited escalation and reduced peripheral damage.

Beyond showing fortitude, he also demonstrated a political acumen for often creating something positive from the tragic. Sometimes it worked. It would be replicated a number of times, such as the passage of the Fair Housing Act after the assassination of MLK. Sometimes it failed or only had limited success. He tried to do the same after RFK's assassination on gun control, but he only achieved partial success.

Beyond crisis management, the book also underscores the centrality of the Vietnam War in the daily affairs of the president as he sought to salvage his legacy in 1968. It caused isolation and resentment, as he refused to acknowledge the mistakes of the past. After Tet, he tried desperately that year to extricate the United States with honor from Southeast Asia. However, Johnson failed because of his inflexibility and unwillingness to accept the shortcomings of his previous efforts, recalcitrant allies, and underhanded tactics by political opponents.

Johnson entered 1968 weakened by the divisive conflict in Vietnam and other factors, including the counterculture movement and race relations. Ultimately, the book shows the full extent of the diminution of power of arguably one of the most influential presidents in US history. After two years in office, only FDR surpassed LBJ in passing his legislative agenda. In 1965, US military forces remained formidable and respected for their prowess, and Americans projected significant economic and cultural power around the world.

However, as the chapters also show, in domestic politics and foreign policy by 1968 the president often failed to shape the world around him. At home, Johnson found himself increasingly swimming against a conservative tide of backlash created by civil rights, free speech, and the war in Vietnam. What followed were stinging defeats in politics, including federal taxes, nominations to the Supreme Court, and gun control. In foreign affairs, events unfolding in Pyongyang, Prague, Moscow, and Saigon underscored the limits of American power, particularly those of the president to sway the outcomes of events unfolding across the globe.

8

Finally, the narrative highlights a complex and complicated man who in 1968 often displayed that he could be magnanimous and sympathetic, even toward those such as the family of his worst enemy or those rioting in the streets. But, then, he could turn on his loyal vice president in a fit of rage over the Vietnam plank. His pettiness often shone through, as well as his stubborn refusal to acknowledge a mistake or flawed policy such as the decisions in Vietnam. It was a trying year and the challenges amplified these traits, both the good and the bad.

In the end, *Time* proclaimed 1968 as: "One damn thing after another, indeed, also one tragic, surprising and perplexing thing after another … events have moved at the pace of an avant-garde movie edited by mad clutter."[26] They were correct and Johnson had a front row seat to the entire drama that he desperately tried to manage under pressures endured by few American presidents.

CHAPTER 1

A Nation on the Brink

The State of the Union Address, January 1968

L ady Bird Johnson woke on Wednesday, January 17 and wrote: "The day of the State of the Union address is always one of such tenseness for me, out of proportion to any responsibility that I have for it."[1]

LBJ began his day a little later than his wife after staying in the White House theater until after midnight with his aides, including Joe Califano, George Christian, Jim Jones, and Harry McPherson, editing the draft of the State of the Union once more.

The president recognized its importance in an election year, as did others. His long-time confidant, Horace Busby, observed: "Whatever he might say, the president's words would be taken as the opening of his campaign for reelection." He added: "Critics, inside and outside Congress, would be attuned to every nuance, listening for false notes that might betray hesitancy, uncertainty, or weakness; listening especially for subtle signals which might reveal a telling unease about their criticisms."[2]

For Busby, the speech also allowed LBJ to silence critics, including senators Eugene McCarthy (D-WI) and Robert Kennedy (D-NY). "If the Lyndon Johnson who appeared on the nation's television screens at midweek was a confident leader, strengthened rather than crippled by the besieging of his presidency, that would be enough." But LBJ's "image as an all-but-invincible politician held more sway over his enemies than over his friends; only an intimation of invulnerability would silence the baying at his heels and turn cautious men of politics to thoughts of 1972."[3]

The president also understood the speech's significance in an election year. As many times previously, he began the process by seeking feedback from multiple sources while having a fundamental idea of what he wanted. Unlike his successor, Richard Nixon, he had a more open approach on some processes that extended beyond his inner circle. Johnson often valued outside opinions, including those from elites in the country's universities and think tanks. While increasingly isolated by Vietnam, Johnson nonetheless wanted some input, hoping to find some new ideas that would further his vision of a better America.

So, LBJ dispatched Califano to meet with academic leaders at prestigious institutions across the country to discuss major issues ranging from foreign policy to resource management. He brought back plenty of suggestions, many related to ending the war in Vietnam.[4]

By May, Califano asked cabinet officers and agency heads for ideas, compiling a large black loose-leaf book of proposals. In late July, Califano reviewed it page by page with the president, who gave one of three responses: fully support; ignore it; or indifference. After that, Califano continued briefing through personal meetings or memorandum in LBJ's nighttime reading, a process that continued into the fall.[5]

As information streamed in, by early December LBJ began outlining his speech. He scribbled some notes about wanting to meet "fundamental national problems" and address middle class concerns of "air pollution, transportation" while focusing on the disadvantaged with "education/health." He wrote: "We can't do it all at once but we have to keep moving toward our goals."

Crime received particular attention, and early on Johnson announced he wanted to "put the Repubs on defensive" by stressing Safe Streets.[6] He fought a losing battle in 1967 on his anticrime bill that called for strong gun control measures and restrictions on electronic eavesdropping. Now, he wanted victories and added anti-riot programs to attract conservatives.[7]

The laundry list of proposals paled in comparison to those from the early Johnson presidency. LBJ and his staff were nearly five years into their tenure, and they had won many victories on civil rights and health care. At this point, they fought to sustain momentum in the face of increasing conservative opposition. The Vietnam War also drained a significant amount of energy as well as resources. In 1968, the country appeared more interested in stopping rioting and crime than expanding the Great Society and its focus on reducing poverty and racism. Thus, an increasingly tired LBJ and his aides struggled to find traction for bold initiatives, something that frustrated the president.

Finally, in late December 1967 at the ranch, Califano presented a series of large charts with dots placed on them. A red dot indicated administrative action needed, while a blue one required legislation. Finally, at the top was a short quotation for the speech giving the philosophy or broad goal. Much haggling followed, with the president making the final determination on priorities and language. Califano returned to Washington to talk with different people, going back and forth four times to hammer out details.

Then, Califano developed one-page summaries, with Johnson deciding whether to include or not. The chief domestic advisor described the process as "essentially like an accordion ... with reports coming in and the accordion has been opened and you squeeze it all down and close it for the State of the Union message, and you open it up again for a series of ten or 15 or 20 special messages."[8]

Throughout the process, Califano observed a "great uncertainty and fierce struggle fermenting among the American people," one that "was also reflected in the administration." Leading up to the speech, he emphasized it "became a battleground for the President's mind."[9]

On one side was Secretary of the Treasury Henry Fowler. Driven by fears of rising inflation, he pressed hard for major cuts in domestic spending to offset the costs of the war. The thought of a large deficit, something that would likely occur if Congress failed to adopt a proposed tax increase, concerned him and others not committed philosophically to Johnson's Great Society, which sought to lift Americans, including minorities, out of poverty and enable them to share in the abundant prosperity of the country through legislation that would create jobs and provide housing.

Fowler's efforts also related to his effort to assuage the obstructionism of the powerful Chairman of the House Ways and Means Committee, Wilbur Mills (D-AR). An opponent of most Great Society programs, he hamstrung the process with his refusal to consider fully funding programs, something strongly supported by conservatives in Congress who railed against Medicare and programs for the poor.

Califano, in particular, pushed LBJ to directly confront Mills, arguing he "wants either (or both) (1) to force ... to your knees or (2) to dismantle great hunks of the Great Society." He sent the president a memo acknowledging that Americans worried about the "lack of leadership" on Vietnam, the riots, and a belief the country "seems to be coming apart at the seams." Califano stressed, "in January the people will be looking to you to show them that you intend to attack these problems and – while recognizing their difficulty – you can give them a sense of hope that they are not impossible of solution."[10]

Califano's admonition to Johnson reflected the frustrations of the country in 1968. The promises of the Great Society, both in economic development and civil rights, remained unmet. A crisis of expectation partly explained the rioting in American cities in the summer of 1967. The strong undercurrent of underfunding of his programs angered Johnson, as conservatives defeated in the major battles of 1964 and 1965 simply used delaying tactics to stymie progress on many fronts such as urban redevelopment, jobs programs, and housing. The chief domestic advisor understood people needed to better comprehend the challenges but have hope that their lives would improve over time, and he wanted Johnson to use his bully pulpit to make such promises.

There were reasons for the president and his advisors to worry about the economy. Deficits had skyrocketed with spending on Vietnam and Great Society programs, estimated at $19.8 billion in 1968. Some analysts feared runaway inflation while others predicted a recession, maybe even a depression. Others worried about trade imbalances and other negative economic trends.[11]

If economic woes concerned the president, his obsession remained Vietnam.

Thus, LBJ planned to open by discussing the thorny problem. He wanted to convince Congress and the American people to support his San Antonio Formula, announced in September 1967, which promised a bombing halt if negotiations began and the enemy did not take advantage of the pause. Rusk emphasized Johnson left details "deliberately vague as an attempt to elicit any kind of response from Hanoi."[12]

But, this highlighted the major problem for Johnson. Since 1965, he floated numerous ideas about sustaining the South Vietnamese

Government (SVG) while pushing the North Vietnamese and their allies toward peace talks that he hoped would ensure Saigon's survival. He often proposed stopping the bombing as a major bargaining chip, but always placed significant conditions on the process that limited any responses from Hanoi. Few innovative ideas appeared to be floating around the White House or Pentagon, although doves increasingly pushed for a phased withdrawal and ending the bombing without conditions to facilitate peace talks.

Deep down, there was something else at play in January 1968. Johnson was a stubborn man, unwilling to admit mistakes, including those made in Vietnam starting in 1964. His special assistant, George Reedy, stressed that LBJ "had never in his entire life learned to confess error, and this quality, merely amusing or exasperating in a private person – resulted in cosmic tragedy for the President." Reedy thought LBJ believed "he had no alternative . . . to feeding more and more draftees into the [Vietnam] meat grinder."[13]

For three weeks, the president monitored the development of the address from the ranch. From the start, LBJ fixated over the length of the speech, wanting a concise and streamlined speech under 4,000 words. After an original draft was longer, one aide reported "both President Eisenhower and President Kennedy have exceeded President Johnson." He included a word count for the preceding four presidents with an admonition: "You might want to plant this information appropriately."[14] It did not matter, the president continually pushed to limit its length.

By January 4, McPherson, a brilliant young lawyer from Texas described by Clifford as "able, witty, and urbane," wrote the first full draft off a twenty-page outline and it arrived in Texas via the teletype. The president started editing and seeking information such as specifics on the programs and their costs.

The early drafts of the speech had many more details and requests for money, reflecting the multiple authors that included McPherson, John Roche, and Larry Levinson. The president began changing words, eliminating some, and adding emphasis on others. It reflected the president's desire to have a tight presentation stressing his priorities on Vietnam and some domestic programs in particular, but it lacked the breadth or innovation of 1964 and 1965, where civil rights and the Great Society

Figure 1 While preparing the State of the Union Address at the ranch in Stonewall, the president took time out to sing with his dog, Yuki, and entertain his grandson, Patrick Lyndon Nugent. (Courtesy of the LBJ Library)

took center stage, although neither lived so deeply in the dark shadow of Vietnam at the time.

Since Vietnam opened the speech, the president sought feedback from many people. Few disagreements appeared other than tightening the wording to prevent any misunderstanding by the North Vietnamese. Reedy, in particular, worried about an original line of "using our antennae" for "exploring through every diplomatic channel . . . signals" that he characterized as having "a hollow ring to it" and called for "some device" to "cut through the fog." The president ultimately accepted his recommendations.[15]

Rostow had a few recommendations, including, "I personally feel there should be no reference to the French. It would cheer up General de Gaulle to make the State of the Union message." The president honored his request.[16]

Others outside the White House were not so supportive. Former secretary of state Dean Acheson wrote Rostow, "I do not like anything about this draft" and called for "its abandonment and a fresh start." He characterized it as "thoroughly boring" and "tendentious, gilding even lilies, and omitting every sear and yellow leaf." The distinguished diplomat minced no words, emphasizing "the Vietnam sections seem a collection of tired clichés."[17]

The old diplomat was correct in many ways. Public presentations by the president and others reinforced the old formula of seeking primarily a military solution, although Johnson increasingly talked about a negotiated settlement that protected the sovereignty of South Vietnam. Many questioned the approach that continued to rely heavily on a series of corrupt and authoritarian regimes in Saigon and ignored the local realities of an ongoing civil war reflecting a struggle for national unification. The proposals for peace made by Johnson had conditions that Hanoi rejected outright, making it appear to some that the peace talks simply constituted window dressing for a military solution. Vietnam continued to demand the lion's share of attention and energy with few indications of a change in the trajectory.

As the president and his advisors continued to work on the speech, on January 14 he returned to Washington.[18] One element escaped the public eye, however, and few besides the first lady knew he was considering a surprise ending by announcing his decision not to seek reelection. LBJ had considered this often, even at the convention in Atlantic City in 1964. Throughout his life, he talked about retiring from political office, but few people took him seriously.

This time, the plan took shape only a few days before the speech. It was a cold and dreary wet day on Sunday, January 14 when Busby received a call from the White House.

LBJ immediately complained: "This goddam draft they've given me wouldn't make chickens crackle if you waved it at 'em in the dark ... It's too long, too dull, too flat, too bureaucratic," he said, adding, "every little two-bit bureau in the government has managed to get at least one line in on their pet project."[19]

He went on: "I get the best minds in Washington together and what do they come up with? Vomit. Fifty pages of vomit."

Then, he got to the point, asking if he would "give up your nap for your country and president?" He then turned apologetic, "Understand I wouldn't bother you if I didn't need a little of Churchill in this thing."

Busby simply thought: "After twenty years, he still aspired to the standard which eluded him."[20]

LBJ's long-time confidant correctly appraised the situation. He had written some of Johnson's most memorable speeches in the early days of his presidency and knew the president had extremely high standards for speeches, albeit often unrealistic ones. It reflected Johnson's lack of confidence in his delivery, something that he knew paled when compared to skilled orators like Franklin Roosevelt and John F. Kennedy. Therefore, he agonized over the words and drove his speechwriters to the brink of insanity by pouring over the drafts and demanding perfection elusive for even the best speakers.

In a short time, Busby arrived at the White House residence and went upstairs. He knew the best gauge of the president's mood was Sgt. Paul Glynn, the president's personal aide. Busby asked for a report, and Glynn simply gave a thumb's down.

Entering the bedroom, the president lay on his bed in his pajamas under the covers. On the bed lay newspapers and official papers.

Impatiently, the president asked: "What do you think of the speech?"

Busby had not read it but echoed a report from Reedy, "Not too bad."

The president snorted in derision, "Hell, don't quote George Reedy to me. You haven't read it."

Then, he motioned Busby over to the bed. He slipped out of the bed and returned with a notepad and pencil.

"I didn't get you down here to waste your time on the State of the Union," he told Busby.

The president outlined wanting to surprise "the living hell out of them" by pulling out a separate sheet of paper and announcing his decision not to seek reelection. However, Busby wondered: "Was I there only to be some part of an exercise in presidential therapy, listening until the emotion spent itself and then forgetting what I had heard?" He knew the president's track record from spending many years with him.[21]

But then, the president said: "The name of this game is to quit while you're ahead. I've always prayed I'd have sense enough to get out when the time came, before they had to carry me out."

Then, a pity party played out: "I do not believe that a man born in my section can lead, or will be permitted to lead, this nation in these times."

Busby dropped the pencil and closed the writing tablet to signify his displeasure.

"All right, all right, have it your way," but the president ordered: "Get this one down."

Slowly the president began: "On that day in November, so long ago, when I came before you for the first time as president, to speak in a time of sorrow and sadness – no make that, tragedy and trial – I said then, 'Let us continue.' We have continued. A thousand days have become two thousand, and two thousand soon will become three. We have done the work of the fallen hero whose place I have labored to fill." He paused and then continued: "We of this generation have kept faith with ourselves, and we have kept the trust of John F. Kennedy. I say again tonight, as my last words to you and to the nation, let us continue."

LBJ asked, "Now, does that possibly, perhaps, maybe meet with your approval?"

Busby nodded affirmatively.

Recognizing the president was done, Busby rose and started to leave.

"Aren't you going to say anything?" LBJ asked.

"Mr. President, we'll have to think about this," Busby replied.

Busby and Johnson did not talk about it for another three months. But that Sunday, Busby thought: "Perhaps great power should not be laid down except for great cause. No such cause existed. Yet if he removed himself from politics, the nation would be vulnerable abroad – and perhaps at home – to the inherent weakness of a lame duck presidency." He would send a note to the White House: "On a matter such as this, every man must step to his own drum."[22]

The day after Johnson talked with Busby, he had a late lunch with Christian and Lady Bird. He told them: "I have been in a hurry all of my life. I have never had time to stay in one place as long as I like. I've always been fighting an uphill fight."

Lady Bird thought to herself: "I could understand his mood so well, because I knew that his mind was lashed, as though to a Siamese twin, to that inescapable problem of: 'How and why do I face up to running again or getting out?'"[23]

But no one outside of Busby, Christian, and Lady Bird knew anything about the surprise. The president often talked the previous year about not running, but few thought he would follow through. But something pushed him to consider it, and he appeared serious to Lady Bird, more so than other times.

To almost everyone, LBJ seemed thoroughly committed to the task at hand. In the days leading up to the speech, LBJ and his advisers continued tweaking it. On January 16, the president requested that cabinet members meet with Califano. They received access to the parts of the speech relating to their offices and not much else.

Vietnam had created a bunker mentality in the White House. Fear of leaks became a constant source of irritation to the president and those around him. Always a man who valued unquestioning loyalty, Johnson increasingly pressured people to shut down the leaks and prevent appearances of internal disputes or a lack of confidence in current policies. Clamping down became more important as the administration continued moving forward, especially in an election year.

For the State of the Union, Johnson feared someone might inadvertently mention them at "some Georgetown party to some columnist who's smarter than they are." Califano acknowledged that by that time, each cabinet member "would be possessed by the fear of God that any leak would cost him his program."[24]

By January 17, aides loaded the final draft onto the teleprompter, a total of 3,799 words with a few last minute changes on topics relating to the Model Cities and removal of some on education because Califano noted, "it merely records what we are supposed to be doing."[25]

Lady Bird reported, "Lyndon spent much of the morning reading the supposedly final draft – I think it was the eleventh version."[26]

Leading up to the speech, Johnson conducted a series of meetings, including an hour-long one with Cabinet members around noon. Liz Carpenter, Lady Bird's closest advisor, attended. Just the day before, she sent LBJ a note with some words of advice. "Take your time. Before each bracketed new beginning, shift your weight, take a glass of water, and get a new breath and start. This helps the listener have time to think through those golden words." She called on him to "get the listener and hold him ... make those bastards sit up with reverence."[27]

Soon after that get-together, he met Lady Bird and Christian, who brought in a draft of the surprise ending that he wrote. Lady Bird characterized it as "a good statement, very well said."[28]

She knew the phrase would come at the end with a statement like, "And now I want to speak to you about a personal matter"

But, she knew it might not come, as she lamented: "He keeps looking from one to the other of us – those close to him – for an answer. But there isn't any answer ... there is nobody who can decide but him."[29]

The whole process reflected bouts of loss of confidence that periodically afflicted the president. It had been there right before the convention in Atlantic City and at other junctures of his career where doubts crept into a person who had deeply seeded insecurities about his education and overall preparation for higher office. Often, it fell to Lady Bird and a few close advisors to prop him up and feed his ego to push him forward. This was just another case of it transpiring at an important juncture of his life.

At 3:45 p.m., LBJ finally sat down for lunch with a heavy emphasis on vegetables complemented by fruit Jell-O. He complained a bit about it, so missing the days before his major heart attack in 1955. Since then,

Lady Bird forced him to surrender cigarettes, fatty meats, and especially rich desserts.[30]

The first lady arrived not long after and encouraged LBJ to go upstairs and get some rest. Instead, Johnson hosted a small group of Republican leaders including House Minority Leader Gerald Ford (R-MI) and Senator Bourke Hickenlooper (R-IA) to outline the main points of the speech before heading to a similar meeting with his cabinet and nearly thirty Democratic leaders led by Speaker Thomas McCormack (D-MA) and Senator Mike Mansfield (D-MT).[31]

After consulting congressional leaders, the president followed his traditional routine before major addresses and headed to the barbershop for his trim. Afterwards, he walked upstairs to change into the suits laid out by his staff and to meet with Mr. Lee Baygan, his makeup man.[32]

About 6:30 p.m., Lady Bird found her husband and handed off Christian's draft with the surprise announcement. They talked quietly, not far from reporters gathering in the Fish Room.

"Well, what do you think? What shall I do?" he asked.

She responded: "Luci hopes you won't run. She wants you for herself and for Lyn and all of us. She does not want to give you up."

Then quietly, she added: "Lynda hopes you will run. She told me this afternoon, with a sort of terrible earnestness, because her husband is going to war and she thinks there will be a better chance of getting him back alive and the war settled if you are President."

"Me – I don't know. I have said it all before. I can't tell you what to do," she concluded.[33]

She thought to herself: "One, either you make a conscious decision to run, in the same state of a mind of a man who is becoming a monk, or some such vocation, going up your life and saying: 'Here it is, I will take whatever comes. I will try to pace the stretch and keep my sense of humor for the next five years.'" She added: "Or, two, you simply make the announcement that you won't run, at a time and in the words only you can choose, but as strong and beautiful as you are capable of."[34]

Then, the president was handed a note from Texas Governor John Connally, his long-time confidant and friend, who already decided not to seek reelection. He wrote: "Go with the statement tonight, because he would never have a bigger audience" and "a live audience would be better than announcing it on the TV or in the papers." Lady Bird acknowledged, "Lyndon had to weigh this against the fact that the whole 1968 program of action would thereby be diluted, if not completely ignored."[35]

No matter what transpired, Lady Bird knew that State of the Union provided high political drama at a time the country felt discombobulated and stumbling in the wake of the summer riots and antiwar demonstrations.

But she also knew that LBJ often cried wolf on the matter, complaining until the very end about the burdens of the job but then moving forward. Anyway, he received good news that day when he learned a new Gallup Poll had him "with a big lead over Reagan, Romney and Nixon and a six-point lead over Rockefeller."[36]

She returned upstairs to dress into a bright red suit with navy trim that fit the patriotic theme of the night. Lady Bird also chose her guests to highlight his accomplishments over the past five years. Before leaving the residence, she studied their biographies and went over a seating chart before heading to the library where everyone congregated.

Downstairs, she mingled with her special guests, who benefitted from the recently implemented Great Society programs. They included a young VISTA worker, a remedial reading instructor in an impoverished D.C. neighborhood as part of the Teachers Corps, and a teen whose high IQ led to his selection as part of the Job Corps to prepare him for college. Finally, there was Specialist Lawrence Joel, a "stocky, middle-aged, smiling Negro" who won the Medal of Honor while serving as a medic in Vietnam. The first lady observed: "They were all so full of enthusiasm and easy to talk to."[37]

The president joined them, talking with the group for a short time. But the Secret Service soon escorted him to his car for the trip to the Capitol building. Inside, he went over the speech one more time, making a few minor edits.

As Johnson traveled to Capitol Hill, James Reston of the *New York Times* went on National Education Television (NET) to contextualize for the audience the feelings of the country. Anticipating possibly the opening of the speech, he stressed the country "isn't a happy mood ... There is a strange awareness of the war and yet I think there is a tremendous difference between people knowing the facts and really not feeling the facts."[38]

He added: "The mood of the Congress, of course, is essentially political." He acknowledged an election year where the "opposition party feels ... this year they have got a chance to win." He properly appraised the situation: "So it will be a very sharp political year, maybe a vicious political year."

Soon, Secret Service agents ushered Johnson into the speaker's chambers, just off the House floor. Waiting on him were some close friends including LBJ's friend and mentor Senator Richard Russell (D-GA). They talked for a few minutes while the crowd gathered.

Then, at 9:01 p.m., the doorkeeper of the House, William "Fishbait" Miller, announced loudly: "The President of the United States." LBJ entered to a thunderous applause that lasted for three minutes.

"He looked wonderful," Lady Bird noted, "the fifteen pound he has lost are all to the good, and I like his hair a bit longer and not slicked down."[39]

For nearly forty-five minutes, the president talked to the congressmen, Supreme Court justices, foreign dignitaries, and the press. Dressed in a somber black suit with a very subdued dark tie, the president opened: "I report to you that our country is challenged, at home and abroad."

"That it is our will that is being tried, not our strength; our sense of purpose, not our ability to achieve a better America."

"And I report to you that I believe, with abiding conviction, that this people – nurtured by their deep faith, tutored by their hard lessons, moved by their high aspirations – have the will to meet the trials that these times impose."

Then, the president launched into a discussion of Vietnam, the most divisive issue of the era. It set the tone for the remainder of the speech and reflected the deep down divisions in the country, ones that would not change without bold, innovative deviations in existing US policy. Most listeners heard none of that, starting the speech off at a disadvantage.

At length he talked about the democratic successes in South Vietnam, including elections with leaders "chosen by popular, contested ballot."

Then, he boasted: "The enemy has been defeated in battle after battle with a million more people living under government control since January of last year."

The president stressed the opponent "continues to hope that America's will to persevere can be broken. Well – he is wrong. America will persevere. Our patience and our perseverance will match our power. Aggression will never prevail."

His first statements sounded eerily familiar to those said over the past three years. Johnson continued pushing an optimistic public message even while harboring private doubts about the South Vietnamese leadership and their ability to rule. He highlighted successes in the ballot box, but ignored the failure of the South Vietnamese Government (SVG) to bring about true democratic reform with economic and social stability for the majority of people. He failed to underscore the failure of the ARVN to win military victories without substantial US assistance. The situation in 1968 looked little different from the day he inherited the mess in Vietnam from Kennedy, but he continued trying to paint a rosier picture than existed.

However, he tried to change the dialogue. "But our goal is peace – and peace at the earliest moment," Johnson stressed: "If a basis for peace talks can be established on the San Antonio foundations – and it is my hope and my prayer that they can ... a really true cease-fire – could be made the first order of business."

Watching the president speak, Califano emphasized: "I felt an urgency as he spoke those words, almost as though he ached."[40] He added: "His delivery was quiet, his tone almost conversational as he looked into the cameras and the eyes of his audience." At points, he caught the president, "leaning his elbows on the podium."[41]

At various junctures, there were loud ovations. Some accused the administration of orchestrating the applause, including journalists Rowland Evans and Robert Novak. They reported that Marvin Watson had middle and lower level White House aides clap and shout as a "pedestrian speech was repeatedly interrupted by applause." Congressman reported they "were sure that they weren't making all the noise."

The two writers stated: "The result was a reception transcending Mr. Johnson's current level of unpopularity on Capitol Hill. The most tepid recommendation was applauded."[42]

But the opening on foreign affairs was lackluster and placed the speech at a disadvantage by starting with Vietnam. The San Antonio Formula had circulated for months, but few believed the enemy would accept its conditions.

Vietnam remained a corrosive topic and no doves, whether listening in Congress or in the streets protesting, believed the president made any commitment toward real change in Vietnam. For many hoping for some major breakthrough, they were sorely disappointed. The absence of peace talks without significant conditions or a start of the withdrawal of US troops made Johnson's words ring hollow and if anything angered the conservatives for discussing peace without military victory. Vietnam continued to poison everything and dilute any hope for expanding the Great Society and healing the wounds the war caused in the American public.

Then, Johnson pivoted to domestic matters. He highlighted the accomplishments of the country, including annual production exceeding $800 billion as well as eighty-three months of uninterrupted growth. "All about them, most American families can see the evidence of growing abundance: higher paychecks, humming factories, new cars moving down the highways," he emphasized.

"Yet, there is in the land a certain restlessness – a questioning."

He tried explaining the discontent: "Because when a great ship cuts through the sea, the waters are always stirred and troubled." But, Johnson noted: "And our ship is moving. It is moving through troubled and new water; it is moving toward new and better shores."

The president continued: "We ask now, not how can we achieve abundance? – but how shall we use our abundance? Not is there abundance enough for all? – but, how can all share in our abundance?"

These questions framed his beliefs about the American dream that he fought for during much of his whole political career, but especially his presidency. His viewpoint reflected populist/progressive principles dating back decades as reformers, including his role models such as FDR, strove to create a better and more equitable country. They wanted people to share in the wealth by providing the less fortunate in society with more opportunities to enjoy the American dream. The Great Society sought to extend this vision, but the conservatives fought back strenuously. So the battle continued in 1968 on many levels.

The president underscored many achievements, but stressed "much remains for us to master." He included joblessness, which was three to four times higher than the national average in some areas. Other pockets had high crime rates, while many locales had polluted rivers and skies harming people.

"We have lived with conditions like these for many, many years. But much that we once accepted as inevitable, we now find absolutely intolerable," he pointed out.

Again, he underscored the past, but noted a new America that rejected the lack of opportunity for some and the inequalities caused by race and environmental conditions. More than any president to that point, he saw correlations between jobs, crime, and pollution and its effects on the least fortunate in society. He also understood the correlation between the different factors and the pent up frustrations in the nation's cities that manifested themselves in mob violence. His empathy was on full display in the words, even though many never believed in his true commitment to the ideas of the Great Society.

Johnson turned to the cities aflame in the summer "where we saw how wide the gulf was for some Americans between the promise and reality of our society. We know that we cannot change all of this in a day. It represents the consequences of more than three centuries."

"But the issue is not whether we can change this; the issue is whether we will change this. Well, I know we can. And I believe we will."

Then, he launched into a series of proposals to address the root causes of the anger and resentment. He highlighted a $2.1 billion manpower program, doubling the funding of Model Cities over congressional allocations, and adding 300,000 housing units for low to middle income families (a threefold increase over 1967). There were other propositions on children's health care and consumer protections, but nothing approximating 1964 and 1965. Even then, he failed to get Congress to fully fund many of those projects, and he continued to face major opposition, especially from southerners angry over government spending on programs they thought primarily served African Americans in urban areas.

But most in the chamber sat up when he announced "that the American people have had enough of rising crime and lawlessness in this country." He told the audience: "They recognize that law enforcement is first the duty of local police and local government" and the frontline of the battle was "the home, the church, the city hall and the country courthouse and the statehouse – not in the far-removed National Capital of Washington."

But, the president also stressed "the National Government can and . . . should help the cities and the States in their war on crime to the full extent of its resources and its constitutional authority."

Johnson outlined passing his Safe Streets Act that allocated more federal money for research on criminal behavior and justice, pushed for more FBI programs dealing with riots and organized crime, and promoted limits on gun purchases, emphasizing "I urge Congress to stop the trade in mail-order murder, to stop it this year by adopting a proper gun control law."

He also issued a warning that "those who preach disorder and those who preach violence must know that local authorities are able to resist them swiftly, to resist them sternly, and to resist them decisively."

Evans and Novak observed it was "the one genuine spontaneous reaction to a Presidential proposal – his anti-crime plan – was magnified to a most uncongressional cheer."[43]

Lady Bird agreed and observed the "most spontaneous and loudest" applause came when he declared: "The American people have had enough of rising crime and lawlessness."[44]

The response led McPherson to write Patrick Moynihan: "The speech as written was not nearly so repressive as Congress's applause made it appear. The audience must have seemed to many people, not only Negroes, in a lynching mood."[45]

Then, the applause stopped when the president launched into a controversial proposal in an election year. Wanting to wage the war in Vietnam and also fund the Great Society, he needed more money to balance the budget without slashing programs. In the "guns and butter" argument, he clearly sought to expand revenues.

He pushed for holding appropriations steady, but for Congress "to act responsibly ... by enacting the tax surcharge which for the average American individual amounts to about a penny out of each dollar's income." He noted it should be a temporary measure not exceeding two years and earlier if Congress wanted, but emphasized, "Congress can never repeal inflation."

Few applauded and few showed any enthusiasm for a tax increase in an election year. Many conservatives like Mills wanted massive cuts in domestic spending, especially to the expansive programs of the Great Society that served the least fortunate in society. On the other side, many liberals wanted to slash defense spending, including the exploding budgets created by the costly war in Vietnam, and take the savings and invest them in domestic programs. None wanted tax increases, and Johnson found himself squeezed between the extremes with little room to navigate.

Nearing the end, he stressed: "Each of the questions I have discussed with you tonight is a question of policy for our people." He acknowledged that each would be debated, but he hoped with "a seriousness that matches the gravity of the questions themselves."

"Can we achieve these goals?" he asked.

"If there ever was a nation that was capable of solving its problems, it is this nation."

"So this, my friends, is the State of our Union: seeking, building, tested many times in this past year – and always equal to the test."[46]

Busby reported as the end neared, "I moved nearer the television screen. The applause swelled. The president nodded toward the audience without smiling. Members rose to their feet, cheers began, and he still stood over the lectern, perhaps hesitating, perhaps not. But his hand did not move to the coat pocket. He nodded again and closed the text. It was over, and he moved away." He wrote that "my visit to the White House on the previous Sunday must have been for the purpose of therapy."[47]

Lady Bird also observed: "As he approached the end, I tightened up in my seat. Would he end with his statement? Did I want him to? Would I be relieved if he did, or if he didn't?"[48]

Later, Christian queried him on why he failed to pull the trigger. LBJ responded forcefully: "Well it was sort of difficult to lay out a big program for the Congress, and say I want you to pass all these things and then conclude with 'Okay, thanks and so long, I'm checking out.' It just didn't work."[49]

A thunderous applause greeted his last statements and shortly he walked down the steps, out of the chamber, and into the speaker's office.[50]

The president waited for Lady Bird to join him. "I had felt a surge of optimism in the Chamber, had listened to the roar of applause," she noted. However, "there was no rush forward" by Cabinet members and congressional leaders, "to say, 'That was a great speech, Mr. President. We'll get to work on the agenda. It is going to be hard, but we'll make it a good year.'" She admitted, "the first maggots of doubt began to gnaw at the good feeling I had."[51]

A little after 10 p.m., Lyndon and Lady Bird climbed into the car with their daughter Lynda and her husband Chuck Robb to return to the White House. There, they moved upstairs to join a large group of people including the husbands and wives of most of his close staff as well as Abe Fortas, William White, and LBJ's brother, Sam.

The first lady had ordered a nice buffet for everyone to enjoy so that they could watch the television commentaries and have a "general rehash which always takes place after a State of the Union Message."

In the bedroom, people gathered to watch a host of experts evaluate the president's speech, particularly NET.

Critics existed in abundance. Arthur Schlesinger, Jr. commented: "The State of the Union Message is not a great art form. It tends toward banality and I would say that President Johnson has once again been faithful to the tradition."[52] Conservative commentator William F. Buckley added: "I think that the speech was a considerable failure, politically and personally."[53]

Nonetheless, Lady Bird acknowledged, "support came from an unexpected quarter, panelists Edwin Reischauer and Patrick Moynihan ... I heard Bill Moyers for just a moment, speaking rather well I thought." She added, "the new Mayor of Cleveland, Carl Stokes, was reasonable and articulate and mostly fair, but of course there is never enough money for urban affairs ... All and all, it was an amusing and entertaining program and I thought we won more than we lost."[54]

Lady Bird also watched "Lyndon, in his bedroom ... busy looking at other networks with a few of the guests. The hall was full and people drifted into the dining room. We had a fire lighted in the Yellow Room for anyone who wanted comfort and a quiet conversation. There was an air of elation, good will, relief ... the wine of success which we had tasted in 1964 and 1965 – or so I evaluated it."[55]

The following day, Lady Bird became less optimistic. "If we tasted the wine of success last night, it was indeed a brief draught. As we looked over the press reports on the State of the Union Message – at least in the Eastern metropolitan papers – they were largely negative or unenthusiastic. This was like working very hard, putting out all you've got, settling back to hear the verdict, and then finding your efforts were not good enough."[56]

There were few supportive editorials, but most were lukewarm at best. One writer correctly noted the speech "reflected the weariness and anxiety of a nation plunged into a seemingly endless war abroad and growing division and disorder at home."[57]

The polls reinforced the bad feelings. A telephone poll on the speech conducted on January 19–20 indicated that 45 percent of the respondents gave it a favorable rating and 55 percent gave it an unfavorable vote. The Quayle poll found it more favorable among those with direct versus indirect exposure (second hand reports). It also uncovered that 40 percent of the Democrats found it unfavorable. The strongest negative came from young men aged 21–49, while older men gave it a higher favorable. It was not what the White House wanted to hear.[58]

But there was some good news. By late January, LBJ's approval ratings climbed to 48 percent, rising ten points since October 1967. People speculated that it turned around because of his renewed "take charge attitude," hopes of progress in Vietnam, and Democrats rallying to his side as the presidential election approached.[59]

The State of the Union address, despite all the time and energy devoted to the endeavor, accomplished very little in building momentum for the president's agenda. It reflected the fatigue of the administration and the nation after years of change and upheaval, bearing a striking resemblance to other times in American history where Americans tired of reform and war and retreated into a search for perceived normalcy.

LBJ wanted to recapture the magic of 1964 and 1965, but the environment had changed dramatically. His principles remained the same, but the country appeared unwilling to proceed along the path he outlined only a few years earlier in inspiring addresses.

The speech also reflected a president who lacked a vision of turmoil and crises laying on the horizon. Even a few weeks beyond that day, dramatic foreign policy challenges headed quickly toward him and the country. In North Korea and North Vietnam, leaders had their own plans for the future that shook the foundations of the presidency of Lyndon Johnson.

CHAPTER 2

Those Dirty Bastards, Are They Trying to Embarrass Us? The *Pueblo* Incident, January–December 1968

Events unfolding in Asia garnered the lion's share of LBJ's attention in the days following the State of the Union address. On January 21, the president carefully monitored the Marine base Khe Sanh, against which the North Vietnamese launched a huge offensive. That same day, reports reached Washington that North Korean commandos nearly assassinated South Korean President Park Chung-hee, significantly raising tensions.[1]

Two days later, Rostow called the president at 2:24 a.m., waking him up to report that the Navy had received a distress signal from the *U.S.S. Pueblo*, an intelligence ship working off the North Korean coast. However, no one seemed overly alarmed and awaited more information. LBJ returned to sleep and awoke early to attend a breakfast with congressional leaders to discuss job growth, not Korea.

Around noon, LBJ met with the American League MVP, Carl Yastrzemski, and baseball legend Joe DiMaggio. The Red Sox star gave the president an autographed bat, and LBJ pretended to lay down a bunt. Yastrzemski chided him: "You have to hit home runs."[2] At no point did the president express concern about the *Pueblo*, even though it became clear the North Koreans had the ship and crew.

Just after noon, the president walked over to the mansion to have his weekly luncheon with his national security team, including Secretary of State Dean Rusk, Secretary of Defense Robert McNamara, National Security Advisor Walt Rostow, and CIA Director Richard Helms.[3]

Also present was General Earle Wheeler, Chairman of the Joint Chiefs of Staff. One person described him as having "a modest and low-key style" and lacking the "Westmoreland theatrical appearance."

He purposely avoided a "blustery style" so common among military men and proved a consummate staff officer who understood Pentagon politics and served as a good bridge to civilian leaders. LBJ respected him, even asking him to serve for a second term despite Wheeler's heart attack in 1967.

Once everyone arrived, the meeting started with some levity. McNamara welcomed his successor, Clark Clifford, the powerful lawyer and lobbyist and long-time confidant to Johnson. "This is what it is like on a typical day," McNamara joked, "we had an inadvertent intrusion into Cambodia. We lost a B-52 with four H-bombs aboard. We had an intelligence ship captured by the North Koreans."

"May I leave now?" Clifford responded.[4]

After the initial laughter, everyone became serious as the focus shifted to the *Pueblo*.

Rusk, whom LBJ described as having "the compassion of a preacher and the courage of a Georgia cracker," opened by reporting Moscow denied any knowledge or responsibility.

Sitting in his chair, the president outlined several options:

1. A direct retaliatory strike against North Korea.
2. Securing a thorough explanation for the hostile act.
3. Capturing a North Korean ship for a possible exchange.[5]

Underlying it all, Johnson wanted to know what happened. Had the ship strayed into North Korean waters? Was it part of a plan to draw US attention away from Vietnam? He could not understand, why now?

Debates arose as Rostow wanted to submit the affair to the UN Security Council, while Rusk pushed for letting the Korean Military Armistice Commission (MAC) handle it.

Again, LBJ queried why now? He answered his own question, stressing it was a Communist conspiracy, likely related to Vietnam. He wrote later: "Our best estimate then, one that I believe holds up well in the light of subsequent events, is that they were aware of the Tet offensive in Vietnam ... They were trying to divert U.S. military resources from Vietnam and to pressure the South Koreans into recalling their two divisions from that area."[6]

As always, Vietnam remained front and center in the president's decision-making process. While he lacked any proof of coordination between the North Koreans and North Vietnamese, even years later he made the accusation. Vietnam was his obsession and, like almost every-thing in 1968 relating to foreign affairs, his perspective flowed through the Vietnam prism that often caused distortions and policy missteps.

LBJ walked away from the meeting with more questions than answers. He knew the "hawks" wanted retribution, but doing so ensured the crews' death. On the other side, the "doves" accused him of manufactur-ing another crisis like the one with Tonkin Gulf in August 1964 to rally public support. He could please neither side.

While Vietnam may have biased his viewpoint regarding the *Pueblo*, Johnson demonstrated a maturity that often eluded him earlier in his presidency in places like Vietnam in 1964 and the Dominican Republic in 1965, where he often acted rashly and relied on military action. This time, he showed patience and restraint, resisting the calls to employ military force, something obviously affected by the huge manpower commitments in Vietnam. However, he ignored critics from both sides and focused on the main goal, securing the release of the hostages. It was not politically expedient, but the right course for those who would have died if the United States responded forcefully early in the crisis.

But the incident also demonstrated the limits of presidential power as a small, relatively insignificant nation seized an American ship and more than eighty hostages. While having major military resources at his com-mand, Johnson had few options. He could employ weapons, but at the cost of the deaths of the US crewmen. It might have been different in 1965, but the diminution of American power caused by Vietnam and its draining of hundreds of thousands of men and billions of dollars as well as clashes in the streets severely restrained LBJ by 1968. This would be the first of many events that unfolded that year that showed just how few options existed when unexpected events occurred far from the White House.

And of course, he showed a significant amount of negotiating skill alongside diplomats in keeping the South Koreans from using the seizure to provoke a conflict that would have dragged the United States into another war on the isthmus. President Park already wanted revenge for the commando attack. The South Korean minister of defense casti-gated Rusk for not responding forcefully to the provocation, positing that it encouraged the North Koreans to take the *Pueblo*.[7]

LBJ also knew Park would squeeze the United States for his own gain. For three years, he had sent tens of thousands of soldiers to Vietnam, winning major economic and military assistance in return. The United States also turned a blind eye to his authoritarian actions. Seoul clearly understood how to manipulate its stronger ally, and LBJ clearly under-stood the situation and worked hard to manage it.

Then, there was Kim Il-Sung, the North Korean dictator. "Why had North Korea flagrantly risked stirring up an international hornet's nest and perhaps starting a war," LBJ wondered.[8]

Few people interacted with Kim, usually only Communist ambas-sadors funneling information that most Americans viewed skeptically. Was he a madman? What was his end game? Was he just coordinating actions with the Soviets and North Vietnamese? No one had answers.

Johnson never acknowledged that Kim staged the entire event largely for domestic consumption. His relations with China had deteri-orated over the years as he moved closer to the Soviets. In return, economic ties suffered: a major source of North Korean revenues. Domestically, food shortages arose, and the people suffered as money poured into sustaining a large military. What better way to demon-strate his power as well as cover up the failed attack on Park than to seize the *Pueblo*?[9]

The lack of information demonstrated that despite all the powerful intelligence resources available to the president of the United States, none could offset the complete lack of data available to him regard-ing the North Koreans. It was typically pure speculation (often faulty) that drove US policy toward Kim. Johnson frequently found himself flying blind in the long contest of wills that unfolded over the following eleven months.

The next day, LBJ again consulted with his national security advisors. McNamara opened by emphasizing that the North Korean action was a conscious effort to test the Americans. He concluded, "the North Koreans have no intention of returning the men or the ship."

The president immediately chimed in, "Did the skipper ask for help?"

General Wheeler responded affirmatively, noting the captain messaged: "These fellows mean business. SOS. SOS."

"Were there no planes available which were prepared to come to the aid of this vessel? Every press story I have seen this morning said that U.S. planes were only 30 minutes away," the president asked.

This was an important question. Why had a relatively unarmed ship been sent so near an enemy coastline without air cover or armed protection?

A long litany of excuses followed from McNamara and Wheeler explaining the aircraft carriers were too far away and American planes on alert in South Korea required hours to change to different bomb racks.

LBJ simply responded, "Until now, I have been under the impression that the ship did not ask for help." He ordered his advisors to "get all the facts and document them well so I can study this matter further."[10]

On another front, Johnson dealt with Congress. Early on, he received a message from Senator John Stennis (D-MS). "For God's sake, do something."

LBJ read it and muttered: "Please thank the senator for his helpful advice."[11]

Others demanded action. Senator Strom Thurmond (R-SC) pushed the United States to "fight if necessary to obtain the immediate release of the ships and all of its personnel."[12] His fellow South Carolinian, Mendell Rivers (D-SC), powerful chairman of the House Armed Services Committee, was even more blunt. "I'd select a target. I'd do like Truman did – let one of them disappear."[13]

On the campaign trail, Republican front-runner Richard Nixon contended the "communist world has been jointly testing the proposition that the United States is over-extended, over-committed, and under-prepared to act." He called the incident a "tactical blunder" as the US military provided no cover for the *Pueblo*. He chastised the administration for allowing "a fourth rate military power ... [to] hijack a United States naval vessel."[14]

LBJ remembered people crying for "strong action ... But we knew that if we wanted our men to return home alive, we had to use diplomacy. If we resorted to military means, we could expect dead bodies. And we also might start a war."[15]

Johnson clearly understood the complexities of the situation unfolding over the *Pueblo*. He knew Americans throughout their history responded unfavorably to aggression on the high seas, dating back to the Barbary Pirates. Political expediency dictated some kind of response, especially as the president geared up for a re-election campaign. Doing nothing constituted inaction that was opposed by his harshest critics in Congress. But, he clearly understood the pitfalls of a military response that ensured the death of the prisoners. He saw the futility of a quick military action that would be unlikely to secure the release of the eighty-two hostages, and would likely lead to their deaths.

On the other side, powerful chairman of the Senate Foreign Relations Committee (SFRC), J. William Fulbright (D-AR), declared the *Pueblo* was "within the territorial waters of North Korea at [the] time of the incident." The day after its seizure, he stressed, "we should be very careful and cautious in our reaction, particularly since some of the precise facts are unknown."[16]

The ghosts of Tonkin Gulf and the lies and half-truths uncovered afterward hung over the discussions. Even normal supporters of the president such as the *Chicago Tribune* admitted on February 7 that Americans were being "a bit hesitant about coming to verbal defense of the nation in this newest crisis because they could not be sure that they had been fed the right facts."[17]

The president worried about the fallout on Capitol Hill when he talked with his advisors on the 24th. "All of the Committees will begin investigations of this incident once it cools down. Should we do anything to head this off?" he asked.

McNamara reacted, "I do not recommend meeting with Congress. They are not interested as much in what happened ... as in what we plan to do."

LBJ then asked where the North Koreans seized the *Pueblo*.

"Our best reports are that the ship was outside of territorial waters," McNamara informed him.

"Is there any chance of error?" LBJ responded.

McNamara reported a less than "1% chance of error in daylight conditions such as existed at the time."

Then LBJ focused on Commander Lloyd Bucher's confession: "How much of a problem does that create for us?"

Rostow answered: "The confession of the Captain appears to have been written by the Soviets. This is not the language of an American ship captain."

Then, the conversation returned to why now? "It appears the North Koreans are doing this in support of the North Vietnamese," Helms reported, adding the Soviets "are putting pressure on North Korea to take some of the pressure off Vietnam."

The president asked: "Would not it be wise now that we have definite information where the incident occurred to tell Senator Fulbright so that he will be more responsible with his statements?"[18] No one answered, and the meeting adjourned.

Even worrying about the location of the *Pueblo*, Johnson still pondered, "assuming that the *Pueblo* had veered off course, that would hardly explain North Korea's sudden bellicose action."[19] Incidents of ships wandering into sovereign waters happened often without incident, making the North Korean aggression more puzzling.

No matter, the president took several proactive steps to prevent the North Koreans from feeling emboldened by the seizure. "On January 25," Johnson underscored, "we called up more than 14,000 Navy and Air Force reserves to strengthen our position in Korea without diverting resources from Southeast Asia." He added: "Our Korean allies were seriously worried that the Pyongyang regime might launch another invasion ... [and] there was a distinct possibility that South Korean forces might be withdrawn from Vietnam."

Johnson also dispatched "more than 350 aircraft to our bases in South Korea ... We assumed that the South Korean army could look after itself, but the North Koreans had a larger air force and we did not wish them to be tempted by that advantage."[20]

Those closest to the president watched the pressures mount because of the *Pueblo* seizure. Lady Bird wrote in her diary: "The city is in a state of tension that has been mounting since Monday when North Korea seized the *Pueblo*."[21]

While searching for answers and taking some preventative measures to send a message to Kim, LBJ also explored more diplomatic options. At a breakfast meeting on the 25th with a small group of advisors, LBJ queried Ambassador Goldberg: "What are the gambles we take by going to the UN?"

Goldberg never directly addressed the question, but responded: "It is best to urge a resolution demanding the return of the ship" as well as condemnation of the act. He proposed asking "the UN to support a return to the Armistice Agreements," although he observed, "of course the Soviets will veto that resolution, but taking this action will satisfy the diplomatic needs."

The president shifted topics: "Was the *Turner Joy* an intelligence ship?"

No, replied McNamara, they "are not the same type of ship."

Then the hawkish Rostow suggested: "As I see it, international law states that the seizure of a ship on the high seas justifies counteraction and equivalent reprisal."

Quickly, LBJ reacted: "Walt, I do not want to win the argument and lose the sale."

Then, Johnson added, if we send "a vast armada, won't the Soviets and the Chinese say that they must be ready to protect their little brothers? Won't that really increase the tension? Is this a move to deter South Korea? What are we going to do after the aircraft are there? Where does all of this lead us?"

The president also worried aloud. "Will this action jeopardize our positions elsewhere, particularly in Berlin?"

McNamara promised, "the 332 aircraft that we are calling up are cats and dogs, but the 303 which are being sent to South Korea are in very good shape."

Finally, the president zeroed in on Congress. "We have got to have a good discussion to see if the Fulbrights represent this country. If they do, we are committing a grave error to send men out. You remember how much trouble we got into on the Tonkin Gulf incident." He stressed: "We need to go to the Congress on this matter."

When Rusk pointed out that Senator Frank Church (D-ID) called for vigorous action, Johnson retorted, "I am sure one the reasons is that he has a Pocatello, Idaho, boy captured out there."

Then, he returned to a common thread. "What concerns me is this. When we get the planes out there and all the forces you have recommended, what do we do then?"

He concluded by calling for several steps, including the dispatch of a letter to Alexi Kosygin explaining the US position to prevent any misunderstanding.[22]

Concerned about the escalating crisis, Johnson moved cautiously, fearful of sparking WWIII if the Russians or Chinese became involved. Many people, like the president, remembered clearly the devastation and divisions created by the frustrations of fighting a bloody war on the isthmus during the Truman Administration. He had few choices other than to wait out the North Koreans or to sacrifice the hostages for a quick but unsatisfying outcome. The most powerful man on earth found himself largely unable to respond forcefully in the face of a much weaker adversary. In many ways, it reflected the same frustrations as Vietnam.

All around the president, people acknowledged the lack of options. Press Secretary George Christian observed that all the planning on responding to the *Pueblo* "was an exercise in frustration; there simply was no pat answer to acts of force or intimidation by a small antagonist against the United States." "Should we bomb Wonsan? That would probably kill the crew, and could touch off another war," he emphasized.

"How about seizing one of their naval vessels?" he continued: "Good idea. Where are the beggars? All they have are a few gunboats, and they're hugging the coast; we would have to violate their territorial waters to bag one. Abandon that scheme. What about the big cannery ship built in the Netherlands which is their pride and joy? Good idea . . . only it's in port and shows no sign of moving onto the high seas."[23]

As Johnson searched for a reasonable response, some Americans expressed compassion for the president. At a White House dinner on the 25th, the first lady and president stood in the greeting line. As people passed, Lady Bird "sensed something of what may be the feeling of the whole country." People pressed her hand and murmured: "We are praying for you." Others "tried to convey sympathy and understanding with a look." She thought to herself that they meant: "You are the President, and we know it is tough and we are in it with you."

Daily meetings followed on the *Pueblo*, distracting LBJ and his advisors from the ongoing battle at Khe Sanh. His critics continued hammering him, asking why the White House failed to defend the American flag or, at the other extreme, why was there another provocation under suspicious circumstances?

With an eye toward the upcoming presidential primaries only six weeks away, the president tried shaping public support by meeting with Hugh Sidey of *Time* and Jack Horner of the *Washington Star* on January 26.

"There should be no attribution to anybody on this," he opened, "I do not want any stories attributed to the President or to the White House. Is that understood?"

They replied affirmatively, and Sidey asked: "What is the mood and the reaction to the North Korean seizure? What are our options?"

Johnson replied: "This is a very serious situation. It is very grave. It does not lend itself to emotion or irresponsibility. At the same time you must do the thing most calculated to get the men back alive and the ship out."

"Our first option is diplomatic," he continued while outlining efforts at the UN, where Goldberg had presented the US case that day.

"This is not an unusual thing – the harassment itself," he pointed out. "What is unusual is the wanton capture of this ship on the high seas and the seizure of the men."

He pivoted, emphasizing: "The Communists are in real trouble in North Vietnam. This action may be tied to that in an effort to draw away forces or attention from Vietnam."

But he returned to a major theme, arguing: "While I know the press and some members of Congress always like to place the blame on their country, this incident to me looks like banditry on the high seas."

Sidey asked about credible intelligence on the matter. In response, LBJ said: "We must continue to keep our cool. We must not lose our heads. I do not know how long we have. I know we must keep our hands out and our guard up."

When Horner queried about what would happen if diplomatic efforts failed, LBJ told him: "I hope it will not be necessary to use military force.

I am neither optimistic nor pessimistic about this. It may be that we will lose the ship and the men, although I do not want to even think about it."

Throughout the opening days of the crisis, the president remained calm and patient, wanting to explore all the options. At Goldberg's urging, he supported asking the UN Security Council to help secure the crew's release. Everyone knew the Soviets would veto the proposal, but it put countries on the record as supporting the United States. "Our primary objective is to gain time, to give all concerned an opportunity for reasoning together. It will give the Soviets time to bring influence to bear on North Korea if they will," the president told his advisors.[24]

Throughout, LBJ continued wondering about Soviet complicity. Soon after the seizure, a Soviet plane left North Korea with large quantities of materials from the *Pueblo*. He also knew that when US Ambassador to the Soviet Union Llewellyn Thompson asked for assistance early on, the Soviets immediately sent a "very negative and chilly response." To him, the Soviets could scarcely have obtained information on the *Pueblo* from the North Koreans, conferred about it, and taken a position so quickly without prior consultation.[25]

Debates continued over possible actions as Rostow continued parroting the hard line. When Johnson pointed out Thompson's observation that Communists react negatively to demonstration of force, Rostow retorted, "this was not the lesson of the Cuban missile crises or the Berlin crises."

The president simply ignored him, having often followed JFK's evaluation of the MIT economist: "Walt has 10 ideas every day, 9 of which would lead to disaster, but one of which is worth having, and this makes it important to have a filter between the President and Rostow."[26] This was one of the nine.

The question of taking North Korean ships rose again, but McNamara pointed out that they only had a few vessels of any consequence, and they rarely left the shoreline. Someone shared that Polish sailors constituted large portions of the crews, and the Polish ambassador made some not too subtle threats about what would happen if the United States seized its citizens.

Ultimately, the president called on his staff to continue to win votes at the UN while communicating with President Park on the ongoing efforts. Finally, he stressed: "I want to get Senator Russell's judgment. He wants the Senate to go back on record in support of what we are doing. Let's not let Congress say we are going to war without consulting them."

He concluded the meeting: "Anytime you have a world crisis we must have our tanks, our caps on and our planes ready. Let's not be accused of being unprepared."[27]

He considered some suggestions of military action. Not long after the seizure, the Navy proposed sailing two destroyers, the U.S.S. *Truxton* and U.S.S. *Higbee*, into Wonsan under heavy air cover with the *Higbee* seizing the *Pueblo* and returning it to sea. LBJ vetoed the idea for fear of inciting another war and also the possible heavy casualties of the *Pueblo* crew killed in retribution.

In another case, the administration explored an attack by a dozen F-105s to sink the *Pueblo*. Colonel John Wright, designated to lead what many considered a suicide mission, gathered his men to brief them. Thirteen pilots appeared, although only twelve planes would fly. Wright gave each the opportunity to avoid the mission, understanding it was likely a one-way mission. A man raised his hand so Wright excused him. "No, that's not it," he replied. "One of the ships is a two-seater, and I'll ride in the back." Wright later said: "Luckily the mission was called off. It would have been certain death."[28]

Repeatedly, Johnson denied the request for action. He wrote: "In each case we decided that the risk was too great and possible accomplishment too small . . . I wanted the officers and crew of the *Pueblo* home alive, and I was prepared to take considerable political heat to achieve this goal."[29]

Beyond freeing the hostages, LBJ focused on preventing another seizure. *Time* magazine concluded early: "What the piracy of *Pueblo* did rehearse for the nation – and its adversaries – was a dismaying litany of military procedures and political assumptions that proved in the crunch to be inadequate, unimaginative and unbelievably overconfident." Editors concluded: "It will probably take years to direct and document all the slippages and oversights that have led the U.S. to the brink of a second front in Asia."[30]

In response to criticisms, Johnson appointed former Undersecretary of State George Ball to lead a committee to investigate the capture of the

Pueblo and to recommend how to limit future seizures. Ball recruited General Mark Clark, General Laurence Kuter, and Admiral George Anderson and others to assist.[31]

They met for several days, and ultimately agreed "unanimously ... on a draft that raised serious doubts about the exact location of the *Pueblo*." Ball added that it "was severely critical of the planning, organization, and, direction of the whole enterprise, and recommended a number of measures to avoid a similar disaster."

Clifford and Ball agreed to give only an oral report to the president to prevent leaks to the press that might cast doubt on the location of the *Pueblo*. "I located all the copies of the document and destroyed them so completely that I did not even keep a copy for my files. I am quite certain that none exists anywhere," Ball remembered.[32]

As more information flooded in, within a few days, LBJ went on national television and gave a flat, rather quick three-minute explanation of why he called for the reserves. "We shall continue to use every means available to find a prompt and peaceful solution." But he acknowledged that the ship had been taken in a "wanton and an aggressive act" and "clearly, this cannot be accepted."

LBJ also continued dealing with Congress on the *Pueblo* by providing information and lobbying for restraint. During a late meeting on the 30th with Senator Everett Dirksen (R-IL) and Congressman Gerald Ford (R-MI), the latter kept pressing the president on the errors made. At one point, LBJ fired back, "I think the mistake was made by the North Koreans. History may prove it wrong. I do not think the mistake was made by us."

Further on, Ford stressed, "their job is to carry out their mission."

Johnson queried, "How would you have done it?"

"If I had known what was on that vessel I might have blown it out of the water myself," he retorted.

When Johnson reported that Wheeler highlighted the fact that no aircraft could have saved the ship, Ford responded, "How could it have been more harmful than having the ship in the hands of the North Koreans? All of you seem to have a good reason for not doing something ... It seems to me your attitude is one of excuse rather than how to prevent it from happening again."

Johnson fired back: "You cannot prevent a man from shooting you tonight as you go home or even prevent a man from killing the President. The North Koreans were the outlaws. You can take the same ship at anytime."

Ford pressed forward, emphasizing: "I do not like the attitude that this was a helpless ship."

LBJ simply responded: "When you send out a spy he sometimes does not come back."

After some more sparring, Ford conceded: "All I am asking is that you check it. We must be able to do better next time."[33]

On January 31, Johnson continued engaging Congress by inviting congressional leaders including Stennis, Rivers, Carl Hayden (D-AZ), and Margaret Chase Smith (R-ME) to the White House. There, LBJ told them: "You won't hear many speeches about the North Koreans' attempt to cut off President Park's head and to kill the American ambassador. All we hear about is how bad our bombing is [in Vietnam]."

"We see both of these actions in Vietnam and in Korea as a coordinated challenge," Johnson said.

CIA Director Helms added, "there is not much doubt that there is a connection between the incursion along the DMZ and the seizure of the *Pueblo*. The reasons for these actions are to divert attention from the attacks in Vietnam and to keep South Korea from sending more troops to South Vietnam."

In addition, General Wheeler told them: "We could not prevent the capture of it under the circumstances."[34]

One senator noted afterward, "I never saw him [Johnson] so grim, serious, and curiously unfriendly. He didn't have the old self-confidence."[35]

That same day, the North Koreans castigated the Johnson administration for proposing a UN discussion. A high-ranking party leader stated "that the US imperialists have illegally brought the *Pueblo* case to the United Nations – although there is a precedent for the treatment of similar cases at the Korean Military Armistice Commission." To the North Koreans, the US decision constituted "a premeditated intrigue for covering up their criminal acts and misleading world public opinion . . . It will be a different story if they want to solve this question by the method of pervious practice."[36]

After much thought, LBJ acceded to Kim's demands and agreed to meetings at the MAC Commission. Since neither side in the Korean War signed a peace treaty, it remained a place to discuss issues related to border clashes, infiltration, and other differences, although most acknowledged it accomplished little other than providing Americans and their ROK allies and the North Koreans a forum to grandstand for the press.

Rear Admiral John Smith led the US delegation at the KMA Commission. He despised the position, describing it as nothing more than "just screaming at each other for the benefit of whomever was interested." He even refused to drink water in advance to prevent asking for a bathroom break as his counterpart, Major General Pak Chung Kuk, (who the American officers called, "Frog Face") would launch into a diatribe about his failure to take the talks seriously. By January 1968, Smith concluded: "These people [the North Koreans] are mad dogs . . . [They] just don't have any feelings. They are completely without scruples or conscience."

With the decision to submit the dispute to the KMA, Johnson tried to prevent an escalation in hostilities. The devastating attacks launched on January 31 in South Vietnam (the Tet Offensive) diverted his attention from the Korean peninsula. But it never meant the president lost sight of the hostages and the ship, but he appeared to have few options other than waiting out Kim. At that point, the challenge according to Rostow became to secure a deal "with the maximum dignity."[37]

The president recognized the ongoing challenges. In early February, a journalist asked the president about his confidence in getting the hostages returned.

LBJ's answer was simple: "No I am not."[38]

But, he persevered in the negotiating path. At a breakfast meeting on February 6 with congressional leaders including Hale Boggs (D-LA), Harry Byrd (D-VA), and Senate Majority Leader Mike Mansfield (D-MT), the president emphasized: "We are having meetings at Panmunjom, but they are getting nowhere." He highlighted, "we are trying to keep them talking." He returned to a common theme relating to Congress: "We are going through some dangerous times. North Korea has a treaty with the Soviets and with China. If a man has nothing to offer as an alternative, I advise that he say nothing."[39]

While trying to limit the criticism from Congress, Johnson continued demonstrating his fundamental commitment to preventing the *Pueblo* Incident from causing another war on the isthmus and distracting from the Tet Offensive in Vietnam. He desperately wanted to prevent over-extending US military commitments while avoiding a direct confrontation with China or the Soviet Union. It remained a politically unpopular position among hawks in Congress and the public who wanted retribution, but a pragmatic choice given the strategic considerations of early 1968.

Outsiders recognized the caution and patience being shown by the president. On February 8, British Prime Minister Harold Wilson joined LBJ at a state dinner. When he gave his toast, according to Lady Bird, he "told Lyndon that his restraint in handling the *Pueblo* incident will earn tribute from reasoning men everywhere, and indeed, from history."[40]

But, the president and others knew they needed to contain their hot-headed allies on the matter. LBJ and others acknowledged the importance of Seoul to the negotiations. "The South Koreans made clear their determination to retaliate if there was one more major provocation by the North," LBJ remembered.

The frustrations mounted with President Park in February. When he hinted at possibly balking at continuing in South Vietnam, the president and his advisors complained bitterly about him. On February 10, Clifford noted: "I am getting a few pains in my tail about the South Koreans. They should remember that we have kept 60,000 men and lost many thousands of American lives in defense of South Korea."

Johnson concurred: "I told Cy Vance last night that Park must understand our problems. Cy must make it clear to him that this talk of pulling out of Vietnam would cause us to pull men out of South Korea."[41]

In response, LBJ dispatched his long-time diplomatic trouble-shooter Cyrus Vance to Seoul in the second week of February. "We knew a major incident could easily erupt into a full-scale war on the Korean peninsula. We were concerned that, in their uneasy mood, the South Koreans might withdraw part of their forces from South Vietnam," the president emphasized.[42]

The skilled diplomat Vance managed to reassure the South Koreans, and tempers cooled measurably by the end of his visit. He told LBJ

Figure 2 On February 9, President Johnson, Secretary of State Dean Rusk, and Secretary of Defense Robert McNamara gathered in the Cabinet Room to discuss major issues, including the *Pueblo* seizure. (Courtesy of the LBJ Library)

on February 15: "In terms of the basic objectives of easing tension and getting a friendly relationship re-established, the mission was a success." But, he added: "in the long run, however, the picture is very dangerous."[43]

Most of the attention during February focused on the MAC. Meetings began almost immediately. Early on, Pak denied any North Korean role in the attack on Park, instead calling it a suicide squad composed of "patriotic" South Koreans. Smith angrily countered, "I want to tell you, Pak, that the evidence against you North Korean Communists is overwhelming, and I am [in] no mood to listen to an obfuscating smoke screen."

Pak changed his focus, calling LBJ a "war maniac" and adding: "They are burning Johnson's effigies today, but tomorrow they will burn Johnson alive." Simultaneously, Pyongyang radio described how the attack on the *Pueblo* "left the U.S. imperialists shivering."[44]

Immediately, Kim demanded the United States apologize for the incursion and end its spying. Of course, Kim wanted the statement before delivering the hostages.

The problem always remained that Kim wanted an embarrassing admission of guilt without first turning over the prisoners. LBJ and his advisors never trusted him to act in good faith, and he did little to dissuade them.

For most of February, even after LBJ offered to allow a third party to investigate the North Korean charge and promising to accept any ruling, Kim held firm on using the KMA Commission to negotiate. He also refused to release the US prisoners until the United States admitted its guilt.

Soviet Premier Alexi Kosygin, likely the only person able to have any influence over the North Koreans, rebuffed US requests for assistance, arguing that it was a bi-national problem and that outsiders would only complicate affairs. He added that an American military buildup in the region showed, "that there were many hotheads in the Pentagon who needed tranquilizers."

By late February, Goldberg told Johnson: "I see no alternative to painstakingly continuing discussions on the hope that we can wear the North Koreans down before they wear us down. It is better to Jaw-Jaw than War-War."[45]

Others supported negotiating, including Undersecretary of State Nicholas Katzenbach. He noted when people talked about attacking the North Koreans as punishment: "If you went and bombed one of their cities or something like that, you wouldn't help get the eighty-two men back and you run the risk of starting a war. So there's not much we've been able to do except talk."

The Pueblo Incident extracted a heavy toll on the president. As the crisis dragged on, Clifford observed that for Johnson, "the seizure of the *Pueblo* was almost too much to bear."[46]

LBJ often highlighted his frustration with the ongoing *Pueblo* stalemate. He wrote later: "If I had to pick a day that symbolized the turmoil we experienced through 1968, I think January 23 would be the day – the morning the *Pueblo* was seized."[47] He moaned, "in spite of every effort we could make, in spite of our patient attempts to balance firmness with reason, and in spite of our innumerable diplomatic moves, eleven miserable months went by before the men of the *Pueblo* were given their freedom. Every day that passed ... the plight of those men obsessed and haunted me."[48]

He desperately wanted a positive outcome, but the North Korean's intransigence created desperation. He told an aide, he would "do anything to get those men back – including meeting naked in the middle of the street at high noon."

As the North Koreans dallied, more Americans grew exasperated. In March, LBJ's brother, Sam Houston Johnson, gauged opinions. One Democratic leader in Louisiana complained bitterly about "getting shoved around all over the damned Orient." He emphasized, "Those little Korean bastards grab our ship and we just twiddled our goddamned thumbs. We ought to serve notice on them to return the *Pueblo* immediately or get themselves blown off the map. That's what you ought to tell Lyndon."

Despite the admonitions, throughout the spring, the administration continued promoting negotiations, something that required keeping the South Koreans from sparking an incident. It was a test of wills and diplomatic tact and sometimes the allies frustrated the White House as much as the enemy.

In April, LBJ flew to Honolulu to meet with President Park, trying to keep the South Koreans in Vietnam and also to prevent them from stoking the fires on the peninsula. Park complained that the United States worried more about the *Pueblo* than the commandos infiltrating his country.

The meeting was often contentious. One person observed: "Park ... demanded stronger commitments from him than he [Johnson] was prepared to give." After listening for a while, LBJ "asked to be excused, turned over the meeting to his aides and retired to the bedroom for a nap." According to Christian, "Park apparently got the message. When Johnson returned an agreement was reached much more to the American liking."[49]

As the sailors' captivity continued, external pressures mounted on LBJ. The families of the hostages, led by the *Pueblo* commander's wife Rose Bucher, lobbied hard in the press and Congress, often criticizing the White House's perceived inactivity. One family picketed Rusk's office, the mother carrying a sign: "I want my son without an apology." A "National Remember the Pueblo Committee" sprung up, handed out "Remember the *Pueblo*" bumper stickers, and pushed the White House and State Department to act forcefully.[50]

The efforts had an impact. In June, Congresswoman Charlotte Reid (R-IL) stood on the House floor and stated: "I have not forgotten the *Pueblo* and its valiant crew ... Neither have I forgotten their wives and families and the heavy burden of sorrow and despair they, too have carried for the past 182 days." On this anniversary (six months in captivity), "we need to reassure them – and the world – that the *Pueblo* and its men have not been forgotten ... that we will not rest until they are home again."[51]

While criticizing the Johnson administration, few people offered reasonable actions to ensure the release of the crew. Christian observed Nixon "told his audiences during the campaign; there would be no more *Pueblos*, just as there would be no more Vietnams."[52] But, he never explained how.

Others recognized the challenges. During the summer, Vice President Hubert Humphrey addressed the issue as he ran for president. He chastised those calling for military action, arguing: "Any damn fool can pick a fight. We've got one war right now and don't need another."[53]

Throughout, Johnson listened to the criticisms and genuinely empathized with the families of the hostages. But, to get them home alive, he had to wait out the enemy. While the initial war fever faded and other events transpired to remove the *Pueblo* from the front pages, including Tet and later the Soviet invasion of Czechoslovakia, the president never lost sight of the ultimate goal of securing the release of the crew of the *Pueblo*. Those who questioned his commitment never fully comprehended the anguish created in a year dominated by one crisis after another.

As the summer faded and the leaves began to fall on Capitol Hill, Kim remained steadfast in his demands. Johnson remained leery, fearful that Kim would renege on releasing the hostages after scoring a propaganda victory. Proposals floated around the State Department proposing the signing of an apology and then immediately renouncing it. However, the North Koreans appeared in no hurry to move forward.[54]

As Christmas neared, the administration hoped for a last minute settlement. Rusk rationalized, "our hope is North Korea will calculate that they are not likely to get more from President-elect Nixon than President Johnson."[55]

With LBJ losing hope on securing the release of the prisoners before the end of his term, the final resolution came from an unlikely source. One night, the State Department country director for Korea, James Leonard, discussed the *Pueblo* with his wife, Eleanor. She argued the United States should repudiate any document before signing an apology, reversing the order of earlier proposals. While some in the State Department opposed it, many seeking the conditional apology first presented in May, others saw a chance to end the crisis and have the hostages home by Christmas.[56]

Undersecretary of State Katzenbach took Leonard's proposal to LBJ. "I said, 'This may sound nutty to you,' and I told him." In response, Johnson said: "It did sound nutty and he couldn't believe it could happen." Katzenbach responded, "Well, can I try it?" The president told him: "If [Woodward is] willing to do it. I'm willing to do it."[57]

Major General Gilbert Woodward, who had replaced Admiral Smith, thought about the "prerepudiated" document: "They'll buy it ... It satisfied their one condition, a signature on a piece of paper ... The North Korean people would never hear about the repudiation. Their propaganda boys would take care of that. And as for the rest of the world, well, they just didn't care."

Not everyone was optimistic, including many in the White House. "Not one of the President's advisers thought this stunt would work ... It was a final shot in the dark and to everyone's surprise it hit its mark," Christian observed.[58]

Simultaneously, the administration launched an oblique attack on the North Koreans. US intelligence knew Kim had purchased a Dutch fishing vessel complete with refrigeration to allow his fishermen to operate in deeper waters. With catches diminishing near coastal areas, the government desperately needed new sources of production.

Thus, the US government learned that the Dutch intended to commission the ship in early 1969. Soon, US officials began inquiring about its departure. Some even questioned insurance giant Lloyd's of London about its transfer to the North Koreans. There was a not too veiled threat to seize it on the high seas. Rusk emphasized, "the ultimate object, of course, would be that such an inquiry on our part get back [to the] North Korean government."[59]

The ruse obviously worked and helped prod an end to the stand-off. When Woodward delivered an ultimatum to Pak on December 17th, the North Koreans' only request was a signature on the right side of the block, Korean style rather than above the line. "If you sign on the right of your name, we are agreeable," Pak soon responded.

Finally, at 10:30 am on December 23, the two sides faced off at the Bridge of No-Return at Panmunjom. Before the hostages arrived, Woodward read a statement: "The position of the United States government with regard to the *Pueblo* as consistently expressed . . . has been that the ship was not engaged in any illegal activity . . . The document which I am going to sign was prepared by the North Koreans and is at variance with the above position . . . I will sign the document to free the crew and only the crew."[60]

Finally, Commander Bucher led a procession across the bridge led by a coffin with the body of Duane Hodges, killed during the initial assault. One of the freed hostages commented, "it's just like climbing out of Hell into Heaven."[61]

Most in the media praised the end of the long nightmare and its resolution. *The New York Times* noted it was a "wise decision . . . to accept some sacrifice of American pride as preferable to a resolution by military force."[62] The president of the VFW wrote "to express the delight of the 1,450,000 members . . . The nation's restraint and patience have paid off, and the men have been returned."[63]

President Johnson and the White House rejoiced, although he immediately ordered an investigation into the treatment of the hostages and their behavior during captivity. However, it was a victory, and he remembered: "In spite of domestic passions and North Korean intransigence, we managed to secure the release of the eighty-two crewmen of the USS *Pueblo*."[64]

In hindsight, Christian appraised the situation well. "The stepchild of American foreign policy for the year 1968 was the communications ship *Pueblo* and its hapless crew in a North Korean prison."[65] He also concluded, "North Korea had shown that gunboat diplomacy could also be used to tweak the nose of a super-power without much fear of retaliation."[66]

In the final analysis, Johnson showed remarkable restraint and patience in dealing with the *Pueblo* seizure. Hawks called for retribution, including Nixon who had to deal with his own crisis in April 1969 when a North Korean MIG-21 shot down a reconnaissance plane, killing thirty-one crewmen. However, Johnson understood any military actions would ensure the death of the crew.[67] He also recognized the limits of American power, especially in the shadow of the heavy fighting in Vietnam in 1968. He wanted to prevent the taking of a spy ship from turning into WWIII, or at the minimum, another war in Korea. In the long term, the perseverance paid off, although not in political terms, as many Americans saw it as further shattering the perceived American invincibility as the country appeared on the verge of crumbling in 1968.

CHAPTER 3

Tet

A Very Near Thing, January–March 1968

L ike so many other days since January 21, the president awoke early in the morning of Tuesday, January 30 to secure reports on "his boys" fighting at Khe Sanh. At 5:37 a.m., he called the Situation Room for an update on the heavily outnumbered Americans.

Over the past week, he often put on his slippers and grabbed a flashlight to navigate the dark hallways to the basement to check on "his boys." The nightmare of another Dien Bien Phu haunted him even as Chairman of the Joint Chiefs of Staff General Earle Wheeler reported that US Commander in South Vietnam, General William Westmoreland, assured him: "We can hold Khe Sanh and we should hold Khe Sanh."[1]

Once in the Situation Room, he usually paced around, asking the staff for updates on casualties and enemy movements. Sometimes, the tall Texan leaned over and studied the sand diorama of Khe Sanh created for him, one flanked by large detailed topographical maps of the battlefield.

The lack of sleep and late night jaunts extracted a heavy toll. He regularly looked tired and disheveled the following day, struggling to stay focused and on task. It could last for long periods of time, and rarely was there a respite.

The 30th was no different, as a tired and restless LBJ made his way through morning meetings until the regularly scheduled Tuesday lunch with his national security team. They discussed the *Pueblo* and Khe Sanh, particularly the latter and its implications.

At 2:35 p.m., National Security Advisor Walt Rostow received a phone call reporting heavy mortar attacks in Saigon near the presidential palace and the American Embassy.

LBJ simply responded, "This could be bad."[2] He was correct.

Unbeknownst to the president and his advisors, the Viet Cong and North Vietnamese had launched the Tet Offensive. While some predicted it, no one anticipated its enormity. One American officer noted, "if we'd gotten the whole game plan, it wouldn't have been believed. It wouldn't have been credible to us."[3]

As observers watched heavy fighting break out all over the country, including inside the perimeter of the heavily fortified US Embassy in Saigon, many shared the feelings of staunch war supporter, Walter Cronkite. In his newsroom in New York City, he asked: "What the hell is going on? I thought we were winning this war."[4]

The offensive pushed the conflict to the forefront, one that caused Johnson so much grief in the three preceding years. After dramatically escalating the war in the summer of 1965, the president found himself approving numerous troop requests that swelled the number of troops to more than 500,000 Americans by January 1968. Throughout, he sought the independence of South Vietnam, although he found the lack of competence of the South Vietnamese Government (SVG) often maddening. Having launched a peace offensive with the San Antonio Formula and the round the world trip in December, Johnson could not find an acceptable solution to extricate the United States from the quagmire, and Tet heightened the problems.

Johnson posed a similar question to that of Cronkite throughout the night on January 31, requesting periodic updates from the Situation Room. For the White House, the surprise attacks constituted the greatest challenge in Vietnam since the introduction of large-scale US forces in 1965. Never had the enemy staged such a substantial offensive. It punched holes into his positive public reports on Vietnam and those of his commanders at the end of 1967 and helped create a crisis of confidence.

After a relatively sleepless night, he rose at 6 a.m. to start digesting the intelligence. It was a cold, dreary day outside, reflecting the mood of the president and others in the White House.

At 7:24 a.m., McNamara called and provided his evaluation. "Well, I think it shows two things, Mr. President. First, that they have more power than some credit them with. I don't think it's a last gasp action."

"I believe we'll deal them a heavy defeat," the secretary of defense correctly predicted, but "I think in other areas it's largely a propaganda effort . . . and I think they'll gain that way."

In response, LBJ digressed and complained about Congress. "Their only interest is to find something wrong," he growled, "people look for something wrong unless you've got so much choking them that is happening."[5]

His preoccupation with Congress and the opposition of the "doves" led by the powerful chairman of the Senate Foreign Relations Committee (SFRC), J. William Fulbright (D-AR), and others including Wayne Morse (I-OR), Frank Church (D-ID), and Albert Gore, Sr. (D-TN) had haunted him since the controversial hearing in January 1966. Sometimes, he referred to the Arkansas representative as "Senator Half-Bright" and the animosity flowed both ways as some in Congress sought to rein in LBJ's power regarding Vietnam.[6]

Johnson went into crisis management over the perceived debacle in Vietnam. Unlike the *Pueblo*, where he sustained a cautious and restrained position, he rarely showed such inclinations on Vietnam. It brought out the worst in him as well as a divided electorate. Soon, he would give people whiplash as his swings between despondency and optimism exceeded normal standards, partly a reflection on the split between his closest advisors on the outcome of the offensive. Tet became the central topic in Washington for nearly two months.

To stem the criticism from Congress and handle the new crisis, Johnson practiced some damage control. He hosted a breakfast for more hawkish congressional leaders, including Senator John Stennis (D-MS), Congressman Mendel Rivers (D-SC), and Senator Margaret Chase Smith (R-ME). Ironically, they met in the family dining room covered by wallpaper honoring the American revolutionaries and a large painting depicting the British surrender at Yorktown.

LBJ sat at the head of the table, his glasses unable to hide the deep circles under his eyes. He opened, "I want to review the problems of the Nation with you. There is now a war spirit in the country, but we do have more sympathizers and 'agent[s] of the enemy' in this country working against us."

He acknowledged the "desperate attack . . . being launched against us in Vietnam" but emphasized, "we have inflicted heavy losses on the enemy." Still, he lamented, "at home many people want to destroy confidence in your leaders and in the South Vietnamese government. I ask you to measure your statements before you make them. The greatest source of Communist propaganda statements is our own statements."

Concluding, LBJ told the group: "If somebody launches a tirade against our people, I hope you will tell them to be responsible. [But] we may have to extend enlistments. We may have to have 100 million dollars for Korea. We may need further call-ups."[7]

The meeting reflected an effort to create a positive spin on the surprise offensive that shocked almost everyone. Whereas the *Pueblo* reflected Johnson's ability to calmly and patiently address problems, anything on Vietnam, including Tet, exposed his obsession with trying to prevent a Communist victory. It often led to him trying to persuade himself, as well as his cabinet and the American people, that events unfolding in Vietnam were not as dire as some portrayed it. He often failed.

As always, he stayed in perpetual motion throughout the day. At one point, his daughter Lynda telephoned around 2:30 p.m. to encourage him to have lunch.[8]

An hour later, he finally arrived, chatting with reporters as he marched through the White House, acting like a man without a worry in the world. In the family dining room, he greeted several journalists, including Hugh Sidey of *Time*, Frank Cormier of the Associated Press, and Carroll Kilpatrick of the *Washington Post*.

As he ate a bowl of soup and a sandwich, downing them with a glass of milk, the journalists asked about his health. In response, he claimed to be sleeping well, a clear contrast to the dark circles under his eyes and weary body posture.

Then, he took the offensive, bragging about the sound whipping being administered to the Communists. He sounded so optimistic, almost to the point of jubilation. However, as one person observed: "They did not believe him."[9]

Despite putting on a brave face, the next day a more contrite and pensive LBJ appeared at the annual presidential prayer breakfast at the Shoreham Hotel in northwest D.C. He told the large audience: "The nights are very long. The winds are very chill. Our spirits grow weary and restive as the springtime of man seems farther and farther away. I can, and I do, tell you that in these long nights your president prays."[10]

However, the more pugnacious LBJ returned at a February 2 press conference, where he characterized the enemy offensive as a "complete failure." He chastised those allowing the enemy to substitute "a psychological victory" for a military one. Confidently, he argued, "when the American people know the facts ... I do not believe that they [the Communists] will achieve a psychological victory."[11]

Mood swings often developed about Vietnam in the months following the Tet Offensive. Johnson vacillated between confidence and self-doubt, sometimes in the same day, as recent reports of casualties from Vietnam often shaped his responses. Also, his talks with either hawkish or dovish advisors played a role, affecting his disposition at that time. Unlike other crises, he demonstrated a less cautious and prudent deliberation and often failed to recognize the limits of US power, driven by an illusion of still hoping to wipe away the stain of Vietnam from his record.

While Johnson argued the enemy would not achieve a psychological victory, he was wrong. As the fighting intensified, media coverage swayed many Americans. Many watched in horror the summary execution of a handcuffed, plaid shirted VC prisoner by Saigon Chief of Police General Nguyen Ngoc Loan on February 1.[12]

The savage act affected many in the American public and some in the president's inner circle, including Harry McPherson. He emphasized the execution showed Americans "not only the inhumanity of an ally, but confirmation of an impression that had been building for years: we were sunk in a war between alien peoples with whom we shared few human values." He added that the nation saw, "Loan, raising his revolver on every channel, turning public doubt into heartsick rage. And carrying us along with him."[13]

Loan's act and Tet changed McPherson's views, a man described by special advisor John Roche as "a guy who used to lay into Johnson, too. I mean he used to really sock it to him." Larry Temple underscored McPherson "was the president's conscience."[14] By 1968, McPherson remained one of the most prominent advisors in the president's inner circle.

Beforehand, McPherson usually accepted Westmoreland's reports.[15] However, after Tet, he stressed: "I put aside the confidential cables. I was more persuaded by the tube and by the newspapers. I was fed up with the optimism that seemed to flow without stopping from Saigon."[16]

The fact his inner circle seemed affected by the negative reporting particularly perplexed Johnson. "I was surprised and disappointed that the enemy's efforts produced such a dismal effect on various people inside the government ... whom I had always regarded as staunch and unflappable. Hanoi must have been delighted."[17]

With some advisors wavering, LBJ grew testier in exchanges with critics. On February 6 at a breakfast meeting, Senator Robert Byrd (D-WV) complained about the poor intelligence. The president objected, responding defensively, "I don't agree with any of that. We knew that they planned a general uprising around Tet. Our intelligence showed there was a winter-spring offensive planned. We did not know the precise places that were going to be hit."[18]

Afterward, LBJ continued complaining about Byrd, lamenting, "there seems to be a great effort to discredit this government and its military establishment."[19] To the president, "this is all part of a political offensive. They say we had the people believing we were doing very well in Vietnam when we actually were not."[20]

Despite the negativity in Congress and the White House, some polls showed the American people initially rallying around LBJ. Gallup and Harris polls displayed a five-point increase for those calling for tougher military efforts to end the war. Fifty-three percent even favored intensifying military operations for "an all-out crash effort in the hope of winning the war quickly even at the risk of China or Russia entering the war."[21]

Yet, LBJ instinctively knew any support remained tenuous. He watched his approval ratings for handling of the war slide from 39 percent in January 1968 to 32 percent a month later. The decline escalated, reaching 26 percent by late March. The hawks wanted more, while the doves sought withdrawal. It was a no-win situation.[22]

The constant criticism and the stress of the war took a heavy toll on Johnson and his family. Lady Bird admitted on February 7 that "these night[s] I am not sleeping much and I dream, sometimes nightmares, sometimes just a long, long dream in which I'm lost and going from

Figure 3 During the tense discussions over the Tet Offensive at National Security Council meeting in February 1968, President Johnson and Secretary of Defense McNamara show the strain of dealing with the crisis in Vietnam. (Courtesy of the LBJ Library)

room to room and can't find my way." She added, "but poor Lyndon – he turns out his lights so late and wakes up so early. Sometimes I think the greatest courage is just to get up in the morning and start tackling the job again."[23]

Infighting in the administration and Pentagon exacerbated the stress on the president. Unlike the *Pueblo*, where most of his advisors supported patience and restraint, there were notable differences in opinion regarding Tet. Hawks in the military led by General Wheeler and their allies like US Ambassador to Vietnam Bunker Ellsworth and Rostow saw an opportunity to further accelerate the search for a military victory. On the other side, doves in the White House and Pentagon recognized the futility of continuing and pushed the president toward a negotiated peace that included a bombing halt to jump start the process.

That job required continuing to worry about "his boys." At a meeting on February 7, LBJ queried, "How do things look at Khesanh?"

General Wheeler responded, "Good."

"Bob, are you worried?" the president asked McNamara.

"I am not worried about a true military defeat."

Then Wheeler jumped in, "Mr. President, this is not a situation to take lightly. This is of great military concern to us."

The president simply responded, "Everything he [Westmoreland] wants, let's get it to him."[24]

Unfortunately, Wheeler interpreted the statement literally and put into effect his political agenda. On February 8, he messaged Westmoreland: "My sensing is that the critical phase of the war is upon us, and I do not believe that you should refrain from asking for what you believe is required under such circumstances."[25]

Now began the long song and dance between the president and the hawks. Initially, Westmoreland's reports optimistically highlighted heavy enemy casualties, an ARVN performing beyond expectations, and victories across Vietnam. Ambassador Ellsworth sent similar messages. Thus, the president thought Tet was a victory, not hard for him to believe as he wanted to escape the sinking feeling of no end in sight.

But on the other side, he was a political realist who watched the nightly news and read the major newspapers, whose reports diverged from Westmoreland's rosy ones. LBJ wanted to believe his general, but he harbored concerns about the US military's ability to win, especially after years of endless promises.

Deep down, something else was at play. LBJ was a man who refused to admit mistakes. His longtime confidant George Reedy stressed that LBJ "had never in his entire life learned to confess error, and this quality, merely amusing or exasperating in a private person – resulted in cosmic tragedy for the President."[26]

The same trait was on full display in February 1968. While Westmoreland fed him positive reports, an inner voice told him that he was right and victory was just within grasp, one ensuring an independent South Vietnam. He would escape the label of being the first president to lose a war. Why would he now reverse course and deny himself a chance to win? If anything, in early February, he appeared ready to double down on a military solution to force an acceptable peace that ensured South Vietnam's survival as an anti-Communist bulwark.

Such bravado was on full display at the state dinner for British Prime Minister Harold Wilson on Thursday, February 8. Flanked by Lady Bird wearing a majestic champagne satin dress under a beautiful gold coat and looking on admiringly, he launched into a toast: "The American and British peoples are not short-distance crusaders. We are veteran campaigners, not amateurs, and we have never been quitters. I have enormous confidence in the character of my own people in their ability to understand and master trial."[27]

Thus, when he entered meetings with the JCS on February 9, he told them, "I want to see what we should do in Vietnam."

His major questions centered on: "Will we have to put in more men? Can we do it with the Vietnamese as they are now?"

After the admirals and generals threw out a few ideas, Wheeler laid down the ultimate end game: more men. He rationalized Westmoreland needed them for reserves and "to prevent the ARVN from falling apart."

"How many men does this represent?" LBJ asked.

"25,000 men ... plus support personnel," Wheeler responded.

Immediately, McNamara interjected, "the total would run about 40,000."

A back and forth continued as LBJ processed the request. McNamara fought to hold the line, but Wheeler sounded alarms: "This emergency is not going to go away in a few days or few weeks," he said.

The president shot back. "All last week I asked two questions. The first was 'Did Westmoreland have what he needed?' (You answered yes.) The second question was, 'Can Westmoreland take care of the situation with what he has there now?' The answer was yes."

Then, he loaded up, "Tell me what has happened to change the situation."

Wheeler explained 15,000 more NVA moved south.

An outwardly skeptical president said, "What you are saying is this. Since last week we have information we did not know about earlier?"

Wheeler pivoted, concentrating on ARVN losses.

Listening, Johnson instead focused on the South Vietnamese carrying a larger share of the fighting. "We have to get the Government of South Vietnam to increase its efforts. Why can't we get them to do as we do, call up 18-year-olds and give the American people the impression that they are doing as much as we?" he queried.

Then, Clifford noted a "strange contradiction" in the administration and JCS message. "On one hand, we are saying that we have known of the buildup ... We have publicly told the American people that the communist offensive was: (a) not a victory, (b) produced no uprising among the Vietnamese ... and (c) cost the enemy between 20,000 and 25,000 of his combat troops."

Then, the incoming secretary of defense stressed, "now our reaction to all of that is to say that the situation is more dangerous today than it was before all of this." He concluded, "I think we should give some very serious thought to how we explain saying on one hand the enemy did not take a victory and yet we are in need of more troops and possibly an emergency call up."

LBJ deflected him, only responding that the enemy changed tactics.[28] However, Clifford continually came back to it over the following weeks.

Not long after, on Monday, February 12, LBJ gave a speech that highlighted his mindset on the first troop request, telling an audience: "Sad but steady – always convinced of his cause – Lincoln stuck it out. Sad but steady, so will we."[29]

But, the urgency of Westmoreland's messages concerned the president and others. When asked for his reaction, Rusk replied: "It looks to me like Westmoreland wants to take advantage of an opportunity to exploit the situation."

The president fought to avoid reflexively deferring to the military brass as he often had in the past. He was not a soldier, despite having received a Silver Star during WWII, and Johnson knew it. But, again, his fallback position was to give the military leaders what they wanted, especially if they thought it could achieve gains.

LBJ responded, "If he [Westmoreland] wanted them to take advantage of the opportunity to do more, I would also send them."

Clifford queried skeptically, "General Westmoreland's telegram has a much greater sense of urgency in it. Why is that?"

Wheeler explained that the general had earlier been conservative in troop requests. However, even LBJ remained leery. "Westy said he could use troops one day last week. Today he comes in with an urgent request for them."[30]

Now, however, with some close advisors such as McNamara and Clifford wavering, Johnson appeared more skeptical than any point preceding February 1968. Yes, he had approved incremental increases in troop levels for three years, but at the same time, he micromanaged the air war and tried to limit the chances of the war provoking WWIII. The Tet Offensive shook his confidence despite the optimistic reports of Westmoreland and Bunker. Clearly, he was not convinced that more troops ensured better results, particularly with the continuing SVG structural issues remaining in place. More doubts crept in over the next few weeks.

Throughout the week, LBJ mulled over the initial troop request. While doing so, he left the White House to visit troops.

On February 17, the president traveled to Fort Bragg in North Carolina and visited with members of the 82nd Airborne before traveling to El Toro, California, to bid farewell to Marines leaving for Vietnam.

In North Carolina, after a short speech thanking the young men for their dedication, he worked the crowd like a campaign stop, shaking hands and talking with many.

At one point, LBJ struck up a conversation with a soldier.

"Have you been to Vietnam before?"

"Yes, sir, three times," he responded.

"Are you married?" the president asked?

"Yes sir," the soldier replied quickly.

Following a natural progression, the president queried, "Do you have children?"

"Yes, sir, one."

"Boy or girl?

"A boy, sir"

"How old is he?"

Then, the president received a shock. "He was born yesterday morning, sir," the soldier replied sadly.

LBJ wrote: "That was the last question I asked him. It tore my heart out to send back to combat a man whose first son had just been born."[31] He knew his son-in-law Chuck Robb would soon depart for Vietnam, perhaps to die or be maimed, leaving behind his pregnant wife Lynda. The lives of those he sent into war clearly weighed on him.

Like everyone, he knew it had been a bad week for the troops in Vietnam. The Pentagon released information that 543 Americans died with another 2,547 wounded, the highest total to that point.

Equally alarming, the US figures were significantly higher proportionally than the ARVN.[32]

The increasing deaths negatively affected the president. His brother Sam observed, "even the loss of one American soldier (and it was never that few) could bring on a mood of sadness and frustrated anger that would keep him awake" all night.[33] In February 1968, there were many restive nights.

As the fighting continued, Tet created other problems for LBJ. Senator Eugene McCarthy (D-MN), who declared his candidacy for the nomination in November, worked hard as the peace candidate in New Hampshire. He told one crowd: "The most important struggle for the future welfare of America is not in the jungles of Vietnam; it is in the streets and schools and tenements of our cities. Yet the commitment of resources and moral energy to the problems of our cities has been but a fraction of the amount committed to the Saigon government."[34]

More threatening, LBJ's powerful nemesis Robert Kennedy also sensed an opportunity. As the heavy fighting unfolded in early February, one of his aides, Peter Edelman, jubilantly announced: "The fig leaf was gone. Tet just ripped the fig leaf right off."[35]

Bobby concurred, emphasizing: "Tet has changed everything, and if I don't go now and make an effort in the primaries, I think I'll be nothing."[36] Kennedy immediately criticized the administration's characterization of Tet as a victory, telling one crowd the offensive "shattered the mask of official illusion with which we have concealed our true circumstances, even from ourselves" and that "total military victory is not within sight or around the corner."[37]

But beyond LBJ's political opponents, the Tet Offensive took a lot of the wind out of the sails of even ardent hawks, including Rusk. By 1968, he admitted: "I was bone-tired" and survived on a daily diet of "aspirin, scotch, and four packs of Larks."[38]

Over time, doubts had crept into his mind. His relatives in Cherokee County, Georgia, asked him, "Dean, if you can't tell us when this war is going to end, well then maybe we just ought to chuck it." He thought, "The fact was that we could not, in good faith tell them."[39]

He turned such opinions into questions for the president. At one point, Rusk told LBJ: "So if my Cherokee County cousins were to say to me, 'Look, if collective security means 50,000 dead Americans every ten years, and it is not even collective, maybe it's not a very good idea.'"[40]

The pressure built, and Rusk snapped. On encountering reporters after a briefing, the normally controlled southern gentleman lost his temper. John Scali, an ABC correspondent (and future US ambassador to the UN under Nixon), hounded him on why the United States failed to anticipate the offensive.[41]

Angrily, Rusk shouted: "Whose side are you on?" Then, he added, "I'm secretary of state of the United States, and I'm on our side! None of your papers or your broadcasting apparatuses are worth a damn unless the United States succeeds ... So I don't know why people have to be probing for the things that one can bitch about, when there are two thousand stories on the same day about things that are more constructive."[42]

With Rusk privately wavering, it appeared only Rostow and some members of the JCS remained steadfast hawks. McNamara clearly flipped by February 1968, and Clifford expressed doubts. Unlike his successor, who had a much tighter circle of advisors, Johnson relied on a fairly large group to provide counsel. This helped ensure the whiplash of LBJ's changing position as he vacillated between military and diplomatic solutions. His shifting opinions reflected the battle for his heart and mind on Vietnam waged throughout the White House, Foggy Bottom, and the Pentagon.

The bureaucratic battles escalated in the capitol by the end of the month. Wheeler returned from Vietnam on the 24th and reported Westmoreland wanted another 206,000 troops. At this point, Wheeler and his allies appeared to want to use Tet to secure not just some replacements, but a massive buildup to expand the war into the border sanctuaries, all the while enhancing pacification programs. Their request sparked an intense debate that dominated all conversations about Vietnam for the next two weeks.

On the 27th, with LBJ at the ranch, McNamara led a meeting of top advisers to discuss the troop increase. The conversation bounced all over the place, from the exorbitant costs and need for higher taxes to the required massive reserve call-ups and extensions of tours. At one point, McPherson simply exclaimed: "This is unbelievable and futile."

Rusk talked about intensifying the bombing. A visibly shaken McNamara, his voice faltering as he held back sobs, laid into the proposition. "The goddamned Air Force, they're dropping more on North Vietnam than we dropped on Germany in the last year of World War II, and it's not doing anything!"

Distraught, he looked at Clifford and murmured, "We simply have to end this thing. I just hope you can get hold of it. It is out of control."[43]

Califano, who rarely attended such meetings, characterized it as "the most depressing three hours in my years of public service." Outside of Rostow, pessimism flooded the room as Undersecretary of State Nicholas de Katzenbach and McNamara "sounded a chorus of despair," while Rusk "appeared exhausted and worn down," Califano remembered.[44]

As Califano and McPherson rode back to the White House, the former admitted to being "physically shaken" and "completely drained."

"This is crazy," Califano said, adding, "It really is all over, isn't it?"

McPherson simply responded, "You bet it is."[45]

The February 27th meeting report notes reached the ranch that evening. The major issues, according to LBJ, were: "What constituted the military strategy and tactics underlying the troops proposals? What budgetary and balance-of-payments problems would these proposals raise? ... What peace proposals should be included ... What was the South Vietnamese capacity to carry the load?"[46]

The next day, Johnson returned to the White House and received a bleak report from Wheeler, who stressed, "the margin of victory was very thin in a number of battles." Nearly one third of the ARVN battalions were "ineffective" and needed months to recover. He emphasized, "pacification is at a halt" and concluded: "1968 will be a critical year in the war. There is heavy fighting ahead."

LBJ listened and asked, "What are the alternatives."

Wheeler alarmingly noted: "Without the reserve, we should be prepared to give up the 2 northern provinces of South Vietnam."

Then, the president turned to Khe Sanh and asked: "What about taking the initiative ourselves? Is there anything we can do other than just sitting and waiting for them to attack?"

When no real response came, LBJ queried: "So he [Westmoreland] really has no initiative of his own other than to interrupt their road building and patrol."

Then, he mused, "Perhaps we have overbuilt Khe Sanh. It looks like the enemy can pick and choose his own time and place."

He also challenged Westmoreland's strategy in the north. Why 206,000 troops at this point if not to wage an offensive? What about prosecuting the war more aggressively? Westmoreland wanted 105,000 by May 1. What were the plans?

For really the first time, LBJ asked some hard questions on Khe Sanh as well as the military plans. Had it been a distraction to allow the enemy to move more toward Hue and the central highlands? Also, would more troops really help the garrison? But in reality, it was only part of a more complex and fluid situation in South Vietnam created by Tet.

Then, the conversation turned to the substantial costs for the buildup. McNamara reported it involved WWII and Korean veterans, men with two years of regular enlistments in the active reserves, and those with six months' training and no active service.[47]

LBJ paused. Throughout the war, he avoided significant mobilization of the reserves and the National Guard, both populated by scions of the influential seeking to escape the draft. He worried many hawks might turn against him if their offspring started dying.

The meeting soon ended, but afterwards, many questions remained. A fundamental one revolved around the effectiveness of the bombing. Rusk admitted, "I have spent all of my professional life dealing with the differences between the promise and performance of air power."[48]

This was important to the president. One of his major bargaining tools in peace proposals was a bombing halt as outlined in the San Antonio Formula. With fewer people believing in its usefulness, it provided an opening to reintroduce it. Negotiations needed a jump-start and using a bombing reduction or suspension might open that door.

After the initial briefings, Wheeler continued painting a drab picture as part of his offensive for more troops. Clifford stressed Wheeler told LBJ that the Tet Offensive was "a colossal disaster for us" and that "we were in real peril." He remembered Johnson was "as worried as I have ever seen him."[49]

Wheeler's allies included Rostow. After the February 28th meeting, he bombarded the president with memorandums strongly supporting the troop request, arguing that the Communists intended to turn 1968 into the year of decision.[50]

At the time, some watching Rostow thought he finally lost his connection to reality. "Walt has a kind of rugby player's view of . . . international events," Clifford observed, "it's sort of a 'pull up your socks – let's get going, let's put our shoulders to the wheel . . . and it's going to be okay' point of view." McPherson was more direct by March 1968, emphasizing Rostow was "utterly neglecting Good Friday and only talking about Easter."[51]

Whatever their individual positions, throughout the debates, everyone planned on LBJ being in office for another four years. This was not a stop-gap measure until after the election. It was a long-term policy decision that would either offset or confirm the past four years of build-ups, ones matched by the enemy. No one in the White House, Pentagon, or State Department, outside of a few close confidants, thought LBJ would not seek reelection. Thus, they thought the decisions made during and after Tet would determine the path in Vietnam for years.

Ultimately, LBJ settled on Clifford to lead a task force, and he gave simple instructions: "Give me the lesser of the evils."[52] LBJ also asked the members to consider some questions: "What objectives would additional forces achieve? What would our budget problems be and could we meet them? If we increased forces, what negotiation posture should we take? What steps should we take to improve South Vietnamese performance? . . . What problems would we face with public opinion?"[53]

The president's decision to create a commission reflected a normal pattern employed by LBJ and others in the face of a crisis, although this one had a very quick turnaround. Putting together a task force provided a chance for many people to weigh in on the issues and, hopefully, create some viable options for the president. But, it also allowed for internecine bureaucratic warfare to expand, primarily in the Pentagon.

Deep down, LBJ wanted negotiations built off the San Antonio Formula, but Hanoi rebuffed the proposal because of the conditions added by the administration and their own desire to initiate their offensive. However, Tet changed their minds, as they experienced heavy losses.

Reports began arriving about a change in Hanoi's position. On February 21, UN Secretary General U Thant reported that North Vietnamese officials said talks could commence immediately if the aerial assault stopped. A few days later, an Indian diplomat confirmed Hanoi promised "substantive" talks within weeks of a bombing halt and a guarantee to meaningfully discuss the 1954 and 1962 Geneva agreements.[54]

With some hope developing on the diplomatic front, simultaneously more doubts crept into the mind of LBJ about a military solution. An important one originated when Cronkite jumped on a plane for Vietnam on February 7. He had visited in 1965, but this time he found shell-shocked civilians choking the roads as well as signs of the death and destruction everywhere. Cronkite encountered military commanders, especially Westmoreland, presenting one version of the war, while the troops and the Vietnamese civilians gave another.

Finally, after a week, he returned home and on February 27, he gave the "Report from Vietnam." The former hawk, the epitome of Middle America with his short-cropped, greying hair, simple dark suit and white shirt, delivered a blistering critique as millions of Americans tuned in.

The man so many Americans trusted and welcomed into their living rooms every night, including LBJ, editorialized: "Who won and who lost in the great Tet offensive . . . I'm not sure." Yet, he added, "we have been too often disappointed in the optimism of the American leaders . . . to have faith any longer in the silver linings they find in the darkest clouds."

Then, he dropped the hammer: "For it seems now more than ever . . . Vietnam is to end in a standoff."[55] Growing more somber, he stressed: "For every means we have to escalate, the enemy can match us." Then, he said: "To say that we are mired in stalemate seems the only realistic, yet unsatisfactory conclusion." In conclusion, he emphasized: "But it is increasingly clear to this reporter that the only rational way out then will be to negotiate, not as victors, but as honorable people who lived up to their pledge to defend Democracy and did the best they could."[56]

His speech immediately affected LBJ, who learned about it while traveling from the ranch to speak at the University of Texas campus in Austin. According to Press Secretary George Christian, he simply said: "If I've lost Cronkite, I've lost the country."[57]

The loss of such a prominent member of the establishment, a man with a megaphone that reached millions, caused Johnson to pause and question his position even more. But, simultaneously, he remained torn about wanting to preserve the mission that he embarked on years earlier in saving South Vietnam from the Communists. Never one to admit a mistake, LBJ held onto some hope that the defeat administered to the North Vietnamese and the Viet Cong would help him salvage the crusade. But, with Cronkite and others increasingly pessimistic, it proved harder each day.

With many people increasingly wavering, so did the president's advisors. Clifford stressed: "There can be no question that [Tet] was a turning point in the war." He complained the military attributed defeat to the media and the antiwar movement but "our policy failed because it was based on false premises and false promises."[58]

Until Tet, he admitted, "I still accepted the military's views that the war was being won in the field." With Tet, "now my faith in our ability to achieve our objectives within an acceptable period of time was shaken and began to erode."[59]

If skeptical before taking over the Pentagon, Clifford's views shifted quickly once in office. He stressed, "fundamental assumptions on which I had based my views crumbled – not with a single dramatic revelation, but slowly and unevenly."[60]

The Clifford Task Force that included the dovish, wonkish Paul Warnke from the Pentagon quickly began deliberations, sparking a divisive bureaucratic battle in the Pentagon. One civilian, Morton Halperin, observed, "we were going to write what we thought even if it meant we all got fired." He concluded the final draft, "really attacked the fundamental motives" of US intervention in Vietnam.[61]

On March 1, the skeptical Warnke read a draft to Clifford and Wheeler. Pessimistically, it questioned whether the "payment on an open-ended commitment" of more troops would break "Hanoi's will to fight."[62] It zeroed in on the fact that the Communists could match almost any troop increase. Instead, the document stressed the large-scale escalation ensured "no early end to the conflict."[63]

The draft also contended forcefully that more US troops further undermined the ability and willingness of the South Vietnamese to fight.

More American troops encouraged "total Americanization of the war" and reinforced Saigon's continued belief that the United States "will continue to fight its war while it engages in backroom politics and permits widespread corruption."[64]

Clifford digested the report and found himself increasingly in agreement with Warnke and other civilians in the Pentagon. On March 4, he delivered it to the president in a meeting with his national security team. It differed from Warnke's version, the secretary of defense throwing some bones to Wheeler and his allies by allowing an additional 22,000 troops. Yet, it emphasized, "this is as far as we are willing to go."

At the heart of the matter, it questioned whether more constituted better. It underscored, "we seem to have a sinkhole. We put in more – they [the enemy] match it."

As the meeting progressed, Rusk said: "Mr. President, without a doubt, this will be one of the most serious decisions you will have made since becoming President. This has implications for all of our society."

LBJ knew it.

He became even more attentive as the discussion shifted to the financial costs. Secretary of the Treasury Henry Fowler reported, "we would need an entirely new fiscal program to offset expenditures dollar for dollar." He predicted another $2.5 billion in expenditures for 1968 and $10 billion for 1969, with cuts in domestic spending of $2–3 billion as well as new taxes.[65]

The president really perked up when Rusk raised the possibility of stopping "the bombing during the rainy period in the North."

"Really get on your horses on that," he ordered.[66]

As the meeting ended, LBJ turned to Wheeler and said: "Tell him [Westmoreland] to forget the 100,000. Tell him 22,000 is all we can give at the moment."[67]

Later, the president remembered: "Some questions were answered in detail; others required additional study and analysis." He highlighted the deep pessimism among the Pentagon civilians but retained some faith in Westmoreland and the South Vietnamese. Still, "on the other hand, I was deeply conscious of the growing criticism we were receiving from the press and from some vocal citizens."[68]

But deep down, he wanted out. However, like often before, he found himself being held hostage by the principle that the only acceptable outcome remained an independent, anti-Communist South Vietnamese government. However, that appeared as unlikely in 1968 to happen without substantial US assistance as in the early days when he took office.

The next day at lunch, LBJ, Rusk, and others debated the bombing halt. The Georgian said the monsoon season limited effectiveness anyway, ensuring no real strategic loss. Rusk pushed to avoid "theological debates about words" and "conditions" and "assumptions" and instead focus on the "*de facto* level of action." He concluded that if Hanoi failed to respond, then bombing should be resumed. "Just take the action and see whether anybody is able to make anything of it," Rusk advised.[69]

On March 8, discussion of the size of the troop allotment returned as the JCS raised their number to 33,000 and selected reserves. When someone mentioned Westmoreland's original request, a discussion ensued. However, it ended abruptly when LBJ forcefully stated: "I am not going to approve 205,000."[70]

Publicly, the pressure mounted on LBJ when a front-page story appeared on Sunday, March 10 in the *New York Times*. The headline read, "Westmoreland Requests 206,000 More Men, Stirring Debate in Administration."[71]

The leak angered Johnson as that day was hard for him. Lady Bird described it as "a day of deep gloom – that is to say, gloom was purveyed in the newspapers and on TV. It weighted the air around me, and I felt it in my very bones." She portrayed Lyndon as having a robust step and telling "hearty stories." He kept working, reading, and moving. "I never took off my hat to him more, or felt more tender toward him," she wrote.[72]

But she also observed the strain manifested in his health. "Those styes are coming back on Lyndon's eyes. First one and then the other, red and swollen and painful." She thought, "wryly, that his life sounded more and more like the tribulations of Job; nevertheless, he is remaining calm, even-tempered, serenely philosophic about politics. But about the war itself, he is deeply worried."[73]

Infuriated by the disclosure, LBJ phoned Clifford, ordering an investigation into the leaks and blaming Pentagon civilians. During the call,

Clifford reported: "He tried to convince himself that he had rejected the Wheeler-Westmoreland troop request the previous week, although in fact he had not done so. In his heart ... he knew that such details did not matter; the damage was done, and it would be virtually impossible to undo."[74]

In response to the controversy, LBJ ordered Christian to state "that no specific request" from his commanders existed at that point. "This might have been correct," Clifford noted, "but it fooled no one and only added to the growing loss of confidence in the Administration."[75]

The rationalization did not matter. Doves, especially those in Congress, seized on the reports and hammered the administration. Antiwar activists outside of Capitol Hill joined the chorus, as many feared another major escalation of the violence in Vietnam. Despite being a tactical victory, Tet certainly had torn away some of the facade about a potential military victory in South Vietnam. More and more, the antiwar faction raised their level of opposition to any further expansion of the war.

Of course, public opinion continually shaped LBJ's moods and responses. Antiwar members of Congress denounced the troop request and Vietnam policy as a whole. On March 11, the Senate Foreign Relations Committee held hearings. Rusk appeared for six and half hours, being peppered with questions from doves led by Fulbright, McCarthy, Gore, and Church. Broadcast on network television, LBJ admitted it "was the most prolonged questioning of a Cabinet officer ever broadcast to the American people."[76]

The senators had good intelligence. One asked about stopping the bombing above the DMZ. "The proposal has been looked at very closely," Rusk replied. However, he added, "It is quite clear from our recent contacts with Hanoi that they would not accept a partial cessation of the bombing as a step toward peace in any way, shape, or form." But, he added, "that does not mean that, as we move into the future, we won't consider examining that and all other proposals."[77]

The next day, Rusk returned for another four and half hours. At the end, LBJ noted: "Secretary Rusk did a magnificent job under trying circumstances. He remained calm, patient, and clear-headed, even under the provocative questioning of some of the most outspoken critics of our role in Vietnam."[78]

Despite Rusk's performance, March 12th was a dark day for LBJ. In the New Hampshire primary, McCarthy nearly defeated the sitting US president. A vigorous opponent of the war, the energized McCarthy traversed the state after Tet telling audiences: "Only a few months ago we were told that 65 percent of the population was secure. Now we know that even the American embassy is not secure."[79] Soon, thousands of young people, a group called "Clean for Gene," for their short haircuts and starched clothes, flocked to the state to work for him.

While most pundits predicted an overwhelming victory for the president, LBJ hesitated. Always known for his political acumen, he observed, "he'll [McCarthy] get 40 percent, at least 40 percent. Every son-a-bitch in New Hampshire who's mad at his wife or the postman or anybody is going to vote for Gene McCarthy."[80]

On March 12, while only a write-in candidate, LBJ won 49.6 percent to 41.9 percent.[81] However, most analysts thought McCarthy would take only 20 percent. The Minnesotan proudly crowed: "If we come to Chicago with this strength, there will be no riots or demonstrations, but a great victory celebration."[82] While later polls indicated widespread discontent with LBJ over the economy and for not aggressively prosecuting the Vietnam War, many interpreted it as an antiwar statement.

As McCarthy continued campaigning, RFK raised the stakes.[83] On March 11, his close confidant Ted Sorenson visited LBJ at the White House. For two hours, Sorenson listened as the president griped about "Vietnam ... the division of the Democratic party, the discussion of his running; the discussion of Bob running." Finally, LBJ asked, "What can I do?[84]

At that point, Sorenson proposed creating a blue ribbon independent commission on Vietnam. The president responded: "Well, Dick Daley made the same suggestion."

He thought a moment and added: "If it could be done without undercutting the Secretary of State and without looking to the Communists as though we're throwing in our hand, that might be useful. I'll think about it."

Then, they discussed commission members. Shockingly, LBJ threw out RFK as chair. Their conversation ended without any commitment, but an agreement to extra talks.[85]

Sorenson, who preferred Bobby waiting to run in 1972, encouraged Kennedy to consider the proposal. Deep down, while saying he would not run if LBJ moved on Vietnam, Kennedy planned to challenge his long-time nemesis, something emboldened by McCarthy's success in New Hampshire.[86]

However, Bobby went through the motions of making a last-ditch effort. On March 14, he and Sorenson met Clifford at the Pentagon. Arriving promptly at 11 a.m., Bobby got right to the point. "One way to correct the policy would be to become a candidate for the Democratic nomination for President. If elected, I could change the policy." But he added, "The other alternative is to find some way to persuade President Johnson to change the policy. Ending the bloodshed in Vietnam is far more important to me than starting a Presidential campaign."[87]

Then, RFK and Sorenson raised the commission. The New York senator acknowledged its membership should respect all viewpoints but must lead toward peace. Sorenson added that the president should publicly characterize the existing policy as an error, hence why he constituted the commission.

Clifford saw right through the ruse. "Ted, you know as well as I do that the President could not issue a statement that this country's policy was a failure."

RFK backpedaled, saying it could focus on reevaluating the Vietnam policy. Then, he outlined membership, including his fellow senators John Sherman Cooper (R-KY), George Aiken (R-VT), and Mansfield. The majority strongly opposed the war, and Clifford knew it.

The politically astute Clifford agreed to deliver the message, but dispensed a few reflections of his own as they left. "First, it is my opinion that the possibility of your being able to defeat President Johnson for the nomination is zero," he stated emphatically. But he conceded that if Bobby gained the nomination, it would split the party and ensure "the Republican nominee would win the election easily," calling the nomination "worthless if you were to win it."

Kennedy acknowledged the obstacles but demanded the president relent. "In an atmosphere that remained polite but was not shadowed with a feeling that a confrontation could no longer be prevented, we parted," Clifford noted.[88]

At 3:30 p.m., Clifford joined Johnson, Fortas, and Humphrey in a small lounge off the Oval Office. After receiving the report, LBJ quickly dismissed the proposal, arguing it would appear that he made a political deal to keep RFK out of the race.[89]

Finally, he zeroed in on the crux of one of the poison pills since all the men suggested by RFK opposed the war. The shrewd Texan recognized a stacked deck.[90]

LBJ instructed Clifford to call Kennedy's Senate Office and ask for Sorenson. He answered but immediately handed the phone to RFK. With LBJ listening on the line, Clifford described the current structure of the commission as a nonstarter. When asked if his removal would facilitate change, Clifford responded empathically: "No."

The call ended and two days later RFK entered the race, stating: "I do not run for the Presidency merely to oppose any man, but to propose new policies."[91] Clifford stressed Kennedy understood the proposal "amounted to an ultimatum and was certain to be rejected." LBJ now found himself having to defend another flank, one created largely by Vietnam.[92] It also reflected the long-running feud between the two men, a rivalry that often defined the decade to that point.

Only a few days after RFK's announcement, LBJ and Lady Bird headed to the ranch, spending Sunday morning with Lynda and Chuck at St. Barnabas Church in Fredericksburg. Afterward, Lady Bird watched Humphrey defend the administration, leading her to lament, "he and Rusk are about the only two who are out speaking for the Administration now." The isolation led her to observe, "I have a growing feeling of Prometheus Bound, just as though we were lying there on the rock, exposed to the vultures, and restrained from fighting back."[93]

The next day, on March 18, LBJ headed to Minneapolis to speak at the National Farmers' Union. Standing in front of a largely conservative audience, he bellowed: "We must meet our commitments in the world and in Vietnam. We shall and we are going to win ... Make no mistake about it – I don't want a man in here to go back home thinking otherwise."[94]

Despite the bellicose language in Minneapolis, once back in D.C., he focused on finding a solution to extricate the United States from South Vietnam. About 6:30 p.m., he hosted the South Vietnamese Ambassador to the United States, Bui Diem. The articulate and well-educated Diem (one of his history teachers was General Vo Nguyen Gap) opened by recognizing the "rising tide of criticism against American involvement" and particularly "the criticism aimed at the Vietnamese themselves and their lack of vigorous action." Someone clearly briefed Diem about the ongoing debates within the White House, as he addressed each in order.

LBJ listened and promised to provide a list of the "inefficient and corrupt commanders" so they could "get rid of them." The president asked a NSC staffer to prepare a memorandum of important US priorities so Diem could present them to President Nguyen Van Thieu. Finally, as the Vietnamese prepared to leave, LBJ forcefully told him to tell Thieu and Vice President Nguyen Cao Ky to "work together and get moving."[95]

Rusk repeated the performance on March 20 with a stern warning to Diem to "emphasize that the problem of public opinion in the United States is directly related to the feeling our people had as to the dedication and performance of the Vietnamese Government and armed forces."[96]

That same day, Clifford chastised Diem and warned: "Your government is facing a clear decision either to broaden the government, clean up corruption, and take measures to gain wide support among the people, or face the loss of American support."[97]

Diem remembered receiving "the distinct impression that the three of them – Johnson, Rusk, and Clifford – had coordinated their message."[98] He was incorrect. However, each agreed the South Vietnamese must take control of their own destiny and quit relying on the Americans. The three signaled forcefully a forthcoming change with a much heavier emphasis on South Vietnamese prosecution of the war.

By March 20, LBJ publicly rejected the troop request of 206,000. It marked one of the first times that he denied an appeal for large numbers of troops. While casualties skyrocketed, the small numbers approved barely replaced those lost or cycling out after completing their tours.

The challenge was what to do next. In an early phone call on the morning of the 20th with Clifford, LBJ thought strategically about messaging the war. He hated being characterized as the "war" candidate, so LBJ ruminated about developing slogans such as "win the peace with honor." He wanted to balance fighting with negotiating to prove "we are the true peace candidate," adding: "We're not the Chamberlain peace – we're the Churchill peace ... We are the Truman who stands up and finally saves Greece and Turkey from the Communists."[99]

Clifford agreed, but pressed the president: "We don't have such a plan."[100]

Later in the day, Johnson met with some advisors and declared, "I want war like I want polio." But, he complained, "what you want and what your image is are two different things."

The conversation shifted to the air war. "Major peace proposals aren't promising unless there is a cessation of bombing," Rusk emphasized. The US Ambassador to the United Nations, Arthur Goldberg, favored a complete bombing halt, while Supreme Court Justice Abe Fortas (a new addition to the inner foreign policy circle) firmly opposed it. William Bundy chimed in, "bombing that far North (north of the 20th parallel) doesn't do that much good" and "I agree with you (Goldberg) on a full suspension."

But, "the bombing keeps lead out of our men's bodies," LBJ responded.

Clifford fired back: "It is not a clear-cut case ... Airpower is not proving to be very effective."

Most advisors remained skeptical on Hanoi responding to a bombing halt.[101] Still, Clifford and others wanted to try, and fought to persuade the president. LBJ appeared torn between getting out through negotiation and becoming the first American president to lose a war. But by late March, he leaned away from new escalations and that was a good start for many who believed the current path provided little hope for a reasonable outcome.

After the final decision on the size of the troop increase unfolded, LBJ encountered another setback as he prepared to address the nation on March 31. Five days before he spoke, he met with the "Wise Men," an advisory group headed by former Secretary of State Dean Acheson. It built off an earlier meeting on February 27 when Acheson visited LBJ at the White House. While the distinguished diplomat expected a consultation, instead the president turned it into an emotional outburst on the war. Angry, Acheson abruptly departed. Rostow followed him and queried why. The older gentleman told Rostow, "You tell the President – and you tell him in precisely these words – that he can take Vietnam and stick it up his ass."[102]

Acheson calmed down and a humbled LBJ requested another meeting. This time, he controlled it. "With all due respect, Mr. President, the Joint Chiefs of Staff don't know what they're talking about." When the president expressed surprise, Acheson added, "Then maybe you should be shocked." By the end, Acheson promised feedback but only if he received sensitive documents to form his own opinion. Johnson complied.[103]

The former secretary of state returned with his colleagues a month later. On the evening of Monday, March 25, a group, named the "Cold War Knighthood" by Clifford, including General Omar Bradley, George Ball, General Maxwell Taylor, and Ambassador Henry Cabot Lodge, gathered at the State Department. At 7:30 p.m., they shared dinner while listening to several presentations by Clifford, influential State Department advisor Philip Habib, Major General William DePuy, and George Carver, the CIA's leading analyst on Vietnam.

The general findings were negative. Clifford characterized the United States as "muddling through," while Carver underscored that pacification efforts suffered significant blows during Tet. Habib focused on the inadequacies of the South Vietnamese leadership and predicted a minimum of five years before progress.[104]

At times, the exchanges proved testy. When DePuy outlined some numbers of enemy dead and wounded during the offensive, Ambassador Goldberg protested, "Who the hell is there left for us to be fighting?"[105]

In another exchange, Clifford asked Habib, "Phil, do you think a military victory can be won?"

He hesitated but replied: "Not under present circumstances."

Clifford followed up: "What would you do if the decision was yours to make?"

Pausing again, Habib answered: "Stop the bombing and negotiate."[106]

At 11 p.m., the meeting adjourned after a series of hard questions for the briefers as well as Clifford and Rusk.

On the afternoon of March 26, the "Wise Men" met with LBJ, who earlier in the day received another fairly optimistic appraisal from

Wheeler.[107] McGeorge Bundy opened with "there is a very significant shift in our position" since the last meeting in November 1967. "When we last met we saw reasons for hope ... Last night and today the picture is not so hopeful particularly in the countryside."[108]

Then, Acheson noted that the majority believed the United States "could no longer do the job we set out to do in the time we have left and we must begin to disengage."[109] Douglas Dillon, Eisenhower's former treasury secretary, agreed. "The briefing last night led me to conclude we cannot achieve a military victory."[110]

At one point, the president quipped, "the first thing I am going to do when you all leave is to find those people who briefed you last night."[111]

A little while later, the president asked for a brief break to talk with Clifford and Rusk. In the hallway, he angrily grilled them. "Who poisoned the well with these guys? I want to hear those briefings myself."[112]

After much discussion about bombing halts and negotiations, Acheson concluded the meeting: "The issue is can we do what we are trying to do in Vietnam. I do not think we can."[113]

Afterward, LBJ complained, "the establishment bastards have bailed out."[114] He was correct, and it angered him. But, it also provided another sobering assessment requiring a different policy.

With most of his advisors, the "Wise Men", and many Americans clamoring for change, LBJ now primarily would seek a successful exit strategy from Vietnam. However, during most of the preceding two months since Tet, his mood vacillated between seeking victory and simply negotiating an honorable exit with an independent South Vietnam, but one without the constant presence of hundreds of thousands of Americans.

During the crisis that followed Tet, Johnson was not the calm and calculating person that he often displayed that year in relation to North Korea and future challenges in Europe. Vietnam brought out the worst in him as the war pulled him in many directions, often leading to horrific outbursts and searches for those he believed had betrayed him. With his advisors split and constantly pushing their own agendas, the president often acted in a schizophrenic fashion, jumping between various extremes depending on his mood and those whispering in his ear. Unlike his successor, who kept a tight circle, Johnson opened debates up to many people, leading to a whiplash regarding what to do next. Thus, LBJ exclaimed: "The two weeks before and the two months following Tet represented a period of activity as intense as any of my Presidency."[115]

But the Tet crisis also highlighted just how isolated the president had become because of Vietnam. Not only did Congress sense weakness, but also the press and many former stalwarts including the Wise Men started counseling changes in the approach, diverging from the path to that point. The diminution of Johnson's power was clearly on display during February and March when political rivals including his nemesis Robert Kennedy also took advantage of the problems in Vietnam to launch Kennedy's presidential campaign. With Hanoi pushing their own agenda, often with support from the Soviet Union and China, and Saigon constantly holding the line on its negotiating and fighting track, Johnson found himself in a quandary on what to do next.

After finally stopping the buildup, LBJ needed an alternative to sell to the American people. He had a few days to work on the ideas to include in the March 31 speech. Many wondered about the final draft, as the bureaucratic battles continued to influence the president. It became one of the most important speeches in his presidency, if not American history.

CHAPTER 4

As a Result, I Will Not Seek Reelection

The March 31, 1968 Speech

S unday, March 31st started with an early morning wake-up call from the White House Operator to the president. LBJ and Lady Bird hurried to dress, and then greeted daughter Lynda, who had taken a late "red-eye" flight from the West Coast, where she left her husband, Marine Lieutenant Chuck Robb, at Camp Pendleton as he prepared to depart for Vietnam.[1]

Tired and several months pregnant, Lynda arrived around 7:00 a.m. at the entrance to the Diplomatic Reception Room. She looked exhausted, so much so that Lady Bird characterized her as appearing "like a ghost – pale, tall, and drooping."[2] LBJ concurred, noting she "seemed lonely and bewildered" as "war and separation were cruel intrusions into her young life."[3]

Obviously distraught from just leaving her husband, Lynda immediately turned to her father and asked, "Why ... was her husband going away to fight, and maybe die, for people who did not even want to be protected?"

Speechless, LBJ "wanted to comfort her ... [but] I could not."[4]

Lynda's question deeply wounded LBJ. Lady Bird found him afterwards, observing, "his face was sagging and there was such pain in his eyes as I had not seen since his mother died."[5]

Vietnam remained at the heart of much of the pain and anguish of LBJ and his family in 1968. "That bitch of a war on the other side of the world," as the president sometimes referred to the quagmire, consumed him.[6] With daily reminders on the television and in the newspapers of the dead and permanently disabled, Johnson rarely went anywhere without protests and denunciations of the devastating war being waged in Southeast Asia. It weighed on him more than any other issue, and contributed to wild mood swings between anger and melancholy, leading often to outbursts and sleepless nights followed by resignation and thoughts of retirement.

By 9:00, LBJ was back in the presidential bedroom, where a large group gathered, including two physicians carefully examining his large hands for skin cancers. They went about scraping samples while the president talked on the phone.[7]

In a corner, Sgt. Paul Glynn and Sgt. Kenneth Gaddis, LBJ's assigned Air Force aides, laid out the president's new suits recently arrived from the tailor. They waited patiently for the inevitable inspection before the president headed out the door for the day.[8]

As LBJ continued his phone call, all attention shifted to the center of the room to LBJ's grandson Lyn. Not yet two, the little boy ignored all the hustle and bustle surrounding him in the bedroom of one of the most powerful men in the world. Wanting to play, Lyn rushed toward his grandfather near the canopied bed. The president leaned over and thrust one of his huge fingers into the waist of the toddler, sending him hurtling backward with his chubby legs flying in the air. Lyn chortled loudly, and his grandfather smiled as they continued the game for a while.[9]

The playful dynamics changed when LBJ's long-time friend and trusted adviser Horace Busby entered the room. He wrote many of the president's most famous addresses before leaving the White House in 1966, but always remained available to the president. The day before, LBJ summoned him to work on the special speech to be given that evening.

Sitting in a rocking chair in a corner, the short, balding head of the United Artists Studio and prominent Democratic fundraiser, Arthur Krim, jumped up and hurried over to Busby. Smiling, he asked: "What do you think of the bombshell?"

"I'm all for it," the Texan replied.

"Gee, I am too. This will make things so much better, so much better. I only wish it could have come earlier."

Busby was unsure what Krim actually knew. Had the president confided in him about not seeking reelection? Or did he just know about the bombing halt? He looked toward the president for guidance, and LBJ simply touched his fingers to his lips.[10]

The president finally hung up and finished with the doctors, telling everyone in the room, "Horace and I have some private business to discuss."[11]

The two men exited the bedroom and headed down the corridor to the West Hall, a room with a broad arching window that looked out toward the Executive Office Building. Busby took a seat on a couch while the president sat in a wingback chair. "Here, take notes," LBJ instructed his old friend.[12]

Before they could start, the telephone operator interrupted. The president simply responded, "Honey, now don't ring me again for a few minutes – I have a very important conference going."[13]

Busby worried the president intended to tell him once more he had reconsidered his decision. Instead LBJ looked earnestly at his friend and said, "I don't know whether I would live out another four-year term here. I want out of this cage."[14]

Busby knew many people opposed this option, including new Chief of Staff Jim Jones and close confidant, Marvin Watson. Nonetheless, Busby encouraged the president forward, stressing, "everyone in the world thinks you would do anything to hang on to power. That impression has colored the whole public reaction to your presidency."

Hesitating for a moment, he continued, "I personally feel that if you take this step it will help in the long term for people to see better all that you have accomplished in your administration."

"Yes, I think that's right, I think it is very compelling," Johnson responded.[15]

After a short pause, the two continued their conversation.

"I rather like what you wrote in January," LBJ murmured.

The president instructed Busby to find White House Press Secretary George Christian, who since the State of the Union had been carrying around a copy of the original draft announcing his decision not to seek reelection.

"Put together another draft, and I'll be back in about an hour and half to read it," the president ordered. As he rose, he told Busby to stay in the Treaty Room and "Don't let a soul know you're over here."[16]

As LBJ headed toward the elevator, Busby summoned up the courage to ask the obvious question.

"What do you think the chances are for going through with this?"

The president stopped and peered down the long hallway toward the Lincoln Bedroom, thinking long and hard.

"Eighty-twenty against it, he replied."[17]

Like in January, Busby and others, including Lady Bird, knew her husband's track record on the matter of announcing his intention to retire. It came at times of high stress and fear of failure during several campaigns in his career, the most recent in 1964 preceding the Democratic Convention in Atlantic City.

But the process also reflected his normal decision-making method. He often liked to gather competing ideas and then formulate his final decision after weighing different perspectives. It worked sometimes, although not always because many people told him what they thought he wanted to hear, fearing the Johnson treatment for voicing dissent like was often the case regarding Vietnam. This time, however, it appeared he genuinely wanted feedback to help him make a difficult decision.

Luci and her husband, Pat Nugent, waited for her father near a White House entrance on a cool, cloudy day. The day before, D.C. had been warm and sunny, alive with the celebration of the Cherry Blossoms.[18] The weather that Sunday morning reflected the somber mood in the White House.

The tall Texan slid into the car with Jones, Pat, and Luci for the short drive to St. Dominic's Catholic Church in southeastern D.C. Soon, they pulled up to the building, one LBJ described as a "somber, gray Victorian-Gothic structure, with twin spires rising above the modern construction." He called it "simple and restful," a place where he went many Sunday mornings as well as unscheduled stops for prayer during the late evening.[19]

During the quiet of the mass, Johnson pondered his momentous decision, perhaps the most important of his public life. Many reasons existed for his not seeking another term. Among the most prominent were health concerns. "I did not fear death so much as I feared disability," he recalled. "Whenever I walked through the Red Room and saw the portrait of Woodrow Wilson hanging there," he added, "I thought of him stretched out upstairs in the White House, powerless to move, with the machinery of the American government in disarray around him."[20] Wilson's debilitating stroke suffered at the end of his presidency terrified LBJ.

His family history also weighed on him. The serious heart attack in 1955 never strayed far from his mind, especially at mealtimes when he counted his calories and fat intake. The long arduous hours that preceded that medical emergency had returned since he assumed the presidency in 1963.[21]

Always, the intense political and foreign policy issues wore on him. The summer of 1967 remained fresh in his memory, a time when African Americans took to the streets to riot. The glow of fires eerily lit the night skies in Detroit, Tampa, Newark, and Chicago. Angry young men prowled the streets, some looting stores and burning cars and buildings.

Policemen in riot gear joined by heavily armed National Guardsmen invaded the inner cities. With their bayonets protruding from rifles and their faces hiding behind gas masks, they launched tear gas into crowds. White clouds enveloped and choked their fellow Americans. Many areas resembled a war zone complete with fortified checkpoints and command posts. LBJ often wondered aloud: How could this happen in his United States? Worse yet, he knew FBI Director J. Edgar Hoover predicted more racial unrest in the upcoming summer.[22]

And then, of course, there was the war in Vietnam. By March 1968, as the debates over Tet demonstrated, Vietnam consumed the president.[23] He stressed, "The issue of Vietnam had created divisions and hostilities among Americans, as I had feared." As he sat in his pew that cold Sunday morning, he pondered wanting "to heal some of the wounds and restore unity to the nation. This speech might help to do that. I deeply hoped so."[24]

The thought of retirement had been in play for months, as highlighted in the lead up to the State of Union address. Yet, most outside of his inner circle always thought LBJ would run. In late 1967, Tom Wicker of the *New York Times* wrote: "it is as likely that Lyndon Johnson will get out of the White House and go back to Texas as it is that Dean Rusk will turn dove, Dick Nixon will stop running, or J. Edgar Hoover will retire."[25] Another commentator, Carl Rowan of the *Chicago Daily News*, added in early March that the odds of LBJ not running "can't be better than a million to one."[26]

If anything, others watched the president become more bellicose regarding the potential political battles, especially after the shock of the New Hampshire primaries wore off. Many thought LBJ relished a fight with Bobby, as a close political adviser, Jim Rowe, observed, "if I ever had any doubts about Johnson's running, I would have lost them the day Kennedy announced because he is not about to turn the country over to Bobby."[27]

Early polling supported Rowe's view. Just days after RFK's announcement, one showed the president winning against all Democratic challengers as well as the Republican contenders.[28]

Yet, a surprise awaited that would shock many, even those closest to the president. He relished drama and political theater, often thriving on it. Johnson liked dropping a bomb and watching people react. It gave him a sense of control and power by keeping others off guard. It was no different this time, although the final decision appeared far from secure.

The time at church was the calm before the storm. Once the family exited the church and entered the car, LBJ reached for the button to close the partition to the front seat.

As it slowly moved upward, he looked across at his young daughter and husband, an airman also heading to Vietnam soon to join Chuck, and steeled himself. He could not help but feel for the vivacious, free-spirited Luci, who was so young, not yet twenty-one. She had a one-year-old and now faced the extended absence of her husband.

As they rode along, LBJ pulled out the short statement that would conclude his speech, one he described as "destined to change ... the lives of all of us." He finished to silence. Then, tears began to flow down Luci's face. "I thought this was what she wanted," he told her. Instead, she tried to smile and simply responded: "It is more complicated."[29]

A wave of emotion swept over LBJ. "They were so very young, and they had such promising happy lives ahead of them," he remembered. Yet, he worried about Pat and also Chuck, who he said he was very proud of, but now, "for a year or more, their wives would wait and pray, as other wives across America would, for their husbands to return to them and their babies."[30]

Deep down, LBJ thought working full-time for a withdrawal with honor constituted his best hope of helping his sons-in-law. The costs of the war, both in gold and blood, had shaken the Republic's foundations, and the debates during the Tet Offensive further underscored the trend. Running again limited his options, as the Republicans would hammer him if he did too much, but also if he did too little. Also, he believed the North Vietnamese might negotiate with him rather than waiting for the possible election of the hawkish Nixon. Now might be the last best chance for exiting the morass and possibly not only assisting his family members, but salvaging his presidential legacy.

After making the announcement to Luci and Pat, LBJ asked the driver to head for the apartment of Vice President Hubert Humphrey. Johnson knew that he and Muriel would leave soon for a conference on nuclear non-proliferation in Mexico City.[31]

As was often the case, LBJ rapidly entered the room along with Jones, exchanged a few pleasantries, and got right down to business. Immediately, he asked Hubert for some privacy. While Muriel and Luci chatted in another room, the president marched into the living room and sat down with the vice president.[32]

The conversation with his vice president demonstrated the complex relationship between the two men that began in earnest in 1964 after years of serving together in the Senate. Humphrey was a loyal warrior who shared many of LBJ's views on civil rights and ending poverty. However, Johnson often derided him because the Texan viewed him as too emotional and willing to compromise on issues such as Vietnam. Nonetheless, like so many others, Humphrey never thought Johnson would surrender the presidency without a fight, so he played along while hoping to run in 1972.

There, with little fanfare, LBJ informed him of his decision, although he told him to wait for a call from Jones to confirm. The Minnesotan, his receding hairline exposing deep furrows across his forehead and his eyes tearing, expressed his dismay and surprise. Johnson reminded him that he told him to start visiting every state and to create a presidential election organization.[33]

According to Johnson, Humphrey took the news "somberly." As they parted ways and shook hands, the vice president simply said that "he hoped to God I wouldn't go through with it."[34]

Then, reality set in. As the president exited, Humphrey's shoulders slumped and voice lowered as he muttered: "There's no way I can beat the Kennedys."[35]

The afternoon remained devoted to continuing the process of assessing the decision while leaving the possibility of pulling it back as evidenced by Johnson instructing Humphrey to wait on a call from Jones. He returned to the White House and immediately headed for the Treaty Room to consult Busby.

As LBJ burst in, Busby noted: "His long face sagged: the firmness was gone, a deep melancholy filled his eyes, and he seemed impossibly tired."[36]

The president looked at his friend and asked: "Well, Judge, how much do we have finished? One sentence or two?" a direct reference to Busby's characteristically slow pace that often included numerous rewrites.

Instead, Busby handed him four pages. Immediately, LBJ's large hands flew in the air as he bellowed, "Damn, you must really want to get me out of town."[37]

LBJ circled the room reading the new draft while one hand played with the coins in his pocket, the jiggling sound disturbing the quiet room. Finally, he exclaimed, "this reads much better!" He slapped Busby's shoulder and laughed loudly, "You may make it as a speechwriter yet."[38]

The president took the draft and left, returning a quarter of hour later. For a short time, they discussed Humphrey's candidacy. Then, the president began staring out the window and across the South Grounds, focusing on the Washington Monument, undoubtedly thinking about the gravity of what he planned to do later that evening.

Always restless, he began pacing the room, moving his eyes toward the ceiling while saying nothing. After ten minutes or so, he moved toward the small circular table in the middle of the room, sat down, took a pen out of his pocket, and started scribbling notes.

As always, he wanted his own words incorporated and proved a tireless editor, poring over and dissecting every word. His days as a student and then teacher led him to search for meaning in every statement. It often proved a maddening exercise for his speechwriters, one often repeated.

As Johnson neared the end, he became transfixed on one statement that Busby had written, "I shall not seek and will not accept the nomination of my party."

LBJ struck out the word, "will" and replaced it with "would."

"No sir, I won't say that. It's too presumptuous," he growled. "They haven't offered me any nomination yet."

Busby protested, worried that "would" might appear too ambiguous. "The press will nitpick every word in that sentence, looking for an escape clause," the Texan protested.

"Well, let 'em, damnit, let 'em," LBJ barked. "I am still not going to reject something that hasn't been offered to me and that's final."[39]

Finished editing, LBJ took the draft and started out of the room but suddenly stopped. "Here, you'd better keep this. I'm going over the West Wing for a while and it might fall out of my pocket." Laughing heartily, he winked, "I don't want this falling into the hands of the enemy."[40]

Despite appearing more firmly committed to his decision, LBJ felt pulled in many directions. He did not want RFK in the White House, but the polls showed his disapproval ratings at all-time highs. On one hand, he hated not completing a job, but the thought of dying in office or becoming incapacitated haunted him. He worried about the boys in Vietnam and what they would think about their commander-in-chief quitting. However, he desperately needed a solution to honorably escape the shackles of the White House.

After leaving Busby, LBJ requested that Lady Bird as well as Mathilde and Arthur Krim join him in the West Hall. Then, always the showman, he watched their reaction as he read them the last section of the speech. Shocked, they sat in astonishment, floored by the last parts of "accordingly, I shall not seek – and I would not accept – the nomination of my party for another term as your President."[41]

Arthur bellowed, "You can't mean this!" while Mathilde murmured, "Oh no, no!"[42]

Stunned initially, soon the composed Lady Bird began scribbling on her small 5 x 7 pad.[43]

LBJ knew his wife's ambivalence. Lady Bird would never shrink from one last fight, and she knew "if we lost, well and good – we were free!" Simultaneously, she also acknowledged, "but if we didn't run, we could be free without all this draining of our friends."[44]

Deep down, she still feared that he would change his mind, something he did numerous times during his political career. But something differed this time, "maybe it was the calm finality in Lyndon's voice, and maybe we believed him for the first time."[45]

Lady Bird knew her husband better than anyone and understood the debates would continue until the eleventh hour. And, they did. At just after 2 o'clock, Arthur and Mathilde, Luci and Pat, as well as Busby, sat down to lunch with the president and first lady.

They gathered in the small family dining room whose windows looked out onto Pennsylvania Avenue and across to Lafayette Park, where protestors often lined up to chant, "Hey, hey, LBJ. How many kids did you kill today?" The dreary morning gave way to an afternoon sun illuminating the painstakingly laid out place settings and the faces of those in the room.[46]

LBJ saw that Mathilde and Luci had been crying, but he remained calm and according to Lady Bird moved into a "quiet state of mind, out of our reach."[47]

Despite LBJ being composed, the lunch proved contentious at times, with Arthur, Mathilde, and Luci forcefully questioning his decision. They argued the president should seek more counsel and wait a few weeks before making such a momentous announcement.

The president listened, soaking in the arguments but refusing to engage. Instead, he let Busby bear the brunt of the offensive. As the rancor increased, LBJ suddenly pushed back his chair and left the room.

After a short time, he returned to a quieter room. When he sat down, the staff moved quickly to remove the dishes of the main meal, most still holding their food as no one had taken time to eat during the heated deliberations.

Once more, LBJ remained silent, hovering over his low calorie pudding. This time, the others joined him, focusing on the plates in front of them. Then, the president dropped his spoon, looked at Busby, and said: "Come on Buzz. I need to see you for a minute."[48]

As they headed down the hallway toward the private bedroom, neither spoke.

But when they entered, the president asked, "Did any of that swerve you any?"

"No, sir, I still feel the same," Busby answered.

Grinning broadly, LBJ exclaimed, "I thought you did rather well. In fact, I think you made an A minus, or maybe an A."[49] LBJ then exited and sent Busby to the quiet Treaty Room to review the speech one more time.

Letting the family, friends, and a close confidant debate the merits of the decision allowed Johnson to continue to devise his final decision. It provided him some clarity on his choices, as the majority of his closest advisors wanted him to resist the impulse or at least wait for a while longer. With only a few, like Busby and Christian, supporting the idea, some, including Lady Bird, worried he might change his mind. Even at the late moment, it was far from certain that he would announce his decision not to seek reelection that evening.

He soon returned, laughing as he entered the room. "You better never go near the West Wing again," he warned. "They're all against you, Buzz, all against you."[50]

Busby thought to himself, "I knew he must only have been testing more reactions, still deliberating, still wanting to know what others thought before he decided finally what he thought."[51]

The president picked up the new draft that Busby tried to write more in LBJ's voice. Reading it, LBJ smiled and then his face beamed, "Why, this is me." As quickly as he had entered, he bolted out.

Despite the praise, Busby thought that the whole process might constitute a therapeutic exercise just like in January. He still thought the president might pull the section from the speech at the last minute, even though he seemed more resolute than before the State of Union speech.

Within a half hour, he returned with his trusted assistant, Marie Fehmer. After making a few minor adjustments, he handed the draft to her with instructions to type it up and then exited.

As Busby sat in the room making a few changes, Fehmer sat next to him, saying nothing, but obviously angry.

"What do you think about it?" he asked.

"I'll type it," she responded.

"Are you for it?"

"I am not," she replied icily.[52]

With so few people supporting the decision, Busby worried about what would happen in the last few hours. During one break, one of his allies, Christian, reported, "it's getting sticky."

But there were allies outside of the White House. LBJ had instructed his press secretary to call John Connally and ask his opinion. The Texas governor bluntly answered: "Tonight is better than tomorrow night and last night would have been better than tonight, because time is running out."[53] He ended that it was the president's decision, but called for no more "agonizing reappraisals."[54]

In response, Busby asked why LBJ did not call directly. Christian laughed heartily, "Haven't you heard? Everything's normal between them – they're not speaking these days." LBJ's appointment of Kennedy loyalist Sargent Shriver as ambassador to France had infuriated the governor.[55]

The debates intensified as the news leaked out about the controversial ending. During the afternoon, Lady Bird joined Luci and Lynda, who she described as "emotional, crying, and distraught." They worried about the soldiers in Vietnam thinking, "What have I been sent out here for? – Was it all wrong? – Can I believe in what I've been fighting for?" The young women feared the troops would believe that they had lost their champion, their father. Lynda, still recovering from a long arduous trip, said with some bitterness, "Chuck will hear this on his way to Vietnam."[56]

Not long after, Lady Bird expressed her daughters' concern to her husband. LBJ acknowledged that he had already thought about the morale issue and called General William Westmoreland. The crusty South Carolinian reported there would be no appreciable effect.

When his wife pressed that Lynda and Luci looked at it from a much closer level as the wives of two soldiers, LBJ snapped, "I think General Westmoreland knows more about it than they do."[57]

By late afternoon, a fog enveloped many people in the West Wing. Lady Bird characterized it as "a strange afternoon and evening," where people met in the hallways and looked at "each other, helplessly, silent, or exploding with talk." She wanted to do something, "but what? And how did I dare do anything, with the decision so momentous, one I could by no means implement, or take the responsibility for making it turn out right." The time just dragged as she "kept looking at the hands of the clock, and counting the hours until 9 PM."[58]

With three hours remaining, Johnson called a meeting with the Soviet Ambassador, Anatoly Dobrynin, one he described as "the most important thing I've done today."[59]

The Russian joined special envoy Averell Harriman and Rostow in the Yellow Oval Room, a room splendidly decorated in Louis XIV furniture framed by Cézanne paintings with a spectacular view of the Tidal Pool and Washington Monument. Lady Bird greeted them with Cokes and exchanged pleasantries, describing the Russian as "affable and talkative." They even discussed the possibility of the Bolshoi Ballet making an appearance at the World's Fair in San Antonio that started a week later.[60]

Suddenly, the doors burst open and Lady Bird observed, "Lyndon came in with that jaunty step that I've seen him rev up under the most intense tension."[61]

Barely stopping for a quick greeting, LBJ boldly announced his intention to seek a peace in Vietnam without endangering American troops. Resolutely, he looked at Dobrynin and called for the Soviet Union to "bring influence to bear for a conference and the making of peace."[62] This included making sure that "in South Vietnam ... the contending parties must give up war and seek a one-man, one vote solution."[63]

Then, Johnson pivoted and tried playing on Soviet fears. He told Dobrynin that the primary beneficiaries of the disorder in Southeast Asia remained Mao and the Chinese. Beijing, the president reminded the Soviet, threatened Moscow's interests. He characterized Mao and other Chinese leaders as getting "cocky" and "chesty."[64]

Once LBJ finished his soliloquy, the Soviet ambassador responded: "Why not have a 100% bombing pause?"

LBJ shot back that the Russians would never have let the Germans continue massing troops and supplies in strategic areas during WWII.

Dobrynin responded that the Soviets never faced the problem.

"But you are helping them," LBJ snapped, adding "our opponents wouldn't have lasted long if it were not for your support, which keeps him afloat."[65]

The conversation continued as the two discussed timetables and the limits of the bombing halt. Then, the president exited quickly and headed back to work on the final edits while the Soviet went off to finish talking with Rostow.[66]

A little later, LBJ caught Dobrynin in the hallway and pulled him aside and away from the curious ears of others. He told him what he planned for the final part of the speech. According to the Russian, LBJ "spoke with difficulty and could hardly hide his emotions."[67]

Not long after running into the Soviet ambassador, LBJ returned to the Treaty Room with Busby, who caught a few mistakes, including how many months the president had served. Originally, he had forty-nine, but the president recalculated that it was fifty-two months and ten days. "That sounds like fifty years," LBJ responded.[68]

"Mr. President, I hate to bring it up," Busby said, unwilling to give up his position.

"But what?" LBJ retorted as he looked down to where Busby had placed his pencil on the last climatic line.

"All right, all right, I guess you've earned something – change it to 'will not accept.'"

Then, the president started to hand the manuscript to Jones, but suddenly withdrew it.

"Somewhere in here, you have me saying I won't give an hour of my time to 'any partisan causes.' We had better change that to read 'any personal partisan causes.'"

Smiling, he said, "Unless you put that in, I might not be able to go out and help Humphrey beat Nixon this fall."[69]

He knew his decision not to seek reelection would shake up the Democratic race for the presidency. He firmly opposed McCarthy and hated Robert Kennedy. Despite his often complex and sometimes rocky relationship with Humphrey, he felt an obligation to support his loyal vice president. It was a way to maintain his legacy, especially on the domestic front, as he often worried that Humphrey lacked the fortitude or commitment to see things through in Vietnam.

Only a couple of hours before the speech, many remained on the fence as to whether LBJ would pull the trigger on announcing his decision not to seek reelection. Some remained adamant in their opposition and gathered in the family sitting room to plead their case one more time while a barber performed the often-repeated ritual of trimming the president's hair before a major address.

"If this happens," Luci complained, "I'll never have a chance to vote for Daddy." She went around the room exhorting people to "do something."[70]

Lady Bird sat quietly, holding her thoughts as Luci zeroed in on Busby sitting in a corner. "Mr. Busby, every person on this floor loves my father – they like him, admire him, understand him, or they wouldn't be here. That includes you."

"But why is it that out of all of the people here you are the only one who wants him to give up this office?" she asked.

Busby thought for a moment, wanting to respond that only the president made the decision, but then lamely retorted, "maybe, it's because I'm the only one here who's not here all the time."[71]

Luci continued trying to get someone to talk with her father when the elevator opened and Watson, the person LBJ called "that tough Marine," entered the room. Busby knew he firmly opposed the decision. As he walked toward the bedroom where LBJ prepared, he looked at Busby and simply stated: "I see you have had a very good day."[72]

Not long after, Krim succumbed to Luci's entreaties and visited the president. Returning quickly, he simply reported, "He says that the decision has been made."[73]

As the time neared for the speech, more people gathered to provide their support. Watson joined Clark and Marny Clifford as well as Walt and Elspeth Rostow, who arrived about 5 p.m.

Quickly, an Army sergeant escorted Clifford and Rostow into the bedroom, where the president fumbled with his tie.

"I'd like you to read this – it is the ending of my speech, you have not seen it before," the president told them as he handed the speech over to them.[74]

Both men read it. Rostow said nothing, but Clifford responded: "After what you've been through, you are entitled to make this decision. No one would be justified in asking you to go on carrying the burdens of the Presidency."[75]

After recovering a bit from the shock, Clifford added: "I understand your decision, Mr. President but that does not keep me from regretting it. If this is your decision, then it becomes my decision. God bless you. I am very sorry."[76]

Looking back, Clifford remembered a meeting in the fall of 1967, where the president asked him about Harry Truman's decision not to seek reelection, that should have alerted him to the very real possibility.

It really never registered with Clifford that LBJ would follow Truman's example. However, sixteen years almost to the date after the Missourian's announcement on March 29, 1952, it appeared another Democratic president would follow his lead.[77]

By that point, it appeared LBJ would follow through, although no one knew for sure. Many people still hoped that he would skip the final paragraphs. As late as 7:45, Watson told his secretary that LBJ "had not made up his mind ... [regarding] saying he won't run."[78]

Lady Bird also wavered, wondering about a repeat of the State of the Union speech. LBJ admitted, "When did I make the decisions that I announced the evening of March 31, 1968? The answer is: 9:01 p.m. on March 31, 1968."[79]

As the speech neared, more signs appeared that he would deliver on his promise not to seek reelection. LBJ instructed people to start calling members of the cabinet, but only a few minutes before the speech started. Watson took his list that included McNamara, Rowe, Chicago Mayor Richard Daley, and AFL-CIO President George Meany.[80] Rostow received orders to contact Wheeler and Westmoreland.[81]

Tension filled the West Wing as the speech neared. Finally, at a quarter to nine, LBJ led a group of people including Rostow and Jones from the private family quarters to his office. Soon after, Luci and Pat followed as well as Lynda and ultimately Clifford, Busby, and Lady Bird.[82]

Johnson passed through the door, just missing Christian and a small group of reporters who stationed themselves near it, each hoping to stake out a good spot to watch and take notes. As he walked by, he thought: "They're in for a surprise."[83]

Into the office strode the president, just like so many times before. He wore a dark black suit and burgundy tie, looking very presidential. Plodding through the maze of cables on the floor to his desk, he looked calm and collected. Sitting down, he fixed his gaze on the teleprompter, adjusted his silver-rimmed glasses, and took some deep breaths.

Just before the start of the 9:00 p.m. (Eastern time) televised speech, Lady Bird walked carefully through the obstacle course of cameras toward the large dark mahogany desk where her husband sat. She noted "the lines in his face were deep, but there was a marvelous sort of repose over-all."[84]

She leaned over and told him, "Remember – pacing and drama."[85]

Then, she returned to her seat, arriving as the president opened: "Tonight I want to speak to you of peace in Vietnam and Southeast Asia. No other question so preoccupies our people."[86]

Throughout the speech, LBJ could look across the room at Lady Bird and Lynda seated in chairs while Luci and Pat stood behind them. Vietnam created a bunker mentality for LBJ, as everywhere he went angry protestors greeted him. This night, however, in this sanctuary under the glare of the lights, he knew that his family loved him no matter what happened next.[87]

Many Americans watched as the president took over all the major television channels that existed in 1968. Briefly, he outlined the successes and failures in Vietnam in the aftermath of the Tet, highlighting the brave defense by the South Vietnamese during the offensive.

At one point, he answered Lynda's question from earlier in the day. "Our presence there has always rested on this basic belief: The main burden of preserving their freedom must be carried out by them – by the South Vietnamese themselves," he said.[88]

But this speech primarily focused on jump-starting the peace process. "Tonight, I have ordered our aircraft and our naval vessels to make no attacks on North Vietnam," he told the national audience. He only made an exception for areas just north of the DMZ where enemy forces continued to mobilize near Khe Sanh.[89]

Then, LBJ voiced his calls to Hanoi to reciprocate with restraint in its operations and to make a sincere effort to sit down at the peace table and negotiate in good faith. "So tonight I reaffirm the pledge," he emphasized, "that we are prepared to withdraw our forces from South Vietnam as the other side withdraws its forces to the north, stops the infiltration, and the level of violence subsides."[90]

After talking at length about balancing the budget and the need for surtax, LBJ transitioned to the last section. As the teleprompter reached it, he paused for a moment and looked directly at Lady Bird. She recognized the moment would change their lives forever.[91]

"With America's sons in the fields far away," he began, "with America's future under challenge right here at home, with our hopes and the world's hopes for peace in the balance every day, I do not believe that

I should devote an hour or a day of my time to any personal partisan causes or to any duties other than the awesome duties of this office."[92]

"Accordingly, I shall not seek, and I will not accept, the nomination of my party for another term as your President."[93]

A collective gasp enveloped the country as hawks and doves listened to the statement and looked around for confirmation that they heard correctly. Few saw this coming, even many closest to LBJ.

He wasted little time moving toward a conclusion with the rhetorical flourish of JFK. "But let men everywhere know, however, a strong, a confident and vigilant America stands ready tonight to seek an honorable peace – and stands ready tonight to defend an honored cause – whatever the price, whatever the burden, what the sacrifice that duty may require."

"Good night and God bless all of you."[94]

People across the country looked at each other, checking to make sure they heard what he said. It shocked almost everyone and constituted the highest form of political theater that LBJ so relished. Few outside his closest advisors (and not even many of them) thought he would surrender the presidency so easily, at least not without a political fight in the Democratic primary. Others questioned how this would really affect the young men fighting in Vietnam. He must really want peace to give up any chance for another four-year term. For many, especially some in the dove camp, it appeared like he was serious, although many still harbored lingering suspicions of the warmonger whom they had demonized for years.

Sitting at his desk as the bright lights dimmed, LBJ felt the weight of the world lifted from his shoulders. All day, he had struggled with the decision. He did it and gladly so. Now, he could escape the dungeon of the presidency, but hopefully not before securing a path to peace in Vietnam and reducing the blemish on his record.

As he finished and reflected on the momentous announcement, the family rushed to embrace LBJ as he moved from behind the desk. Lynda kissed him, fighting back the tears. Then, Luci hugged him tightly and comforted her father, something she excelled at during such times.[95]

Deep down, Lady Bird expressed relief. Until the end, she had not known whether he would do it, but he had and now a new life lay before them.

Figure 4 After giving his speech to the nation on March 31, 1968 announcing his decision not to seek reelection, the president and his daughter, Luci, watch the playback of the address. (Courtesy of the LBJ Library)

The family exited the office and moved to the second floor where others waited. There, friends greeted them, including Christian, Leonard Marks, Doug Carter, and Wilbur Cohen. Lady Bird observed, nearly everybody looked stunned and struck silent.[96]

Then the phone started ringing as calls flooded in. One of the first came from Chicago Mayor Richard Daley, who said: "We're going to draft you. You dropped the biggest bombshell by announcing that you will not be a candidate for nomination for another term as my President."[97] Others came from Rusk, Bill Moyers, and Alice and George Brown.

At one point, Lady Bird took a call from Abigail McCarthy, who told her, "when he made the announcement, I could only think of you standing in front of the Wilson portrait." Lady Bird understood the reference, knowing it symbolized the toll that the presidency exacted on those who held office.[98]

While he had been up for nearly fifteen hours, the night was not over for LBJ. He changed into a blue turtleneck and worked the room, thanking everyone and appearing genuinely happy and relieved.

Then, he left at 11 p.m. to meet a group of thirty-five reporters gathered in the Yellow Room.[99] LBJ enjoyed the sight of the shocked reporters, each clamoring to know more, as the Texan certainly dropped a bombshell on almost everyone in America.

One reporter forcefully asked: "How irrevocable is your decision?"

"It is just as irrevocable as the statement says," LBJ snapped. "Completely irrevocable. You just take the statement and read it. There were no shalls, no woulds, no buts; I just made it 'will.'"[100]

Several reporters continued the line of questioning, obviously not convinced of his sincerity. Aggravated, Johnson shot back: "My statement speaks for itself. I don't see why we should have these high school discussions about it."[101]

Later, another asked whether he felt as if he had sacrificed himself. LBJ responded: "No, no, I am not sacrificing anything. I am just doing what I think is right, what I think is best calculated to permit me to render the maximum service possible, in the limited time left."[102]

Finally, the press conference ended and the president retired to his living quarters. At about midnight LBJ sat down with Arthur. He looked at his friend and said, "I never was any surer of any decision I ever made in my life, and I never made any more unselfish one." He zeroed in on the "525,000 men whose very lives depend on what I do, and I can't worry about the primaries. Now I will be working full time for those men out there . . . the only guys that won't be back here by the time my term ends are the guys left in the last day or two."[103]

He truly believed that he could pull off the miracle, and now he had a new crusade, likely one of his last. The effort to find a way to extricate the United States from the morass in Vietnam became an all-consuming effort, one that dominated the last nine months of his presidency. It ensured some gains, but ultimately ones undermined by his inability to let others, including the vice president, shape the outcome as well as Nixon undermining a last minute breakthrough after negotiations began in Paris. Burnishing his legacy became a fundamental mission of his remaining time in office.

Finally, about 1 a.m., all the guests departed and LBJ and Lady Bird prepared for bed. As he fell asleep after an exhausting day, she wrote: "At last the decision had been irrevocably stated, and as well as any humans can, we knew our future!"[104]

The next day, the benefits of the decision rolled in. His brother, Sam, sent a note, "Last night was the happiest moment of my life. I am proud to be your brother."[105]

The newspapers echoed the good feelings. The *Washington Post* shared the views of many when its editors wrote that LBJ "made a personal sacrifice in the name of national unity that entitles him to a very special place in the annals of American history . . . The President last night put unity ahead of his own advancement and pride."[106]

His colleagues added more accolades. A long-time antagonist on Vietnam, Senator Albert Gore (D-TN), called the pronouncement "the greatest contribution toward unity and possible peace that President Johnson could have made."[107] New York Republican senator Jacob Javits stated, "in a grave hour of war and national doubt, the President has lifted the office of the president to its proper place, far above politics."[108]

Most important to the life-long politician, his popularity soared. A Harris poll for April 1 found that LBJ's ratings shifted from 57 percent disapproval to 57 percent approval almost overnight.[109]

When LBJ traveled to Chicago and New York soon after, instead of picketers and hecklers, the president received standing ovations for putting the country's needs over his own. It reenergized him and his agenda.

Yet, one journalist, quoting W. B. Yeats, noted that for the country after the announcement: "We are closed in, and the key is turned on our uncertainty."[110] It was unquestionably so.

In the final analysis, the decision shook the country. It reflected an honest commitment to break the deadlock in Vietnam and his genuine sacrifice of his political career for the betterment of the country. Of course, selfish concerns regarding his health and desire to buttress his legacy drove his decision, but he could have easily set those aside like he had before and moved forward in the Democratic primary against McCarthy and Kennedy, who likely would have split votes. Tet, however, destroyed many of his illusions about Vietnam, especially that military force would accomplish his goal of an independent SVG able to stand on its own. It was a difficult decision, but one that reflected for the moment a desire to put the needs of the country ahead of his own desires. Many regained some hope for a new beginning to what had started as a very difficult year.

CHAPTER 5

The Days the Earth Stood Still

The Assassination of Martin Luther King, Jr., April 1968

For our euphoric days passed after LBJ's big announcement. Letters and telegrams poured into the White House praising his decision. Public opinion polls skyrocketed, flipping overnight from 57 percent disapproval to the same number in support.[1] Positive editorials flooded major newspapers across the country as LBJ often read them to his aides.

The jubilation gave LBJ a new bounce in his step, and he exuded a fresh excitement and confidence, declaring: "We're going to get this show on the road again."[2]

The pace accelerated as he pushed to complete legislation held hostage in Congress on civil rights and antipoverty measures. Lady Bird observed, "Lyndon was going at an even faster pace than before he made known his decision Sunday night."[3]

Good news continued arriving as the week progressed. On Wednesday, April 3, the North Vietnamese signaled their willingness to negotiate. "Perhaps," LBJ wrote, "a real breakthrough has arrived at last" as he prepared to travel to Hawaii to meet Westmoreland.[4]

Johnson savored the moment unlike any since 1965. As a man of action, the decision not to seek reelection provided him a much-needed boost of energy and enthusiasm. Beyond focusing on Vietnam, he would push forward on the Fair Housing Act, gun control, and other domestic measures to solidify his legacy. It was a new day and with the clock now ticking down on his presidency, he gained much-needed momentum.

His mood only improved the following day when he traveled to New York City to attend the investiture of Terence James Cook as the new Catholic Archbishop of New York. Accompanied by Luci and Lyn, LBJ landed by helicopter in Sheep's Meadow in Central Park on a beautiful spring day as the temperatures climbed into the low 70s.[5] Pink and white blossoms dotted the trees, the explosion of spring mirroring the new attitude emanating from the presidential limousine that whisked the entourage to St. Patrick's Cathedral.

The motorcade sped from the park along Madison Avenue to the cathedral. Along the sidewalks of the bustling city, hundreds lined up to cheer as LBJ passed, lifting his spirits even more.

Arriving at the beautiful neo-Gothic church, Johnson quickly entered the cavernous structure and headed down the center aisle. As he passed, thousands rose simultaneously as they recognized him. Spontaneous applause erupted throughout the huge cathedral, the sounds resonating off the high ceilings. According to LBJ's escort, only Pope Paul VI received such a similarly rousing welcome, in 1965.[6]

LBJ sat in the front row, thoroughly satisfied with his enthusiastic greeting. Soon, Archbishop Cooke took to the large white marble dais. The forty-seven-year old New York native opened his sermon: "Let us pray with all our hearts that God will inspire our president. Mr. President, our hearts, our hopes, our continued prayers are with you."

He zeroed in on what motivated many in the audience to greet the president so enthusiastically. "In the last few days, we have all admired his heroic efforts in the search of peace in Vietnam. We ask God to bless his efforts with success." He concluded, "May God inspire not only our president, but also other leaders and the leaders of all nations of the world to find a way toward peace."[7]

At the end of the ceremony, LBJ triumphantly exited the cathedral, only stopping for a short conversation with Jackie Kennedy. He marched out and into the New York spring, exhilarated at the turn of events over the past few days and adulation heaped on him for making the political sacrifice to focus on Vietnam. The chance to reduce US involvement in Vietnam (one he largely helped create), provided a chance to end a conflict that tore apart the country and undermined his ability to accomplish more on the social and economic fronts. He felt confident that he could maintain the momentum and redoubled his efforts by looking to all options to assist in the process.

As a last minute decision, Johnson instructed Chief of Staff Jim Jones to arrange a meeting with US Ambassador to the United Nations Arthur Goldberg, who he hoped would arrange a quick meeting with Secretary General U Thant.

They sped from Central Park to UN Plaza, where Goldberg waited in the main lobby. The president and entourage went to the 38th floor and Thant's office. There, the Burmese diplomat reported: "Hanoi really wants to talk to you." Later, he promised, "I am at your disposal. My sole concern is to contribute as best I can to bringing peace." LBJ left pleased and admitted later, "Hanoi's agreement had given all of us a great lift."[8]

On board Air Force One for the short flight back to Washington, the president spent time working the press, including some of his harshest critics. He seemed to enjoy doing so for the first time in a long while. Toward the end, he made his way to the back of the plane to check on a napping Lyn, carrying his tired grandson into the White House after the helicopter ride from Andrews Airbase. People noticed a different man, one more relaxed with his guard down.

When he entered the West Wing, he found a very quiet and comparatively deserted space. Many of the staff had already departed for the day as some headed out to Andrews Air Base with their bags and equipment so they could board the planes leaving for Hawaii later that evening.

He observed: "The world that day seemed to me a pretty good place."[9]

Meanwhile, more than seven hundred miles away, Martin Luther King, Jr. rested at the Lorraine Hotel in Memphis. Tired, he had run for weeks between planning the Poor People's March in Washington and backing the predominantly African American sanitation workers striking in Memphis.

For three years, the relationship between LBJ and King had deteriorated after the voting rights victory in 1965, particularly when King criticized US conduct in Vietnam at a speech in the spring of 1967, when he declared, "I could never again raise my voice against violence of the oppressed in the ghettos without having first spoken clearly to the greatest purveyor of violence in the world today: my own government."[10]

Others poisoned their association, especially FBI Director J. Edgar Hoover, who accused King of being a pawn of the international

Communist movement. The director constantly funneled reports to LBJ's Chief of Staff Marvin Watson and Attorney General Ramsey Clark about King's leftist influences and marital infidelities.[11] The lurid details of the affairs seemed of little interest to LBJ, but his paranoia over Vietnam fueled his anger toward King.[12]

Back in Memphis, the lifting of an injunction against marching renewed King's energy on the warm evening of April 4. Exiting Room 306 of the Lorraine Motel, King joked around with his friends and staff, stepping out onto the balcony at 6 p.m. and yelling down to Ben Branch, a trumpet player from Chicago to request his favorite song, "Precious Lord, Take My Hand."

He shifted his attention to the limo driver, Solomon Jones, who looked upward and said, "Dr. King, it's going to be cool tonight. Be sure to carry your coat."

Then, a loud noise rang out as a bullet struck King in the jaw and shattered his spinal cord. As he bled, his long-time friend Ralph Abernathy cradled him while King's close confidant Andrew Young wept, "Oh my God, my God, it's all over."

After a short time, an ambulance arrived and carried him to St. Joseph's Hospital, where people gathered to pray for a miracle.[13] Millions across the country joined once the news leaked out.

In the Oval Office, LBJ talked on the phone with Robert Woodruff of Coca-Cola. He hurried things along because he needed to dress for a fundraiser at the new Hilton Hotel on Connecticut Avenue, where he planned to deliver a short speech.

Suddenly, LBJ's special aide Tom Johnson walked into the room at 7:30 p.m. and handed him a note on a plain white piece of paper that read: "Mr. President: Martin Luther King has been shot."

Shocked, the president remembered, "a jumble of anxious thoughts ran through my mind. What does this mean? Was it the act of one man or group? Was the assassin black or was he white? Would the shooting bring more violence, more catastrophe, and more extremism?"[14]

The president had little time to digest the gravity of the situation. At 8:20, Christian delivered the message: "Mr. President: (the Department of) Justice has just advised that Dr. King is dead."[15]

Figure 5 On the day of the assassination of Martin Luther King, Jr., Secretary of Defense Clifford and a staffer react to the news of the death of the civil rights leader. (Courtesy of the LBJ Library)

LBJ lamented, "a President's limitations are never more evident than when he hears of the death of another man. In that ultimate situation a President is only a man and can do little or nothing to help. I rarely have felt that sense of powerlessness more acutely than the day Martin Luther King, Jr., was killed."[16]

Now, a crisis mode engulfed the White House, like none since the assassination of John F. Kennedy. Within minutes, the president canceled his speech, telling Califano to encourage the organizers to say a prayer and end the dinner. Word went out that he would postpone his trip to Hawaii until further notice.

With only a short time in which to work, he scribbled notes for a speech to the nation. While Christian and several others worked on it, he headed to the White House barbershop as customary before giving a televised address. There, he called Coretta King in Atlanta, offering his sympathy and promising assistance in returning the body.[17]

At 9:07, he went on camera to tell his countrymen: "America is shocked and saddened by the brutal slaying tonight of Dr. Martin Luther

King." He pleaded, "I ask every citizen to reject the blind violence that has struck Dr. King, who lived by nonviolence." He extended his sympathy to the King family and stressed "I know that every American of goodwill joins me in mourning the death of this outstanding leader and in praying for peace and understanding throughout this land."

Then, he called for order: "We can achieve nothing by lawlessness and divisiveness among the American people. It is only by joining together and only by working together that we can continue to move toward equality and fulfillment for all our people." The president concluded, "I hope that all Americans tonight will search their hearts as they ponder this most tragic incident."[18]

Johnson understood instinctively that he must recognize the sacrifice of King in promoting the civil rights movement despite his lingering animosity over the civil rights icon's opposition to the Vietnam War. However, LBJ knew he needed to try to find ways to neutralize violence in America's inner cities. He wanted people to look to the future for hope and honoring King in some way provided an opportunity, but he realized the challenges that lay on the horizon.

Once back in the Oval Office, a flurry of activity followed. At one point, LBJ sighed as he told Califano, "Everything we've gained in the last few days we're going to lose tonight." He slumped in his green leatherback chair and signed a stack of papers, keeping him preoccupied rather than sinking further into despair over the senseless act.[19]

Everyone remembered the horrible days in Watts in 1965 and Detroit in 1967 and hoped for calm. Unfortunately, rioting broke out all over the country, including 14th and U, only a few blocks from the White House. Some marchers threw bricks into primarily white-owned businesses, opening the way for looters and eventually arsonists. Black smoke started floating into the warm, humid sky.

Johnson's crisis management style came into focus. He remained calm but active, constantly moving and indefatigable, trying to deal with the large scope of the violence that erupted all over the country. He would cajole, exhort, and threaten, typically trying to prevent an overreaction by local officials that would enflame embers into a raging fire. He would use the lessons learned the summer before to use federal resources to try to prevent the confrontations from digressing into slaughter, always searching for ways to limit casualties and constrain the use of force, fearful of establishing precedents his successors might employ with much more harmful results.

In addition, unlike local leaders, he sought to understand the multiple, holistic factors that sparked the violence, often showing empathy toward those in the streets. He wanted to contain the violence and also provide some hope to those feeling dispossessed to quell their anger and frustrations. Finally, he tried to mobilize leaders within the African American community to his support efforts. It was a significant task that had many challenges and pitfalls.

As riots began, LBJ jumped on the phones, talking to mayors and governors all over the country. He reached out to his friend Governor Buford Ellington in Tennessee, who sent the National Guard to Memphis, much to the great consternation of Attorney General Clark. He feared inciting more violence with a show of force.

Trusted advisors joined the president as the tragedy unfolded. Busby arrived at the White House and stressed, "I had rarely seen him so subdued or so alone within himself." LBJ prowled the room, reading the Teletype and watching the news, his body becoming more rigid as Secret Service agents handed him updated reports.

On the phone to black leaders and other government officials, he told them to go to the ghettos, "For God's sake, go see the people, let them see you, let them know you care, that we all care."

Then, he shifted his focus to preventing bloodshed. "Both sides," he warned the mayors, feared each other. "Don't, please, send your skinny little rookies out with great big guns and all by themselves – if the shooting starts, it may never stop," the president pleaded.

After a while, he put down the phone and lamented: "I'm not getting through. They're all holing up like generals in a dugout getting ready for war."[20]

LBJ also worried that jubilant whites celebrating King's death would further incite African Americans. One of those attending the Democratic fundraiser at the Hilton told columnist Mary McGrory: "Of course, I'm from the South, and I am glad."[21] Halfway around the world in Vietnam, some white G.I.s dressed like Klansmen and paraded around Cam Ranh Bay celebrating his murder.[22]

To stem the growing tidal wave of violence, LBJ ordered his staffers immediately to arrange a meeting with prominent civil rights leaders. He understood the need to have them out in the streets and on television and the radio trying to prevent more violence. Unlike many other politicians, he had created a lot of good will with his support of the civil rights bills and appointment of African Americans to prominent positions in government including the Cabinet and Supreme Court. He wanted to use all the resources available to the White House in this time of mourning and crisis.

Quickly, they reached a large number who agreed, including Bayard Rustin, Executive Director of the A. Philip Randolph Institute, distinguished African American jurist, Leon Higginbottham, Walter Fauntroy of the Southern Christian Leadership Conference (SCLC), and Justice Thurgood Marshall.

His staff also reached out to Martin Luther King, Sr. and delivered a message: "The President wants you to know his prayers are with you." The well-liked elder King simply responded, "Oh no, my prayers are with the President. And I want so badly to be there tomorrow to do whatever I can."

A nurse took the phone and reported that health issues prevented travel, and that he needed to preserve his strength for the funeral. LBJ acknowledged, "I understood completely and I admired his ability to think of his country at a time of such private grief."[23]

While a flurry of activity continued in the White House, a well-timed thunderstorm hit the capitol late in the evening, sending most rioters scrambling for cover. However, by that time, looters had ransacked 150 stores and arsonists set eighteen fires.[24]

Finally, about 11 p.m., LBJ retired to the White House residence for dinner. Luci, Pat, Lynda, and Lady Bird joined him as well as Secretary of Defense Clark Clifford, close friend Arthur Krim, and devoted administrative assistant Marie Fehmer with Busby popping in and out.[25]

Lady Bird played host, having slipped out of her flame-colored chiffon dress she planned to wear to the fundraiser and into something more practical and comfortable. Always observant, she stressed: "Dinner was a strange, quiet meal. I thought, and maybe everybody else did that we had been pummeled by such an avalanche of emotions the last four days that we couldn't feel anymore." Yet, she concluded, "here we were, poised on the edge of another abyss, the bottom of which we could in no way see."[26]

By midnight, positive reports on the unrest funneled in, indicating the riots lacked the feared rage. Nonetheless, Busby observed LBJ "thought the calm was misleading." To him, "Friday night would be the critical time." Busby noted, "once again, it was move, move, move."[27]

As late as 1 a.m., the president called Califano to expand the list of invitees for the morning meeting. LBJ also instructed him to arrange a memorial service at the National Cathedral and to request that the Archbishop of Washington, Patrick O'Boyle, have his parishes hold services honoring Dr. King. He asked someone to call Jackie Kennedy, Coretta King, and King's father to request that they issue statements calling for nonviolence to honor the fallen leader.[28] Trying to remain proactive, he understood the worst likely lay on the horizon.

Near 2 a.m., he tried to sleep after digesting updated intelligence and news reports from across the country. Unable to sleep, he got on the phone and ordered Clark and Chairman of the Equal Employment Opportunity Commission Cliff Alexander to jump on a plane for Memphis. He needed eyes and ears on the ground since he distrusted the notoriously racist mayor of the city, Harry Loeb.

After a long night, LBJ finally fell asleep, not waking until about 7 a.m., late by his standards. When he arose, he immediately worked the phones, not even changing out of his pajamas as staffers entered and exited his bedroom.

In one conversation, he told a mayor: "Your men didn't get any sleep last night; they're going to be tired, scared, irritable, and trigger-happy tonight." He encouraged him to address the issue forcefully, arguing: "It's easier to stop shooting before it starts."

In other calls, LBJ stressed, "Don't wait till dark to holler for help."[29]

But some leaders pushed back, one proudly crowing, "the crisis is past."[30]

"I hope you're right," LBJ responded, but quipped: "We shall see what we shall see."[31]

Throughout the morning, he worked on a speech to give right after the meeting with the civil rights leaders. At one point, Johnson decided to add a section on addressing a joint session of Congress on Monday because he wanted to present a comprehensive program for African Americans. Busby and Clifford were unenthusiastic, wondering how in such a short time the White House could develop such an ambitious proposal.

Frustrated, LBJ barked. "Goddamn it, this country has got to do more for these people, and the time to start is now."[32]

Not long after, Clifford arrived to update the president on plans to deploy troops into the major cities if crises developed.[33] The president wanted to be ready this time around with federal troops, learning significant lessons from the previous time when he waited too long and the situation worsened before he could use troops to enforce some semblance of calm.

By 11 a.m. he entered the Cabinet Room and sat down.[34] Flanked by Justice Marshall and NAACP leader Clarence Mitchell, Jr., LBJ looked across the table at Humphrey sitting next to Wilkins and Young. Throughout the room, prominent civil rights activists including Walter Fauntroy, Dorothy Height, Leon Sullivan, and D.C. Mayor Walter Washington waited. Clifford, Christian, and Califano along with congressional leaders including Mansfield and House Speaker John McCormack sat interspersed among the distinguished assembly.

Following a script prepared beforehand, the president began that King "held deep convictions about the great issues of the day. Some of them did not agree with mine. But on the issue of human dignity, there was no difference between us."[35]

For nearly forty-five minutes, the group discussed the assassination and the next steps. From the start, violence was a central focus. LBJ believed that militants like Stokley Carmichael and H. Rap Brown had already fueled the fires from the previous night. The president reported talking with John Gardner of the Urban Coalition and encouraging him to have African American leaders denounce violence, something many already had done the previous day.

Those sitting around the table desperately wanted to avoid a repeat of Watts and Detroit. Each knew the destruction accomplished little and ensured a significant white backlash. In response, LBJ read a telegram from Martin Luther King, Sr.: "Please know I join in your pleas to

American citizens to desist from violence and permit the cause of non-violence for which my son died not be in vain."

At this juncture, LBJ looked up to acknowledge the feelings of those in the streets protesting. "If I were a kid in Harlem. I know what I'd be thinking right now: I'd be thinking that the whites have declared open season on my people, and they're going to pick us off one by one unless I get a gun and pick them off first."[36]

But, LBJ wanted to prevent rioting even though Mayor Richard Hatcher of Gary, Indiana, angrily replied that "racist" America caused the rage. In response, LBJ told him that the death of King should not make anyone believe violence solved racial problems.

The president agreed with Sullivan about the heart of the matter: "The large majorities of the Negroes are not in favor of violence ... but we need something to fight back with: we need something positive to carry to the people. Otherwise we'll be caught with nothing. And the people just won't behave in a vacuum."[37]

At one point, several participants prodded LBJ: "We need more than patience and non violence. We need funds for the cities." LBJ responded that he had already made numerous efforts to help the inner cities, especially the young people. "How well I have gotten through remains to be seen."

Then, he queried, "How well have you gotten through?"[38]

Then, LBJ turned his attention to the congressional leaders sitting around the table, complaining about efforts to root out racism "sitting too long in the Congress."[39]

His commitment to change impressed many in the room. Rustin believed the president promised "that he would put all the forces of government to work to find out who it was who had done this heinous act, and that in the meantime he wanted to reassure the community that things would be done ... the very fact that we were there I think helped."[40]

Afterward, Assistant Attorney General Warren Christopher evaluated the president's performance, observing: "The event featured Lyndon Johnson at his best. He preached, he cajoled, he pleaded at least temporary acceptance of the conclusion that the shooting was the work of one deranged man, not a manifestation of white society's attitude about race."[41]

Christopher was correct. This was the LBJ of 1964 and 1965 working a room full of people who could aid his agenda. He desperately needed them to take to the streets, airwaves, and churches and push people to stay out of the violence and condemn those perpetrating it. He understood the limitations of the president in affecting the African American community.

He worked the room flawlessly, but missed a major part of the equation: the increasingly radicalized young people in the African American community, tired of the broken promises and angry over continued police brutality, lack of educational options, and fed up with the long-time leaders who they thought too often kowtowed to the white establishment. However, the message of Carmichael and other radicalized leaders resonated more among African American youth than those of the people sitting in the room. The violence reflected it.

Near noon, the participants boarded vehicles for the short drive to the National Cathedral. By the time the distinguished group arrived, more than 4,000 people crowded into the large Gothic structure, many young and white and scions of the Georgetown elite.

The president immediately made his way to the front of the great hall. As he walked, all rose and sang, "We Shall Overcome." Wearing a dark black suit, LBJ took his seat by Justice Marshall, Mayor Washington, and Robert Weaver, Secretary of HUD and first African American cabinet member. They sat not far from where MLK gave one of his last sermons, only five days earlier.

The choir opened by singing, "Precious Lord, Take My Hand," the same song MLK asked his friend to play right before the bullet struck.

As the song ended, Fauntroy gave a prayer. "Forgive us for our individual and corporate sins that have led us inevitably to this tragedy. Forgive us. Forgive us, God, please forgive us."

The service was brief as Humphrey fought back tears, as did many others in the large crowd. At the end, the 24,000-pound church bell rang, its sound muffled by leather covers to reflect a time of mourning.

When the service ended, the presidential entourage led the procession out into the beautiful spring day. As they exited, a group of young boys and girls spontaneously began singing, "We Shall Overcome." Soon, the entire cathedral erupted with the anthem of the civil rights movement.[42]

LBJ had little time to absorb the events unfolding around him as more work remained, as everyone expected more disturbances that night. As they sped back toward the White House, smoke spiraled skyward from the previous night's riots, casting an ominous black cloud over the capitol.

Once back at the White House, LBJ went on national television flanked by the civil rights leaders. He opened: "Once again, the heart of America is heavy – the spirit of America weeps – for a tragedy that denies the very meaning of our land." Highlighting the strain on the very fabric of the country, he stressed, "if we are to have the America that we mean to have, all men – of all races ... must stand their ground to deny violence its victory in this sorrowful time and all times to come."

He focused on King's contributions and sacrifice of his family. "No words of ours – and no words of mine – can fill the void of the eloquent voice that has been stilled." He emphasized King's dreams did not die with him, and that people, both black and white, needed to join together to let the nation and the world "know that America shall not be ruled by the bullet, but only by the ballot of free and just men."

Then, he turned to the near future and acknowledged that "we have rolled away some of the stones of inaction, of indifference, and of injustice," but "our work is not yet done. But we have begun." He called on everyone in government from the halls of Congress to schools and churches to "move with urgency, with resolve, and with new energy" to accomplish all possible "until we do overcome."

This section of the speech reflected a recurrent theme throughout his presidency. Much more remained to be done to move the country toward realizing the dream of equal opportunity and away from the dark, prejudiced past. He realized the deep-seeded racism that plagued America was a potent and powerful force standing in the way of progress, not just for African Americans but all minorities. The task started in 1964 on ending segregation and discrimination to honor President Kennedy had progressed but not far enough. Johnson correctly recognized it was a project only partially fulfilled that helped fuel the anger and resentment spilling over into the streets after King's assassination.

Finally, he asked for the leadership of Congress to host him at the earliest possible day so that he could outline plans to honor the slain leader. "Together, a nation united, a nation caring, a nation concerned" and one that set aside self-interest, "that nation can and shall and will overcome."[43] Then, he signed a proclamation declaring Sunday, April 7, as a day of mourning.

After the television address, LBJ sat down with some advisors for lunch and gave a sincere prayer: "Help us, Lord, to know what to do now." As he finished and raised his head, he smiled and said, "I thought I'd better get specific about it, fellas."[44]

As the meal opened, a series of reports arrived on the relative calm in New York City, Atlanta, and Cleveland. But as lunch progressed, those in the White House watched history unfold just outside. Unlike events in Vietnam or Detroit, what transpired that day occurred in real time. There were no paper reports to read or phone calls to take. People simply went to the windows and watched.

It began when secretaries returning from lunchtime reported that salespeople in downtown stores had started clearing out customers and closing. Another staffer's wife described mounting fear as whites fled the area, many on foot as traffic jams developed.

Several people rose from their chairs and walked to the windows overlooking Pennsylvania Avenue.

One simply said, "Gentlemen, I think you better see this."

Instead of noticing the spring beauty of Lafayette Park, they saw an "ugly flood" of traffic "bumper to bumper, curb to center stripe, with Washingtonians surging out toward the sanctuary of their suburban homes."[45]

Then, their gaze shifted to the east. "Through the pale leaves, beyond the gray buildings, smoke leaped into the sky, and we could see the first flames," one observed.

LBJ never left his chair, as he instinctively knew what was happening. Busby watched as the president, "attempted to establish contact with municipal authorities" as reports of looting and arson flooded the White House. The rioters quickly overwhelmed the Washington police force, and LBJ knew it. However, he required a request from city officials before he could send in the military to help restore order. Suddenly, the crisis became extremely personal for everyone in the room.

Once more, Johnson encountered a crisis in the inner cities where African Americans took to the streets in violent mobs. He had watched in horror as Watts exploded in 1965 in Los Angeles and in the summer of 1967 in Detroit. However, he ignored the recommendations of the Kerner Commission that he created after Detroit that included dispersing people out of large public housing units and pushed for the migration of African Americans into the suburbs. Now, LBJ found himself trapped inside the White House as throngs of terrified whites fled the city. It appeared an intractable situation, and some conservatives took glee in highlighting that it confirmed all their fears about breaking down the old system that contained blacks.

Washington D.C. was in the throes of chaos. Angry young African Americans left school early, as packs of looters crashed through the doors and windows of businesses, many near the White House. Once they ransacked the store, people carrying Molotov Cocktails appeared and threw the incendiary into the building. Only a few businesses escaped the mayhem, mainly black-owned ones. Soon, huge plumes of black smoke reached up into the spring sky.

Around 2 p.m., the president and his staff moved into a sitting area overlooking the Rose Garden. Someone opened a window, but instead of the scent of flowers, the smell of burning timbers wafted into the room.[46]

By this point, the president had already dispatched a number of people, including Christopher and DC Director of Public Safety Patrick Murphy, to reconnoiter the city as the overwhelmed communication systems failed and reliable intelligence disappeared.

While waiting, someone asked the president for permission to close the federal offices and let workers leave. Standing at a window, LBJ hissed, "Who in the hell do they think is still around to dismiss?"[47]

Also, preparing for the inevitable, LBJ ordered troops readied. Rapidly, units began gathering on the perimeter of the city, as the Pentagon started implementing well-developed contingency plans built off lessons learned in Detroit. He also ordered Califano to get a "proclamation or order, whatever I need to send troops into Washington to maintain order."[48]

The president showed remarkable foresight on several levels as the request went out for the military. He pushed his advisors, including his legal counsel, Larry Temple, to think about the future. "Before going into this thing," he told them, "I want to know how we are going to get out."[49]

While they waited for a request from Mayor Washington for troops, LBJ sought to avoid turning the riots into a bloodbath and replicating the bloody confrontations in Watts and Detroit, again demonstrating noteworthy restraint. He called General Harold Johnson, chief of staff for the Army at the Pentagon.

"General, I know I've been over this with you before, but I want to go over it one more time," he spoke into the phone.

"Number one, are you sure of your commander? Are you sure he has control of his men? Are you sure he isn't one of those who is willing to use a little more force than necessary to set an example?"

Then, he went on, "Number two, are you sure of these troops? Make sure none of them are trigger happy? No question of discipline? ... The whole world will be watching tonight. I don't want anybody – repeat, anybody, shot if it can be avoided. You understand that, don't you, General?"

The president listened intently to his response, his brow furrowing and face becoming red. Suddenly, he slammed down the phone and stormed out of the room.

He returned a few moments later and sank into a chair. "Gentlemen, I want you to know you can sleep well tonight," LBJ said sarcastically: "The commander in chief," he added, "just concluded five minutes of instruction of the chief of staff of the Army ... over one of the goddam military's supersecret, hotline connections."

He continued, "And when the commander in chief finished, the good general said, 'Gee, I'm sorry sir, I can't hear you on this line. Let me see if I can borrow a dime ... and I'll call you back from a phone booth outside.'"[50]

Meanwhile, the president waited on a report from Christopher, Murphy, and Vice Chief of the US Army, General Ralph E. Haines, Jr. They scoured the city, seeing hundreds of fires and panicked people fleeing, with rioters moving freely. They tried using a police radio to report the mayhem to the president, but the overloaded system failed.

Finally, they found a pay phone at an abandoned gasoline station. They stood in line and waited their turn, not wanting to identify themselves. After a long wait, Christopher borrowed a dime from Murphy and called the White House at around 4 p.m.

As the anxious crowd behind them waited, Christopher reached the president.

"Where have you been!" LBJ screamed. "I've been trying to reach you for an hour."

Christopher explained the situation, watching the crowd behind him grow more restless. He pointed excitedly to his watch and mimed that it would not take long.

Haines took the phone, reinforcing the need for the troops. The president curtly cut him off, simply responding, "Fine. We'll send in the troops."

Once the president put down the phone, he secured a formal request from Mayor Washington for the deployment of federal troops. Quickly, LBJ signed a proclamation calling for the rioters to cease and desist as well as an executive order federalizing the National Guard and ordering the military into the capitol.[51]

By 5 p.m., soldiers, many Vietnam veterans, flooded into Washington. As they plowed through the exiting traffic, some people left their cars to applaud them. A steady stream of jeeps and large trucks turned into a torrent as troops from the surrounding bases at Fort Meade and Quantico occupied the capitol. They dispersed, setting up machine guns on the steps of the Capitol Building, leading a journalist to write that it looked like a "parliament of a new African Republic."[52]

Soon, they surrounded the White House and piled sandbags at strategic points. Inside, nervous White House staffers gathered, one emphasizing: "We were scared to death. The country was exploding, and it was pretty hard to figure out how the hell we were going to contain it."[53] The building now resembled the embassy in Saigon more than the home of the leader of the free world.

Once they secured major buildings, the troops moved into the ravaged areas. With strict orders not to fire unless given permission by an officer (they fired only three bullets during the occupation), the soldiers scattered the rioters.[54] As they gained a foothold in the worst areas, they apprehended looters and curfew violators, turning them over immediately to the police. Slowly, the military established some semblance of order by midnight.

The devastation overwhelmed many people. Returning home from Memphis, Attorney General Clark had his pilot circle the capitol. A passenger observed: "Coming up the river, looking out the window, I saw a big orange ball with a needle in it." Then, he exclaimed, "Holy shit, that's flames, and the needle I'm seeing is the Washington Monument. The city looked like it had been bombed from the air."[55]

Some criticized the invasion, as Senator Russell complained about the Marines guarding the Capitol building lacking live ammunition. But LBJ remained committed to preventing additional bloodshed. He told Califano: "I don't want Americans killing Americans. I may not be doing the popular thing, or even the right thing, but no soldier in Washington has killed a civilian yet."[56]

Even the height of the crisis, LBJ maintained a sense of humor. Reports circulated that Carmichael organized a group at 14th and U Streets and planned to march on the "posh" homes in Georgetown of the newspaper editors and columnists who loved to criticize him.

The president smiled when he read the report and bellowed, "Goddamn! I've waited thirty-five years for this day!"[57]

Not long after, LBJ received a boost when Cyrus Vance arrived from New York about 7 p.m. When he heard about the rioting, Vance jumped on a plane for National Airport and battled the D.C. traffic to reach the White House. The skilled troubleshooter personally observed and studied the Detroit Riots in 1967, and he led a task force that issued a formal report on how to handle similar events. Always calm and collected, his appearance steadied the president and his advisors.

Throughout the evening, LBJ manned the phones, receiving reports from Vance, who moved over to the DC command post of Mayor Washington. Also, other cities began to burn, including Pittsburgh and Chicago.

It was a long day, the president waiting until nearly 11 p.m. to have some dinner with some close advisors. LBJ focused on the television showing coverage of the riots and briefly mentioned a FBI report on a possible attempt on the life of Chicago Mayor Richard Daley.

But foremost on his mind already was the visit to Congress on Monday. He turned to Busby and told him that it "can make or break us." He acknowledged the 31st speech accomplished a great deal, but the King assassination erased it. Busby listened intently as LBJ unburdened himself about constructing another monumental speech, a process exacerbated by the absence of McPherson, whose daughter had been injured in a fall.[58] A long weekend lay ahead.

The president stayed up late into the night and early morning on the 6th. At about 3 a.m. on Saturday, Vance returned from the D.C. command center. Obviously exhausted after a long, stressful day, he also nursed a herniated disc in his back that caused great pain. He asked for a drink, and Califano obliged.

As they enjoyed a scotch and soda, a pajama clad LBJ burst in and surprised the two men. He faked rage, exclaiming: "No wonder the nation is going up in smoke and riots and looting. My two top advisers are sitting around drinking."[59]

The president barely slept as he manned the phones gathering intelligence and haunting Califano's office, the unofficial War Room.

That evening, the president under advisement from the Secret Service, decided not to attend Dr. King's funeral in Atlanta. An inordinate number of death threats had flowed into the White House, and the FBI warned Ku Klux Klan members "possessing highpowered rifles ... are capable of making an attempt to do bodily harm to the president." The Secret Service highlighted the logistical nightmare of protecting the president among a teeming mass of tens of thousands.[60] The president also feared being seen as trying to take political advantage of the event, something some civil rights leaders accused Nixon and Kennedy of doing.[61]

By April 6, LBJ awoke to the headline in the *Washington Post*, "4000 Troops Move Into District After Day of Looting and Arson." Other bylines on the front page read, "Arrest in Slaying 'Close,' Clark Says" and "Curfew Imposed As Roving Bands Plunder and Burn." It also included one, "Carmichael Warns of Retaliation," where the previous day he said "when white America killed Dr. King last night, she declared war on us" and encouraged those in the streets to "take as many white people with them as they can."[62]

Such statements infuriated congressional leaders, who criticized the lack of deadly force employed on the rioters. On April 6, Senator Robert Byrd (D-WV) pushed the president for a curfew to be "re-inforced immediately, and looters should be shot, if they are adults (but not killed; just in the leg)." He added: "The time for restraint is ended" and complained that LBJ failed to impose martial law.[63]

The president's actions further angered the hard-liners like Byrd and many of his fellow senators and congressmen, especially those from the south who shared his convictions. But, it went beyond them and to many whites, who complained bitterly about the rioting and how it reinforced their convictions that African Americans could not handle the newly legislated rights. Deep down, they longed for the days where African Americans knew their place.

However, Johnson instinctively rejected his southern, lower middle-class roots. Clamping down would further cement the anger and resentment spilling over into the streets. LBJ understood the violence hurt the cause of civil rights and that many simply participated in it not out of political angst, but for personal gain from looting. However, he would not allow the trigger happy racists to start a race war, and he desperately wanted to find a way to do more to ameliorate the years of exploitation and discrimination.

Despite improved conditions in D.C., the president and his staff never relaxed. They spent the day considering a series of proposals for the speech to Congress, including new programs ultimately totaling more than $5 billion. Debates broke out on their focus. Gardner Ackerly, chair of the Council of Economic Advisors, called for a "Bill of Economic Rights" and a reordering of priorities to inner-city work programs and properly funding housing and welfare. He stressed that "even people who can't be appealed to on the basis of conscience ought to recognize that the choice is between engaging the thirsts of the poor or repressing their violent protests at incalculable costs."[64]

Other debates arose over how to pay for them, including tax increases and shifting money from space exploration and defense and into programs starved by Congress. People needed jobs and hope, especially young blacks, whose unemployment rates far outstripped their white counterparts.

But there was also realism within the White House on what Congress might accept in an election year. Raising taxes was a nonstarter. Shifting money from other projects was an uphill battle in districts dependent on government spending. More important, McPherson observed, "on the Hill, and probably for a majority of the country, this [new spending] seemed dangerously like a protection racket." People in power "were not convinced that public funds and programs would be more successful in changing them in the future as in the past." He added, "they simply saw no relationship between the issues of racial justice . . . and people stealing television sets from gutted stores."[65]

Here the reality of the riots affected any efforts to promote positive change. It was tough to overcome the visuals of African Americans looting businesses and burning buildings, often in their own neighborhoods. The actions further confirmed to many critics of the Great Society that the focus on civil rights and economic programs for the poor only encouraged them to act badly. Few blue collar or middle-class workers sitting in their living rooms watching the news understood why the blacks reacted in such a manner, having little empathy for their fellow Americans. Instead, Nixon and conservatives like Senator Strom Thurmond (R-SC) and Alabama Governor and presidential candidate George Wallace exploited the anger and resentment for political gain, making it nearly impossible for Johnson to squeeze out more support for those in the riot-ravaged areas.

Throughout Saturday, the staff worked on proposals and the speech outlining them. However, they lost momentum as LBJ grew more pessimistic. Others around him expressed frustration with congressional obstructionism. One aide told a reporter: "What's the use of escalating the demands for the Negro when Congress won't move on what we've already sent up there?"[66]

While the staff focused on the speech to Congress, LBJ shifted attention to Vietnam, although always keeping his eye on the cities. Westmoreland arrived after the president canceled the Honolulu meetings. Traveling to the White House, the South Carolinian observed downtown Washington, "looked considerably more distressing than Saigon during the Tet Offensive."[67] He quipped that the British burned down the city in 1814, but this time its inhabitants seemed intent on doing so.[68]

Despite focusing on Vietnam, throughout the day, LBJ took a number of calls from Mayor Daley in Chicago. On Friday night, the south side ghettos burned with 575 fires, nine people dead, and thousands arrested. One journalist observed, "the looters, like vultures, fed on the ashen carcasses of scores of stores. Loaded with booty, they looked like an army of worker ants as they scurried off to the side streets and alleys."[69]

The events in Chicago surprised no one. For many years, race relations in Chicago simmered in a stew of corruption and discrimination, exacerbating tensions between the Chicago police force and the African American community. Mayor Daley and other leaders provided little relief to the burgeoning ghettos that grew astronomically during WWII with a massive exodus of African Americans into the city. The assassination of MLK just blew the lid off the toxic mix that had evolved over the years.

Saturday opened little better, as deaths mounted and the police failed to curtail the violence. The obstinate Daley and Illinois officials sent in the National Guard, but they proved equally ineffective as the numbers of fires and violence increased.

Finally, in the late afternoon acting Illinois governor, Samuel Shapiro, requested federal troops. LBJ responded in a telegram, "I have directed troops ... to proceed to O'Hare Field and to the Glenview Naval Air Station." He promised immediate deployment on arrival to assist the police and national guardsmen. Soon, troops left Ft. Hood for Bergstrom Air Base just outside of Austin, the president's home airport. Others from Fort Carson in Colorado boarded planes, many of them battle-hardened Vietnam veterans.[70]

Wanting to know more, the president dispatched Christopher to Chicago. On landing at O'Hare in the evening, he immediately took a helicopter ride over the riot-ravaged areas. Christopher could tell that "even at a thousand feet, it was evident the situation was grave."[71]

Immediately, Christopher got on the phone and called the White House at 1 a.m. LBJ answered, not having gone to bed. "He sounded weary and disheartened," Christopher remembered.[72]

Not long after, Califano entered the president's bedroom with a proclamation and executive order sending federal troops into Chicago.

"Johnson's eyes were heavy with fatigue, his jaw sagging," his aide remembered, "Lying on his back in bed, he signaled me to hand him a pen, and signed the papers as he held them up over his head, which he was too exhausted to raise from the pillow."[73] He finally fell asleep, but not before ordering 20,000 troops into the Windy City.

When he started the next day at 6:32 a.m. in the Situation Room, the conditions had improved in Chicago. However, other cities, especially Baltimore, appeared primed for an explosion. So, it was more of the same.

The president had early meetings with Westmoreland, but took time to talk with Daley as well as Lady Bird in Texas, where she entertained members of the foreign press on the ranch and at the World's Fair in San Antonio. He also met with Califano and others as they strategized about the speech to Congress.

Around noon, he headed to St. Dominic's for Palm Sunday Mass with Luci, Pat, and Califano. Only a week earlier, he sat there contemplating the speech declaring his intention not to seek reelection. Now, he pondered new questions.

The homily gave him solace as the priest Norman Haddad told the audience, "I saw the reflection of Christ's passion in Martin Luther King, accepting his cross. Let us reflect how we stand in our attitude toward this crucifixion." The pastor also prayed that "the president and the leaders of the country be given the wisdom and guidance to help bring about a responsible peace and that those who are filled with anarchy and the psychology of mob rule be brought to the realization that the way to violence is not the way to peace."[74]

As the service ended, the president walked toward the exit. The eight hundred congregants rose in unison but remained in place. Califano observed, "as we left the church, the congregation . . . gave the President warm, supportive, understanding smiles and nods."[75]

Throughout the afternoon, he boarded a helicopter heading to Andrews Air Base to deposit Westmoreland on his plane. Returning, Johnson asked the pilot to fly at a low altitude to view the destruction. They went up 7th Street and down 14th Street as dark black smoke continued to rise from the burned out buildings. A horrified president silently looked down on a scene straight from a war zone.[76] Somberly, he exited and returned to the safe environs of the White House. It was quite a contrast from the places only blocks away.

On arrival, LBJ turned to the task at hand. While reports of violence filtered in from across the country including Pittsburgh; Tuskegee, Alabama; and Wilmington, North Carolina, the most pressing problem lay only forty miles away in Baltimore. The night before, city officials reported 250 fires, 273 arrests, and three dead.

In the late morning, fresh reports of violence arrived as the police and National Guard failed to disperse the growing crowds. Within a short time, fighting in the poverty-stricken areas consumed more than a thousand square blocks. White vigilantes roamed the streets, while heavily armed storeowners prepared to defend their businesses. Violence spiraled out of control with no relief in sight.

By late Sunday afternoon, Baltimore and Maryland officials surrendered and requested federal troops. Governor Spiro Agnew phoned Clark, who relayed the message to the White House. Within a short time, the president ordered troops stationed near the city to advance. He sent a telegraph to Agnew: "I have already directed the troops you requested to proceed at once to Druid Hill Park."[77] Soon, members of the 82nd Airborne headed northward from Andrews Air Base to engage the rioters. However, it was not until 10:15 p.m. that LBJ finally signed the official proclamation.[78]

By the next day, more than 10,000 troops occupied Baltimore. Their presence and the curfew quelled the looting and arson. Washington and Chicago remained under the watchful eyes of US soldiers, but the police now gained the upper hand and arrested thousands. It was a step forward, but one accompanied by the pain of burnt homes and businesses, civilian deaths, and overflowing jails.

It was not a scene LBJ savored, but one he understood as he told Christian: "What did you expect? I don't know why we're surprised. When you put your foot on a man's neck and hold him down for three hundred years, and then you let him up, what's he going to do? He's going to knock your block off."[79]

Unlike Wallace or Thurmond, LBJ instinctively understood the root causes of the rioting. His experiences in South Texas as a teacher and seeing the poverty in the Mexican American community and its accompanying problems gave him insights that they lacked. Genuinely, he wanted a better America with expanded opportunities for all its citizens, but he understood huge obstacles existed, especially for those of color who lacked access to proper housing, education, and job opportunity. It was not politically expedient to reach out to the dispossessed whose anger he comprehended, but he truly believed it was the right thing for the United States if it would ever realize its vast potential.

A very small glimmer of hope existed on Sunday for new programs to address the roots of the rioting, but by that evening LBJ fully abandoned the plan to speak to Congress. Earlier, he lamented to McPherson about passing new legislation. "I'm the only one who can't do these things. Bobby, Gene, Nixon, any one of them would get a honeymoon from Congress in their first year. But not me. Cuz I've been, I've asked Congress for too much for too long. And they've tired of me."[80]

But at the heart of the matter lay the inability to formulate a reasonable proposal, one that Congress likely would pass. Busby remembered the president receiving a sheaf of paper of recommended actions. The president's face sagged. "We don't have the ideas we used to have when I first came to town," he lamented. Pointing to the stack of recommendations, he characterized them as "all vanilla; they wouldn't begin to touch our problem."

Then, he cut to the heart of the issue. "Until we all get to be a whole lot smarter, I guess the country will just have to go with what it has already."[81]

By this time, it was clear that his power had waned, something exacerbated by his announcement of his decision not to seek reelection. This diminution of power from the heady days of 1964 and 1965 became all too apparent in a country exhausted by rapid socioeconomic change, the war in Vietnam, and disillusionment caused by the assassinations of JFK and MLK. It was hard for the president to accept, but increasingly it became apparent to him that he would have to find other avenues to push the country forward.

With few options, LBJ borrowed from his playbook following the assassination of JFK and settled on honoring Dr. King with a substantial piece of legislation: the Fair Housing Act. As early as 1966, Johnson proposed legislation ending discrimination in the sale, rental, or lease of housing. He characterized it as a basic human right challenging segregation all over of the country.

Not everyone agreed with the decision. Clark opposed it, stressing "it would raise expectations; and it would manifest an unwillingness of the American people to really come all the way toward equal justice."[82] Johnson persisted, and it went to Congress.

While many congressmen ran from it, fearful of inciting a white backlash in the suburbs, the House passed it. However, in the Senate, Minority Leader Everett Dirksen (R-IL) opposed it for assaulting private property rights. Many of his constituents agreed, believing African Americans in their neighborhoods would drive down housing prices, diminish schools, and cripple their way of life. Twice, LBJ's allies failed to break cloture, so the president accepted defeat.

The battle for fair housing wounded many supporters, including the president. Califano remembered, "when Johnson sent his fair-housing bill to Congress in 1966, it had prompted some of the most vicious mail LBJ received on any subject and the only death threats I ever received as a White House assistant."[83] McPherson stressed that the Watts riots allowed opponents to "justify the worst feelings of the racists in Congress and the press."[84]

The midterm elections further demonstrated the volatility of the issue. Several prominent Democrats, including Senator Paul Douglas of Illinois, lost their seats, partly for supporting the Fair Housing Act. The party also lost significant numbers in the House, particularly in the suburbs. When Congress reconvened in 1967, Democrats clearly understood backing fair housing constituted a significant liability.

Undeterred, in February 1967, LBJ once again submitted the act. He stressed "there should be no need for laws to require men to deal fairly and decently with their fellow men" but such regulations were "decent and right. Injustice must be opposed, however difficult or unpopular the issue."[85]

But once more, opponents marshaled a spirited campaign, arguing the legislation abridged their First Amendment rights to freedom of association. LBJ denounced critics using slogans such as "Open housing is forced housing" and "A man's got a constitutional right to sell to whomever he wants." In particular, Republicans warned "LBJ's bureaucrats" would be "swarming over every neighborhood setting up Negro-white quotas, forcing homeowners to sell their property, and encouraging vicious gangs of rioters and looters to destroy neighborhoods which dare to resist."[86]

Again, the act failed to advance, never even exiting committee in the House. Some of LBJ's frustrated lieutenants encouraged him to circumvent Congress and issue an executive order. He balked, arguing, "without the moral force of congressional approval behind us, the struggle for open housing would be lost before it had even begun."[87]

So, in January 1968, the president sent the bill back for a third time. Cracks appeared in the opposition as Dirksen shifted his position in late February. The Illinois senator observed, "one would be a strange creature indeed in this world of mutation if, in the face of reality, he did not change his mind."[88] By March 11, the bill reached the Senate floor, where supporters defeated a filibuster. That afternoon, it passed by a vote of 71 to 20.[89]

But obstacles remained in the House, where southern conservatives in the Rules Committee refused to move on the matter. However, the assassination of King changed the dynamics and presented LBJ with an opportunity.

Almost immediately after King's assassination, LBJ told Califano, "We've got to show the nation that we can get something done." He particularly wanted to demonstrate to African Americans, many at the time protesting in major cities, that he could still secure gains.[90]

On April 5, the president sent a message to Speaker John McCormack urging passage of the Fair Housing Act. He called for the Congress to ensure the American "right of a man to secure a home for his family regardless of the color of his skin." Johnson stressed, "in your hands lies the power to renew for all Americans the great promise of opportunity and justice under law."[91]

Republicans in the House, led by minority speaker Gerald Ford (R-MI), opposed the bill, strongly toeing the line of the National Board of Realtors. However, twenty-one Republican moderates, led by the ranking member of the House Judiciary Committee, William McCulloch of Ohio, broke ranks. When the Republican caucus met on the matter, he challenged his fellow Republicans to remain true to the vision of Lincoln.[92]

Even so, passage of the act remained in doubt. On Monday, McCormack met with supporters of the bill. "I'm not sure we are going to accomplish anything," he told them. Afterward, Democratic leaders sat down and looked for fifteen to twenty names needed to win. Doing so, they worried about success.

But, in classic LBJ style, the White House initiated a full court press with legislative liaison Harold "Barefoot" Sanders leading. Such efforts inspired *Time* correspondent Hugh Sidey to observe, "he would lie, beg, cheat, steal a little, threaten, intimidate. But he never lost sight of that ultimate goal."[93] Quickly, they found one vote when Jake Pickle (D-TX), who represented LBJ's old congressional district, received a $1.4 million grant for housing. Sanders asked the president to call House Democratic whip Hale Boggs of Louisiana and former Republican house leader, Charles Halleck.[94]

With the White House and their allies actively seeking votes, Tuesday arrived and provided some momentum. In Atlanta, a thousand people gathered for King's memorial service inside his father's Ebenezer Baptist Church. Vice President Humphrey, Clark, Weaver, and Katzenbach represented the president, while RFK, McCarthy, and Nixon joined the assembly, the latter receiving a spattering of boos. Dignitaries including Jackie Kennedy, Wilt Chamberlain, and Henry Fonda crowded into the church, while thousands waited outside to march with King's body.[95]

Millions watched the service on television, including people at Camp David, to where the president had moved for meetings to discuss Vietnam. They observed Pastor Ron English pray: "Deepen our commitment to nonviolence so that the country will not be run asunder by a frustrated segment of the black masses who would blaspheme the name of Martin Luther King by committing violence in that name."[96]

Television crews continued covering the ceremony as the pallbearers carried the coffin to a mule-drawn wooden wagon. A long procession snaked through downtown Atlanta to Morehouse College. Crowds flooded into the quadrangle as Mahalia Jackson opened with a stirring rendition of "Take My Hand, Precious Lord." More than five hours after starting, the memorial ended with a keen sense of loss remaining.

Throughout it all, LBJ requested constant updates on Atlanta as he met with US Ambassador to Vietnam Ellsworth Bunker and General Wheeler at Camp David.[97] Secret Service agents reported a "church ... very much over-crowded" and that during the play of King's last sermon "at this time persons became very emotional and tension was felt among those in the church." They also highlighted that there were "no incidents of concern to this service" even though Carmichael attended.[98]

By 4 p.m., Ellsworth departed and the president joined his staff in the living room of the Aspen Lodge to watch the coverage of King's funeral. After a short meeting with Admiral U.S. Grant Sharp, LBJ returned to digest the media coverage of the memorial service and long processional. The mules pulling the green wagon carrying the body of the slain leader hit close to home for many in the room who had watched JFK's body delivered to Arlington Cemetery by a horse-drawn carriage. It was another sad day for the country.

Throughout, the president also monitored debates in the House. The main battle revolved around getting the Senate bill out of the House Rules Committee. Leaders scheduled a vote despite protests by the committee chairman William Colmer (D-MS), who complained bitterly about being forced to do so amid an atmosphere of rioting. When it finally occurred, seven voted for and seven against, leaving Illinois Republican John Anderson as the tiebreaker. He flipped his earlier vote and broke ranks with the Republican leadership, ensuring the legislation emerged from committee.[99]

With that victory and the White House continuing its full court press as the president returned to the capital, the House convened the next day to debate the fair housing bill. It featured impassioned speeches from both sides. Democrat William Fitts Ryan (D-NY) argued that Congress should honor King and "pass the bill which is before us to guarantee open housing and the free exercise of civil rights." On the other side, opponents smeared King, including William Tuck (D-VA) who claimed that his nonviolence tactics provoked conflict. "Violence followed in [King's] wake wherever he went, North or South, until he fell a victim to violence."[100]

When the final vote occurred, 152 Democrats joined 77 Republicans in supporting the bill. 89 Democrats and 106 Republicans voted against it, creating a final tally of 229 to 195. It passed by a much larger margin than anyone envisioned.[101] In a press conference, LBJ proudly stressed, "through the process of law, we shall strike for all time the shackles of an old injustice."[102]

The passage of the legislation marked a stunning victory that appeared unlikely only weeks before King's assassination. With determination and grit, Johnson and the White House used his death to jumpstart the process. He captured the old magic of 1964 in outmaneuvering much of the Republican leadership and conservative southern Democrats. He understood the urgency of needing to exploit the tumult created by the death to try to accomplish something positive to honor the fallen civil rights leader. While handicapped politically compared to 1964, he still found a way to pass the legislation along with allies in Congress, giving him a victory during a difficult time. It was classic Johnson.

Once the voting ended, LBJ traveled a short distance across the hall to the Fish Room to address the nation. "This is a victory for every American because the only true path to progress for a free people is the one we will

Figure 6 President Johnson stands with Clarence Mitchell after the signing of the 1968 Civil Rights Act on April 11, 1968. (Courtesy of the LBJ Library)

take when this legislation is made the law of the land," he opened. He acknowledged that only a short time earlier, "there were very few who thought that in our time we could bring this justice to all Americans." But, he observed, "Congress today has shown that if we have the will, there is a way."[103]

While happy, LBJ wanted more and stated: "I call upon the Congress to now complete its work of hope for millions of Americans by passing the measure recommended" by the White House in twenty messages and fifteen appropriation bills "in order that we can move forward with our programs of social justice and progress."[104]

While winning on the Fair Housing Act, he would not have such victories on these other activities. People in Congress could be persuaded to support such a monumental bill, but the smaller fights ensured more personalities and individual concerns played out in appropriation bills. Those were a much harder sale and reflected closer to the president's diminution of power over the previous two years.

The following day in the late afternoon, a large crowd of more than 200 gathered in the East Room for the official ceremony. Standing around LBJ were prominent civil rights leaders, a significant number of whom had joined him only a week before to discuss King's death. Some strained to watch the signing from various vantage points, including Clarence Mitchell who realized his long years of struggle for fair housing finally culminated in victory.

Flanked by Lady Bird in a bright green dress that contrasted with the dark suits, LBJ beamed at signing another monumental civil rights bill. Then, he took a seat to place his signature on it, painstakingly using a hundred pens to sign out his name. He distributed one to each person in the room as a memento.

After finishing the process, the president rose and went to a lectern. There, he highlighted the long battle over the legislation and proudly exclaimed, "Now, with this bill, the voice of justice speaks again. It proclaims that fair housing for all – all human beings who live in this country – is now a part of the American way of life."

With an eye toward the rioters, he added, "I would appeal to my fellow Americans by saying, the only real road to progress for free people is through the process of law and that is the road that America will travel."

Yet, he also warned, as he would do often over the next five years, "We have come some of the way, not near all of it. There is much yet to do."[105]

LBJ wrote later, "As I returned to my office, I thought to myself how different the mood of this day was from that just one week earlier."[106]

It certainly was a special day but only the beginning of more battles. Days after the rioting, Senator Thurmond sent out flyers to his constituents: "We are now witnessing the whirlwind sowed years ago when some preachers and teachers began telling people that each man could be his own judge in his own case."[107] The dark clouds of backlash rose even as LBJ lay down the pen.

But, for the moment, LBJ could look back over the week with some satisfaction. With substantial assistance from people at many levels, he managed the country through a major national crisis. He beat back calls for more violence against the rioters, showed wisdom in limiting the amount of force applied, and always pushed for an exit strategy.

In addition, much like after the assassination of JFK, he succeeded in ensuring the passage of a landmark civil rights bill. It was a significant victory on housing and opened the way for ending some of the *de facto* segregation in neighborhoods and schools, further chipping away at the bastions sustained since *Brown* v. *Board* in 1954.

However, much like with his major achievements in civil rights in 1964 and 1965, he encountered a recalcitrant conservative opposition, both in the Republican Party and reactionary southern and western Democrats. His own fatigue and lack of new ideas to address the endemic racial and socioeconomic conditions in the country, particularly among African Americans, plagued him. He wanted to do more, but accomplishing it as a lame duck president in an election year provided more challenges than opportunities. It had already been a long year, and it was only April, with much on the horizon, including a presidential race that would ensure more drama.

CHAPTER 6

He Hated Him, but He Loved Him

The Assassination of Robert Kennedy, June 1968

I n the early morning of June 5, the president retired to his bedroom about 12:50 a.m. after a long day of work, staying up to watch the results of the California campaign where his nemesis, Bobby Kennedy, appeared to be winning. However, at 3:31 a.m., Walt Rostow woke him with the news that an assassin had shot RFK at the Ambassador Hotel.

The groggy president rose and began gathering information. At that time, little existed other than scattered reports about the assassin's identity and questions on the severity of the wounds.

Just after 4 a.m., Lyndon called Lady Bird and asked. "Will you come in here?"

She found him "propped up against the pillows, looking as though he had never been asleep." All the television sets glowed as "he was listening intently, and I realized at once that something serious was happening." She found "all three faces of the three television sets were on and the scene was total confusion" as every few minutes a tabulation of the votes total scrolled across the screen.

The Johnsons watched as the stations replayed the whole event, the newsmen catching the whole affair on camera, including the "light crack of the gun. We saw Senator Kennedy lying on the floor, a pool of blood under his head," Lady Bird observed.

She watched, as "every few minutes the flashbacks would come on the screen – the smiling face of Senator Kennedy, tasting the wine of victory, making little jokes with Ethel by his side. And then the whole nightmare would start over again."[1]

The first lady perceived "an air of unreality about the whole thing – a nightmare quality. It couldn't be true. We must have dreamed it. It had all happened before."[2]

From the start, LBJ worked the phones. His first calls went to the Secret Service with orders to give protection to all the candidates. "If there weren't enough Secret Service men they could borrow from the FBI or from the Marines ... assign them now," he barked.[3]

Ironically, several weeks before RFK's assassination, LBJ asked Congress to adopt legislation allowing for Secret Service protection of presidential candidates. The large crowds and general unrest in the country left him "deeply concerned."[4]

However, Congress failed to act, and tragedy struck.

Knowing he clearly overstepped his authority by ordering Secret Service protection, LBJ immediately tried to remedy it. At 5:30 a.m., he called Senator Mike Monroney (D-OK), chairman of the subcommittee overseeing Secret Service budgets and urged him to get the bill out of committee "right now – today." Within a few hours, it reached the Appropriations Committee and eventually the Senate floor.[5]

For the second time in five years, LBJ faced a major crisis caused by an assassin's bullet striking down another member of America's royal family, or at least the closest thing approximating it. Proactive, he employed many of the lessons he learned when John Kennedy died and some from a few months earlier with King's murder. He sought to reassure the country once more the assassin could not tear down the country and tried to prevent violence, all the while using the death to push reforms to honor the fallen. It would put his vast political talents fully on display.

The attack on RFK followed a whirlwind of a campaign after Johnson announced his decision not to run. Everyone knew animosity remained between the two men, dating back years. The two men interacted little, the last time in early April when Bobby requested a meeting with the president.[6]

RFK was a political animal and understood LBJ's departure from the race made Humphrey the biggest challenge lying in his path. He recognized Johnson retained influence with his vice president and sought to gauge the president's position.

The president agreed to a meeting on April 3rd in the Cabinet Room.[7] Bobby entered and symbolically took a seat directly across from the president, one typically occupied by Humphrey, while Sorenson sat to RFK's left and Rostow to the president's left. White House aide Charles Murphy was near Kennedy, ready to take notes.[8]

The president opened the meeting by saying he was "pleased at its spirit and wished to explore whether they could find areas in which the Senator could be helpful to the nation at this critical time."[9]

They talked for a while, the president stressing that "he and Senator Kennedy would not be far apart if they sat at the same table." The discussion shifted to Vietnam, and Sorenson chimed in about the March 31 televised addressed: "I thought the language of the speech was just right."

Then, Johnson promised Clifford would provide briefings to Kennedy, and he would gladly accept suggestions; LBJ emphasized: "I want everybody to get together to find a way to stop the killing."

Finally, Bobby probed Johnson on the presidential race, the real purpose of the meeting. LBJ responded he would "have his own judgments and would exercise them, but except for a few fundraising dinners, he planned to keep out of campaign politics."

Kennedy pressed him a bit: "Will people in your administration be free to take part in pre-convention politics and support candidates?"

"I will need to think about that," Johnson replied.

"If you decide later on to take a position, can we talk to you prior to that?" Bobby queried.

"Yes, unless I lose my head and pop off, I will try to honor your request," the president responded.[10]

At this point, he stressed he had no enmity toward Bobby, but noted quite "frankly that he felt much closer to the Vice President, who had been everything the President could ask as Vice President."

As the conversation neared its end, the president emphasized he "never thought of his administration as just the Johnson Administration, but as a continuation of the Kennedy–Johnson Administration" and concluded, "the next man who sits in this chair will have to do better."

RFK simply commented: "You are a brave and dedicated man."[11]

They parted amicably, but the suspicions remained. LBJ secretly recorded the meeting. When he asked for a transcript, there was nothing on the tape. Unbeknownst at the time to Johnson, Bobby carried a scrambler to the meeting to prevent any recording and manipulation of the conversation. The misgivings about each other died slowly.

Afterwards, Murphy reported: "There is a real chance of influencing the campaign to minimize vindictiveness and divisiveness. This meeting broke up with an obligation, express or implied, on both side to try to do this." But, he concluded: "The relationship with Senator Kennedy will not be really cordial, and a guarded attitude on both sides can be expected. To make this work, and to reap for the country the benefits of the unity for which the President has already paid so high a price, the game will have to be played straight."[12]

He was correct, and many foreign observers understood neither man liked the other. Soviet Ambassador to the United States, Anatoly Dobrynin, told Averell Harriman about a "joke going around the Diplomatic Corps of President Johnson's preference for successor: First, Hubert Humphrey; second, Nelson Rockefeller; thirty, McCarthy; fourth, Nixon; fifth, Ho Chi Minh; sixth, Kennedy."[13]

Despite the mistrust and longstanding animosity, when the assassin's bullet struck Bobby, the president rose to the occasion and showed leadership. Califano noted: "Since he was well aware of his own psychological baggage, in no situation did Lyndon Johnson try harder to do the right thing – for the country, the Kennedy family, and himself – than in the hours and days following the shooting of Robert Kennedy."[14]

Johnson performed admirably in the following days, seeking to assist the family with the arrangements for the funeral and burial and showing compassion toward the Kennedys despite his long-standing rivalry with Robert Kennedy. Putting aside his own pettiness that often reared its ugly head, especially when dealing with RFK, Johnson showed statesmanship and leadership in another time of crisis, something happening frequently in 1968.

After learning of the tragedy, Johnson reached out to the family to show his concern. LBJ sent a telegram to the Kennedy matriarch, Rose Kennedy: "Our fervent prayers are with you and the Ambassador."[15] He also reached out to RFK's brother, Ted: "Our thoughts are with you and Joan as we read every sentence and see every picture of this dreadful time. Added to the sharp pain of grief, we are aware of the weight and the burden you carry for your whole family. Please know that our prayers are with you."[16]

Beyond prayers and condolences, Johnson helped the family with logistics. He immediately made available a Jet Star airplane for three of

Robert's children so they could fly to Los Angeles. It left Andrews Airbase on one hour notice with Robert Jr. and then picked up the other children in New Hampshire and Boston before heading west.[17]

During the day, LBJ also focused on preparing a statement to give that evening, working with speechwriters to try to hit just the right tone.

Around 6 p.m. on the 5th, White House assistant Mike Manatos reported that former legislative aide Chuck Roche had called from Los Angeles. He was at Good Samaritan Hospital and observed the Kennedy people looked "gloomy." He left with the impression that only prayer could help, but acknowledged the family recognized the "President's willingness to do whatever he can."[18]

As Johnson prepared his address, special White House assistant George Reedy encouraged him to make sure of "no action be[ing] taken to feed the flames" such as those of civil rights activist Charles Evers (brother of activist Medgar assassinated in 1963) who said that anyone who spoke for the poor risked their lives. "That is simply not true. The truth is that no man in this, or in any other country, can be prominent without risking his life." Finally, Reedy argued: "It seems to me of great importance that no steps be taken, other than that of physically protecting the candidates, until the situation is clear. The nation cannot afford to wallow in another orgy of self-flagellation."[19]

As the day progressed, the president and his staff prepared for the worst. Joe Califano, Warren Christopher, and others discussed putting 600 National Guardsman in the capitol and keeping at least 600 policemen on the streets. They also developed contingency plans leading to the scheduled demonstration on June 19 by people camped in Resurrection City and over 4,000 college students participating in the Poor People's March organized by King to highlight poverty in America.[20]

Despite the concern, Mayor Walter Washington reported a quiet city. However, Califano worried "enough people will get stirred up ... so that there could be trouble later in the day." The mayor requested army officers as liaisons in police precincts and asked for troops on a thirty-minute alert. Everyone desperately wanted to avoid a repeat performance of April.[21]

Johnson also focused on what to do next. He invited Senate leaders Everett Dirksen (R-IL) and Mike Mansfield (D-MT) to the Oval Office.

After pouring them a drink, they talked for nearly an hour about the ills of the country and how to respond to RFK's increasingly likely death. Fearing a circus of investigations, LBJ encouraged the men to oppose congressional inquiries, promising none himself. Instead, he proposed a commission on violence headed by Milton Eisenhower to study the root causes and suggest possible solutions. The two agreed.[22]

The president clearly wanted to prevent another wave of conspiracy theories regarding the assassination of a Kennedy. He had organized the Warren Commission, and its findings never satisfied some, who even blamed Johnson for playing a role in JFK's death. Johnson wanted to appear proactive and address the rising level of gun crime in the country, something Robert Kennedy spoke out against only a few weeks before his death. He clearly wanted something more than just focusing on one death and sought to address the continuing problem of gun violence in America.

As LBJ managed the crisis, many in the country mourned another fallen hero.

Distinguished journalist Eric Sevareid went on the evening news on June 5 and characterized the Kennedys as "a star-crossed family; and this generation, like the audience to a remorselessly unfolding Greek drama." He stressed such "events psychologically disorient the whole nation; there is no logic, not dignity involved."

As if supporting Johnson's plan to honor RFK by pushing gun control, he argued: "We are no longer the open, frontier America ... For we live today, not on the frontier, but in a crowded theater. It has always been a crime to set a fire in a crowded theater. And the right of free speech does not encompass the right to shout 'fire' in a crowded theater." He finished: "It will be very important to see if the teaching of a generation be redirected and the young taught to spell the world [sic] 'duties' before they learn the word 'rights.' Of necessity, the former precedes the latter in the lexicon of freedom."[23]

As the evening progressed, LBJ worked feverishly on his statement. Near 9 p.m., the White House received information from the Los Angeles Secret Service that RFK's "heart [was] getting weaker" and the doctors "asked all members of the family to gather at the hospital."[24]

At 10:07 p.m., the president went to the Fish Room and talked again about a tragedy.

Looking tired and drained, LBJ opened: "My fellow citizens, I speak to you this evening not only as your President, but as a fellow American who is shocked and dismayed, as you are, by the attempt on Senator Kennedy's life, deeply disturbed, as I know you are, by the lawlessness and violence in our country, of which this tragedy is the latest spectacular example."

In one of the strongest statements, he stressed: "Tonight this Nation faces once again the consequences of lawlessness, hatred and unreason in its midst. It would be wrong, it would be self-deceptive, to ignore the connection between that lawlessness and hatred and this act of violence."

Forcefully, he raised his voice slightly and said: "200 million Americans did not strike down Robert Kennedy last night any more than they struck down John F. Kennedy in 1963 or Dr. Martin Luther King in April of this year."

"But those awful events give us ample warning that in a climate of extremism, of disrespect for law, of contempt for the rights of others, violence may bring down the very best among us. A Nation that tolerates violence in any form cannot expect to be able to confine it to just minor outbursts."

Johnson felt the need to avoid issuing a blanket condemnation of his fellow Americans. Instead, as was often the case, he tried to find a common ground that appealed to the best in the country and asked for collective action to stop the carnage. He instinctively understood the limits of the nation accepting responsibility but definitely wanted to build momentum for a crusade against guns and the violence they caused.

"My fellow citizens," he emphatically said, "we cannot, we just must not, tolerate the sway of violent men among us. We must not permit who are filled with hatred, and careless of innocent lives, to dominate our streets and fill our homes with fear."

"There is never – and I say never – any justification for the violence that tears at the fabric of our national life; that inspires such fears in peaceful citizens that they arm themselves with deadly weapons; that set citizen against citizen or group against group."

"Let us put an end to violence and to the preaching of violence."

Then, he underlined a major point: "Let the Congress pass laws to bring the insane traffic in guns to a halt, as I have appealed to them time and time again to do. That will not, in itself, end the violence, but reason and experience tell us that it will slow it down; that it will spare many innocent lives."

"Let us purge the hostility from our hearts and let us practice moderation with our tongues."

Toward the end, he highlighted his commitment to a commission whose membership included Judge Leon Higginbotham and Archbishop Terence Cooke to "look into the causes, the occurrence and control of physical violence across this nation, from assassination that is motivated by prejudice and by ideology, and by politics and by insanity, to violence in our cities' streets and even in our homes."

"This is a sober time for your great democracy," he concluded, "but we are a strong and resilient people who can, I hope, learn from our misfortunes, who can heal our wounds, who can build and find progress in public order. We can. We must."[25]

Afterward, LBJ worked the phones to push the legislation on Secret Service protection of the presidential candidates; something passed easily the following day and signed into law by late afternoon.

Finally, at 1 a.m., he joined his trusted advisors, Larry Temple, Califano, George Christian, and Harry McPherson for dinner. One observed LBJ's "anguish was visible. His presidency had erupted out of the assassination of John Kennedy, a man who in death had assumed heroic proportions that LBJ would not achieve in his life." But with Bobby's death, "a murdered Kennedy would likely leave a legacy of what-might-have-been that would rival his brother's. In life Robert Kennedy had been a political hammer; in death, he would be a haunting nightmare" for the president.[26]

The conversation was somber, with the president often picking up the phone and asking the Secret Service, "Is he dead yet?" Several times, he asked Califano, "Is he dead? Is he dead yet?" He checked with White House staffer Larry Levinson and also the Secret Service, telling them: "The President wants to know whether Bobby Kennedy has died." Watching the clearly distraught president, Califano observed, "I couldn't tell" what he wanted to know "because Johnson didn't know whether he hoped or feared the answer would be yes or no."[27]

At 2:20 a.m., the president retired, having been awake for nearly twenty-four hours.

But, his slumber ended quickly. At 5:01 a.m., Rostow called and reported: "Mr. President, it has just been announced that Senator Kennedy is dead."[28]

LBJ and his advisors now faced a myriad of challenges after RFK died. Many revolved around Bobby's final resting place. The family wanted him interred in Arlington near John, but he was not a veteran. The president and his advisers worked on the matter, Rostow telling a State Department official that there must be places reserved for high government officials.[29]

There were also discussions over what constituted an "official" versus "state" funeral. Califano secured information from White House aide Jim Gaither, finding only presidents and vice presidents had state funerals where the body could lie in the rotunda of the Capitol. Others received an "official," which could be for the chief justice, cabinet members, and other government officials and foreign dignitaries deigned by the president.[30]

Late in the morning, Califano briefed the president on the burial site within the 3.2 acre plot reserved for John Kennedy, reporting Robert McNamara was making final plans. Califano reported Nicholas Katzenbach took charge of arrangements for the arrival of the body at Union Station and its journey to the Arlington Cemetery. Finally, an aide stressed the family "does not want any military participation – no taps and no honor guard. They are trying to get some musical college group to sing some hymns at the grave site."[31]

The White House also carefully monitored the unfolding investigation of the assassin, Sirhan Bishara Sirhan. Within a day, the FBI sent Attorney General Ramsey Clark a memorandum highlighting that he graduated from John Muir High School in Pasadena in 1963. School records described him as "friendly, cooperative, well mannered." However, agents uncovered writings at his family home advocating the overthrow of the government and calling for the assassination of Robert Kennedy.

The FBI also provided other information. At the Ambassador Hotel, two witnesses remembered him being in the area around 9:30 p.m. and making a statement condemning "rich people" and in particular RFK, blaming him for wanting to "buy the presidency." He appeared alone, according to the people who interacted with him beforehand. Agents found .22 caliber shells in the glove compartment of his car and also his identification.[32] The FBI believed he was a lone assassin, something sustained in subsequent investigations.

This was good news on one level for Johnson and the White House. It helped remove the possibility of a link to a foreign organization or domestic group that might flame the anger and lead to violence.

For most of the day of June 6, LBJ focused on funeral arrangements, including the use of government planes to fly the body and family members back to New York for the mass as well as Ted Kennedy and his wife to Washington, D.C.[33]

He also worked on a short television and radio statement. In it, LBJ praised RFK, noting he "affirmed this country – affirmed the essential decency of its people, their longing for peace, their desire to improve conditions of life for all." He concluded: "Our public life is diminished by his loss."[34]

After watching the replay, LBJ complained that the bad lighting and makeup highlighted too many lines on his face. He did another version, but Califano remarked: "Even better makeup and lighting couldn't remove the lines from his face on this grim afternoon."[35]

Equally important, the president began formulating actions to honor RFK, just as with JFK and Martin Luther King after their tragic endings. This time, he focused on guns, something RFK's campaign had highlighted on the campaign trail. On May 27, Kennedy told an audience in Roseburg, Oregon: "If someone sent a gun to a man on Death Row in Kansas, he could receive it. It happened. Does that make sense?" When confronted by pro-gun activists, he added: "All we're saying is when someone purchases a gun by mail he must be competent to . . . So protest your right to keep and bear arms. The legislation doesn't stop you unless you're a criminal."[36]

LBJ zeroed in on guns and the escalating violent crime caused by them. Since 1963, he had sought stronger gun controls, particularly after JFK's death. He already had submitted legislation labeled the Safe Streets and Crime Control Bill in February 1968. It called for much tougher laws, more money for local police through federal grants, and tighter control of wiretapping and other surveillance procedures.[37]

But Johnson and his allies faced a powerful opponent in the form of the National Rifle Association (NRA). One observer noted: "Pro-gun control forces were poorly organized and the NRA's efforts against the administration proposals were relentless."[38]

However, support for proposals built after the murders of MLK and RFK. Johnson sent a strongly worded letter to the House and Senate on June 6 as part of the renewed effort to strengthen gun control.

"Criminal violence from the muzzle of a gun has once again brought heartbreak to America," he opened.

After outlining the deaths of more the 750,000 Americans from firearms since 1900 and the average of 6,500 murders a year in the country, he underscored the main argument: "Far too many [guns] were bought by the demented, the deranged, the hardened criminal, and the convict, the addict, and the alcoholic. We cannot expect these irresponsible people to be prudent in their protection of us, but we can expect the Congress to protect us from them."

He complained bitterly about the Senate only passing watered down legislation involving handguns while allowing mail order purchases of shotguns and rifles to continue, even "fifty-five long months after the mail-order murder of President John F. Kennedy."[39]

Johnson emphasized: "So today, I call upon the Congress in the name of sanity, in the name of safety – and in the name of an aroused nation – to give us the Gun Control Law it needs." He wanted the mail order business stopped, guns out of the hands of young people, and an end to the interstate sales of weapons.

But he wanted Congress to respect the wishes of the majority, reasoning, "the voice of the few must no longer prevail over the interests of the many."[40]

Even before throwing down the gauntlet, LBJ understood the challenge. In the immediate aftermath of the shooting, he told Califano: "We have only two weeks, maybe only 10 days before the gun lobby gets organized. We've got to beat the NRA [National Rifle Association] into the offices of members of Congress."[41]

LBJ pushed forward quickly, although his own party stood in the way, as Senator Joseph Tydings of Maryland proposed an even more strident bill in committee that delayed a vote. It worked against the legislation because every day it sat, the more the NRA mobilized and people moved beyond the murder of Kennedy.

With Congress debating and the president and his staff lobbying on gun control, the preparations for the funeral continued. They culminated on Saturday, June 8, when Lady Bird awoke and wrote: "This was a day completely detached from the normal, a capsule of time suspended in unreality."[42]

The president rose early and hurried out to the helicopter pad accompanied by Lady Bird, Califano, Jones, and Rufus Youngblood, his trusted secret serviceman since Dallas in November 1963.

They traveled to Andrews Air Force Base and took a Jet Star to the US Naval Air Station (Floyd Bennett Field) in Brooklyn, disembarking for a short helicopter ride over to Sheep's Meadow in Central Park. LBJ entered a large black limousine with Lady Bird for the short drive to St. Patrick's Cathedral.

Unlike nearly two months before when the president and first lady traveled to the investiture of Archbishop Cooke, there were no crowds to greet them or bustling streets, as uniformed policemen stood shoulder to shoulder at the intersections.

Instead, Lady Bird found them "lined with people who stood silent, motionless." She remembered, "for three days the television had been invoking the phrase 'like a Greek tragedy,' and indeed, there was much of a Greek drama about this, these mute crowds, the voiceless chorus."[43]

Youngblood saw similar expressions as the limousine slowly traversed the route. "I looked out at the somber faces lining the avenue," he wrote, "and it brought back that day in 1963 when we had followed the caisson bearing the body of John F. Kennedy." He remembered it being "a different day" as "different people were packed along the route, but the feeling and the sounds were the same. There was a hush ... broken only by the sound of people sobbing."[44]

The Johnsons arrived at St. Patrick's Cathedral at 9:40 a.m. with the first lady exiting to characterize it as a "magnificent setting – equal to any sorrow or any job." More than two thousand people crammed into the building as the Johnsons and their small entourage quickly made their way to the front.[45]

Trailing the president, Califano observed it was "a difficult entrance; the church was uneasily tense." People in the room, most Kennedy loyalists, understood the tension between the two "political enemies" who had been "ruthless political street fighters, and most of the congregation in St. Patrick's had walked on the Kennedy's side of the street." He felt most thought RFK's death resulted from an illness in America, and "they blamed LBJ for making society sick." "A good number in these pews had expected to ride to power in the White House with Robert Kennedy and were bitterly disappointed," he added and acknowledged, "Johnson knew all this. I could feel it as we walked down the aisle."[46]

The feud between the two men would not dissipate in tragedy. It had deep roots dating back nearly a decade to when John Kennedy selected Johnson as his running mate. LBJ genuinely liked and respected JFK despite tensions, but Bobby remained a constant source of irritation. His loyalists joined the senator in holding Johnson in contempt and believing he took away the rightful place of two Kennedy men. LBJ knew he sat in a comparatively hostile room, but he made every effort to not show anything other than respect for another fallen Kennedy.

They entered the second pew on the left, sitting right behind a number of Catholic dignitaries. Lady Bird entered first, allowing Lyndon to sit on the aisle, a short arm's length from the dark, shiny coffin draped in a flag in the middle of the center aisle.

Soon a gaggle of Secret Service agents, whom LBJ derisively called his "Mexican generals" followed. Auspiciously, right in front of the casket facing the crowd remained a single Secret Service agent, having a full view of the congregation, including the president and Vice President Humphrey, who sat four rows back and away from the president for security reasons. One person noted, the "Secret Service agents ... have come to symbolize the fear for the nation's public men."[47]

Then, a stirring occurred just as the first family took their seats. "The congregation silently and without signal, had risen," someone observed. To the left entered Jackie Kennedy in black accompanied by her two children. LBJ and Lady Bird immediately stood as she passed in front of them and sat on the opposite side on the front row with other members of the Kennedy clan.[48]

Lady Bird described the whole affair as "one of staggering drama and beauty." In the altar area sat high officials wearing robes of different shades of red from "deep purple red and the bright orange red," with Cardinal Richard Cushing "on his throne – the most commanding figure there."

A *New York Times* reporter observed: "Mr. Johnson sat through the 90-minute service in New York's St. Patrick's Cathedral grave-faced and perspiring beside his wife and the flag-draped coffin of his slain challenger."[49]

LBJ listened intently as Ted Kennedy eulogized his brother. Ted, with whom LBJ enjoyed a good relationship, was "strong and composed, though his eyes were red-rimmed," Lady Bird noticed. Toward the end of a heartfelt tribute, he asked everyone to remember Bobby as "a good and decent man, who saw wrong and tried to right it, saw suffering and tried to heal it, saw war and tried to stop it." He closed with the memorable statement by his brother: "Some men see things as they are and say, why? I dream things that never were and say, why not?"[50]

It was a powerful service as one person reported: "Lyndon B. Johnson knelt beside another Kennedy through a solemn requiem mass this morning reflecting on the family tragedy that had also become his own."[51]

Near the end, Lady Bird and Lyndon watched RFK's eight children "the girls dressed in white or navy, their long blonde hair caught back with ribbons and hanging down their backs" joined with "the little boys in dark suits" as they "walked up to the altar in pairs, carrying an offertory, while an orchestra of violins was playing a beautiful melody." The director of the music, according to Lady Bird, was "a study – an expression of the utmost passion, of torment and talent – a magnificent element in this whole tragic mosaic." Then, it struck her; it was Leonard Bernstein.[52]

In conclusion, Cardinal Cooke acknowledged the president by saying 200 million Americans did not kill Kennedy. He urged his countrymen not to sink into despair or inaction. "For, to permit this to happen would be to fail utterly to grasp the message of hope and optimism in Senator Kennedy's life," he concluded.

When Cooke finished, one of the Catholic dignitaries leaned over to the president, and told him that he should leave first.

LBJ rose as Ted crossed over to shake his hand and exchange some words.

Then, the president and first lady passed in front of the family seated on the front row opposite where they sat. Both expressed their sympathy to Ethel.

"You have been so kind," she told LBJ.

They stopped to give their condolences to the children and Rose before talking to Jackie.

"I called her name," Lady Bird remembered, "and put out my hand. She looked at me as if from a great distance as though I were an apparition. I murmured some words of sorrow and walked on ... It was somehow bewildering."[53]

Soon, the Secret Service agents ushered them out of a side entrance and into the limousine. As they retraced their path back to Central Park, Lady Bird saw still silent crowds lining the streets, although "occasionally a hand went up in greet or there was a slight smile."[54]

The flight home was quiet, although there was some good news. Someone informed Johnson that agents had arrested James Earl Ray in London, giving some closure to the King assassination.[55] Lady Bird wrote that the capture somehow said: "This government will not be mocked."[56]

Arriving home about 1 p.m., the president and first lady retired to their personal quarters. While only the early afternoon, it had already been a long day. And, like the tired country, they knew it was not over and the emotional toll would linger.

Uncharacteristically, the president made no phone calls or held any meetings for over four hours. Finally, he emerged from his quarters for a couple of meetings including one with the president of Ireland, Eamon de Valera, but mainly he waited on the arrival of the train from New York carrying RFK's body.

Lady Bird struggled, acknowledging: "I could not bring myself to work. There was so much to be done – so much piled on my desk and my little sitting-room office that required concentration and the best thinking I could give it. But in this interval of time, between the funeral ceremony and the burial, with everyone in a sort of emotional trance, I could not detach myself and work."[57]

She admitted, "so I gave up and looked at TV endlessly." But the tragedies continued as the funeral train struck two people, killing them and hurting five others, delaying it for several hours.[58]

There were a couple of reprieves for the Johnsons as Princess Grace of Monaco and her brother asked for tea with the first lady, momentarily distracting her.

For LBJ, the arrival of Reverend Billy Graham provided some solace. They met in the Cabinet Room before sharing dinner with the first family. Lady Bird and many around him knew that LBJ valued Graham's spiritual advice and comforting words. He certainly needed them.

As they ate, they waited. Planners predicted a 4:30 p.m. arrival of the body, but it was already dark by the time the first couple received word of the train nearing Union Station, around 8.

The Johnsons, accompanied by Jim Jones and Califano, exited the White House as a light rain shower began. They headed south on 15th St. over Constitution Avenue, taking the path in reverse from the route the motorcade would follow once the Kennedy family retrieved the coffin from the train.

Arriving just before 9 p.m., they waited in the limo, where House Speaker John McCormack and Muriel and Hubert Humphrey joined them. Lady Bird noticed the normally "ebullient" Humphrey looked "drained and empty."

"Eric Sevareid sure had it right for once when he said, 'whoever gets the Democratic nomination, it will be a tarnished shield,'" the vice president lamented.

Lady Bird concurred. "For reasons more emotional than rational, it seems to me, this whole tragedy turns the nation toward the Republican Party."[59]

After twenty minutes or so, the party entered Union Station through a side door. Lady Bird remembered walking through the "great vaulted concourse," remembering the last time she visited during the funeral of General Douglas MacArthur in 1964, when she stood by Bobby.

Suddenly, a flurry of activity enveloped LBJ. Someone informed him that Cardinal Cushing had a heart attack on the train and needed a doctor. Taking control, LBJ ordered his own doctor to provide assistance. Then, he told an aide to make arrangements to use a government plane to fly him back to New York.[60]

Finally, at 9:25 p.m., pallbearers including McNamara and General Maxwell Taylor prepared to move the casket from the train to a waiting hearse. LBJ conferred with Archbishop Cooke before joining the Humphreys. He and Lady Bird moved to the back of the hearse, standing on the right side, with the vice president and his wife on the left behind family members as the pallbearers put the body into the vehicle.

Then, Johnson took time to talk with Ethel, Ted, and Robert Kennedy, Jr., before returning to his car. The Johnsons waited their turn, the fifteenth limousine in line among a long caravan of cars heading toward Arlington National Cemetery in the dark June evening. According to Califano, the president insisted that no one "impose his office on the Kennedy family."[61]

The motorcade headed toward the Justice Department, where Clark led employees out onto the street to stand and honor the slain leader. Then, they moved to the Lincoln Memorial, where people from Resurrection City honored their champion by singing to him from the steps of the Lincoln Memorial.

During the ride, LBJ proved particularly introspective, something rarely on display. Califano talked about him speaking in soft tones about Rose and her "extraordinary difficult life" punctuated by "her husband's philandering, her son Joe's death in the war, Jack's and now Robert's assassination." Tears streamed down his cheeks with Lady Bird reaching across and placing her hand on his arm. He reflected: "That woman has suffered more than anyone I know. Her religious faith is what brings her through these tragedies."[62]

As they passed the throngs of people lining the streets, Lady Bird saw, "one curious, touching thing that carried its own message. Every now and then in the crowd you could see a small light. Sometimes it was just a lighted match or a cigarette lighter ... And sometimes a candle." Once they began their ascent up the hill into the cemetery, "the glow of the candles increased."[63]

Unknown to LBJ and Lady Bird, the Kennedys had asked for candles rather than bright lights on the lawn near the burial site. Only flickering flames and television camera lights illuminated the dark night as the Johnsons exited. They moved toward the burial site on a "gently sloping mound with two lovely magnolia soulangiana trees shading it" not more than 100 feet from John Kennedy's grave.[64]

It was a short service, not exceeding fifteen minutes because the family wanted no rifle salutes or elaborate music, as only members of the Harvard Band played "America the Beautiful." LBJ and Lady Bird participated in the recitation of the Lord's Prayer and knelt on damp artificial grass with Ethel at the gravesite, rising and offering their heart-felt condolences to her and the family before leaving quickly to prevent any traffic jams.

As they walked to the limo, Lady Bird noted: "There was a great white moon riding high in the night – a beautiful night. This is the only night funeral I ever remember. But then this is the only such time in the memory of our country – an incredible, unbelievable, cruel and wrenching time."[65]

The car departed Arlington Cemetery and headed back to the White House. As the Johnsons traveled, Califano observed: "Throughout the entire ride back, the President uncharacteristically did not say a word." Ten minutes before eleven, they arrived back at the White House, emotionally spent by the entire affair.[66] "LBJ left the car silently," Califano added, "went up to the living quarters, and retired with Lady Bird for the evening."[67]

Throughout the day, Johnson showed empathy toward the Kennedys despite the long hostility that had existed between him and RFK. He particularly identified with Rose, not understanding how she remained so strong after burying three of her four sons, all dying tragically during service to the country. While not often apparent, he exhibited an emotional depth rarely on public display. He clearly rose to the occasion that day despite the challenges.

The Kennedys appreciated the president's efforts. Afterward, Jackie Kennedy wrote the Johnsons a note. "I do thank you . . . for all you did in those sad days, to make it possible for him to be laid to rest with all the love and care and nobility that meant so much to those who loved him." She concluded, "Sometime there are no words to say things – only this – I am deeply grateful."[68]

LBJ reciprocated the gratitude, writing Ethel Kennedy a week after the funeral in response to her letter thanking him: "Thank God you have so many who love you nearby, that you have been blessed with so many fine children, and with a strong affirmative spirit in yourself." He concluded: "If there is ever anything I can do to help you or yours in the future, Ethel, I hope you will let me know. So long as I have the power to help, please know that I have the desire to do so."[69]

Immediately following the funeral, the president turned his attention to the National Commission on the Causes and Prevention of Violence that he announced in his June 5th speech. After meeting with the committee on the 10th, he signed the executive order officially creating the group in front of a large group of reporters in the Cabinet Room.

Then, he made a long, strong statement. "This troubled world will long remember the scar of the past week's violence, but when the week is remembered, let this be remembered, too: that out of anguish came a national resolve to search for the causes and to find the cures for the outbursts of violence which have brought so much heartbreak to our Nation."

Then, he outlined the commission duties. "My charge to you is simple and direct: I ask you to undertake a penetrating search for the causes and prevention of violence."

Johnson hoped the commission would find an understanding of why violent crime "struck down public figures and private citizens alike" and what role the disrespect for law and order played. Finally, he wanted them to highlight "practical actions to control or prevent these outbreaks of violence."

Then, the president encouraged the commission to ask questions on what role "permissiveness toward extreme behavior" encouraged violence and what "the public's airwaves, the screens of neighborhood theaters, the new media" played, along with mental illness.

Then the president focused on his main goal to honor RFK: gun control. He strongly believed guns ensured mass carnage and daily violence. Johnson knew Lee Harvey Oswald effortlessly purchased a high-powered weapon that made it possible to shoot JFK. Other acts, including the slaughter by Charles Whitman at the University of Texas in Austin in August 1966, further highlighted the deadly nature of these weapons of mass destruction. Every day, the violence intensified and more Americans died due to what LBJ perceived as lax gun laws and easy accessibility for everyone, including young people, criminals, and the mentally deranged.

So, in his statement, Johnson asked: "Can our society any longer tolerate the widespread possession of deadly firearms by private citizens?"

In conclusion, LBJ acknowledged: "The truth you seek will yield stubbornly to search. But I do want to be sure that the search is made, and that search must be started now."[70]

While guns remained his immediate focus, Johnson and many others knew that there were many reasons for the escalating violence in the country, including drugs, the breakdown of traditional respect for the law, and rising crime associated with the changes sweeping much of the country. Despite creating the commission, he knew pinpointing the problems would accomplish nothing without positive and proactive solutions. These were far more complex to put in place, as few could agree on the causes, much less the solutions. But, LBJ firmly believed people should at least try.

After the funeral, LBJ devoted more time and energy to the Safe Streets Act of 1968. Two days after the country said goodbye to RFK, legislation emerged from the House and Senate that differed significantly from LBJ's original proposals. Assistant Attorney General Christopher emphasized: "The bill is far more a reflection of the fears, frustration, and politics in the times than an intelligent carefully tailored measure."[71]

There were several major disagreements. The bill pushed block grants to states and gave governors more control under only vague federal guidelines, rather than centralized distribution with common plans and goals. Equally important, Title III of the legislation took away eavesdropping capabilities of individuals, but provided significant ones to the government, leading a Califano aide to complain, it "may do more to turn the country into a police state than any law we have ever enacted."[72]

Gun control also emerged weakened. The efforts to add licensing of gun owners and registration of guns failed. Tydings could not even get the bill out of the Senate Judiciary Committee, and Califano stressed:

"The President believed that liberals, like Tydings, had been their own worst enemies."[73] Ultimately, only watered down proposals relating to handguns survived.

For a week, LBJ debated vetoing the bill, encouraged by others including McPherson who wrote: "I recognize that you must sign this bill ... But it's the worst bill you will have signed since you took office."[74]

Attorney General Clark also vigorously opposed the wiretapping provisions and warned about potential abuses by overzealous government officials. "From a practical standpoint, the result might be a worse bill. The mood of the country and the Congress indicate a crime bill will be passed this year ... If the Congress acted again it might ... limit the jurisdiction and *habeas corpus* powers of the federal courts. This would be disastrous."[75]

Ultimately, Califano noted: "Reluctantly, we all felt the lesser of two evils was for the President to sign the bill."[76] LBJ finally relented, noting the act contained "more good than bad."[77] He had other business with the Senate Judiciary on the horizon with Supreme Court nominations and needed to move on.

LBJ signed the bill on June 19, noting he sent a bill "designed to help America rid herself of the plague of crime" over sixteen months earlier. "The bill I sign today bears little resemblance to my original proposal. It contains many provisions that I strongly disapprove. Nevertheless, I sign the bill because it is an urgently needed first, if faltering, step in the war against crime."[78]

As for stricter gun control, it took until October for the president to win a victory, albeit only a limited one. The Gun Control Act of 1968 ended mail order sales, purchases by minors, and stopped the importation of cheap handguns from other nations, but failed on national registration, gun licensing, and other limits.

At a press conference afterward, the president hammered home: "I think we need a stronger gun control law, so we can keep them out of the hands of the maniac, the insane, the delinquent and the minor."[79]

Later, he issued a blistering critique of the bill. "The voices that blocked these safeguards were not the voices of an aroused nation. They were the voices of a powerful gun lobby, a gun lobby, that has prevailed for the moment in an election year . . . we have been through a great deal of anguish these last few months and these few years – too much anguish to forget so quickly. So now we must complete the task which this long needed legislation begins."[80]

Both the efforts on Safe Streets and gun control further highlighted the increasing diminution of power of the president as his presidency wound down. It reflected the rising power of powerful conservative forces in Congress, particularly Midwestern and western Republicans and southern Democrats, who increasingly pushed for decentralization of power and also limits on the power of the federal government to regulate in many areas, including guns.

The episode showed how powerful lobbies like the NRA lined up their supporters to push back on gun control, even those ideas generally thought of as common sense approaches. There was little Johnson could do to defeat the rising coalition of conservatives and lobbyists for powerful interests, unlike four years earlier. The country was moving to the right, a process accelerating in 1968.

The battle continued until he left office and turned over the issues to his successor. In December 1969, the Eisenhower Commission presented its findings to President Nixon and called for addressing the root causes of violence including poverty and lack of opportunity as well as guns. Nixon simply ignored the findings.

Little changed, and the slaughter continued. LBJ found himself on a losing side against a mighty lobby as his desire to honor RFK fell flat. The Republicans used the idea of law and order with great effect, including in battles on the horizon on the nomination of Abe Fortas as chief justice of the Supreme Court. It became a strong wedge issue, one often blending with appeals to racial prejudices. While Johnson and his allies sought positive change from the tragedies associated with guns and crime, the GOP and conservative Democrats used it to successfully mobilize working class and lower middle-class whites, shifting political power all over the country. Years later, the issue of guns and crime remained a hot button issue with little change likely, just like in 1968.

Despite the legislative defeats, the president performed well during a time of tragedy. Given the longstanding animosity between LBJ and RFK, it would have been easy for Johnson to drag his feet and provide limited support for the family while doing little, if anything, to honor him. However, he put aside his often petty and vindictive nature and did what was best for the Kennedy clan and the country. He would not always do so in the coming months, as frustrations grew with Congress and elements of his own party, but in this particular moment, the president performed admirably and struck the right tone in an another crisis.

CHAPTER 7

The Big Stumble

The Fortas Affair, June–October 1968

A tired president tried to recover after the emotional days following the assassination of RFK. Even as he battled on the crime bill, he received a surprise.

On June 13th, Chief Justice Warren wrote: "I hereby advise you of my intention to retire as Chief Justice of the United States effective at your pleasure."[1]

The letter never stated it, but the seventy-seven-year-old Warren worried about Nixon's possible victory. Their paths often crossed in California politics, and Warren considered the likely Republican nominee unethical and overly partisan. He wanted Johnson to appoint his successor before Nixon won.[2]

It was another opportunity for Johnson to shape the Court, building from replacing Arthur Goldberg with his close friend, Fortas, in 1965 and appointing Thurgood Marshall in 1967. As Califano observed: "While the President had won most ... battles in Congress and the Executive Branch, the contest would inevitably play out in the courts long after he left the White House, and he intended to win them as well after he had gone."[3]

LBJ considered only Fortas for chief justice. Their friendship dated back to 1948 when he represented Johnson in his disputed Senate primary race against Coke Stevenson, which Johnson won by a mere eighty-seven votes. Even as a justice, Fortas advised the president on matters of domestic and foreign policy, often blurring ethical lines with regular visits to the White House to discuss matters pending before the Court. Johnson genuinely trusted Fortas to continue his vision of equality and opportunity.

But the issue of who should replace Fortas was more contentious. From the start, the president zeroed in on his old friend, Homer Thornberry. He took over LBJ's congressional district in Central Texas in 1948 and proved a capable, progressive legislator. Thornberry held that office until 1963 when President Kennedy tapped him for the US District Court for Western Texas. Two years later, Johnson nominated him for the Fifth Circuit Courts of Appeals. The president thought his southern roots would appeal to Russell and others from the Old Confederacy, partially offsetting their animus toward a Jewish liberal.

But several people recognized the challenges. White House special counsel, Larry Temple, told Johnson that nominating Thornberry invited charges of cronyism. Sarcastically, Johnson rebuffed him: 'What political office did you ever get elected to? ... don't come to me as any great knowledgeable expert until you've run and gotten elected to a political office ... then I'll listen to your political judgment."

Lady Bird interrupted, "Lyndon, he may be right about that, and that's what worries me about Homer – although I'd love to see him on the Supreme Court."[4]

Others echoed Temple's concerns. Clifford visited the White House on June 22 to discuss Vietnam, accompanied by Fortas. Afterward, as LBJ changed into his pajamas for an afternoon nap, he asked for Clifford's reaction on Fortas and Thornberry.

"Mr. President, it is a splendid idea, but I am concerned it may not survive in this form. I regret to say this, but I do not think you can sell that package to Congress," the long-time Washington insider had said.

"What do you mean? Abe is already on the Court, he is well respected. What's wrong with it?" the president queried, genuinely surprised by Clifford's response.

The defense secretary replied: "Mr. President, the Republicans are convinced they are going to elect the next President. They would probably accept Abe on his own. But if his nomination is tied up with Homer Thornberry's, I am afraid that they will find some way to sidetrack it."

Angrily, LBJ fired back: "Homer is a fine man, he has a good record, he has written some good decisions down there in Texas. Dick Russell will support him. They are not going to find anything wrong with him."

"That's not the point," Clifford counseled, "the Republicans will not look into the merit of the matter. They will oppose Homer simply on the grounds that you are trying to pack the court with your friends at a very late date in the political calendar. They will try to stall both appointments until after November."[5]

LBJ quickly retorted: "What do you suggest?"

Clifford immediately answered. "For the opening on the Court, select a nonpolitical, prominent Republican, someone who stands high at the bar . . . but has not been down in the political pit fighting the Democrats. There are plenty of men who fill the description."

The president stared sharply at Clifford and snapped: "Well, I don't intend to put some damned Republican on the Court."

Fortas and Clifford departed as LBJ headed to his bedroom. Outside, Fortas told Clifford: "I understand exactly what you were trying to do. I don't know if the President can bring this off, but I couldn't very well sit there and disagree with him when he wants to make me Chief Justice."

Clifford wished him luck and promised his support. However, he thought to himself: "If only I had known about Thornberry before the meeting, perhaps I could have talked to Abe privately and convinced him to join me in opposing it."

A couple of days later, Clifford offered the name of a prominent Chicago lawyer, Albert Jenner. But it was too late. Johnson stayed with Thornberry, leading Clifford to assert: "The die was cast."[6]

The president ignored the admonitions of his close associates and terribly misread the political landscape relating to Thornberry, but mainly Fortas. He failed to fully recognize the changed conditions in the country since 1965 when the Senate confirmed Fortas. As the Warren Court upheld liberal (and some libertarian) ideas on free speech and rights of accused criminals, the country swung further right, fueled by the backlash against civil rights and perceived moral descent caused by permissiveness on pornography and abortion as well as removal of school prayer. Conservatives saw an opportunity to undermine Johnson and prevent the court from moving further left.

LBJ moved forward, despite ominous warning signs, especially from conservative southerners. On June 25, his assistant focusing on legislative affairs, Mike Manatos, brought word back from Senator James Eastland,

Chairman of the Senate Judiciary Committee. The Mississippian said: "Abe Fortas cannot be confirmed as Chief Justice."

Manatos wrote: "He told me that he talked to Roy Cohn today," and reported Dirksen "is opposed to Fortas, contrary to the impression he may be giving."

Some senators appeared spoiling for a fight. During a ride in a subway car with Senator John McClellan (D-AR), Eastland listened as the aging veteran told him to have "that SOB formally submitted to the Senate" to allow a fight, one he relished.

More important to the White House, "Eastland indicates also there will be a filibuster against Abe Fortas should his name be submitted to the Senate."[7] This changed the numbers game significantly and broke with recent precedent regarding the Supreme Court, where the Senate typically accepted the nomination on a majority vote.

On the 26th, Johnson met Eastland at the White House, where LBJ opened by highlighting a talk with Russell, "hoping that the judgment of that respected Southerner would moderate Eastland's position." LBJ observed: "My reference to Senator Russell's statement did not faze him in the slightest."

Instead, Eastland went into his "strenuous objections to Fortas" and expressed his irritation at a recent speech in which "Fortas had said the battles between the black man for equality in America were essentially the same as those of the Jew." Johnson detected that Eastland "interpreted that statement as a conspiratorial call for Jews and Negroes to take over America." The president added: "He said that he was aware of Senator Russell's position but that he did not think that in the end, when all the debate was over, Senator Russell would support Fortas."[8]

Here, Johnson overestimated his ability to influence Russell, and by extension the southern Democrats. His old mentor chafed at losing civil rights battles and watched with consternation as the country changed, especially the south. He also understood LBJ had lost ground because of Vietnam and the riots as well as the decision not to seek reelection. While outwardly cordial and still coming to the White House for dinners, the relationship was not the same as in 1964. It reflected the continuing degradation of Johnson's power since 1965, one especially apparent in 1968. Without Russell, LBJ knew the odds of overcoming a filibuster deteriorated significantly.

Despite Eastland's pessimistic report, on June 26, the president sent forth the names of Fortas and Thornberry to the Senate for confirmation.

At a subsequent press conference, a reporter asked, "Do you antici-pate having any trouble in having the Senate ratify these?"

Johnson responded, "I would suspect that they would review their records very carefully. I believe when they do that they will meet with the approval of the Senate."[9]

But the opposition mobilized quickly, led by Robert Griffin (R-MI). The junior senator attacked: "If a 'lame duck' President should seek at this stage to appoint the leadership of the Supreme Court for many years in the future, I believe he would be breaking the faith with our system," he argued.[10] Defiantly, he threatened a filibuster and announced that the nomination "smacks of 'cronyism' at its worst – and everybody knows it."[11]

On the campaign trail, Nixon told a crowd that "a new President with a fresh mandate" should choose the chief justice. Seeking to win conser-vative support, he added, "Supreme Court appointments of his would be strict constitutionalists, rather than men who call social considerations as well as the Constitution into play."[12]

The nominations sparked interest across the country. As Lady Bird visited Oregon, she found people talking about Fortas and Thornberry. "Indeed, everyone came up to me with questions or expressions of interest, but I was unable to assess the color of their thinking, approval or disapproval." She observed quickly: "There is a tremendous difference in the whole thinking of the rest of the country outside of Washington. Political events are important, yes, but they are not the whole universe . . . I love Washington, but it is a self-important town."

While the country discussed the nominations, the early opposition centered on the procedural, although it was clear Fortas raised the ire of conservatives. Reports filtered in that Robert Byrd (D-WV) would do "everything in my power" to stop Fortas, branding him a "leftist." According to Manatos, Byrd "indicated he would not have voted to con-firm his nomination had he known the sort of record he would have made on the bench."

Manatos also emphasized: "Russell Long classifies Fortas as 'one of the dirty five' who sides with the criminal against the victims of crime."[13] Conservatives from both parties remembered his defense of accused Communist scholar and writer Owen Lattimore during the McCarthy hearings and his representation of Clarence Gideon, an indigent defendant whose case led to everyone indicted receiving a lawyer if they could not afford one. His support of civil rights in the Court strike further angered southerners.[14]

With the opposition so vocal, Califano emphasized that by Saturday, June 29, Johnson "assumed personal direction of every detail of the effort to secure confirmation of his friend Fortas."[15] It was his last major political campaign and quickly became a very nasty one. An aide observed: "Even during Lyndon Johnson's White House years, political contests rarely came brass-knuckled as the bout the President set off ... when he nominated Justice Abe Fortas to succeed Earl Warren as Chief Justice."[16]

Johnson put his personal reputation as a deal maker on the line with the nomination of Fortas and Thornberry. During past major legislative battles, ones that often stretched his immense talents, the president usually won. However, it was a different time with a tsunami of conservative reaction developing. The Republicans and conservative southern Democrats wanted a confrontation and decided to politicize the Supreme Court nomination process in an election year.

Johnson recognized many of the challenges. Califano stressed that LBJ "never expected quick hearings and floor action" and feared that the longer the battle lasted, the worse it would become. He particularly worried about Dirksen. "We've got to get this thing through ... early, because if it drags out ... Dirksen will leave us," LBJ warned. When Califano underscored Dirksen's public support of Fortas and Thornberry, Johnson responded: 'Just take my word for it. I know him. I know that Senate. If they get this thing drug out very long, we're going to get beat ... Even Dirksen will leave us."[17]

From the White House, Johnson and his aides began a full court press. On June 28, the White House counted sixty-two supporting, five probably supporting, twenty-two opposing, six probably opposing, two doubtful, and two not contacted.[18] By this total, they almost had enough (if counting those leaning toward support) to stymie the filibuster threat.

The battle heated up in late June as Johnson worked hard. He reached out to Henry Ford II through Califano: "Tell him I didn't bring about the resignation ... Warren handed me his letter resigning. I had to look at the Court and the country ... it wouldn't be a good thing for the first Jewish Chief Justice to be turned down." Johnson wanted Ford to urge the National Alliance of Businessmen to pressure Griffin and other Republicans into stopping their opposition.[19]

Johnson looked everywhere for votes. In the African American community, he asked a prominent Republican lawyer, William Cohen, to push African American senator Edward Brooke (R-MA) to support the nomination.[20] Then, he contacted prominent civil rights activist Judge Leon Higginbotham in Philadelphia and requested that he contact African American lawyers in Pennsylvania to lobby Republican senator Hugh Scott.[21]

In the South, LBJ and his aides reached out to several people, including Paul Austin, CEO and Chairman of Coca-Cola. It was not a hard sell, as one aide reported: "Austin feels very strongly that the conservative Republicans and southern Democrats are insulting not only you, but the office of the Presidency."[22] From his office in Atlanta, Austin began calling Russell, Herman Talmadge (D-GA), Harry Byrd (D-VA), and several others, stressing the importance of supporting the president on the matter.[23]

The cornerstone of LBJ's southern efforts became the effort to persuade Russell. Early on, he hosted the Georgia senator for dinner, at which Russell expressed his feelings that Fortas was not "an ideal appointment" although he thought he was "an extremely able man" and "more stable and conservative" than Goldberg.[24]

LBJ correctly appraised Russell's feelings on Thornberry, who at one point was his hunting partner. He thought he was "a good man, an able man, and a fair man."[25]

There were many other efforts spanning the country. LBJ asked Clifford and the DuPonts for assistance with the Rhode Island senators.[26] The White House had Attorney General Ramsey Clark contact several progressive Republican senators, including Mark Hatfield of Oregon and Jacob Javits of New York.[27] Johnson also wanted "John Harper [head of Alcoa] to call [Howard] Baker," the Tennessee Republican and Dirksen's son-in-law. Everywhere, LBJ pushed his people to use whatever connections possible to lobby for the nomination.

Johnson and the White House adopted a two-pronged strategy. First, he appealed to the southern Democrats, seeking some party unity by using Russell as the point man but also applying pressure through prominent businessmen and political leaders throughout the region. On the other front, the president reached out to more liberal and moderate Republicans, people often less partisan and also open to continuing the liberal leanings of the court. The goal was holding the sixty votes needed to stymie the threat of a filibuster, and early on it appeared likely to happen.

The president also played up Fortas within the Jewish community. He pressed White House aide Ernest Goldstein to "get every Jew out in Illinois to go up to Dirksen to thank him for his support." LBJ asked Califano to "enlist the aid of David Brody and Hyman Bookbinder, heads of Washington offices of the Anti-Defamation League and American Jewish Committee."[28]

The Jewish question was important. "From the moment Griffin announced his opposition, there were charges of anti-Semitism," Califano remembered. He acknowledged it was something "Johnson encouraged." Griffin felt the heat and responded he would back Goldberg returning to the Court. "Johnson told me to get someone to point up the inconsistency between this position," Califano emphasized, "and Griffin's previously asserted opposition to any appointment by a lame-duck president."[29]

But the Jewish question brought some levity into the conversations. When McPherson found a picture of Fortas and philanthropist David Lloyd Kreeger wearing yarmulkes during a violin duet at a charity event, he told Johnson: "I'll circulate it and try to get the Jewish groups behind us."

Johnson looked at the photograph and quipped: "This doesn't mean a damn thing. I've had on more of those than Abe has."[30]

Nonetheless, Johnson recognized the importance of the question. While anti-Semitism thrived in many areas of the country, including the south, he knew its ability to put Republicans on the defensive in key states like New York, Illinois, and California. It also allowed LBJ to rationalize away some of the opposition to Fortas, preventing him from seeing some of the ethical and moral shortcomings of his friend. It was significant as he tried to create a coalition to defeat the filibuster threat. The calculus had changed over the last three years, but he remained confident in his abilities and those of his allies to emerge victorious.

The White House efforts achieved positive results. At a news conference in early July, Dirksen stated: "Fortas and Thornberry are going to be confirmed" and "there will be no filibuster against confirmation."[31]

There were other successes. B'nai B'rith organized in favor of Fortas as one official referred to Griffin and others in the statement: "On the basis of long experience, a move under respectable auspices always brings the bigots out of the woodwork." Another spokesman noted: "We think it would be bad for the status of all minority groups if the move against Fortas were allowed to succeed."[32]

Both sides fought hard in the court of public opinion.[33] The opponents increasingly questioned Fortas' close relationship with Johnson and his willingness to blur lines between the Supreme Court and the Executive Branch.

There was some foundation for the criticism. In his political career, there were a number of junctures at which Johnson showed little regard for normalized standards of behavior and faced accusations of crossing ethical lines for political or personal gain. None stood out more than his relationship with Bobby Baker, the secretary to the Senate Majority Leader. Their relationship led to a major investigation in 1963, during which rumors and accusation swirled around Johnson, some speculating Kennedy would drop him from the ticket in 1964. The assassination of JFK ended it, but the episode underscored a weakness of Johnson that carried over into his relationship with Fortas.[34]

A number of people raised questions about the appearance of impropriety in the relationship between Johnson and Fortas after 1965. One person emphasized, "during the Johnson years, Fortas was part of the judicial branch and, as well, an unofficial member of the executive branch." Between when LBJ took office and July 2, 1968, there were 145 meetings between the two men. This fails to take into consideration phone calls or casual encounters outside the president's standard daily diary.[35]

Others observed that Fortas often bragged about knowing secret entrances to the White House from both the Treasury Building and Executive Office. Some knew he had a special telephone line to the president.[36] As Califano observed, "Fortas was unwilling to step away from the exhilaration of involvement in the most exciting and challenging matters his client ever faced."[37]

But LBJ rationalized away the issue. "Our history is filled with examples of Supreme Court Justices who not only advised Presidents but carried out political chores for them, and those examples go back to Chief Justice John Jay of George Washington's administration."[38]

Others speculated on the matter. Califano emphasized that "he [Johnson] refused to be denied access to his best attorney just because he had given him to the Supreme Court. It was not in LBJ to think there was any advice or information to which he was not entitled." He went on "if he was trying to get the first fair-housing bill in history passed, certainly the President was entitled to know whether a forthcoming Supreme Court decision might endanger the bill and, if necessary – though I don't believe it ever was – to get his friend Abe Fortas to delay its promulgation until after the vote on Capitol Hill."[39]

By 1968, many understood the symbiotic relationship between Johnson and Fortas. An aide noticed: "Fortas was so consistently present and Johnson so often directed me to consult him that the Supreme Court became part of the staff and his involvement so routine that early shock and concern over time faded, like Fortas himself, into the woodwork of the White House."[40]

This was a problem that, while not acknowledged by the president, constituted a major challenge for many people, including a number of his allies. LBJ and Fortas clearly violated the spirit of the separation of powers ingrained in the Constitution and American political culture. Many of those closest to the president understood the issues, and his opponents clearly wanted to exploit them. He opened himself up to these criticisms, and while he continued having a blind spot on the matter, they came back to haunt him as the nomination fight continued.

As both sides mobilized, a major problem developed with Russell over the nomination of Alexander Lawrence to be a US District Judge for the Southern District of Georgia. Some in the administration, including

Attorney General Clark, firmly opposed him on the basis of his civil rights record. Johnson originally vacillated, but came to support him out of political expediency and after Lawrence received support from the progressive editor of the *Atlanta-Constitution*, Ralph McGill.

But the White House stumbled badly, demonstrating a lack of focus and clarity that existed during the major legislative battles of the first two years. On May 22, Tom Johnson met with Russell and reported to the president that the senator vehemently defended the nominee. "We are fighting a shadow on this one. Those who accuse Lawrence of speaking out against Negroes do not exist. I cannot find anybody who has made any such statement." As they finished, Russell delivered a stinging rebuke: "Ramsey Clark is no great asset to the President."[41]

After announcing the nominations of Fortas and Thornberry, Johnson and Russell talked. The senator emphasized: "I will support the nomination of Mr. Fortas for Chief Justice, but I will enthusiastically support Homer Thornberry."[42]

But the conditions changed quickly as Russell chafed at delays, often referring to Lawrence's critics as mongrels, "fanatics, mystics and publicity seekers."[43] On July 1, an angry Russell sent a letter to the president complaining that "over three months having elapsed, on May 20th, at your suggestion I wrote you again with respect to this appointment and concluded by making a personal appeal (the first I have made to any President of the United States) for you to forward the nomination of Mr. Lawrence to the Senate."[44]

Then Russell really hit hard, stating: "To be perfectly frank, even after so many years in the Senate, I was so naïve I had not even suspected that this man's nomination was being withheld from the Senate due to the changes expected on the Supreme Court."

"Whether it is intended or not, this places me in the position where, if I support your nominees for the Supreme Court, it will appear that I have done so out of my fears that you would not nominate Mr. Lawrence," he added.

"This is, therefore, to advise you that, in view of the long delay in handling and the juggling of this nomination, I consider myself released from any statements that I may have made to you with respect to your nominations," he concluded, "I shall undertake to deal objectively with the nominations you have made to the Supreme Court, but however I may vote, I want you to understand that it is not done with any expectation that I am buying or insuring the nomination of Mr. Lawrence."[45]

Immediately, LBJ tried damage control. He wrote Russell. "As I indicated to you several times in the past week that I intended to send Mr. Lawrence's nomination to the Senate. I did so because I was convinced that he was qualified for the post ... This transpired weeks before I was notified by the Chief Justice of his intention to retire."

Then, Johnson stressed his decision on Mr. Lawrence "had and has no relationship, direct or indirect, to the nominations of Mr. Justice Fortas as Chief Justice and of Judge Thornberry as Associate Justice." He emphasized his "intention to send Mr. Lawrence's name to the Senate."

He concluded: "I am sure that you will vote for or against the nominations of Justice Fortas and Judge Thornberry as your conscience dictates. I am frankly surprised and deeply disappointed that a contrary inference would be suggested. Both my own standards of public administration, and my knowledge of your character, would deny such an inference."[46]

The president also tried making personal entreaties to assuage Russell's anger, but nothing worked. Califano observed, "the President knew that his misstep had placed Fortas's nomination in terminal jeopardy. Hurt and angry at himself ... [Johnson] asked him [Russell] to destroy all copies" of the letter and then quickly nominated Lawrence (who ironically became a strong defender of civil rights).[47]

Privately, LBJ complained bitterly about Clark destroying "one of the great friendships I've had with one of the great men that has ever served this country."[48]

Some in the administration fired back. Temple characterized Russell's argument as "just false. It was just a lie ... Russell was way off base. He was wrong. He was completely wrong." LBJ tried to excuse Russell, believing another southern senator who hated Fortas had poisoned the well.[49]

People outside the White House detected the estrangement between the two men. One newspaper noted: "President Johnson has cut his communication lines with one of his oldest friends and advisers, Sen. Richard B. Russell." It resulted from "a difference of opinion over a matter Russell doesn't even discuss with friends."[50]

The damage was done. Johnson and his advisers clearly failed to see the political importance of the issue to Russell. There was likely a great deal of blame to go around, but especially for Clark. But, it appeared to be a bigger problem of a lack of focus as the White House scurried around in the last six months of office, concentrating on issues, including the peace talks in Paris, the nuclear arms reduction summit in the Soviet Union, and influencing the Democratic Convention in Chicago. It was a costly misstep that delivered a significant blow to the president's court plans.

In addition, Russell appeared much more willing to break ties with the president after his announcement on March 31. He no longer needed Johnson for his long-term ambitions of representing Georgia and the south. It allowed him to extract some revenge on Johnson for his betrayals over the past five years, particularly related to civil rights. He was not finished with the president and their personal and professional relationship suffered.

But the blowback from the Russell controversy extended much further. The White House initially did not know that Russell went beyond his pledge to treat the nomination "objectively." Soon after breaking with the president, he asked Griffin to his office. On arrival, Russell asked Griffin if he had eighteen firm no votes and would they hold firm no matter the pressure.

Griffin responded affirmatively. In a heavy southern drawl, Russell said: "We're with you ... but as far as the group that I'm with is concerned, namely the Southern Democrats, we'd rather not get out front because we would hurt your chances more than we'd help."

Once he heard those words, a big grin enveloped Griffin's face. Now, he had Democrats and the charges of partisanship flew out the window. Griffin had the element of silent support that immensely strengthened his position.[51]

With LBJ losing his long-time friend and mentor, the battle shifted clearly in favor of Johnson's opponents. While not knowing the full extent of Russell's duplicity, the president understood the numbers game shifted clearly to Griffin and his allies. Without southern support, the ability to stymie the filibuster became much more difficult. The reality, however, remained that even with Russell in his corner, many of the southern Democrats would have joined recent defectors to the Republican Party like Thurmond and voted against cloture at the minimum to defeat Fortas. But, Russell's defection provided leadership to the movement and gave conservatives a chance at vengeance.

With Russell on board, Griffin increased his attacks. "I have every reason to believe the White House is pulling out all stops" he said after noting the president "has a lot of leverage" and highlighted that he knew of senators receiving calls from executives of companies with government contracts. When asked for details and whether they originated from White House pressure, he noted: "I just think it is quite obvious."[52]

As Griffin fought on, Ford reported in late June that despite his pressure, he refused to back down. Califano informed Johnson that Griffin "takes exception to anybody being appointed [by a lame-duck president], and [he says] Abe Fortas is still the President's lawyer."[53]

To combat the opposition, LBJ had his staff prepare two different sets of analyses of Fortas' opinions; one tailored toward conservatives and another for liberals.

Johnson asked Califano to edit them. After reviewing them, he warned "the two different analyses might be exchanged and find themselves in the wrong hands. Fortas is essentially a liberal Justice and perhaps we should put our emphasis on that."

The president asked, "remember the Texas schoolteacher during the Depression?"

Califano knew the story well. At the height of the Depression, a young man went for a job interview. He endured intense questioning from school board members. At the end, they looked down at the perspiring schoolteacher and the redneck chairman asked, "Do you teach that the world is flat or do you teach that the world is round?"

He thought for a moment and responded: "I can teach it either way."

"The point is that the high school teacher wanted the job," Johnson stressed, "just the way we want Fortas confirmed for Chief Justice. The teacher knew damn well that the world was round and everyone knows damn well where Fortas stands. But we've got to give each senator ammunition to justify his vote."[54]

While LBJ and his staff lobbied, Fortas went in front of the Senate Judiciary Committee for four days of questioning on July 16. Never before had a nominee for chief justice been subjected to such a spectacle. However, Fortas opened with a statement, "I want to say that I am very happy to be here. And I am happy to answer any and all questions that the committee may ask." He believed his experience in 1965 and on other occasions before Senate committees provided him a forum to win the support of senators sitting on the fence.[55]

Senator Albert Gore, Sr., a long-time friend of Fortas, opened the hearings: "Justice Fortas is an able lawyer, an eminent jurist, and dedicated to the welfare of the country." The fireworks began.[56] Many anticipated a focus on his rulings, but the first witness, Senator Griffin, went after Fortas' close association with Johnson. He called him a presidential "crony." Griffin probed, "If the doctrine of separate powers is important, what justification could be offered in the event of a member of the judicial branch should actively participate on a regular, undisclosed basis in decisions of the executive branch while serving on the Bench?"[57]

Others followed Griffin's line of attack.[58] They alternated between questioning his judicial decisions, which he successfully parried, before concentrating on his relationship with the president. He tried to argue he simply followed the example of many other justices from John Jay to Louis Brandeis who advised presidents. Fortas also downplayed his role in the Johnson White House in shaping debates or policy.[59]

His answers often caused concern within the White House. When Fortas denied advising LBJ on cases before the court and writing the president's statement on sending federal troops to Detroit in 1967, Califano underscored: "Fortas's testimony was so misleading and deceptive that those of us who were aware of his relationship winced with each news report of his appearance before the Senate committee. Cronyism was now the least charge some of us feared."[60]

The charges stuck with some senators and the press. A *Washington Post* editorial welcomed Fortas' admission on his relationship with LBJ, arguing most in Washington already assumed it. But, the editorial board added "neither the Justice's explanations of the situation in which he gave the President advice nor his historical citations showing that other Justices have advised other Presidents make the relationship wise or proper."[61]

Afterward, some, like senior senator from Michigan Phil Hart, tried to spin the hearings positively. He emphasized: "He (Fortas) is just superb. He made me feel like a plumber listening to him." Nonetheless, the damage was done and the opposition gained ground.[62]

Johnson watched the hearings closely and recognized the political harm. He knew in his heart, "the truth is that Abe Fortas was too progressive for the Republicans and the southern conservatives in the Senate." To him, they "were horrified at the thought of a continuation of the philosophy of the Warren court." But perhaps most important, "the opposition was strengthened by the fact that the Republicans and Southerners were convinced that Richard Nixon, if elected, would choose a conservative Chief Justice."[63]

He was only partly correct. Griffin's early line of attack laid doubts about the independence of Fortas, especially as a chief justice. It raised issues about the damage that would occur to the credibility of the court and separation of powers. Finally, it ensured that significant questions about the ethics and integrity of Fortas were asked. The relationship clearly crossed the accepted norms of behavior and any effort to dismiss it by rationalizing that it was about Fortas' ideology ignored that reality. It remained a blind spot for the president as well as his dismissal of critics who charged that his appointment of Thornberry was blatant cronyism, despite the fact that by this time, few people even focused on the Texan.

Despite growing concerns, Johnson sought for a committee vote to throw the nominations out to the Senate before the opposition gained further strength, especially as a summer recess approached.

It appeared it might happen. In a meeting with Manatos on July 25, McClellan reported no longer planning to delay the vote. The aide reported: "Senator McClellan admits that Fortas is probably the most able lawyer he knows. He wonders, however, about his philosophy as it applies to crime ... McClellan also brought up the question of which he considers pornographic. He thinks every member of the committee ought to see it."[64]

As the White House maneuvered, Thurmond intensified his fight, arguing vigorously that Fortas had enabled pornographers to peddle smut with his First Amendment rulings. Buoyed by the testimony of James Clancy of the Citizens for Decent Literature during the hearings, a man who provided magazines and even a film for the committee, Thurmond chastised Fortas for his liberal interpretation of the First Amendment and contended it corrupted young people and promoted violence.[65]

As the White House mobilized to respond to the new attack, Johnson lost his temper with Sanders, Temple, and Califano. He lashed out, "We're a bunch of dupes down here. They've got all the wisdom. All the sagacity is reposed up there. They're just smarter than we are. We're a bunch of ignorant, immature kids who don't know anything about this ... They're whipsawing us to death because they're dragging their feet." He concluded, "We've got to do something."[66]

Johnson should have recognized that there was little that the White House could have done. There was a clear record on Fortas and free speech, civil rights, and criminal rights. Being identified with the perceived liberal Warren Court had its problems. The growing conservative backlash on cultural issues such as pornography, school prayer, integration, and school choice put the liberals on the defensive by 1968.

Figure 7 Johnson and Justice Abe Fortas meet in the Cabinet Room in late July 1968 to discuss the ongoing battle over his nomination to Chief Justice of the Supreme Court. (Courtesy of the LBJ Library)

The conservatives had the momentum, buoyed by other issues, including rising crime, the perceived breakdown of civil society, and the riots in the inner cities.

By late July, it became more apparent that the tide had turned. On July 29, Mansfield and Manatos met with Eastland to try to push a vote on Fortas when the Judiciary Committee convened on July 31. "Eastland has told us he cannot guarantee a vote. As a matter of fact, his best judgment is that Strom Thurmond will delay Committee action on Wednesday . . . Eastland further states that the possibility of gathering together a quorum is unlikely," Manatos reported.[67]

Such delays aggravated LBJ, but he held his tongue publicly. In a press conference on July 31, a reporter asked him: "Are you discouraged with the proceedings in the Senate and the treatment that has been accorded your appointments to the Supreme Court?"

Johnson answered: "I don't know that I can improve the situation by any comments that I would make. I certainly don't want to inflame it any." He only stressed: "It is a very rare thing to find a man with the unusual qualifications of our Associate Justice, Justice Thornberry."[68]

In early August, warnings of the impending doom increased. One analyst observed: "Where Mr. Johnson's crystal ball failed was in its inability to foresee the reaction of Southern Democrats . . . In his three years on the bench, Fortas has associated himself with a liberal philosophy offensive to Southerners."[69]

Nonetheless, by mid-August, a Harris poll showed overwhelming support for the nomination with 69 to 14 percent saying the president had the right to promote someone from within the present court. The same poll found a significant majority believed Fortas was an able man.[70]

With some public support, LBJ continued pushing forward. Renewed efforts included the creation of a Lawyers Committee on Supreme Court Nominations to back Fortas. However, there were warning signs. When the White House could not find a single prominent lawyer from Mississippi to join (until McPherson prodded a friend), Califano noted it confirmed to Johnson "that the opposition to Fortas was rooted in bigotry and opposition to his civil rights program."[71]

Therefore, he observed: "Johnson dug in, and we all tried harder."[72] But, the opposition delayed the nomination, and Johnson knew the longer it went, the less likely a successful outcome.

It became a desperate situation, and Johnson tried to regain the magic of years earlier, but as a lame duck president mired in a host of quagmires with few novel ideas to offer, it appeared unlikely to occur.

On August 9, LBJ received a call from Eastland while at the Texas ranch. He was in San Antonio and asked to visit. When he arrived, the president took him on a ride. "I made one more attempt to bring the Senator to my point of view. He would not give one inch," the president remembered. "He told me flatly," Johnson added, "Fortas would not be confirmed as Chief Justice and that therefore there would be no vacancy for Judge Thornberry."[73]

At that point, Johnson realized "that we probably could not muster the votes to put the Fortas nomination through." He believed Eastland received assurances from Republicans that Nixon would win and name someone as chief justice more to the liking of Eastland and other conservative southern Democrats. Johnson emphasized: "I had learned over the years that Jim Eastland was one of the best sources of intelligence in the Senate on what the Republicans were doing. He bent over backward to support legislation they wanted, and he was often a partner in their maneuvers."[74]

At the same time, some in the White House argued that Mansfield should keep the Senate in session around the clock. Temple stressed, "I don't know whether this was because he didn't think that he had the votes and support to keep them in session or whether that wasn't his cup of tea as it was Lyndon's Johnson's cup of tea to keep them in session to break the filibuster on civil rights back in the 50s." He also acknowledged that other business, including the Non-Proliferation Treaty, limited Mansfield's options.[75]

But LBJ refused to surrender without a last-ditch effort. He had watched Nixon finesse the subject by talking about appointing conservative justices who avoided social activism, while stressing he deferred to the Senate prerogatives on the matter. But, Johnson thought if he could at least have Nixon oppose a filibuster, he might have a chance for victory.[76]

LBJ asked Krim to reach out to Whitney Young of the Urban League and Walter Thayer of *International Herald Tribune* to pressure Nixon to publicly oppose a filibuster. Young reported that he "spoke rather forcefully to Nixon," while Thayer said he talked "pointedly" on the matter. Neither could persuade the Republican nominee.

It would not be until mid-September when Humphrey accused Nixon of "paying a political debt" to Thurmond for attacking Fortas that Nixon finally responded. "I don't oppose Fortas," he said, "I don't support him. I oppose a filibuster. I oppose any filibuster." But one White House aide emphasized: "By this time, however, it was too late."[77]

The attacks by Thurmond and Griffin extracted a heavy emotional toll on everyone involved. Temple remembered Fortas being "a very tormented man throughout the whole nomination process because he could not fight back." He believed Fortas viewed everything as a symbol of the "bitter, corrosive opposition to all that has been happening in the Court and the country: the racial progress, the insistence upon increased regard for human rights and the dignity in the field of criminal law."[78]

While Fortas despaired, Johnson got mad. In early September, he told Secretary of Agriculture Orville Freeman that he wanted to retaliate against the southern Democrats. He focused on the farm bill, where the government gave huge payments to wealthy southern farmers including Eastland, who received $157,000 annually to leave thousands of acres fallow. The threat fell through when Freeman told him that it would cost the Democrats in the election.[79]

Again, Johnson had few weapons left in the arsenal to use against his opponents. By 1968, the demographics had changed with the defeat of a number of leading progressives, including Paul Douglas (D-IL) in midterm elections in 1966. The Vietnam War and urban unrest appeared likely to unseat other liberal Democrats, including Wayne Morse (D-OR), in the fall of 1968 as Humphrey's presidential campaign and Johnson's unpopularity handicapped Democrats other than the southern conservatives residing comfortably in their seats.

When the committee finally convened on September 13, the White House and Fortas took another blow. Griffin and Thurmond supposedly had explosive new materials. Johnson and others queried Fortas about "any other vulnerability." Fortas answered "he couldn't think of anything."

Right before the committee resumed its hearings, Fortas' confidant and fellow lawyer, Paul Porter, asked Califano for a meeting. When he arrived at the White House, he produced a letter he had sent to several prominent businessmen asking them to contribute to a fund to pay Fortas to teach a seminar for the American University Law School. He had raised $30,000, of which half went to pay Fortas for his work over the summer.[80]

Problems immediately appeared in the arrangement. Porter admitted several people he approached were prominent businessmen who expected to have business before the Supreme Court. According to Califano, "Porter tried to justify the arrangement, saying it wouldn't influence Fortas's behavior in the Court, but his eyes teared as he talked to me." The lawyer admitted Thurmond planned to call the dean of the law school, B. J. Tennery, before the committee when it reconvened.[81]

Afterward, Temple and Califano went to the president with the news. As he digested the bombshell, Johnson went silent for a minute or two before saying: "We won't withdraw the nomination. I won't do that to Abe."[82]

Then, he pivoted after fully understanding that they could not break the filibuster. But he wanted at least a vote to show that a majority supported him. With it, "he'll be able to stay on the court with his head up. We have to do that for him."[83]

The new revelations further weakened Fortas' position and confirmed Johnson's instincts that the battle was over. On September 16, Manatos reported that Mansfield and Dirksen "agree that the 'dirty movies' issue has taken its toll on Fortas, and that the $15,000 fee, while a secondary issue, has been hurtful." He added, "Mansfield and Dirksen both believe floor debate on pornography will be dirty, that Thurmond tastes blood now, that the 'crony' charge has fallen of its own weight ... and that the movies were what the opposition needed to make their positions jell."[84]

Thurmond clearly understood the political landscape, particularly in Middle America in the Midwest and Bible Belt South. Pornography was a relatively new addition to the culture wars being waged across the country against the purveyors of smut that terrified mothers everywhere – about the corrosive influence on their sons – as well as prominent clergymen across the country. It was salacious and played well in various conservative news outlets, especially those with strong ties to various grassroots Christian organizations springing up across the country in support of school choice, school prayer, and protection of traditional family values.[85]

The bad news kept coming as the debates continued. Russell wrote the president on September 26 confirming his vote against Fortas. He highlighted, "the last hearings of the Committee, which revealed the nominee's actions in accepting a $15,000 honorarium for nine lectures before classes at American University and the manner in which it was handled make it impossible for me to support Justice Fortas ... the fact that these funds were collected by a former law partner from the most affluent clients of their law firm ... in my opinion raises a very grave question of ethics and propriety." He concluded: "Due to all of the circumstances, I felt in duty bound to tell you frankly and in all candor of the conclusions to which I have been driven in this case."[86]

Just as Johnson predicted, Dirksen abandoned ship and refused to support any efforts to suspend debates. Finally, on October 1, the White House secured a vote on ending the filibuster. It won a majority, 45–43, but fell far short of being able to ensure cloture. It was a small victory, but signaled the end of the battle.

Soon, Fortas wrote Johnson: "I note the failure of the motion to end the filibuster in the Senate with respect to my nomination as Chief Justice of the United States." With a new court term starting on October 7, he emphasized: "In view of these circumstances, I ask you to withdraw my nomination as Chief Justice. Continued efforts to secure confirmation of that nomination, even if ultimately successful, would result in a continuation of the attacks on the Court." He concluded: "Attacks of this sort would be especially inappropriate and harmful to the Court and the nation if they continue while the Court is in session, engaged in the adjudication of issues of great importance to the nation as well as the litigants. I do not want to provide the occasion for a situation of this sort."[87]

Soon after, LBJ issued a statement: "With deep regret I have accepted and concur in the request of Mr. Justice Fortas and am withdrawing his nomination as Chief Justice of the United States. I believed when I made this nomination, and I believe now, that he is the best qualified man for this high position. The action of the Senate, a body I revere and to which I devoted a dozen years of my life, is historically and constitutionally tragic."[88]

The last time the Senate failed to confirm a nomination for the Supreme Court (John J. Parker because his views were deemed as too reactionary) was in 1930, the only time it had withheld its advice and consent on the Chief Justice since 1795.[89] It was a significant blow to the president, but also to the constitutional system.

After some thought, Johnson and his staff decided not to nominate anyone else. On October 10, he praised the qualifications of Fortas and Thornberry, stressing: "Had the Senate been permitted to vote, I am confident that both ... would have been confirmed." But, he lamented: "In ordinary times I would feel it is my duty now to send another name to the Senate for this high office. I shall not do so. These are not ordinary times. We are threatened by an emotionalism, partisanship, and prejudice that compel us to use great care if we are to avoid injury to our Constitutional system ... Under the circumstances, the foundations of government would be better served by the present Chief Justice remaining until emotionalism subsides, reason and fairness prevail."[90]

The loss hit everyone hard. Johnson blamed himself and the White House staff on the matter. Privately, he told a journalist: "The Fortas appointment would have been different if he had another four-year term."[91]

He was correct. The original line of attack by Griffin focused on Johnson's lame duck status, believing it gave his party an opening with the likely Nixon victory in November. While the focus shifted over time to Fortas' positions and ethics, it opened the door for Griffin and others to delay the process until they developed more issues to undermine the nomination. The March 31 decision not to seek reelection definitely played a role in the Fortas/Thornberry defeat.

Others shared Johnson's anger regarding the process. Late in September, the Johnsons invited Fortas and his wife Carol to dinner. Lady Bird worried whether they wanted to see the first family, "the unwitting architects of all the agony they had been going through." She lamented that over the years, she watched different people "maligned, torn apart ... and life questioned by Congress and press" but "there was a wise, able, and compassionate guide for them to turn to" in the form of Fortas.

But now, he had been "pilloried, where is there an Abe Fortas for him to turn to? There isn't anybody."[92]

The two entered and the first lady observed, "Carol was bouncy and strong and expressed her observations in salty and, I thought, healthy language." On the other hand, "Abe was very quiet, contained, and dignified."

During the evening, they talked about the presidential campaign and "likelihood that there might be a swing to strong conservatism." "And we talked of the heritage of [Joseph] McCarthy the first and [Eugene] McCarthy the second," Lady Bird emphasized, adding: "What days we have lived through here."[93] They parted friends, but ones depleted by the whole experience.

The sting of defeat stayed with everyone. A couple of years later, Johnson reflected: "The Fortas incident left me with a sense of deep foreboding," he recalled. "I feared that Congress's action would eventually lead to a conservative Court, a reversal of the philosophy of the Warren court, and a dissipation of the forward legislative momentum we had achieved during the previous eight years." He observed: "In the end, the result of the 1968 Presidential election foreshadowed such a swing to the right, and it came as the final blow to an unhappy, frustrating year."[94]

In the final analysis, a combination of factors shaped the failure of the Fortas/Thornberry nomination process. In ways, LBJ's instincts failed him. His unwillingness to separate Fortas from his inner circle (or even consider another court member) when he went to the Court sabotaged his chances, something he refused to acknowledge. The charges of cronyism with Thornberry also stuck and undermined his campaign. Like Vietnam, he could not see beyond his own personal desires, something exacerbated by Fortas' own bad behavior that led to him resigning his seat in disgrace in May 1969 after another scandal involving payments engulfed him.

But, there was also the rising conservative tide that crashed the attempt. It reflected the diminution of the power of the president from only a few years before and the growing anger and resentment created by the perceived attacks on conservative institutions by people of color and those not aligned with the Christian faith. The growing resentment of the southern conservatives allowed a sense of revenge for the civil rights victories and made the clash even more vicious and mean-spirited. When combined with the partisanship of the GOP in an election year, the president faced a much more difficult task than originally anticipated by many observers.

But, Johnson was right in the end, partly in recognizing the forces aligned against Fortas, in particular, and their origins. More important, the battle in the summer of 1968 clearly set the tone that followed in the years after and through the modern era. The Supreme Court became increasingly politicized, as evidenced by the bruising battle in 1969 over Nixon's nomination of two southerners, Clement Haynsworth and G. Harrold Carswell, that went down in defeat after massive resistance from labor and civil rights groups. Others followed over the years, including Robert Bork during the 1980s. However, 1968 proved a major turning point in the history of the court and the tensions of that year would spill over for many more to come.

CHAPTER 8

The Tanks Are Rolling

Czechoslovakia Crushed, August 1968

Residents of the White House awoke to a hot and humid day on Tuesday, August 20th. LBJ started his day a little late, having returned the previous night after giving a rousing speech on Vietnam to the VFW meeting in Detroit.[1]

As he scurried between meetings in the morning, Lady Bird observed: "There was an air of excitement in the White House, more than usual staff coming and going, a feeling of tenseness, of something about to happen."[2]

She eventually cornered Walt Rostow and asked: "Is there anything good going to happen in the next day?"

Without hesitating, he responded: "It looks as if the Russians have emptied their out-basket to us. They have answered all of the President's correspondence." Lady Bird knew good news when she heard it.[3]

Since the Glassboro, New Jersey, meetings in August 1967 with Premier Alexi Kosygin, where LBJ and the Russian discussed a series of topics including arms reduction, the president had hoped for a chance to ease tensions with the Soviet Union. In particular, he hoped to reach an ambitious deal on further reducing nuclear weapons. Building off the recently agreed on Non-Proliferation Treaty (NPT), both sides wanted an Anti-Ballistic Missile Treaty (ABM) to improve relations further. So, it appeared a summit might take place in the Soviet Union, the first one in many years between the US and Soviet leaders.

But, it went beyond nuclear weapons. Johnson wanted the Soviets to push their North Vietnamese allies to the negotiating table. On the Soviet side, Kosygin and his allies thought easing tensions might reduce spending on the military, allowing more money to flow into the Soviet economy that continued to stagnate. They also wanted to undermine the growing Chinese threat as Mao Zedong competed with Moscow for influence in the developing world, claiming his superiority in national liberation and ideological orthodoxy.

With the minutes ticking down on his presidency and the Democrats lagging far behind in the polls against Nixon, LBJ wanted to make a big splash and try to cement his legacy as a global statesman. With the summit and also potential progress in Paris with the North Vietnamese, he hopefully would dilute the stain of the war in Vietnam and help Humphrey in the last days of the presidential election. He thought the forthcoming summit provided an excellent opportunity to facilitate this process.

Thus, the Soviets agreed to issue a joint press release simultaneously on August 21 announcing a summit between Kosygin and Johnson in the Soviet Union in October. The meetings appeared to offer positive steps in recovering from what to that point had been a tumultuous and trying year for Johnson and the country.

But storm clouds had been gathering on the horizon that threatened to further cement 1968 as a year of a continuous nightmare for Johnson. In January 1968, Czech reformers led by Alexander Dubček began dismantling a conservative regime to establish "socialism with a human face."[4] Originally, Moscow acquiesced, but during the early summer, alarm bells went off in the Kremlin as Czechs moved toward liberalization of the economy and a more independent foreign policy outside of the Warsaw Pact. The "Prague Spring," as it became known, sent shockwaves through Eastern Europe.

For months, the president and his staff closely monitored events unfolding in Czechoslovakia. While preoccupied with Vietnam and domestic disturbances, many in the White House looked favorably on the changes. However, they said little and kept a low-key profile, a policy that Department of Defense official George Elsey characterized as one of "non-action."[5]

Most feared creating another situation like Hungary in 1956, in which the Warsaw Bloc believed the United States and its allies fomented the uprisings. As Senate Majority leader, LBJ learned painful lessons in 1956 that shaped debates in 1968. He supported President Dwight

Eisenhower but later worried how US rhetoric molded Hungarian resolve and also Soviet suspicions, leading to the crushing of the movement.[6]

In this case, LBJ understood the limits of US power. Since 1945 when the Iron Curtain descended on Eastern Europe, Americans had cautiously approached the region, relying on propaganda and some covert action to undermine Soviet control. However, Johnson watched in the mid-1950s as the overheated rhetoric of people including Secretary of State John Foster Dulles pushed the Hungarians into action. Eisenhower's fear of provoking WWIII prevented a forceful response, and Soviet tanks crushed the Hungarian fighters. Johnson clearly learned from the lesson.

As the heat and humidity built up in the capitol, LBJ held his regularly scheduled Tuesday lunch with his national security team. Clifford noted that after some tense days, inside the air-conditioned White House, that day "the mood was better than it had been in weeks."[7]

As the group convened, LBJ shared a glass of sherry with each man. "Gentlemen, let us drink to a summit conference in the Soviet Union in October. This could be the greatest accomplishment of my administration."[8]

Clifford acknowledged as each raised their glasses, "for once our Administration, so bitterly divided on Vietnam, was united." Looking at the president, he noted: "I could see that arms control held the same importance to Lyndon Johnson in international affairs as civil rights did in the domestic arena." It would become LBJ's lasting legacy in foreign policy, "not that dreadful war in Southeast Asia."[9]

There was reason for optimism. Rusk planned to travel to Moscow in late August to start hammering out the details for the first summit that would be held since 1961. LBJ wanted face-to-face talks to push his agenda, and just like FDR, he believed personal diplomacy could overcome ideological differences. He wanted to push Kosygin toward concessions that likely would fall to his successor to ratify, but he would receive credit for initiating the process.

As the lunch on the 20th continued, the talk shifted to Czechoslovakia. Rusk sounded optimistic, stressing that the Soviets would not invade after agreeing to a summit announcement. On the other hand,

CIA Director Helms voiced concern, noting the Central Committee had convened for an emergency session that day.[10]

But for the most part, the meeting revolved around the president and his aides basking in the glow of the forthcoming summit, quite a feat for a lame duck president. Unfortunately, much like the days following the March 31 speech, circumstances beyond his control threatened the positive turn of events in the next few days. Such quick changes reflected the impossible nature of 1968 when one crisis after another undermined any equilibrium in domestic and foreign affairs.

Once more, Johnson faced a crisis not too dissimilar to the *Pueblo* and Tet where foreign powers tested his diplomatic mettle. Once more, he avoided overreacting and recognized the limits of American power in accomplishing any goal other than extracting as much propaganda value from the Soviet aggression. His response reflected both his ability to remain calm during an international crisis and the fact that the president of the United States faced significant limits in shaping events unfolding in the world.

Unbeknownst to LBJ, Soviet Ambassador to the United States Anatoly Dobrynin had received instructions to request an urgent meeting with the president. He pulled out a previously unused personal phone number for LBJ provided by Rostow.

He made the call, already knowing about the impending Warsaw Pact invasion of Czechoslovakia. His superiors wanted him to deliver personally the formal "explanation," but stressed it must be done in the early evening just as the tanks rolled into Prague.

As instructed, the veteran diplomat phoned Johnson. Without hesitating, LBJ invited Dobrynin over. The Russian wavered, trying to keep to the strict deadline imposed by his bosses. He deferred, telling the president he needed time to translate the message into English.[11]

Afterward, the president queried Rostow: "What's your guess. Is it Czechoslovakia?"

"It could be," Rostow responded.[12]

Dobrynin arrived just after 8 p.m. and aides ushered him into the Cabinet Room, where only Johnson and Rostow sat around the huge table under the watchful eyes of the portraits and busts of Lincoln and Kennedy.

The president, recently returned from a haircut as he prepared to leave for the ranch the following day, greeted the Russian cordially. He opened by telling Dobrynin about a color movie he recently watched of the Glassboro meetings where he praised Kosygin for his political acumen, noting: "Well, you would have thought he could be a Country Judge of New Jersey, or President of the United States, or anybody."[13]

The pleasantries continued over discussions of Eisenhower's recent heart attack, LBJ's need to lose weight, and an offer of a soda to quench the Russian's thirst.

Then, Dobrynin changed course: "Mr. President, I have an urgent instruction from my government to you about a serious business. I will read it."

Dobrynin outlined the "conspiracy of the external and internal forces against the existing social order in Czechoslovakia" and how the "Czechoslovakian Socialist Republic approached the allied states, the Soviet Union among them, with a request of rendering direct assistance," including military force.

LBJ sat passively while Rostow quietly digested the information. Dobrynin continued by highlighting the Soviet treaty obligations and "the threat to the Socialist order in Czechoslovakia constitutes at the same time a threat to the foundations of European peace and world security." He concluded: "We proceed from the fact that the current events should not harm the Soviet-American relations to the development of which the Soviet Government as before attaches great importance."[14]

For some reason, LBJ seized on the last statement. While Dobrynin observed that Rostow "sat with a lowering face," he stressed that LBJ "apparently did not immediately appreciate the significance of the news" and added, "much to my surprise he did not react to it all."[15]

Instead, Johnson pivoted and returned to discussing the summit. It caught the Russian off guard, Dobrynin stressing, "he looked cheerful and said he attached great importance to his forthcoming meeting with the Soviet leaders" where he hoped to discuss many topics including the Middle East and Vietnam. LBJ bragged that he "had more freedom of action" after declaring his intention not to seek reelection.[16]

It was surreal. For a man who often launched into a tirade for the slightest insult or perceived slight, LBJ listened impassively as the

Soviet ambassador rationalized the violation of Czech sovereignty by the Warsaw Pact on some trumped up charges of ideological heresy and protecting the Czechs from themselves.

But, the president appeared in denial. He really wanted the summit and showed his tendency at various points in his life to disconnect from reality to create an alternative one that he desired. He could convince himself of what he wanted to hear, rather than hear what was actually said. It was on full display that evening, when Johnson ignored Dobrynin's ridiculous claims in favor of returning to the question of the forthcoming summit, so intent on not wanting to lose his last chance for redemption on foreign policy. For the Soviet ambassador, it was a complete shock that Johnson responded in this manner.

Soon, the discussion drifted to whether Dobrynin wanted a whiskey, to which he admitted, "I would have agreed to drink anything at the moment!"[17] LBJ told stories about the origins of the Lone Star flag of Texas, the birth of his new grandchild, and even Johnson's grandfather who fought in Hood's Brigade during the Civil War. It concluded around 8:45 p.m. with the president praising US Ambassador to the Soviet Union Tommy Thompson and Dobrynin, noting "it would be good for this country and for your country too, if we had men of quality like you and Thompson."[18]

After a short meeting with Rostow, the president went to dinner with some guests as well as Lady Bird and Luci. While dining, the first lady remembered watching Rusk testify before the Platform Committee of the Democratic Convention, where he told members, "We anticipate early and important talks with the Soviet Union on the limitation and reduction of offensive and defensive strategic missiles."[19]

LBJ joined her, observing an aide approach the secretary of state to deliver a note. Rusk looked up and requested a delay. Johnson knew what the young man said as Lady Bird observed "there was a churning air of expectancy and excitement in the room" as "Lyndon ate hurriedly and went back to his office."[20]

By 10:15 p.m., LBJ returned to the Cabinet Room for a meeting with his national security team, including Humphrey. While LBJ zeroed in on the concept: "It is one country invading another Communist country.

It is aggression. There is danger of aggression anywhere."[21] The severity of the message delivered by Dobrynin apparently sank in over dinner.

But he continued to focus on the summit. For LBJ the major question on the matter remained: "Can we talk now after this ... Does our presence look as though we condone this movement?"

Rusk forcefully responded. "I am surprised by the time of this action. I am disappointed, particularly in light of their favorable messages" on the summit. Then, he highlighted "we do not know yet if the Czechs will raise a voice" like Hungary in 1956.

He urged caution outside of forceful denunciations in the United Nations and the press. Deep down, Rusk worried about Soviet responses, especially in Berlin, emphasizing Khrushchev called the city "the testicles of the West" and that "when he wanted to create pressure he squeezed them."

He concluded: "We must decide what moral force and political force we should bring to bear," but acknowledged, "the big question is what the Czech reaction will be. I would not move ahead in the next day or so."

Others, like Clifford, worried about bigger issues. "Czechoslovakia is just one piece on the chess-board," he warned, "this march will have effects on Poland, Bulgaria, Rumania and Hungary." He called for delaying the summit announcement scheduled for the following day.

US Ambassador to the United Nations and long-time Johnson foreign policy aide, George Ball, raised the issue of its timing and the ghosts of Hungary, reminding people in the room that the Russians launched the attack in 1956 right before the Democratic National Convention. "They have been concerned about the internal structure of the Warsaw Pact and about not destroying the relationship with the United States," the veteran diplomat observed, carefully noting the tightrope the Kremlin seemed to be walking.

Then, General Earle Wheeler weighed in on the matter, decisively noting: "There is no military action we can take. We do not have the forces to do it."[22]

Vice President Humphrey summed up the frustrations of many in the room, stating "The Czechs touched the heart of the Communist revolution. All you can do is snort and talk."[23]

The vice president was right. Unless committed to starting WWIII in Central Europe, Johnson had few options. LBJ knew the Europeans, despite the recent ghosts of Adolf Hitler's soldiers marching through Prague in 1938, would not support fighting over Czechoslovakia. Few Americans would risk nuclear Armageddon over the country where Communists led the revolution to reform, not end, authoritarian rule. Johnson correctly recognized the constraints and pushed only to punish the Soviets for their actions in other realms and to prevent a repeat of the mistakes of 1956 in Hungary.

In the end, the president had Rusk cancel the joint statement on the summit. He told Dobrynin the United States would never condone the illegal invasion and emphasized the Soviet action "was like throwing a dead fish in the president's face."[24]

However, Johnson did not remove the possibility of a summit as he sought to test the pulse of the nation. It was not a harsh condemnation, as LBJ continued to want the summit. He and others hoped the crisis would subside through some miracle such as the Soviets immediately withdrawing and allowing elements of the Prague Spring to continue to flower.

It was wishful thinking. The only real options left open to Johnson remained trying to prevent the Warsaw Pact from replicating its actions in Romania, where reformists had control, or Yugoslavia that continued to serve as a model of socialist republics not completely subjugated by the Soviets. There was also the potential to exploit the Soviet aggression in the international community, as Washington struggled in efforts to win friends because of the vocal denunciations throughout the non-industrialized world for its activities in Vietnam. Other than that and flickering hope of the summit, the limits of the American presidency in 1968 were on full display.

To accomplish the goal of battering the Soviets in the court of international opinion, the president ordered Ball to return to the United Nations and organize opposition to the Soviet invasion. "George, the matter's now in your hands: do what you have to do," Johnson told him.

Rusk added, "that means put on your hawk's beak, go into the Security Council, and give the Russians hell."[25]

Afterward, Johnson contacted Nixon about events unfolding in Czechoslovakia and the damage done to the summit as well as the negotiations on nuclear arms. The Republican nominee conveyed his appreciation for the information on the matter and promised not to make his job harder.

"You know how I feel. To hell with the election. We must all be firm on this," he told LBJ.[26]

Dismayed and frustrated, the president stayed up late in the little lounge talking to Tom Johnson, Jim Jones, and George Christian. At 4:30 a.m., he finally went to bed, lamenting that the following day should have been a triumph. Instead, "a story that would have produced banner headlines around the world was never written."[27]

Once more, his grand plans crashed into the realities of the world around him. His hope for a triumphal announcement vanished because the Soviets feared losing control of Eastern Europe. It was another body blow, joining the many others of the year of the continuous nightmare, as he characterized it. He awoke the next day, hoping deep down the Soviets would reverse course, allow him to save face, and move forward toward the summit. However, the pragmatist in him knew that would be unlikely to happen.

Lady Bird joined him in lamenting the events of the day. She wrote in her diary: "And so our high hopes for this morning were dashed. For a few hours it had looked as though we were making a step forward with Russia. And then suddenly, catastrophically, the word had come that the Soviet forces were moving into Czechoslovakia." She continued, "I, at least, felt a little like Moses, glimpsing the promised land from the mountaintop – and then suddenly having it disappear like a mirage. I was in bed by midnight, knowing that this day would shape many of the days to come, but not knowing how."[28]

Others agreed with the Johnsons' appraisals. Clifford described the invasion as "a shattering moment, not only for Lyndon Johnson and his dreams, but for the nation and world. History was taking a turn in the wrong direction that day, and there was nothing that anyone could do about it."[29]

He was only partly correct. The Johnson Administration could have made a stand in Czechoslovakia, but it chose not to do so because it wanted to avoid a military confrontation at a time when it found itself stretched far too thin by the war in Vietnam. Furthermore, the *Pueblo* standoff continued, meaning the Korean peninsula remained a potential flashpoint. But, the choice was correct for many reasons, especially wanting to prevent a nuclear war. That was of little solace to the Czechs, who for the second time in three decades found themselves being crushed by an authoritarian foreign power. Johnson would have to accept the limitations and try to manage the crisis to prevent it from spreading and to also win some rhetorical victories.

The following day, the president read the headlines, including the *Washington Post* with a huge byline, "Soviets Enter Czechoslovakia," while the *New York Times* emphasized: "Czechoslovakia Invaded By Russians and Four Other Warsaw Pact Forces; They Open Fire on Crowds in Prague."[30]

Throughout the morning, he worked on a public statement that he released from the Fish Room just after noon. It differed greatly from his interaction with Dobrynin the night before and better reflected the reaction most Soviet leaders expected.

He opened: "The tragic news from Czechoslovakia shocks the conscience of the world. The Soviet Union and its allies have invaded a defenseless country to stamp out a resurgence of ordinary human freedom."

Attacking the basic arguments of the Kremlin for the invasion, he stressed the Czechoslovakian government "did not" request its allies to intervene and denied any external aggression as serving as a justification.

"The action of the Warsaw Pact allies is in flat violation of the United Nations Charter," the president added.

Johnson concluded, "in the name of mankind's hope for peace, I call on the Soviet Union and its associate to withdraw their troops from Czechoslovakia ... It is never too late for reason to prevail."[31]

The administration also intensified efforts at United Nations to secure a denunciation of the act that evoked memories of Hitler sweeping through the country in 1938. From Africa to Asia to Latin America, condemnations arose, hurting the Soviets standing in international affairs, something they never fully appreciated until afterward.

Ball went to work on the evening that LBJ received Dobrynin. Working primarily with the Canadian and British ambassadors, he called for an emergency Security Council meeting. "Our first piece of business was to get the Czechoslovak crisis inscribed on the agenda," Ball wrote.[32]

The Soviets opposed the move, as Soviet Ambassador to the United Nations, Yakov Malik, emphasized the Czech government requested the intervention "in view of the threats created by the external and internal reaction" against the country's "socialist system."[33]

Ball countered by calling the invasion "an affront to all civilized sensibilities" and that the Soviet Union and its allies had sought "to impose by force a repressive political system which is plainly obnoxious to the people and the leadership of Czechoslovakia."[34]

By a vote of 13–2 the Council voted to debate the Soviet invasion, as the Americans pushed a resolution to condemn Soviet aggression.[35] The debates were contentious. When Malik argued the Soviets intervened for reasons of "fraternal solicitude," Ball fired back that Czechoslovakia was exactly "the kind Cain showed Abel." At one point, the Soviet ambassador bitterly called for the "distinguished United States representative" to "stop pounding his fist at [him]." Ball simply denied doing it, and added he had "not even pounded my shoe."[36]

The debates in New York continued for days and, as *The Economist* reported, Malik and Ball spent time "savaging one another."[37] The president monitored them daily, wanting some form of victory to be salvaged from the obvious defeat of the forces of progressive change in Eastern Europe.[38]

And, in the end, Ball acknowledged, "the Czechoslovak debate was carried on before the television cameras and no doubt served the purpose of exposing Soviet brutality to the world."[39] LBJ and the United States won a symbolic victory, but failed to achieve anything substantive to assist the Czech revolution, whose fire the Soviets extinguished under the tracks of their tanks.

Despite some victories at the United Nations, LBJ became angrier as the crisis continued. To Clifford, the president railed about being "double-crossed" by the Soviets, especially the premier. "Maybe I was sucked in by honeyed messages about the summit from Kosygin," he complained bitterly.[40]

Clifford responded that "perhaps Kosygin had not been the central figure in the decision" and that it might have been an eleventh hour choice to invade. The secretary of defense warned that it might signal Kosygin losing power in the Central Committee, something later borne out by the rise of Leonid Brezhnev.[41]

He correctly characterized it as a last minute decision. Only three days before the invasion, the Central Committee hardliners pushed Kosygin to challenge the Czech liberalizers. Fear drove them as they watched other challenges originating in Romania, fearing the Czech virus would infect Hungary and Poland. Not considering its effects on the summit, they brought down worldwide condemnations and damaged their efforts to paint the United States as an aggressor in Vietnam.

Of course, LBJ and his advisors knew little of the inner workings of the Central Committee, where some Soviet leaders clearly opposed the decision, albeit not publicly. They believed easing tensions with the United States ensured a strengthening of the economy, enabled reduction of costly defense expenditures, and allowed them to play the Americans off against the Chinese.[42]

However, this pointed to the challenges for the president, especially in the tumultuous year of 1968. Events beyond LBJ's control thousands of miles away in Moscow and Prague largely determined the outcome. He lacked proper intelligence on the matter, both on the ground and in the Kremlin. The whole episode highlighted the fluid state of international affairs during the period, one where domestic or regional factors could throw the best laid plans into disarray and destroy the president's plans for shaping his legacy.

But, as the crisis unfolded, some people questioned how Johnson could criticize the Soviets in Czechoslovakia. Was it any different than the US intervention in 1965 in the Dominican Republic? There, the United States used the Organization of American States (OAS) to remove a perceived threat by the leftist Juan Bosch to US hegemony. To some, both were simply great power politics sustaining regional supremacy.

Rusk directly defended the administration's actions in the Dominican Republic in an interview two days after the invasion, complaining about the "moral myopia that passes my understanding." He highlighted "all the difference in the world between acting to meet the common danger under a treaty of mutual security and to enable the people of the country work out their own future."

In contrast, he characterized the Soviet involvement as "an attempt to prevent the people of a country from having their own government, working out their own internal policy and government as is the case in Czechoslovakia." To him, it was a case of the "difference between black and white."[43]

There were many critics of the White House regarding Czechoslovakia. The *New York Times* editors suggested America's "over involvement" in Vietnam hurt its ability to respond.[44] Others tied it to Indochina, including Senator George McGovern (D-SD). "It is difficult if not impossible to order the internal affairs of even a small nation," he said, "This is one of the lessons we must learn from our own intervention in the affairs of the Vietnamese people."[45]

But, on the other side, Nixon exploited the affair, calling it "an outrage against the conscience of the world." He railed: "It violates the basic tenants of the international law, it violates both the letter and spirit of U.N. charter; it violates the basic spirit of human decency." He called for the Soviets to withdraw and "reconsider this brutal act."[46] While not outlining a course of action, Nixon clearly appealed to hardline anti-Communists who opposed LBJ's outreach to the Soviet Union. Once more, Humphrey found himself siding with the White House with little maneuvering room.

At this point, Johnson found himself in a position to please few people. The lack of forceful action against the Soviets, and even the absence for some of virulent rhetoric condemning the intervention, alienated conservatives. On the other side, the liberals attacked Johnson for his policy in Vietnam and previous interventions in Latin America for showing the hypocrisy of the United States. It was an election year and both sides sought to score points on the matter.

The White House had few answers and Johnson's crisis management style focused on patience and recognition of the limited options presented to the United States. Therefore, he tried managing expectations and preventing a world war and learning from the past to avoid a situation like that in Hungary in 1956. There was little else to do other than pressuring the Soviets in the United Nations and hoping for a quick resolution that would allow the summit to proceed.

On the 22nd, LBJ met with members of the cabinet and advisors to discuss Czechoslovakia. He highlighted several important points:

"We have no commitment to intervene militarily. It would not be in the Czech interests or ours."

"We have been ... deceived."

"The 'Cold War' is not over."

But ironically, given the situation, he emphasized: "We would go anywhere at any time to further interests of peace." He concluded: "We want to achieve peace."[47]

With the crisis continuing, the administration left open the door for a summit. Christian told reporters on the 22nd, "I think the President has said and indicated many times he would go anywhere to further the cause of peace, if his presence were required."[48]

LBJ recognized his dearth of options in confronting the Soviets in Czechoslovakia, understanding Rusk's point, "if there were a military intervention, there would be world war."[49] The United States lacked the military strength to respond against a firmly entrenched enemy in Czechoslovakia. Vietnam strained US resources to a breaking point, leaving few routes available even if Johnson wanted to make a show of strength and solidarity. This, along with his passionate desire for a summit, affected his management of the crisis.

Furthermore, NATO, especially the West Germans, appeared very unlikely to support any military action. In the months leading up to the invasion, Bonn firmly opposed maneuvers on the border and any hardened rhetoric on Radio Free Europe. Few in Europe and the United States wanted to start a world war over Czechoslovakia, despite the ghosts of 1938 and charges of appeasement.

Most agreed the president had few choices. Katzenbach argued: "Given the cold war atomic standoff, there was really nothing we or our NATO allies could do apart from issuing strong verbal protests and denunciations of the invasion." Once more, the ghosts of 1956 arose. "We did not want to repeat the unfortunate fiasco of 1957, when, incredibly, the CIA encouraged a Hungarian uprising that caused the deaths of hundreds of brave freedom fighters and we were able to do nothing to help," he emphasized.[50]

On the 23rd, the president communicated these ideas and others to congressional leaders, including powerful senators Everett Dirksen (R-IL), J. William Fulbright (D-AR), and Bourke Hickenlooper (R-IA).

These men had radically different views of the world as did their House counterparts Gerald Ford (R-MI), Mendel Rivers (D-SC), and Clement J. Zablocki (D-WI). Sitting in the Cabinet Room, they listened to the president and his advisers report on Czechoslovakia as well as Vietnam and the Middle East.

Trying to make a positive out of negative, Johnson had a political agenda that reflected his crisis management style on display during most of 1968. For months, some in Congress sought dramatic reductions in troop levels in Western Europe. They wanted significant cutbacks from 300,000 to 50,000 men. From the start, LBJ adopted a "hard, hard, hard line," according to Clifford in opposition to the decreases. The president promised there would be "no cutting forces in Europe by even one man during his administration."[51]

LBJ played up the ongoing Soviet threat with the help of General Wheeler, who stressed, "the Soviet Union is substantially increasing its military strength." By the end, Johnson observed: "The situation in Central Europe today indicates it would be less than prudent for us to further reduce the U.S. military presence there." Instead, "we should take the lead in maintaining our strength" and work with allies to improve their capabilities.[52]

The Soviet invasion gave LBJ all the ammunition he needed to beat back his opponents. Congressmen who previously supported reducing troop levels switched sides and backed sustaining a large deterrent against Soviet aggression. It also helped provide momentum for a renewal of the NATO Treaty appearing on the horizon in 1969. LBJ, the consummate politician, won a small victory in the face of a larger defeat, much like after the deaths of King and RFK.

The Soviet troops remained in place as the president headed off to the ranch for a summer break on the 24th. As he settled in back home to watch the drama of the Democratic National Convention in Chicago, he received periodic updates on the Czech crisis. He performed some small acts such as cancelling the second inaugural flight of a Soviet commercial jet to the United States.[53] But, overall, he lacked the power and the will to do more, paralleling Eisenhower's impotence in 1956.

While in Texas, LBJ and his advisors focused more on threats to prevent the Soviets from crushing similar movements in Eastern Europe.

They hoped the crisis might pass and Warsaw troops withdraw quickly, thus tamping down the anger in the United States and allowing the president to move forward on the summit front. But, they also prepared for any further escalation in other countries by speaking forcefully on the matter.

To contain the Soviet aggression, Johnson also sent the Soviets a warning about Romania and Yugoslavia. Some worried they might replicate their activities, especially against the Romanians under Nicolae Ceausescu, who challenged the Soviet Union over foreign policy after taking office in 1965. He reduced Romania's participation in the Warsaw Pact and eased censorship of the press. In tandem with Josip Tito, many thought Ceausescu represented a new path for the Eastern European Communist nations, particularly after he refused to participate in the invasion of Czechoslovakia and strongly condemned it.[54]

The administration wasted no time in warning the Soviets on the matter of Romania. In meetings on August 23rd between Rusk, Ambassador Thompson, and Ambassador Dobrynin, Rusk laid into the ambassadors. He asked Dobrynin whether "in any way" he had "been misled by the manner in which he had discussed the Czechoslovakia problem." He acknowledged fully understanding LBJ's feeling on the invasion and the damage done.[55]

Then, he focused on other possible actions against others in Eastern Europe. Rusk reported: "We have received in the last few hours a number of alarming rumors about the possible Soviet invasion of Romania," stressing independent sources, not the Ceausescu government, had issued the report.

Dobrynin immediately responded that "he had neither seen nor heard any indication whatever of any contemplated Soviet action against Romania, and he did not believe that there was anything to these rumors."[56]

Nonetheless, fearing more military actions, LBJ delivered a blistering speech in San Antonio at the Milk Producers Association convention in front of a crowd of 3,000. While not naming Romania, the president stressed: "There are even rumors late this evening that this action might be repeated elsewhere in the days ahead in Eastern Europe."

Referencing the "heavy heart" that developed over the events in Czechoslovakia, he stressed: "But I repeat tonight, let no would-be aggressor misjudge American policy during this Administration. I express hope and the belief that there will be no condoning of aggressors and no appeasement of those who prowl across national boundaries." He went on: "So I say to you tonight and to the world tonight, we cannot and we must not in the year 1968 return to a world of unbridled aggression."

Referring to the UN Charter on the fundamental right of all nations to exist, "there should not be any doubt in the minds of anyone as to where the United States of America stands on a question so fundamental to the peace of the entire world." He concluded: "So let no one unleash the dogs of war, let no one even in this period of highly charged domestic debate in our country even doubt what the true views of the American people are on these matters."[57]

The Soviets made numerous efforts to tamp down the rhetoric and rumors over Romania, and their labors apparently succeeded. At a NSC meeting on September 4, Ambassador Thompson reported: "The Soviets are unlikely to invade Romania. There is no current threat to the Communist system in Romania. The situation is quite different from the threat to Soviet and Communist power which was rising in Czechoslovakia."[58]

Being proactive paid dividends. In moments of crisis, Johnson sought to keep moving and looking for ways, often small ones, to try to create something positive out of an incredibly dismal situation. In this case, he successfully beat back the congressional efforts to reduce US forces in Western Europe and pressured the Soviets to prevent similar actions in Romania. Johnson employed the use of political and diplomatic tools at his disposal in dealing with domestic and foreign opponents and successfully salvaged some minor victories. He showed more skills of tact and diplomacy than his opponents on both sides of the political spectrum often gave him credit for having.

While monitoring Romania, the White House also devoted energy to the humanitarian crisis, like the one after Hungary in 1956. Rostow reported to the president that arrangements existed to admit Czech refugees under the Parole Authority of the Immigration and Nationality Act. Rusk planned to seek a $20 million increase in the Refugee Assistance appropriation from Congress because nearly 100,000 Czechs resided outside the country when the invasion occurred.[59]

The president supported the idea of bringing the Czechs to the United States and issued a press release on supporting the admission of refugees. At a September 4th meeting of the NSC, Johnson stressed: "We can accept those who desire to come to the United States but not encourage them to come."[60] He and others feared a massive exodus and the stress it would place on Germany. They also feared Communist agents infiltrating the west among the refugees.

With the distractions of the presidential race and Fortas nomination, the White House and most Americans moved on from the Czech crisis. There was little anyone could do other than deliver rhetorical attacks in the UN and publicly. The lack of bloodshed like that experienced by the Hungarians in 1956 limited the world outcry and with Vietnam and the violence in Chicago taking center stage on the nightly news after the first couple of days of the invasion, peoples' attention turned elsewhere very quickly.

But the invasion had long-term effects beyond intimidating those in the Eastern Bloc and damaging East–West relations.[61] Several weeks after the Soviet invasion, LBJ told a colleague: "The Czechoslovakia situation has made problems in Europe more acute." He particularly worried about Senate ratification of the NPT Treaty. "You live in one of the most dangerous periods in history. It would be easy for the Russians to take further moves. They got away with Czechoslovakia. If they thought this government was prostrate till January 19, I don't know what you would do. You cannot trust a totalitarian country."[62]

The Soviets upped the ante in late September when *Pravda* announced the Brezhnev Doctrine, something reiterated publicly the following month that stated: "When forces that are hostile to socialism try to turn the development of some socialist country towards capitalism, it becomes not only a problem of the country concerned, but a common program and concern for all socialist countries." It basically justified the type of interventions in Hungary in 1956 and Czechoslovakia in 1968.[63] The statement alerted the Americans and others within the Eastern Bloc that force would sustain Soviet hegemony.

LBJ argued later, "the invasion of Czechoslovakia did more than postpone the summit meeting." With the NPT already under consideration, "many Senators were in no mood to approve agreements with

Moscow in that charged atmosphere." He considered calling a special session to debate the treaty, but his friends in the Senate counseled against it, arguing the tactic would "cause bad feelings and increased resistance." LBJ complained "it was clear leaders in the Republican party wanted to delay approval of the treaty until after the inauguration" to allow Nixon the chance to "at least share credit for this historic move." He was right, as the Senate approved the treaty in March 1969.[64]

Everyone speculated on what might have been if LBJ went to Russia in 1968. He wanted a legacy of being a peacemaker, not a warmonger. Even as late as November 11, the Russians showed some interest in hosting a summit and talking about nuclear arms reductions, something McNamara, now president of the World Bank, reported after a personal invitation to meet Kosygin.[65]

Even Humphrey recognized the importance of what might have been. One journalist noted the vice president "has no doubt that the spectacular Presidential visit would have made a significant difference – perhaps the crucial difference – in the outcome of the election campaign that he was then waging."[66]

The president was skeptical, as were many of his advisors, including Rusk, who argued Czechoslovakia remained too close in the public's memory. LBJ complained that he thought the Russians would use the summit "to take some of the polecat off of them."[67]

But, he considered the request seriously, never wanting to let go of a chance to cement a positive chapter in his record on foreign affairs. After several attempts in September and October, the president had Rusk query Dobrynin one last time just after the election, hoping for meetings in mid-December.[68] At the end of November, LBJ had Ambassador Thompson suggest a meeting in Geneva right before Christmas.

LBJ even reached out to president-elect Nixon on the matter. "Mr. Nixon," Johnson noted, "considered the possibility and finally decided against it." The president then suggested, "he chooses a trusted adviser to go with me as an observer and full participant in the talks." Nixon responded affirmatively, proposing a retired diplomat Robert D. Murphy.

However, the final efforts were for naught. "I believed the Soviet leaders had been persuaded that it made more sense for them to deal with the incoming administration," he stressed, adding: "I had a strong feeling that they were encouraged in that view by people who were very close to the Nixon camp."[69]

The crisis in Czechoslovakia represented another major challenge to Johnson. He handled the invasion with patience and restraint, trying desperately to avoid a confrontation that would spark WWIII or replicate the disaster in Hungary in 1956. His response reflected his recognition of the lack of options available to him including the overextension of American troops, the lack of support for military action on the domestic and international fronts, and the overall limits of American power in Eastern Europe.

Like so many other points in 1968, Johnson found himself in a reactive position as events beyond his control threatened to spiral out of control. Moscow's decision to crush the Czech experiment further highlighted how his efforts at peace failed not just in Vietnam, but also on the grand scale in 1968 and ensured that the nightmare of a year continued. Unfortunately, more disappointments and challenges unfolded in Chicago simultaneously and added to the tensions of an already exhausting nine months.

CHAPTER 9

The Perfect Disaster

The Democratic National Convention, August 1968

The road to the Democratic Convention in Chicago began immediately after LBJ announced his decision not to seek reelection on March 31. That night, Mayor Richard Daley talked about drafting him for the nomination, but at the time Johnson appeared resolute in his decision.

LBJ consistently dismissed the notion of returning to the field as it became crowded with Eugene McCarthy, Robert Kennedy, and Hubert Humphrey. But the summer months brought the death of RFK and most polls showed the other two men losing badly to Nixon. Thus, the Draft Johnson movement gained steam as polls showed him leading Nixon by 7 to 8 percentage points.

It even came from unlikely sources. In the immediate aftermath of Kennedy's assassination, Kennedy loyalist Pierre Salinger had McCarthy's advisor Dick Goodwin ask for a meeting with the candidate. When the Minnesota senator arrived, Salinger remembered: "We told him that in light of what had just happened, the best thing for everyone concerned would be for McCarthy to fly to Washington as soon as possible, meet with Lyndon Johnson, and convince him that he should change his mind and run for reelection."

"It's our only hope of winning," the two men told him, adding, "you can't get the nomination, and Hubert can't win the race for President."

McCarthy acknowledged the logic of their argument and promised to mull it over. "Of course, he never did it," Salinger emphasized.[1]

Kennedy's death sparked others to push for Johnson to run. Richard Moose, a former NSC staffer, contacted Johnson's aide, Tom Johnson, who reported. "Dick said he is of the opinion that the President should be prepared to accept the nomination of the Democratic Party." He concluded: "He doesn't think Humphrey can beat Nixon, and unless the President runs, Nixon will be President."[2]

The visions of Johnson sweeping in and saving the Democratic Party at the national convention in Chicago played right into his massive ego and vanity. The same rationales for not seeking reelection remained in place, especially his concern over his health. However, his desire for validation pushed him forward to at least consider the nomination if asked, along with his animosity toward Republican front-runner Richard Nixon and lack of confidence in Humphrey. Still, many around him thought he would revel in the accolades, but simply decline after receiving the honor. But, no one knew for sure at the time.

The talk of LBJ seeking the nomination constituted only one part of the controversy surrounding the lead up to the Democratic National Convention. The president continually denied having any interest in Chicago, but few believed his denials.

By mid-May, rumors abounded of the interference of the White House in planning the details of the Chicago Convention. A leak to the press infuriated the president. Tom Johnson wrote a memorandum about tracking down journalist Merriman Smith, who had written stories about LBJ's interference based on an anonymous source close to the president. He told the well-respected veteran journalist that the president had no involvement in planning the convention. He denied any cooperation between Johnson and Daley, emphasizing "the President hasn't asked that nuts and bolts planning be submitted to him for approval."

In response, "Smitty" stressed: "Tom, you're wrong."

He highlighted a long conversation "with the same man who told me earlier that the President would not seek or accept renomination. I didn't print what he told me then, but in light of how that came out I believe he knows what he is talking about."[3]

Johnson concluded: "It looks as though somebody has filled Smitty in very well. We do not know who it is, but Smitty is not the type of correspondent who writes this type of story without hard facts and a good source."[4]

Temple launched an inquiry into who leaked the information. First, he contacted Horace Busby, who denied speaking with Smith, stressing he had not talked with him in two years. Christian said the same and emphasized: "He said he knew absolutely nothing about these plans or any conversation relating to them." The president was not happy with the leak, especially when the staff failed to track down its source.[5]

The whole episode showed Johnson in denial about his role that everyone knew was substantial. He had been in control of the party for five years, and he would not surrender the reins of power so easily. The president liked the clout, and he rationalized he had the experience at Atlantic City in 1964 and remained the sitting president at a time the contest for the nomination was in doubt in the early summer of 1968. While issuing public denials, no one who knew Johnson thought he would remain above the fray, especially with major issues like Vietnam and the unit rule remaining hotly contested among delegates as the convention approached in August.

From the beginning, the White House played an active role in shaping the convention. Johnson chose Chicago as the site for the convention, ignoring others including Humphrey who wanted Miami, far away from the riots of the summer of 1967 and those that occurred in April after King's assassination. Miami was further from major regions that might ensure an influx of antiwar and leftist protestors. Finally, many feared Daley's strong-armed tactics and those of his security forces would jeopardize actions inside and outside the convention halls.

LBJ also helped make sure that Congressman Hale Boggs of Louisiana became chair of the Platform Committee, despite Humphrey wanting Edmund Muskie.[6] Johnson also made sure his loyal supporter and prominent Democratic National Committee member, John Criswell, served as the executive director of the event. Thus, instead of Humphrey leading and putting his imprint on the convention, Johnson selfishly clung to control with negative outcomes resulting.

As the convention approached, LBJ's role became even more apparent. Califano stressed: "Johnson wanted to present himself as aloof from the party process and position," but "because the President was still his party's leader, our people organized the convention and virtually dictated the platform."[7]

Johnson also devoted a great deal of time and energy to sustaining his legacy. The convention provided him with a chance of possible redemption by his swooping in and taking the nomination from McCarthy or Humphrey, who few believed could defeat Nixon. This would be the supreme validation of his political career and march him into another four years. Also, it provided him a platform to frame the accomplishments of his administration, even if he chose to resist the calls for a draft movement. It would provide one last opportunity to seize the political stage in front of thousands of party loyalists as well as a national audience.

Thus, LBJ dispatched his aides Harry McPherson and Lawrence Levinson to Hollywood to work with writers on a script as a tribute to his achievements for the delegates in Chicago. Ultimately, they secured a twenty-eight-minute highlight film of Johnson's accomplishments narrated by Gregory Peck. As one observer noted, the film was a "cinematic and political tour de force."[8]

Simultaneously, he worked to prevent the Kennedys from upstaging him. Teddy emerged from self-imposed exile as the convention neared and talk of drafting him for the vice presidency (and maybe even the presidency) escalated.

In late July, LBJ's special assistant, George Reedy, received a visit from a Kennedy supporter, Jack Sutherland, emphasizing: "He said he suspected that John Connally had 'knocked down' the Ted Kennedy Vice Presidential candidacy at your instructions. I told him I had not talked to you about it but that I could not imagine your doing any such thing when you had announced your determination to stay out of the campaign. I also pointed out that this was not a very logical way of 'knocking down' the Kennedy candidacy."[9]

But the Kennedys concerned the president. On July 30, a Kennedy brother-in-law, Stephen Smith, contacted Califano regarding showing a movie at the convention about the life of RFK.

Califano went to the president and asked about it. He simply responded: "I've got no choice, so O.K."

But it was not that simple. Seeing the film as a ploy to help Ted, Johnson insisted that the film be shown on Thursday night, long after the nomination process ended.[10]

Old habits died hard for Johnson. While he had less personal animosity toward Ted, LBJ resented the perceived attempt to upstage a possible

Draft Johnson movement, or at the least, the convention honoring him during the process. At the minimum, he wanted to prevent another Kennedy from entering the limelight and perhaps upstaging Humphrey, who represented some continuity to his legacy. Maybe just as important, he wanted to limit the attempts to honor his nemesis, RFK. While he was gracious in the aftermath of his death, Johnson had no desire to perpetuate the myths of Bobby by the end of summer 1968.

With Johnson and the White House orchestrating much of the convention from the White House with the assistance of Daley and Criswell on the ground in Chicago, the Draft Johnson campaign received a bump in the aftermath of the Republican convention (August 8–11). The Gallup Poll taken immediately afterward had Nixon leading 45 percent to Humphrey with 29 percent and Wallace garnering 18 percent with 8 percent undecided. In the race to the convention, Humphrey led McCarthy by only 4 percent, ten points less than in late July.[11]

The president and other Democrats watched the polls. A likely Nixon victory inspired more speculation that LBJ should enter the race. Given that most of the delegates were party stalwarts not committed to any particular candidate outside of a few states where primaries mattered, the maneuver was possible. Even more so, the unit rule allowed people like Connally and Daley to control the votes within their state delegations, giving the president allies willing to push his name forward if he desired it.

Thus, some like Criswell and Daley continued pushing a Draft Johnson movement. Criswell (using the pseudonym of Bert) wrote on August 9 from Chicago: "In my judgment, the president should come to the convention," but provide "no indication of a presidential appearance." He wanted every effort made to ensure an illusion "that he isn't planning to be here."

Criswell hoped "the president could make his appearance on Tuesday night. It's just the right time," one day before the nomination process. "An appearance and birthday celebration on Tuesday night would be ideal," Criswell reported. To him, the arrangements committee would stress it would be "appropriate for the convention to hear from the president, the man who built the record on which the party would have to campaign in the fall."

He even proposed a fireworks display for the president along the lakefront with Johnson watching from his Hilton suite. "There is no question in my mind that the president should attend and that he will be pleased, perhaps even surprised, by the reception," Criswell reported.[12]

Mayor Daley "brightened up right away" when informed of a possible Johnson visit to Chicago and stated: "He shouldn't be down in Austin or somewhere when the convention is going on. He should come here and let us whoop it up like it should be."

Criswell concluded: "I think he is afraid to come on Tuesday night because he's afraid we'll draft him – and that's what I am for . . . I'm for a draft, and I'll start it if there is any chance he will do it."[13]

As some debated the likelihood of drafting the president, LBJ and his aides focused on the most contentious issue leading into the convention: the Vietnam plank. While Johnson pushed primarily for the San Antonio Formula, the doves wanted a bombing halt without conditions, a phased withdrawal of US troops, and expedited negotiations.

The focus on Vietnam by Johnson continued throughout the summer of 1968. He continued pressing the North Vietnamese to negotiate while pressuring Saigon to compromise on several issues, including the role of the Viet Cong. He also pushed forward with shifting the combat operations to the South Vietnamese and cajoled President Nguyen Van Thieu to focus more on land reform along with pacification programs. Nonetheless, the Paris Peace talks floundered, as the North Vietnamese remained suspicious of American intentions while the South Vietnamese worried about the United States fashioning a peace with little of their input. All of these tensions put Johnson further on edge, as his commitment to peace appeared not to be advancing quickly enough.[14]

Early on, Humphrey found himself caught between the two competing forces of the president fighting while negotiating and the peace faction aligned with McCarthy and others who wanted the United States out of Vietnam as soon as possible. He hoped to fashion a compromise and prevent a major clash at the convention over the Vietnam plank.

But the efforts to create a compromise placed Humphrey right in the firing line of the president, who grew increasingly agitated and frustrated over his lack of success in brokering a peace in Vietnam. It brought up years of Johnson's overall lack of respect for his vice president, who he thought too often sided with the liberal peaceniks on Vietnam. While Humphrey remained a loyal and dedicated member of the administration, Johnson often failed to repay the loyalty. He often chastised Humphrey for lacking the backbone to confront his enemies and accused him of vacillating, especially on Vietnam. It created tension between the two, especially as the vice president tried to establish his own place in the political arena in the summer of 1968.

In late July, at the urging of some of his aides, Humphrey planned a speech to distance himself from the president. On July 25, the vice president showed Johnson a draft. The president exploded, saying he "would be jeopardizing the lives of his sons-in-law and endangering the chances of peace. If I announced this, he'd destroy me for the presidency," Humphrey reported. Johnson began charging Humphrey as "disloyal" according to Clifford.[15]

But as the convention neared, Johnson calmed down and told Humphrey that he would support the plank as long as Rusk approved.[16] So, for weeks, he labored with people from the Kennedy and McCarthy wings, including David Ginsberg and Theodore Sorenson, as well as Charlie Murphy from the White House to fashion a compromise.

Finally, after much wrangling between the parties, a promising statement evolved on the Saturday before the convention. Ginsberg contacted Humphrey, who took down the resolution, making only a few minor changes. Then, the vice president remembered: "I reached Secretary of State Rusk on the phone and we went over it together. He made one or two suggestions I readily accepted and he said, in effect, 'It isn't all we'd like, but under the circumstances, it will do. It's a constructive, sensible plank. We can live with this.'"[17]

Humphrey then got on the phone with Rostow who supported it without any reservations. He reached out to others including Boggs and labor leader George Meany, who raised no red flags so he stressed: "I called Ginsberg back, said, 'Go ahead. It meets with everybody's approval. Let's go with it.'"

He concluded: "About 80 per cent of the McCarthy demands were directly met; the text had been cleared with State and Defense; Ginsberg had talked to virtually every member of the platform committee and had checked it with Larry O'Brien." He thought: "It appeared that we had been able to work together with disparate groups in the convention on the most complex, delicate question and come to an agreement ... leaving only a small group of hardline McCarthy people in opposition."[18]

As one person noted about the last group, deep down, Humphrey likely understood that even if he supported a watered-down plank, it would win him little support among some delegates. One observer noted: "Nothing, would bring the real peaceniks back to our side unless Hubert urinated on a portrait of Lyndon Johnson in Times Square before television – and then they'd say to him, why didn't you do it before?"[19]

Despite still facing some hard liners, Humphrey was supremely satisfied with the compromise. But, LBJ was not. He thought it would send a wrong message to the North Vietnamese that seemed to undermine his harder line position at the peace talks in Paris.[20] His obsession with Vietnam threatened not only him but the Democrats' chances of emerging from the convention unified instead of hopelessly divided.

On Sunday, Ginsberg called Jones at the ranch to discuss two or three minor points that Murphy raised. However, in the background, Ginsberg heard an increasingly aggravated Johnson grow louder and angrier. It was a sign of things to come.

As the convention opened the next day, Watson, acting as the self-described "eyes and ears" for Johnson in Chicago, asked for a meeting with Humphrey, on the instruction of the president. The vice president went to the postmaster general's suite where Watson expressed Johnson's displeasure.[21]

Humphrey responded: "Well, Marvin, I cleared this with the Secretary of State, and I've cleared it with Walt Rostow."

"That doesn't make any difference. It's been looked over again and it just doesn't meet with the President's approval," Watson responded.[22]

The back and forth continued for a while, but as the meeting concluded, Watson emphasized: "You must stay the course on Vietnam if you expect to be nominated."[23]

Humphrey immediately returned to his suite angry and upset. He did not even know what the president wanted, so he called him at the ranch.

"I understand that you or some of your people are not pleased with this plank," the vice president opened.

Johnson curtly responded: "We're not."

"Dean Rusk approved it," Humphrey fired back.

"That's not what I hear," LBJ replied.

"Well, he did, and so did Walt Rostow," he lobbed back.

Then, Johnson unloaded: "Well, this plank just undercuts our whole policy and, by God, the Democratic party ought not to be doing that to me and you ought not to be doing it; you've been a part of this policy."

Humphrey simply responded that the plank was acceptable to Rusk and Rostow.

"Well, Mr. President," Humphrey concluded the discussion, "we'll have to do the best we can. Possibly we can get something that is acceptable, but I'm afraid we're going to have serious troubles here."[24]

To Humphrey, it remained unclear what the president wanted other than to have his plank as written. He seemed almost irrational, as often the case on Vietnam, as nothing seemed to please him. The inscrutable Humphrey had not misunderstood Rusk or Rostow. The vice president had shown real statesmanship in crafting a compromise, but Johnson clearly sabotaged the process by rationalizing that it might send a confusing message to the North Vietnamese or South Vietnamese. It was hard to tell at this point also if the president's reaction might have related to the Draft Johnson movement. No matter, Vietnam once more damaged the Democratic Party, particularly the likely standard bearer.

Others piled on the vice president, including Connally, already angry at him for supporting abolition of the unit rule that gave control of many of the state delegations to a few people who determined the votes. He told O'Brien. "If Humphrey thinks he's got the nomination locked up, he better count the delegates again, because all hell will break loose if we're kicked around. He'd better remember that we in the South can deny him the nomination if we withdraw our support."

Not long after, O'Brien noted that the Texas governor "hinted that if Humphrey wasn't careful, Lyndon Johnson would be entered in nomination."[25]

For a while Humphrey debated supporting the plank as written. However, the president pressured him. He asked Boggs and Senator Jennings Randolph (D-WV) to return to the capitol. There, Westmoreland briefed them on the dangers of suspending the bombing in Vietnam, highlighting how the NVA would move men and supplies into the south if it happened.[26]

After returning to Chicago, Boggs visited Humphrey's suite, where he made it clear no compromise would advance without Johnson's approval.[27] The vice president capitulated and supported the president's plank. Thus, a battle that could have been avoided turned into a very ugly one. The president's clear obsession with Vietnam and unwillingness to turn over the party to Humphrey damaged the Democrats and prevented any chance of emerging at least partially unified from the convention. The only real winner in the matter was Nixon.

With the president focused on the Vietnam plank, talk continued to swirl around him being drafted. Jones reported that Jake Jacobsen, the president's former chief legal counsel, had reported on the brewing battle on the unit rule and complained: "No one is in charge of the convention. There is a real vacuum."[28]

Most importantly, Jones reported: "Jake says this convention is going to draft the President if there is the slightest indication, the draft will be accepted."[29]

The weekend before the convention, LBJ traveled to speak at his alma mater, Southwest Texas State College. Despite Connally highlighting "a growing sentiment" within the Texas delegation to put the president forward for the nomination, LBJ emphasized to his youthful audience: "I am not a candidate for anything, except maybe a rocking chair."[30]

Despite the public denials, LBJ had Connally gauge interest in a Draft Johnson movement. The Texas governor reached out to southern counterparts, a number already mad at Humphrey's liberal positions on civil rights and opposition to the unit rule. Connally emphasized: "I believe in his heart he wanted the moment of drama, the emotion of a convention swept away as in olden times, and the vindication it would present."[31]

However, Watson denied that the president was a candidate, "although if he had wished it, he could have been the Party's nominee in a heartbeat." Instead, Watson arrived two days before the convention to "achieve tangible results; namely, an acceptable platform and candidates committed to carry out his programs, particularly regarding Vietnam."[32]

Nonetheless, Watson queried some prominent Democrats about drafting LBJ. People in the New York delegation said any Johnson effort to take the nomination would likely "blow the Party apart."[33]

The desire to have the convention nominate him combined with frustrations over Humphrey's position on the Vietnam plank and the unit rule caused Johnson and some aides to undermine the vice president. Humphrey had been extremely loyal and often a leader in civil rights and other social programs. But, deep down, LBJ did not respect him, feeling he lacked the intestinal fortitude for hard fights like Vietnam and too often proved willing to compromise when he needed to fight. It created tensions in August 1968, as Humphrey desperately needed to emerge from Johnson's shadow, but the president would not let him.

Thus, Johnson rarely supported the vice president publicly, claiming to want to follow Eisenhower's tradition and remain above the fray as he had done in 1960. During the summer, however, LBJ told a reporter about Humphrey: "He cries too much." When asked to elaborate, Johnson simply answered: "That's it – he cries too much."[34]

In another case, he joked about seeing Humphrey and McCarthy holding tearful babies. "That's the way I feel when I look at the two candidates, like crying," Johnson said.[35]

At times, the White House humiliated Humphrey. When his campaign requested more phones and floor seats and another 500 seats, Criswell gave the news that they could have 2 percent of the request.[36]

It became so bad that Humphrey sent one of his sons each day to wait in line to collect passes for the family and their friends.[37]

At one point, a White House aide described Humphrey as "wounded, hurt, and baffled as a child" as he asked a friend to confirm rumors on whether Johnson planned to seek the nomination.[38]

Humphrey should have been treated much better by the president. The vice president had waited loyally in the wings as Johnson proved a hard-driving taskmaster. His argument about staying above the fray showed in his own way a lack of loyalty to his devoted vice president. It also demonstrated an unwillingness to surrender the limelight, much like his refusal to turn over the convention planning and implementation to Humphrey's people, which would have helped the campaign dramatically. The diminution of Johnson's power since 1966 likely played a significant role in the process, despite his having delusions of the party still willing to rally behind him at the eleventh hour. It was not the best of Lyndon Johnson on display after times during the year when he showed statesmanship and character. However, the party politics and personal ambitions brought out the worst in him.

While the president worked behind the scenes on Vietnam and continued hoping for a Draft Johnson movement, a powder keg threatened to explode in Chicago as thousands of protestors from across the country descended on the city.[39]

An ominous portent of things to come occurred on the Friday night, August 23rd. Yippies, a group of youth counterculture and antiwar activists, led by Abbie Hoffman and Jerry Rubin, gathered outside the Chicago Civic Center. There, in dramatic political theater, they nominated a swine called "Pigasus."

A reporter asked: "Why are you here?"

Rubin replied: "We want to give you a chance to talk to our candidate, and to restate our demand that Pigasus be given Secret Service protection and be brought to the White House for his foreign-policy briefing."

A minor confrontation occurred when Chicago police seized Pigasus and arrested several Yippies. The group simply found another pig and continued their antics.[40]

The minor clash foreshadowed more serious ones. Twelve thousand policeman complemented by 6,000 National Guardsmen and 7,500 regular Army troops on call waited to confront the demonstrators and possibly poor African Americans that many feared would arise again like in April.

In advance, Daley denied the marchers permits to occupy some public spaces and imposed curfews. The security forces ringed the Chicago Amphitheater where delegates convened with a seven-foot-high barbed wire fence, poured tar over manhole covers to prevent sabotage, and placed bulletproof doors in the entranceways. Along the lakefront, barricades sprung up and the police and guardsmen readied for battle.

By Sunday evening, a major confrontation erupted in Lincoln Park just north of the downtown area where many delegates gathered in hotels and restaurants. The police angered the crowd by refusing to allow a flatbed into the park to host a scheduled concert.

Shouts of "Pig, pig, fascist pig!" and "Pigs eat shit!" filled the park.

At 10:30 p.m. the police ordered the park vacated. When some protestors refused, heavily armed and angry Chicago police moved in, clubbing them, including several journalists from *Newsweek* and *Life*. It marked only the start of the violence.[41]

On Monday, August 26, the convention opened with Aretha Franklin singing the national anthem at 7:38 p.m. Johnson, at the ranch, retired to the small living room to watch the convention, eating his dinner on a tray while glued to the televisions. All three major channels were on, although he usually only listened to Cronkite while muting the others.

The convention opened with little fanfare. Watson gave an interview to CBS around 10:30. When asked if he "controlled" the convention for Johnson, Watson vehemently denied it. He said he had no knowledge of the president even contacting people. When queried if he had heard rumors of drafting the president, Watson simply responded he did not know if anyone planned anything.[42]

As Watson finished, a major floor fight broke out. It focused on the unit rule that allowed party functionaries, especially powerful people within each state delegation, to decide the votes of the group. Many delegates saw it as undemocratic and allowing the state bosses and powerful politicians to control the process.

In advance, Humphrey wrote a letter to the convention supporting its abolition. He broke a promise to Connally on the matter, angering many southerners as well as others, including Daley, who threatened to pull their support.

Determined foes battled each other on the matter, voices raised and tempers flaring. Connally rose and defiantly announced: "Mr. Chairman, Texas, voting under the unit rule, casts 104 votes no." However, the southerners lost and the convention abolished it.

Then, another battle dear to Johnson and his loyalists broke out. Some delegates challenged Connally's selection of the Texas delegation, arguing it failed to reflect the diversity of the state, especially its absence of African Americans and Mexican-Americans.

A long debate broke out, lasting into the early hours of the morning. In the end, the Connally supporters ultimately won 1,365 to 995.

The Johnsons watched the drama unfold. Lady Bird observed: "The Convention had grown so exciting Monday night that I had stayed up until 3 – I, who love to go to bed early! When some contingents had had the presumption to contest the seating of the Texas delegation, I couldn't possibly go to bed until John Connally had won that fight!"[43]

The president joined the first lady in staying up into the early morning, taking a few breaks to swim and walk around the ranch. He and many others watched the convention finally disperse late in the night as delegates still debated the seating of the Georgia delegation. Finally, at 3 a.m., he headed to bed still harboring dreams of possibly traveling to Chicago the next day.

All summer, he had held onto the possibility of visiting Chicago to give a speech on his sixtieth birthday. His aides, including Harry Middleton and Horace Busby, worked hard on it, as Califano noted, "none anticipated a triumphant appearance more than Lyndon Johnson."[44] The president insisted on secrecy and by August 25th, a draft arrived at the ranch. For two days, he edited it in preparation for a triumphal trip to Chicago.

In the speech, LBJ underscored: "For many millions of our citizens, life is better now because of the promises that the Democratic Party made four years ago." He concluded with a flourish: "And I pledge to you that so long as I have a breath in my body, I shall use it to encourage my country in its pilgrimage toward a freer, braver, more responsible and united America."[45]

It was an inspiring discourse that likely would have stirred many delegates and the millions watching on television. However, he never delivered it as Califano acknowledged the "1968 Democratic National Convention" became "Lyndon Johnson's political crown of thorns."[46]

Even so, those around him watched with great interest as he continued holding onto a dream of possibly being drafted. Christian said that Johnson was "fantasizing that the convention would be such a mess that he would go in and be acclaimed as the nominee."[47]

Califano emphasized: "It became apparent to Temple at the ranch and me back at the West Wing of the White House that LBJ hoped, and probably anticipated, that the convention delegates in Chicago would offer to draft him to be their party's candidate, a draft he intended to turn down but one that would validate his presidency in the eyes of fellow Democrats."[48]

However, by the end of the first day, some saw the handwriting on the wall. "When the Convention virtually erupted on Monday [over the unit rule], the likelihood of our making the trip seemed to me to dwindle to almost nothing," Lady Bird concluded.[49]

The next morning, a warm muggy August day in the Texas Hill Country, she woke and noted: "This whole week has been a sort of suspended-in-space time." She acknowledged that March 31 marked the irrevocable end of the run, "but there was a special saying good-by this week to our whole political life" unfolding in Chicago.

"The Convention would be choosing from among others, and for us it was really over – no matter that it was over by choice," she noted.[50]

She added, "And so on Lyndon's sixtieth birthday I woke to a sense of void and yet excitement. I called Mrs. Dick Daley to thank her for her invitation to a luncheon and to say that we had no plans to be there."[51]

The president woke after only a few hours of sleep and stayed in his pajamas while making and taking phone calls. Temple and Jones popped in as well as Lady Bird, Luci, and Lyn to wish him a happy birthday. Most of the time, he focused on the television commentators reporting from Chicago, still debating whether to go or not.

In the late morning, Dirksen called to talk primarily about the Paris peace talks. He asked the president: "Are you any closer to going out there to that convention?"

LBJ answered: "No, no. I haven't made any plans to go and rather doubt that I will. I might change my mind, but I have not made any plans to go and I don't know what I can contribute."

He added: "I think they'll have a big knock-down drag-out with the pacifists and the fellows that Hanoi has been working on. But it looks like the vote has been pretty good. They took Kennedy and McCarthy and McGovern, and they wrapped all their doves together, and they couldn't get but 30 votes."[52]

While LBJ monitored things from the ranch, Connally held a private meeting with the southern governors and queried whether they would support a draft of Johnson. They answered unequivocally, no. They understood his unpopularity in the south over civil rights and liberal policies and feared its effect on the party.[53] When combined with Daley wavering and even toying with the idea of supporting Ted Kennedy's run to stop Humphrey, the draft talk died quickly.

Many of the president's closest advisors also saw the danger of his presence. Watson admitted: "Even Cabinet Officers such as myself could leave our hotels only with the greatest difficulty. Clearly, if the President were to appear, it would be like red meat to the demonstrators, giving them a focus that would only intensify their violence." He counseled against attending.[54]

Even so, during the day, Johnson announced: "I would go" to help the presidency and country, but emphasized that there were those who thought he would "hang on to the presidency to the end but it didn't come out that way. I suppose they think I would do the same thing about the convention."[55]

In the early afternoon, Johnson gave a last-minute press conference. He continued to insist: "I am not talking to the convention. I am not sending any emissaries. I don't have anyone reporting to me other than Cronkite."[56]

That was untrue, although he convinced himself to the contrary. Johnson obviously dispatched Watson to serve as his eyes and ears, just like in 1964. Also, he contacted Connally and Daley on a regular basis as evidenced by a steady stream of phone calls.

However, he rationalized he did not interfere by adopting a rather bizarre way of communicating. As Califano noted in the ruse, "instead of phoning Chicago himself, the President would have Temple or Jones place the call while he listened on another line. When LBJ had a question, he would put his hand over the receiver and tell Temple or Jones, 'Ask John Connally' this or that, and Temple or Jones would repeat the question so the President could hear the answer," Califano remembered.[57]

The president was disingenuous, and his elaborate ruse reflected his ability to find ways to avoid the hard truths and mislead the media, and by extension the American people. He lied about his role in Chicago and the efforts he made to influence everything from the composition of the leadership and choice of sites to behind the scenes efforts to shape the platform, particularly relating to Vietnam. Everyone knew Johnson would not surrender control of the party so easily, despite his protests. It further undermined his credibility among the press and those in the party.

After a swim and lunch at the pool with Lady Bird and Congressman J. J. Pickle, the president returned to his bedroom. He made a series of phone calls to Watson, Daley, Christian, and Criswell (a total of eight) between 2:03 p.m. and 4:15 p.m. The plane remained on standby, and the staff wondered if he might still try to go to the convention, either to give his speech or simply enjoy a birthday celebration in his hotel suite complete with fireworks on Lake Michigan.[58]

Finally, at 4:45, Johnson called Humphrey, and reported he would not attend the convention as some speculated. Soon, after, Connally informed the Texas delegation they would support Humphrey. Finally, at 5 p.m., Christian told the press one final time that the president would not go to Chicago.[59]

It was a tough pill to swallow, but he had few options. Connally's report along with those from Watson clearly indicated LBJ had little, if any, support by that time for a Draft Johnson movement. The clashes in the streets and battles over the unit rule fully underscored he had little to offer and, if anything, might provoke a very negative response by the protestors and people in the convention. It was a prudent decision.

It was so different than four years before in Atlantic City, where he received an enthusiastic reception. The last year in particular had severely damaged his reputation, particularly the ongoing war in Vietnam and the riots in America's cities. He had lost so much ground and his inability to legislate and govern the way he did in his first two years stood in marked contrast to only a short time before August 1968.

After making his decision, LBJ announced wanting to fly to Austin to visit Luci. While there, he would let photographers take pictures of him cutting cake and opening presents. Lady Bird stressed: "With all vestige of a possible trip to Chicago ruled out, I began to call some close friends, all of whom were standing by, to come on over and celebrate Lyndon's birthday tonight."[60]

At about 5 p.m., the family boarded the helicopter for the short flight over to Camp Mabry in Austin. The presidential motorcade drove to Luci's house, where miraculously Luci and her friends created according to Lady Bird a "table with a beautiful array of cakes and punch, polished candle sticks, newly shined silver, wedding present china." Soon, a hoard of people including the press arrived even though the first lady noted "the big news was more than a thousand miles away."[61]

As the party unfolded, the president sat on a big sofa. He smiled as Luci brought him a big piece of cake with a single candle on it. LBJ grabbed Lyn and put him in his lap and let him start devouring it, making his grandfather very happy. Crumbs fell everywhere, something their dog Yuki immediately cleaned up.[62]

At one point, the press sang "Happy Birthday." Afterward, he answered a few questions. Lady Bird described the journalists as "rather subdued" and highlighted her husband "talked at length and in mild good humor. But it was all very low-key and, somehow, this added to the sad atmosphere."[63]

They stayed for a couple of hours, even after the press left. Then, the group headed back to Mabry for the return trip to the ranch with the sun still shining in the late August evening.

Once home, LBJ headed off for a drive around the countryside with Tom Johnson and Pickle, stopping to pick up a couple of guests arriving by plane including Supreme Court nominee, Homer Thornberry, and his wife. It was not until nearly 9 p.m., they returned to the main house where a large group waited including Luci, Lynda, Jones, and Temple.

Everyone crammed into the living room to watch the convention. Lady Bird admitted that as people arrived, "we stopped to greet all our good friends and then to turn our faces back to the television – to the wilderness of the scene in Chicago."

She added: "More than twenty of us congregated in the living room and we simply couldn't break it up for dinner," which the staff prepared for the large dining table. "Finally I had Mary put the dinner out on the buffet in the dining room and," she noted, "as we could tear ourselves away, we filed in, filled our plates, rushed back and took our seats and watched the spectacle."[64]

Lady Bird described the scene unfolding as "a three-ring circus! There was a Stop Humphrey movement by McCarthy and McGovern and a Draft Teddy Kennedy movement, with the TV commentators running in a circle from one Kennedy supporter to another, trying to stoke the fires under it. You would have thought there were no delegations to the Convention except those from New York, California, and Wisconsin."

But then Lady Bird noted: "Finally the forces of the South moved in and favorite son delegations began releasing their delegates for Humphrey ... first Texas, then South Carolina, and then Tennessee."[65]

Throughout, the only recognition of Johnson occurred when Anita Bryant sang, "Happy Birthday" to him.

Then, Lady Bird highlighted: "The Convention moved on toward the bitterest fight of all, the crucial Vietnam plank in the platform. And so, in spite of all the hell raised on the floor and in the city, the work of the Convention did go forward."[66]

But, the contest over the Vietnam plank was only beginning. That night, Humphrey's forces tried to bring a quick vote on it just after midnight when some delegates began returning to their hotels.

The antiwar forces organized quickly, demanding an adjournment. Loud shouts of "Stop the War" echoed throughout the cavernous hall. When convention chairman Carl Albert sought a vote, the antiwar delegates protested so vigorously that Daley finally signaled for him to stop it all. Albert surrendered and gaveled the convention into recess for the night.[67]

The desire for a quick victory that avoided the drama of the confrontation with the antiwar delegates during primetime was a last ditch effort to try to limit the damage of a full-scale debate on the matter. The procedure failed and damaged both Johnson and by extension Humphrey, who still smarted from not being able to push through his compromise in the face of LBJ's opposition. The president bore responsibility for the contentious fight started that night that continued into the next day. He put his own needs above those of his vice president and party and doomed the Democrats to a desperate fight on the floor and in the streets as once more Vietnam took center stage in the rancor of 1968.

The president stayed up late into the night. At 2:02 a.m., he called Watson at his hotel room and talked for nearly half an hour. Finally, he went to bed about 2:30 a.m., having hoped that his sixtieth birthday would have been another moment of glory and adulation. Instead, it was a low point in his life and career.

Always the astute observer, Lady Bird wrote in her diary: "Today, Lyndon's sixtieth birthday, was probably as strange and dramatic and, in a way, sad a birthday as any he will ever have."[68]

Another person close to the president, a White House intern, Doris Kearns, admitted that she received a call from the president about that day. She stressed: "He said how horrible he felt, that he couldn't even come on his birthday, they hated him that much. He sounded so low. I thought, 'My God, he's been destroyed by this too.'"[69]

But, Johnson could not escape the pull of the black hole of Vietnam. His obsession with the war, one that appeared to momentarily dissipate on March 31, remained the Achilles ' heel of the administration that refused to compromise, Johnson fearing it might undercut his credibility in the negotiating process that in August looked like it was going nowhere. He just could not let it go and allow his vice president to break even the slightest from his position, helping guarantee anger and resentment toward both men. It was just a plank, some argued, and committed him to nothing. But, he would not even let that go and move forward toward a compromise. The all or nothing of Vietnam continued to plague him and became even more personal as he moved forward with his supporters at the convention.

After the long night and crushing realization of no triumphant trip to Chicago, the president woke up after only a few hours of sleep and jumped on the phone by 7:29 a.m. to talk with Rostow and, a few minutes later, Rusk about Vietnam.

Of course, the forthcoming battle in Chicago on the Vietnam plank loomed large. LBJ took some time in the later morning for a swim with Thornberry and then a short drive around the Hill Country with his good friend. But, for the majority of the morning, he marshalled his forces in Chicago on Vietnam.

After lunch, the president parked himself in front of the televisions in the living room to watch the convention. For hours he watched the drama unfold as the pro-Johnson/Humphrey forces clashed with the antiwar McCarthy/McGovern factions.[70]

Senator Muskie opened by taking to the stage and telling the delegates that there were "real differences" between the Johnson/Humphrey plank and the antiwar ones. However, he stressed, "the dividing line is not the desire for peace or war; the dividing line is limited to means not ends."[71]

Then, Salinger, working for McGovern, rose in support of the antiwar plank.[72] He evoked the memory of RFK, claiming that had he lived, he would have supported the peace proposal. Not long after, Sorenson characterized the Johnson/Humphrey plank as "one which, Richard Nixon or even Barry Goldwater could run with pleasure."[73]

Others piled on. The distinguished, grey haired Albert Gore received a rousing standing ovation from the antiwar delegates when he pointed out the loss of more than 25,000 young men and asked for what? "An erosion of the moral and spiritual base of American leadership, entanglement with the corrupt political clique in Saigon, disillusionment, despair here at home and a disastrous postponement of imperative to improve our social ills."[74]

As the debates continued, loud chants of "Stop the War!" began in the California and New York delegations, spreading throughout the hall. When Boggs took the stage and read a statement from General Creighton Abrams that said the enemy would increase its abilities fivefold if the bombing stopped, the jeers intensified as delegates pushed and shoved each other, screaming obscenities as the images of the mayhem filled television screens.

After three hours, the roll call finally occurred with the Johnson/Humphrey plank winning 1,527 ¾ to 1,041 ¼. At 5 p.m., the spectacle finally ended amid choruses of "We Shall Overcome," as many of the delegates put on black armbands and dispersed for dinner. Any thoughts of Democratic unity after leaving Chicago disappeared that late afternoon.[75]

Immediately, critics arose, including journalist Drew Pearson who stressed: "The most disruptive debate was that over peace in Vietnam. It left wounds that probably not heal, either before or after November. The tragedy is that it didn't have to happen. If LBJ sitting at his ranch in Texas had taken his hands off the reins of the convention it would not have happened at all." "But he did not," he continued, "instead he seemed more interested in vindication for his own Vietnam policy than in the election of Hubert Humphrey."[76]

Those close to the president agreed. Clifford acknowledged Johnson's victory on the Vietnam plank "was a disaster for Humphrey. At the moment when he should have been pulling the party back together to prepare for the battle against Nixon, Humphrey had been bludgeoned into a position that had further split the party and given more evidence of his own weakness."[77]

However, the spectacle of the fight on the convention floor paled in comparison to that unfolding on the lake front, particularly Grant Park, right across from the Hilton Hotel where the candidates and many delegates stayed.

As the evening began, more than 15,000 people gathered for a rally by the National Mobilization Committee. They had permission for the gathering but no march, as many hoped would occur, to the Amphitheater. Organizers handed out flyers to the police that read: "Our argument is not with you ... This nightmare week was arranged by Richard Daley and Lyndon Johnson."[78]

As the crowd gathered, a young shirtless protestor ran toward a flag pole, planning to turn it upside down to signal distress. The police moved in, obviously aggravated by the attack on the national symbol. They tore into the protestors, most having discarded their badges and any other identification amid shouts of "Kill, Kill, Kill." They slung their belly clubs, knocked people to the ground, and hauled away anyone who resisted.[79]

Author Norman Mailer watched from his room in the Hilton. "The police attacked ... like a chain saw cutting into the wood, the teeth of the saw the edge of their clubs, they attacked like a scythe through grass, lines of twenty and thirty policemen striking out in an arc, their clubs beating, demonstrators fleeing. Seen from overhead, from the nineteenth floor, it was like wind blowing dust, or the edge of waves riding foam on the shore."[80]

As journalist Theodore White watched the riot, he scribbled into his notebook: "The Democrats are finished."[81]

Watson also acknowledged LBJ "realized that the television coverage of the convention – with all its violence and anger – had been a disaster for the Democratic Party. Instead of giving the Party and Humphrey a lift, as Party conventions normally do, the net effect was the creation of a mountain of adversity that had to be overcome if victory was to be achieved."[82]

Democrats in the convention hall also watched in horror the mayhem in the streets, the tear gas sometimes choking delegates walking near the battlegrounds. At one point, liberal Connecticut senator Abraham Ribicoff rose to the podium and bellowed: "With George McGovern as president ... we wouldn't have to have Gestapo tactics in the streets of Chicago."[83]

An angry Daley, his fist pumped into the air, fired back: "Fuck you you Jew son of bitch you lousy motherfucker go home."[84]

Ribicoff simply responded: "How hard it is to accept the truth. How hard it is."[85]

As delegates sparred, the nomination process started. Earlier in the day, an attempt to embarrass the president unfolded when a Kennedy loyalist, William vanden Heuvel, threatened to place Johnson's name in nomination to protest the Vietnam plank. He argued Johnson "is the only one who can run on the Vietnam plank they have given us."

In tandem, Goodwin mockingly said: "Why take the dummy when you can get the ventriloquist?"

An infuriated Johnson sent an aide to confront vanden Heuvel. For an hour, he jawboned the New Yorker about insulting the president and his office. Ultimately, he retreated and withheld the nomination.[86]

Johnson had already sent a note to Carl Albert that the congressman read to the delegates. In it, he stressed his decision not to seek another term was "irrevocable ... I ask therefore that my name not be considered by the Convention." He added: "During the remaining months of my terms as President, and then for the rest of my life, I shall continue my efforts to reach and secure those enduring goals that have made America great – peace abroad and justice and opportunity at home."[87]

As many Americans went to bed in the late evening, the process progressed as LBJ and millions of others watched the count for Humphrey increase. While some votes rolled in for McGovern and McCarthy, the vast majority went to the vice president. By 11 p.m. he had enough to win after delegates from Pennsylvania announced their votes. He celebrated by jumping up and running around the room, taking time to kiss the television showing his wife. However, in this moment of triumph, just outside his hotel the raging battle continued in the streets of Chicago. It was a bittersweet victory.[88]

Not long afterward, at 11:50 p.m., Johnson called and congratulated him. He had watched it all on television in the living room with Lady Bird, Luci, Lynda, and his aides, Temple, Johnson, and Jones. He was happy for the victory for the Vietnam plank and seemingly validated by Humphrey's selection. However, everything else underscored his world coming apart at the seams. It had been a long and sad day for him and the Democratic Party.

The following morning, he slept late before beginning a flurry of phone calls, first to Boggs, Criswell, North Carolina Governor Terry Sanford, and Watson in Chicago. He also made a number to Attorney General Clark to discuss the violence in Chicago. Even though he was not there, Johnson managed to have a significant presence.

There were also four phone calls in a matter of hours to Humphrey at his suite in the Hilton Hotel.

For weeks, Johnson had paid close attention to the vice presidential process. At one point, Watson "outlined to Humphrey the names of the President's suggestions for Vice President: Governors John Connally, Robert McNair, and Buford Ellington." He admitted the president "did not insist" on anyone, but wanted "a Humphrey running mate who would shore up Humphrey and prevent him from wandering from his commitment to support the programs of the President, including especially Vietnam."[89]

Watson remembered LBJ had accepted Humphrey's choice of Muskie, especially after the Maine senator gave an impassioned speech in defense of the administration's Vietnam policy. While Johnson thought Muskie brought little to the ticket, he knew Humphrey genuinely liked and respected him.

While making a flurry of calls during the day, LBJ took some time for a lunch with the family and staff before taking a ride around the countryside with Luci and finally a long nap. He awoke and called Muskie and then Daley before taking another drive over to the Danz Ranch.[90]

Figure 8 Johnson and his family join him in the bedroom to watch the Democratic National Convention on television on August 28. (Courtesy of the LBJ Library)

Finally, just after 8:30 p.m., he sat down once more with dinner trays in the living room to watch the last night of the convention. There were chants of "We Want Daley" as his partisans packed the gallery with signs, "We Love Mayor Daley," trying to erase some of the bad publicity from the night before in Grant Park.[91]

Early in the evening, the convention went quiet as the delegates watched the memorial film put together for Robert Kennedy. As it ended, people began singing loudly, "The Battle Hymn of the Republic," which continued for a while even as the chairman Albert tried gaveling a call to order. When Daley's people tried drowning out the singing with "We Love Daley," the other side began chanting, "We want Teddy!"[92]

Finally, nearly two hours late, Humphrey rose to give his acceptance speech. He opened by acknowledging the "deep sadness that we feel over the troubles and the violence which have erupted, regrettably and tragically, in the streets of this great city." He quoted St. Francis of Assisi. "Where there is hatred, let me know love. Where there is injury, pardon ... Where there is despair, hope. Where there is darkness, light."

He also praised abolishing the unit rule "in the proud tradition of Franklin Roosevelt, and Harry Truman and Adlai Stevenson and John F. Kennedy." Cheers followed the naming of each man.

Then, Humphrey courageously added "and Lyndon Johnson." Daley's supporters and southerners cheered while a chorus of boos rained down from the antiwar delegates.

Sitting in the hall, William White wrote: "It was the first time in this correspondent's attention that the name of Lyndon Johnson, sitting President and chieftain of his party had been mentioned since John Bailey had dropped the name on opening night."

Humphrey, loyal to the end, continued amid more boos: "I truly believe that history will surely record the greatness of his contribution to the people of this land, and tonight to you, Mr. President, I say thank you. Thank you, Mr. President."[93]

He went on and discussed Vietnam and made the closest thing to a break with the president: "If there is any one lesson that we should have learned, it is that the policies of tomorrow need not be limited by the policies." He promised if elected, "I shall apply that lesson to search for peace in Vietnam as well as to all other areas of national policy."[94]

Then, he focused on peace at home along with party and national unity, ultimately concluding: "Believe in what America can do, and believe in what America can be, and ... with the help of that vast, unfrightened, dedicated, faithful majority of Americans, I say to this great convention tonight, and to this great nation of ours, I am ready to lead our country."[95]

Balloons and confetti fell from overhead as many delegates tried putting on a good face for the national audience, but Humphrey's words failed to ameliorate the divisions in his party and the country.

Thus concluded what Luci described, with reference to the week, as "the longest wake I ever attended."[96]

Afterward, LBJ acknowledged the disaster in Chicago. He wrote: "Fighting between police and students at the Democratic National Convention in Chicago proved to every television viewer in America how deep the cleavage was in our society, how intense the hatreds, and how wide the gulf between law enforcers and those who had nothing but contempt for the law. These conflicts also exposed the ugly side of the so-called New Politics, in spite of its claims of idealism."[97]

Humphrey also recognized the damage, lamenting: "After Chicago, I was like the victim of a hurricane, having to pick up and rebuild but with too little time to do the job."[98]

Chicago had been a disaster of epic proportions for everyone involved, including LBJ. His hope for a triumphant visit to the convention collapsed along with most chances of the Democrats retaining the White House. However, he played a large role in the dysfunction of the convention. His refusal to surrender control to Humphrey and his people doomed the process from the start, as it might have unfolded differently in a more isolated location, far away from Daley's authoritarian rule in the amphitheater and the streets. The leadership of the convention if led by someone like Muskie would have likely been more moderate and less concerned about sustaining Johnson's legacy and more focused on a Humphrey victory.

But, the problem that continued to ravage the Democratic Party remained Johnson's obsession with Vietnam. Humphrey worked hard to fashion a compromise plank that gave the McCarthy and Kennedy people the feeling of being heard, limiting the rancor at least inside the convention. But, Johnson would not let Humphrey have the victory for fear of it hurting his peace agenda that appeared to be going nowhere in August. His pettiness in undercutting Humphrey on Vietnam, as well as other slights, clearly showed a darker side of the president. It was clearly on display in the days before, during, and after the convention in Chicago.

Thus, the nightmare year continued its pattern of trying the souls of Johnson and everyone around the president. The battles in Chicago became a symbol of the type of year unfolding and reflected how he created it. However, the turmoil was far from over as a presidential election in November loomed large, and Richard Nixon appeared the largest winner of the Democrat's dysfunction in the Windy City.

CHAPTER 10

Is This Treason?

The October Surprise that Wasn't, October–November 1968

A busy day on October 28 turned into a long night for the president. While most of Washington slept, a flurry of activity enveloped the White House in the early morning of the 29th, all avoiding the probing eyes of the press.

At 2:30 a.m., a small group of national security advisers including Dean Rusk, Clark Clifford, and Richard Helms gathered in the Cabinet Room. General Creighton Abrams, commander of US forces in Vietnam, awaited them. Johnson entered and greeted him, thanking him for secretly flying to the capitol from Saigon.

LBJ opened by discussing the three requirements for the long-anticipated bombing halt, including NVA respect for the DMZ, no attacks on southern cities, and talks incorporating the South Vietnamese Government (SVG).

For three hours, the group weighed the pros and cons of a bombing halt, most agreeing that the weather limited its effectiveness anyway and why not give Hanoi a chance to fulfill its promises to talk if the aerial bombardment of the north ended.

Finally, Johnson pointedly asked General Abrams if he had any reluctance in stopping the bombing above the 19th Parallel. Abrams answered unequivocally: "No, Sir."[1]

Convinced, the president agreed to the bombing halt that he hoped would spark the long-awaited peace process that had started in Paris in May. He admitted enjoying not seeking reelection, stressing: "Tough to be a candidate and peace seeker at the same time."[2]

The group took a break and then reconvened around 6:20 a.m. Quickly, Rusk reported that President Nguyen Van Thieu could not get a delegation to Paris within the three days mandated. Johnson responded: "Looks like a delay. May be something to report that Nixon is trying to handle this like another Fortas affair. That's the old Nixon. He may be jittery."

Rostow handed a memo to LBJ from his brother Eugene, who reported receiving a call from a New York friend who had lunch with several close associates of Nixon. "One of them explained" that Nixon "was trying to frustrate the president, by inciting Saigon to step up its demands," he underscored.[3]

His source was prominent banker Alexander Sachs. So, Rostow asked his brother to "go back" and "see how much further detail he can get on the people involved and how close, in fact, they are to Nixon." Soon, Eugene produced another memo from that conversation that his brother delivered to the president.

LBJ faced another crisis, one of many during 1968. This one, however, remained out of the public spotlight, although its potential ramifications remained high as the election approached. Once more, he went into crisis mode, remaining cautious and considering all the political consequences of his actions. But, he also remained angry that anyone would endanger his last chance at redemption on Vietnam. It would be a very long few weeks in the White House.

Johnson gathered Jim Jones, Harry McPherson, George Christian, and Tom Johnson in the sitting room and showed them the original report. He told them to have all the candidates ready for a conference call at 5 p.m.

"Have a phone they can cram right up their butts," he snarled.[4]

They moved to the Cabinet Room and joined the national security team. LBJ read Eugene's second memo from his source who "thought the prospects for a bombing halt or a cease-fire were dim because Nixon was playing the problem as he did the Fortas affair – to block ... They would incite Saigon to be difficult, and Hanoi to wait."

He added that Nixon's strategy relied on "an expectation [that] an offensive would break out soon, that we would have to spend a great deal more (and incur more casualties) ... These difficulties would make it easier for Nixon to settle after January. Like Ike in 1953, he would be able to settle on terms which the President could not accept, blaming the deterioration of the situation between now and January or February on his predecessor."

In response, Johnson instructed US Ambassador to Vietnam Ellsworth Bunker to tell Thieu, "we realize political forces are saying things to him and to Hanoi, but we are going to act in the best interests of South Vietnam," and he wanted Bunker to report "we have these intercepts from the political forces here." Then, the president emphasized: "The question is whether we go with him or without him. And tell him also that we are responsible for the conduct of the government until January 20th."[5]

Again, Vietnam took center stage in the life of Lyndon Johnson, even into the last days of his presidency. For months, he agonized over getting the peace process moving in Paris. For the most part, he fulfilled his promise from March 31 to devote himself to the matter. In July, he flew to Honolulu to personally pressure Thieu into supporting his efforts, although the South Vietnamese complained about incorporating the NLF into the process. But, now he had forward movement that looked like it might push negotiations and give him one last opportunity to cement a peace process and possibly suppress some of the horrible legacy of Vietnam. However, people in the United States and South Vietnam had other plans.

While the early morning meetings on the 29th exposed that the Nixon campaign was undermining the peace process, the Republican nominee's people had conspired for months to prevent an October surprise that would aid Humphrey.

The primary provocateur was Anna Chennault.[6] The Chinese-born widow of the famed Flying Tiger leader, Claire Chennault, used her husband's connections and money to become a power player in the Republican Party. Gregarious and sophisticated, Chennault became a regular attendee at major party events and raised hundreds of thousands of dollars for GOP candidates. She traveled extensively in Asia and had many connections with virulently anti-Communist groups, including those in South Vietnam.

As early as July 3, 1968, Dick Allen of the Nixon campaign reported Chennault asking for a meeting. He stressed it should be an "absolute top secret" and "this would be a good opportunity to get filled in on events in Paris and other developments." Nixon wrote: "Should be but I don't see how – with the S.S. [Secret Service] if it can be [secret] RN would like to see – if not – could Allen see for RN?"[7]

Nevertheless, a week and a half later, Nixon met with Chennault and the South Vietnamese Ambassador to the United States, Bui Diem, at his Park Avenue apartment. She introduced Diem to the presumptive Republican nominee as well as his close advisor, John Mitchell. She wrote that Nixon told Diem: "Anna is my good friend. She knows all about Asia. I know you also consider her a friend, so please rely on her from now on as the only contact between myself and your government." He also reportedly said that if he won, he would ensure "Vietnam gets better treatment from me than under the Democrats."

Diem remembered that as he left, Nixon said "his staff would be in touch with me through John Mitchell and Anna Chennault." He added: "In the rush of flying back and forth between Paris and Washington, with side trips to Saigon . . . I soon forgot the Nixon meeting. Within a couple of months, though, it would come back to haunt me."[8]

A month later, Chennault headed to Saigon and met Thieu. She wrote about "delivering a message from Nixon requesting that I be recognized as the conduit for any information that might flow between the two." Once home, she reported to Mitchell and Nixon that Saigon "remained intransigent" regarding "attitudes vis-à-vis the peace talks."[9]

Her efforts and those of others had an effect. In late August, the SVG Minister of the Economy, Au Ngoc Ho, said: "I think Nixon finally has the presidency in the bag this time and I think that means not much change in the course of the war."[10]

With Chennault spearheading efforts to reassure the South Vietnamese that Nixon provided their best ally, Johnson moved forward on another front. In August 1968, the president addressed the VFW national convention, where he declared: "I want peace in Viet-Nam. I want it perhaps more than any single living American individual. But the pursuit of peace in this Administration is going to be governed by America's abiding interests as we see them."[11]

Afterward, he renewed efforts to push the enemy to the bargaining table. He continued prodding the South Vietnamese to participate in negotiations and a North Vietnamese promise to respect the DMZ.

Hanoi countered by demanding a bombing halt without preconditions. However, by October 11th, the North Vietnamese (under pressure from Moscow) promised to consider the US proposal if the bombing stopped.[12]

With some positive momentum developing, people in the Nixon camp began worrying that the peace initiative would aid Humphrey, especially since the polls showed the race tightening in mid-October.

This led Nixon to instruct Haldeman on October 22 to "keep Chennault working on SVN – insist positively on the 3 Johnson conditions." The aide noted Nixon asking: "Any other way to monkey wrench it? Anything RN can do." Finally, he told Haldeman to get his personal secretary, Rose Mary Woods, to contact the prominent Chinese business-man, Louis Kung, to tell Thieu to "hold firm."[13]

In response, Chennault and others intensified lobbying the Thieu government. On October 23, NSC officials intercepted a cable from Diem to Thieu: "Many Republican friends have contacted me and encouraged us to stand firm. They were alarmed by press reports to the effect that you have already softened your position."[14]

While Nixon publicly praised the president for his efforts at a "just peace in Vietnam," privately he worried about his election prospects.[15] With first-hand knowledge of events transpiring in the White House through an undisclosed "double agent" as well as Henry Kissinger, who worked as an informant, the Nixon people pushed harder to undermine the Paris talks.[16]

In response, on October 25, Nixon released a statement. He disin-genuously praised Johnson for resisting the impulse to create a "fake peace" and swore "not to play politics with this war." "I am also told that this spurt of activity is a cynical, last minute attempt by President Johnson to salvage the candidacy of Mr. Humphrey. This I do not believe," he said.[17]

Such statements infuriated the president, who still maintained a healthy disdain for Nixon, one dating back to his vicious attacks on Helen Gahagan Douglas during the 1950 California Senate campaign. While they shared humble roots, Johnson believed that Nixon lacked character and was overly partisan and reckless.

But, LBJ also liked Nixon's position on Vietnam that paralleled his own, much more so than many Democrats. He clearly believed the

Republican nominee would less likely cut and run in Vietnam. Nonetheless, Johnson recognized Nixon would manipulate every political issue possible for his personal gain, especially at this late date when polls showed Humphrey quickly closing the gap. This set the stage for tensions between the two strong-willed men.

A day later, Nixon called CBS evening radio and argued a coalition government in South Vietnam was a "thinly disguised surrender ... Far from ending the war, it would only insure it resumption under conditions that would guarantee Communist victory."[18]

He wrote about taking the offensive: "The only way to prevent Johnson from totally undercutting my candidacy at the eleventh hour was for me to make public the fact that a bombing halt was imminent." He said, "I wanted to plant the impression ... that his motive and his timing" were political.[19]

In response to Nixon's statements, LBJ characterized him as shallow and deceitful as often portrayed. He called Nixon's statements "ugly and unfair charges" by a man "who distorts the history of his time."

With Johnson and Nixon feuding, the White House sought a direct link between Nixon and the conspirators undermining the peace process. However, it proved elusive, although clearly Chennault and other prominent members of the campaign worked against Johnson.

A major issue inside the White House remained how to frame the Nixon campaign's actions. Some in the administration characterized it as treason. But, that was a very serious charge that required proof of collusion with an enemy.

Others examined different avenues. In 1967, Assistant Attorney General Nicholas Katzenbach discussed applying the Logan Act of 1799 to African American activist Stokley Carmichael that prohibited individual citizens from negotiating with foreign governments in conflict with the United States after he traveled to Havana and Hanoi. But, Katzenbach acknowledged it had not been applied in more than 150 years.[20]

However, some in the president's cabinet, including Clifford and several Pentagon advisors, discussed applying the Logan Act against the Nixon people.[21] But, that was as far as it went. The main actors, including Johnson, never seriously considered its application. The fact was the crisis unfolded so quickly and applying the Logan Act appeared an unlikely alternative and made the challenges of how to go forward more apparent, although a well-placed leak or direct statement by the president on the matter remained alternatives.

As the election neared, the Nixon campaign used multiple channels to undermine the peace process beyond Ambassador Diem. Nguyen Tien Hung, a close advisor to Thieu, stressed that the South Vietnamese president remained leery of Diem, who remained loyal to Vice President Nguyen Cao Ky. Thus, he reported: "Thieu sent his own messengers to Washington to contact Mrs. Chennault, and he relied heavily on his brother Nguyen Van Kieu, who was South Vietnamese Ambassador to Taiwan. Mrs. Chennault often sent messages to Thieu through aides of his brother."[22]

It was clear that Thieu needed little persuading to delay the peace process. He recognized that Nixon would likely win, and with assurances of a better deal from the Republicans, Thieu had little incentive to support the lame duck president. Less than three months before leaving office, Johnson had little leverage, reflecting the diminution of power over the past nine months since announcing his plan not to seek reelection. However, the fact that the Nixon campaign interfered in the process angered him and showed the extent that it would go to win.

Despite the interference, on October 27, the North Vietnamese agreed to start peace talks on November 6. Special envoy Cyrus Vance telephoned the State Department from Paris: "We've got everything we asked for."[23]

Finally, it appeared that a major breakthrough was on the horizon, one that would help Johnson partially wipe away the stain of Vietnam. Furthermore, it might help Humphrey and his beloved Democratic Party in the November elections. People within the White House were more optimistic than ever about the potential for a peace process that sustained their vision of an independent South Vietnam, but extracted the United States directly from the quagmire.

But the interference by the Nixon people continued. That same day, an intercepted cable from Diem to Thieu read: "The longer the present situation continues, the more we are favored ... I am regularly in touch with the Nixon entourage," which included Chennault, Mitchell, and Senator John Tower.[24]

Diem also told Thieu that he "explained discreetly to our partisan friends our firm attitude" and "plan to adhere that position," which could make it hard for Johnson "in forcing our hand." Another cable showed Diem "had been informed that if Nixon were elected he would first send an unofficial emissary to Thieu and would consider going to Saigon himself prior to Inauguration."[25]

By this time, the president had the information provided by Eugene Rostow. On the 29th, Johnson ordered an FBI wiretap on the SVG Embassy in Washington. He soon requested round the clock surveillance on Madame Chennault. Walt Rostow became the primary person transferring information to the president through almost daily briefings.

On October 30th, FBI Deputy Director Cartha "Deke" DeLoach sent over a memo on Diem receiving a call from an unidentified woman that he obviously knew ("the FBI believes this woman to be possibly Mrs. Anna Chennault"). She apologized for not talking to the ambassador the day before at a party, but worried about too many people being around. She asked about the situation and Diem "responded that 'just among us' he could not go into specifics on the telephone but something 'is cooking.'" The ambassador invited her over to "talk with him as time is running short." She agreed to do so after lunch with Mrs. Spiro Agnew.[26]

Later that day, Chennault visited the South Vietnamese Embassy for over an hour and returned the following day for another thirty minutes.[27]

Inside the White House, Johnson and his staffers monitored her movements and those of other Nixon operatives. Califano wrote: "Johnson now suspected that Nixon had acted on Chennault's advice and treasonably, to his thinking, subverted his own government in order to win the election." Jones remembered when Johnson learned about Chennault's activities, he affirmed: "This is treason!"[28]

With the peace process moving forward while the Nixon campaign tried to undermine it, Johnson planned a national address to announce the bombing halt and progress in Paris. Beforehand, he decided to speak with Humphrey, Wallace, and Nixon at 6:05 p.m. on the 31st.

With his national security team listening, he reported on Hanoi's agreement to meet his demands. Then, he delivered a strong message to Nixon, who had close ties dating back years to a group characterized as the China Lobby. It maintained close ties to Chiang Kai-Shek on Taiwan after the Communists drove him from the mainland in 1949. They had worked tirelessly to promote his government as the legitimate one of China, supported military defense of the island, and battled efforts to normalize relations with Peking.

During the conversation, Johnson complained: "Some of our folks are, even including some of the old China lobbyists, they are going around and implying to some of the embassies and some of the others that they might get a better deal out of somebody that was not involved in this. Now, that's made it difficult and it's held up things a little bit. And I know that none of you candidates are aware of it or responsible for it."[29]

As the president obliquely chastised Nixon and the China Lobby, McPherson observed: "He looked around the room at us with a wicked grin."[30]

Johnson knew that Nixon and his aides, especially those with close ties to the China Lobby, would undermine any negotiations with the Communists. They argued that the duplicitous Communists often won the peace. Nonetheless, he hoped the phone call might put Nixon on notice and also allow Humphrey to use the information to call out the underhanded tactics of the GOP nominee.

After the conversation ended, almost immediately, Humphrey phoned back. In the discussion, Johnson highlighted having Thieu on board, but "in the meantime, Nixon's folks – I don't know whether he had anything to do with it or not; don't charge that he does, I can't prove it – but some people supporting him told Hanoi that they could – that he has no connection with this war, wasn't involved, that he could be more reasonable, didn't have any commitments, than anybody fighting them for about 5 years."

Conversely, LBJ stressed: "Then on the other side of the track, they told the South Vietnamese if they don't sell out – let Johnson sell them out here at the conference table and bring into it the NLF – Humphrey is going to get beat, and they will have a bright future. So they have been holding for two weeks."[31]

The revelation about the Nixon campaign's interference was no surprise to Humphrey. As early as September 27 an aide told him that

NSA intercepts showed SVG concerns over the peace process and Chennault's role in stoking fears.[32]

William Bundy visited Humphrey to explain what the White House knew about the phone taps and intercepts. Afterward, Humphrey met with several advisors including his press secretary Norman Sherman who wanted to expose Nixon. Humphrey responded that they lacked evidence and "it would have been very difficult to explain how we knew about what she [Chennault] had done."

In the last stages of the campaign, Humphrey would issue a mild rebuke of Thieu, but he passed on the chance to throw the charges at Nixon. His aide Ted Van Dyk stressed: "Ninety-nine out of a hundred men with the Presidency at stake would have had no inhibitions – they would have demagogued it."

Others agreed, including journalist Theodore White, who emphasized: "I know of no more essentially decent story in American politics than Humphrey's refusal to [exploit it]; his instinct was that Richard Nixon, personally, had no knowledge of Mrs. Chennault's activities; had not hand in them; and would have forbidden them had he known."

On the flip side, Humphrey emphasized about Johnson's knowledge: "The President will do nothing about it."[33]

While Humphrey and Johnson wrestled with the information over the last few days of the campaign, on the evening of the 31st, the president announced the bombing cessation and also the start of a four-party plenary session in Paris on November 6.

In the televised speech, he highlighted the process and how it unfolded. He included a veiled threat to Nixon and his people, something not apparent to outsiders. "In this critical hour, we just simply cannot afford more than one voice speaking for the nation in the search of peace," he stressed near the end.[34]

With only a few days left before the American people went to the polls, Johnson had the chance to report the interference by the Nixon campaign. Once more, he wavered because he feared revealing sources and being accused of partisanship. Also, the president believed it was likely that Nixon would win and such charges, especially if proven true, would create a constitutional crisis and damage the office of the presidency. Nonetheless, he could have been more forceful, along with

Humphrey, and likely changed the outcome of the election. Ironically, his greatest fear of undermining the presidency occurred only a few years later with Watergate, where once again Nixon's dirty tricks arose, ultimately leading to his downfall.

While optimistic about the peace initiative, the White House continued monitoring Chennault. On November 1, Rostow forwarded reports on her activities. "Herewith the Lady tries again but got something of a brush off, yesterday afternoon. Also, attached is a significant intelligence report from today's *Washington Post's* society section."[35]

In a telephone conversation that day with his friend Jim Rowe in the Humphrey campaign, LBJ complained: "Nixon ... is in deep telling Thieu ... and all of them not to go along with me on anything because said here that he wouldn't pay a damn bit of attention to them, and so what they better do is wait for him and he'll never sell them out, that he'll stay with them. Hell, he didn't think we ought to have sold out China."

The president groused: "Because he (Thieu) thinks that we will sell him out, and Nixon has convinced him, and this damn little old woman, Mrs. Chennault, she's been in on it."

Rowe simply replied, "I wouldn't doubt it."[36]

The frustrations with Thieu's foot-dragging infuriated the president. The strong-willed and shrewd Vietnamese politician hardly needed convincing that the hardline Republicans would give him a better deal. He proclaimed his government would not become a "car that can be hitched to a locomotive and taken anywhere the locomotive wants to go." He saw the Johnson proposal as a "clear admission of defeat."[37]

With Thieu exerting his independence despite heavy pressure from Ambassador Bunker, more intercepted messages fueled anger within the White House. On November 2, Chennault contacted Diem and gave a message "which her boss (unidentified) wanted her to give personally to the ambassador. She said the message was that the ambassador is to 'hold on, we are gonna win' and that her boss also said, 'hold on, he understands all of it.'" She said he "had just called from New Mexico," where Spiro Agnew spoke that day.

There were some within the administration who thought the American public should know about the interference. On November 2, Rusk told Jones that the press should be given a background briefing on the

China Lobby's interference to explain the uncertainty of the South Vietnamese going to Paris, although he stopped short of naming members of the Nixon entourage.

Others sounded off as Rostow asked LBJ to invite senators Everett Dirksen and Mike Mansfield to review the evidence of the Nixon campaign's machinations. Then, he wanted the White House to go to Nixon and say that if the activities continued, officials would release information that would "destroy him and any effectiveness he would have if he's elected." Rostow wanted to remind Nixon: "His first duty is to tell Saigon to get their delegation to Paris as fast as possible."[38]

Some of Johnson's inner circle also sought to contain the damage being done by Nixon's operatives without going public. Clifford encouraged Johnson to call Dirksen, so on November 2nd, he took the advice and phoned him.

LBJ opened: "We're skirting on dangerous ground, and I thought I ought to give you the facts and you ought to pass them on if you choose. If you don't then I will a little later."

He talked about the bombing halt and having Thieu on board weeks earlier. "Then we got some of our friends involved, some of it your old China crowd, and here's the latest information we got. The [FBI] agent says that she's – they've just talked to the 'boss' in New Mexico, and he says that 'you must hold out' – just hold on until after the election. Now, we know what Thieu is saying to them out there. We're pretty well-informed on both ends."

Then Johnson stressed the Nixon people should stop interfering. "Now, I'm reading their hand Everett. I don't want this to get in the campaign. And they oughtn't to be doing this. This is treason," the president underscored.

However, he offered an escape route. "Now I can identify them because I know who's doing this. I don't want to identify it. I think it would shock America if a principal candidate was playing with a source like this on a matter this important. I don't want to do that."

But, Johnson added, "And my judgment is that Nixon ought to play it just like he has all along, that I want to see peace come the first we can, that it's not going to affect the election one way or the other . . . Now, if Nixon keeps the South Vietnamese away from the conference, well, that's going to be his responsibility. Up to this point, that's why they're not there."[39] He concluded: "Well, now, what do you think we ought to do about it?"

"Well, I better get in touch with him, I think, and tell him about it," Dirksen responded.

Johnson noted: "I know this – that they're contacting a foreign power in the middle of a war."

Dirksen replied: "That's a mistake."

Johnson continued, "and it's a damn bad mistake. Now I don't want to say so, and you're the only man I have confidence in to tell them. But you better tell them they better quit playing with it."

Then, he hammered home his point: "Well, you just tell them their people are messing around in this thing, and if they don't want it on the front pages, they better quit it."[40]

Johnson's conversation with Dirksen highlighted what he wanted from the Nixon campaign. He sought to end their interference while not outing his sources or possibly creating a direct confrontation that led to post-election fallout. It gave the Nixon people a chance to retreat and possibly help the process, but it hurt Humphrey who supported the peace process and would have continued Johnson's efforts. It was a tactic that some in the White House questioned, some believing a simple leak of the information might have tightened the presidential election.

Not long after the two men completed their conversation, Dirksen called Nixon. Bryce Harlow, a Nixon campaign staffer, answered. The senator talked about Johnson wanting to know if Nixon or "his troops" were telling the South Vietnamese "not to go along."

Alarmed, Harlow "skinned upstairs" in the Century Plaza Hotel in Los Angeles and found aide John Haldeman standing guard over Nixon's door.

"I've got to talk to the boss," he said.

Haldeman responded: "He's in bed and he's asleep. You can't talk to him."

"Oh, yes I can, and I'm a gonna. I've got to talk to the boss. You'll have to get him up."

They went back and forth, but ultimately, Harlow won.

After waking Nixon, he told him: "You've got to talk to LBJ. Someone has told him that you're dumping all over the South Vietnamese to keep them from doing something about peace and he's just about to believe it. If you don't let him know quickly that it's not so, then he's going to dump . . . He tells Ev Dirksen and Ev called me." Harlow pleaded: "You've got to do it."[41]

Now began a song and dance between Johnson and Nixon as the election neared. To try to counter the threat, Nixon employed several people, including Senator George Smathers (D-FL). He reached out to Johnson in the early afternoon on November 3rd and told the president that Nixon feared: "You were getting ready to charge him with the accusation that he connived with John Tower and Anna Chennault to bring about the action of the Saigon government not participating." Smathers said Nixon insisted "this was first not supported by the truth, and secondly, unfair, and thirdly, unfortunate."

Instead, Nixon offered the president "his full cooperation, and he would offer to go to any place that you might want him to go" to end the impasse over Paris.

Johnson responded: "The problem is not his traveling anywhere. The problem is the people on both sides of the fence getting the impression that they can get a little more for the house if they'll wait a week to sell it."

Johnson told Smathers he had proof of the plot and "started personally watching the traffic" with intercepted telegrams that told the SVG "that Nixon is going to win; therefore, they ought to wait on Nixon. So what's he doing – my judgment is – he was – on the surface he was playing that he didn't want to undercut me. Under the table, his people – and this I think you can tell him for sure, there's no doubt about it."

Johnson outlined, "all he got to do is just go back through the same sources and tell them, 'You go on, I'm gonna support the President, and you better get to the damn conference, because these people are not going to support you if you refuse to even go talk when you've got a chance to.'"

Smathers tried defending Nixon. "You seem to think . . . that Tower and Chennault have made these contacts. But he [Nixon] said he doesn't know whether they have or they haven't. He doesn't think that they have."[42]

"Well, you tell him . . . He's got to keep his Finches and his Lairds (referring to Nixon campaign staffers) and his Chennaults and the rest of them from running around and messing up the broth. And it's messed up – there's no question about that," Johnson answered emphatically.

Smathers replied: "I'll pass this word back to him, that goddamnit, you had it set and that someone – his people – are screwing it up."[43]

Knowing that LBJ could drop a huge bomb three days before the election, Nixon personally appealed to Johnson in the early afternoon of the 3rd. Nixon called and opened: "I just wanted you to know that I feel very, very strongly about this, and any rumblings around about somebody trying to sabotage the Saigon government's attitude certainly – certainly have no – absolutely no credibility, as far as I am concerned."

Johnson replied "That's – I'm very happy to hear that, Dick, because that is taking place."

Nixon tried to interject, "No, I –."

Cutting him off, Johnson said: "Now here is the history of it. I didn't want to call you, but I wanted you – "

Nixon returned the favor: "That China Lobby is something – "

Not to be outdone, the president interrupted: "I wanted you to know what happened. The UPI ran a story quoting, I guess it was [Robert] Finch, [who] said 'a highly placed aide to Nixon today said the South Vietnamese decision to boycott the Paris talks did not jibe with the assurances given the major Presidential candidates by Johnson.'"[44]

Johnson was already angry that Finch had told reporters that South Vietnam refused to join the Paris talks in response to "evidence that Mr. Johnson had ordered the bombing pause unilaterally and hastily to further the Humphrey candidacy."[45]

The president continued laying out a chronology including Thieu's promises.

"Then the traffic goes out that Nixon will do better by you. Now that goes to Thieu. I didn't say, as I said to you the other day, I didn't say that it was with your knowledge. I hope it wasn't," LBJ emphasized.

Nervously laughing, Nixon lied and told Johnson: "As a matter of fact, I'm not privy to what you were doing of course."

Then, he deflected by stressing: "And, of course, there is some thought that Hanoi would rather deal now than deal later."[46]

He tried to reassure the president: "Good God, we want them over in Paris. We've got to get them to Paris, or you can't have peace."

Johnson countered: "Well, I think that [if] you take that position, you're on very, very sound ground."

The president further outlined the chronological narrative and focused on the October 31 conference call, where he highlighted again "some of our folks, including some of the old China Lobby are going around and implying to some of the folks that they might get a better deal out of somebody that was not involved in this. Now that's made it difficult on me, and it's slowed things down some."

Nixon declared: "I just want you to know that I'm not trying to interfere with your conduct of it. I'll only do what you and Rusk want me to do. But I'll do anything."

Johnson simply responded: "Well, that's good, Dick. "

After talking some more about Finch's statement, Johnson once more reminded the Republican nominee: "You just see that your people don't tell the South Vietnamese that they are going to get any better deal out of the U.S. Government than a conference."

Immediately, Nixon fired back: "Yeah, and also, we've got to make sure that Hanoi knows they're not going to get a better deal."

As the conversation wound down, Nixon could not help himself in trying to make a point. "You understand, of course, that this business – some of Humphrey's people have been gleeful. They said the bombing pause was going to help them, and so forth, etcetera, and our people say it hurts."

Johnson simply replied: "I'll tell you what I say. I say it doesn't affect the election one way or the other." Nixon agreed, even if he privately did not.

In closing, LBJ reminded Nixon that on the 31st, all three candidates said: "We'll back you, Mr. President."

"Right," Nixon simply responded. Not long after, the conversation ended.[47]

Despite outward appearances of cordiality, the president and others in the White House remained very skeptical of Nixon's denials. With only three days left, some wanted to go public. But, Johnson vacillated. While angry, he worried about the damage done to the likely winner, who would inherit a constitutional crisis on the day he took office, the exposure of the sources, and fear of the accusations of partisanship.

However, the clock was ticking down with little time left to change the course of the election with the bombshell revelations.[48]

With the end near, the Nixon people kept up their efforts. Thieu's close advisor, Hung, emphasized: "During the closing week of the election, Nixon's campaign manager, John Mitchell, called her [Chennault] 'almost every day' to persuade her to keep Thieu from going to Paris for peace talks with the North Vietnamese. They thought their calls were being tapped by the FBI and she joked about it, asking Mitchell playfully: 'Who is listening on the other side?' Mitchell did not find it funny and told her, 'Call me from a pay phone. Don't talk in your office.' Mitchell's message to her was always the same: 'Don't let him go.'"[49]

At one point, Mitchell telephoned: "Anna, I'm speaking on behalf of Mr. Nixon. It's very important that our Vietnamese friends understand our Republican position and I hope you have made it clear to them."[50] Thieu understood the message, and the Nixon people said it often enough to prevent any misunderstanding.

As the White House continued monitoring the principal participants, reporters got wind of the intrigue. It gave Johnson a potential opening to expose the Nixon campaign's complicity by simply affirming the validity of the story or leaking something simultaneously.

In late October 1968, a *Christian Science Monitor* reporter in Saigon, Beverly Deepe, received information from South Vietnamese sources about the GOP efforts to undermine the peace talks. On October 28, she sent a memo to the Washington bureau: "Check out report that [South Vietnamese Ambassador to the United States] Bui Diem had sent a cable to the Foreign Ministry about contact with the Nixon camp."

After receiving no response, she fashioned an article that started: "Purported political encouragement from the Richard Nixon camp was significant factor in the last-minute decision of President [Nguyen van] Thieu's refusal to send a delegation to the Paris peace talks – at least until the American Presidential election is over."

Her editors never published the piece. They told her "that my lead had been 'trimmed and softened' because the editors could get no confirmation and thus without it, they could not print such sweeping charges before the election."[51]

Nonetheless, a colleague of Deepe began asking questions. On November 4, *Christian Science Monitor* reporter Savelle Davis visited the South Vietnamese Embassy. A FBI bug picked up the conversation between Davis and Diem as he highlighted receiving a story from a correspondent in Saigon.

An alarmed Rostow immediately contacted the president at the ranch. "Davis said that the dispatch from Saigon contains the elements of a major scandal which also involves the Vietnamese ambassador and which will affect presidential candidate Richard Nixon if the *Monitor* publishes it. Time is of the essence inasmuch as he has a deadline to meet if he publishes it."

Soon after, Davis requested a White House response. It gave LBJ a final chance to uncover the Nixon campaign's duplicity. He hesitated, still unsure whether he wanted to make the charges and stand accused of aiding Humphrey.

Thus, on November 4, the last day to have any real impact in the newspapers and media before the election, Johnson consulted with Rostow, Rusk, and Clifford.[52]

Clifford advised: "Some elements of the story are so shocking in their nature that I'm wondering whether it would be good for the country to disclose the story and then possibly have a certain individual [Nixon] elected. It would cast his whole administration under such doubt that I think it would be inimical to our country's interests."

Rostow emphasized: "The information sources must be protected and not introduced into domestic politics; even with these sources, the case is not open and shut."

Finally, Rostow summed up opinions: "So far as the information based on such sources, all three of us agreed: (A) Even if the story breaks, it was judged too late to have a significant impact on the election. (B) The viability of the man elected as president was involved as well as subsequent relations between him and President Johnson. (C) Therefore, the common recommendation was that we should not encourage such stories and hold tight the data we have."[53]

Johnson reluctantly concurred.

Afterward, an administration spokesman responded to Davis: "Obviously I'm not going to get into this kind of thing in any way, shape or form."[54] The story died before having any impact.

Johnson could have confirmed the story or even used his office to make an announcement condemning the interference, but he chose not to do so. He lacked definitive proof of Nixon's collusion, the only real evidence that might have swayed many people. The fears of being charged with partisanship after spending most of the election claiming he had stayed above the fray likely influenced him. He missed an opportunity to possibly save the country the heartbreak of Watergate and the tarnishing of the presidency by Nixon and his aides. However, LBJ would not live long enough to watch the tragedy unfold.

The next day, on November 5, the American people went to the polls. Nixon won by a very narrow margin. A Nixon campaign spokesman, Herbert Klein, said afterward that Johnson's bombing halt five days before the election never really hurt Nixon. "During the first 48 hours 'it gave a major shot in the arm to Mr. Humphrey and Democratic party workers,' he said, but later, when it became apparent that the South Vietnamese were reluctant to go along with the plan, things 'started swinging back to us.'"[55]

On the other hand, some South Vietnamese officials crowed about their role. "We helped elect an American president," a top official noted. "Fifteen days would have done it," said one cabinet minister, "but four days wasn't enough, and we saw to that."[56] Another "expressed the opinion that the move by Saigon was to help presidential candidate Nixon, and that had Saigon gone to the conference table, presidential candidate Humphrey would probably have won."[57]

The victory of Nixon removed Saigon's incentive to go to the bargaining table. Johnson had few tools to leverage participation. The end of 1968 saw the ally that Johnson sacrificed so much to support ultimately reject his peace initiative in favor of a perceived harder-line approach that ultimately extended the war another five years for the Americans.

Even after Nixon emerged victorious, the White House continued gathering intelligence. On Friday, November 8, Rostow forwarded a message marked "Literally Eyes Only," from November 7 with information on Chennault contacting Diem to advise that "date from South Vietnamese President Thieu 'which our boss' was alright. She advised she had given 'them' everything when she finally got back to her office to call, that 'they' got the whole message."

Figure 9 President Johnson and Richard Nixon share an elevator ride in the White House soon after the presidential election of 1968. (Courtesy of the LBJ Library)

The report also highlighted: "Senator John Goodwin Tower had talked to her today. Tower is planning to return Sunday and Chennault and Tower plan to meet Diem either Monday." There were other messages that day outlining her being at a suite at election headquarters "in [an] area of Nixon's party awaiting to descend [to the] ballroom."

Even at this late date, an angry Rostow wrote: "First reactions may well be wrong. But with this information I think it's time to blow the whistle on these folks."[58]

Even with the information, Johnson appeared unwilling to continue. On the 7th, the White House called DeLoach and requested an end to the surveillance of Chennault. However, the tap on the South Vietnamese Embassy was maintained until January 6.[59]

Johnson refused to tarnish the new president-elect with the information gathered during the days before the election. It was too late, and he knew it. For many of the same reasons as before, LBJ failed to release the information. By this point, protecting his sources shaped his response. He also sustained his desire to protect the office of the president that clearly influenced him despite the continuing anger over the interference.

Into the following week, more evidence reached the White House, much zeroing in on vice president-elect Agnew as the prime suspect managing Chennault within the Nixon campaign. On the 11th, the White House requested the phone records of Agnew from the FBI.[60]

The following day, Rostow reported: "These new times on the gentleman in Albuquerque on November 2 suggest he had ample time to make the telephone calls to the Lady and Secretary Rusk while in Albuquerque, before departing to Texas." It noted the "phone call to the Lady was at 1:41 p.m. EST and to Secretary Rusk at 1:55 p.m. EST." According to Rostow, Agnew had plenty of time to call her.[61]

Information continued flowing to the president into late November. White House staffer Bromley Smith sent a message to the president at the ranch: "Here is further evidence of the continuing activity of the lady with South Vietnamese Embassy officials." It showed Chennault contacted Diem's secretary and requested the ambassador call when he returned. She also asked the counselor of the embassy, Nguyen Hoan, to meet at her Watergate Apartments for an exchange of correspondence.[62]

Even on December 10, Rostow wrote the president: "The lady is still operational," as reports of her arranging meetings with people like Senator Karl Mundt (R-SD) for Diem and others continued to circulate.

LBJ wrote on the memo: "Keep all these in one file for ready reference."[63]

The command marked a termination of efforts by the White House on the matter. He would not attack Nixon, lacking the smoking gun directly tying him to the plot by Chennault and others within his campaign to torpedo the negotiations in Paris. To him, it would have no positive effect and instead handicap any efforts by Nixon to rule. It would also splatter on to him, as he would have to admit he spied on the campaign and his allies.

At this point, Johnson tried to hide the whole affair from the public to protect his reputation. He had Rostow gather all the materials into one file (that became known as the "X" File) that the NSC advisor took when he left the White House.

In June 1973, a few months after LBJ died, Rostow wrote a memo to Harry Middleton, Director of the LBJ Library. He argued the "X" File should remain in the library under "conditions I judged to be appropriate" and stressed: "my recommendation to you that this file should remain sealed for fifty years from the date of this memorandum." He emphasized it related to the "activities of Mrs. Chennault and others before and immediately after the election of 1968." After 50 years, the file "might be opened for research" but only after proper screening.[64]

Middleton ultimately overruled the request and opened it in 1994. By that time, the Watergate scandal and its aftermath made the Chennault Affair seem like a minor indiscretion and only reinforced the belief in the dirty tactics employed by Nixon and his associates.

But the question of Chennault haunted Nixon, who also wanted it to remain a secret as many had questions about the president's culpability. William Safire wrote in 1975 on the question of whether Chennault was an agent of candidate Nixon: "Dammit, the answer appears to be yes and no. I cannot positively assert that she did so, or if she did, that it was at the direction of Mr. Nixon or his aides."[65]

Others weighed in on the matter. When queried about Nixon's responsibility, Harlow answered: "No, I'm not convinced that it was not true. It was too tempting a target. I wouldn't be a bit surprised if there were some shenanigans going on."[66]

Nixon himself worried about disclosures and consistently denied interfering. After a series of stories after the election by journalist Tom Ottend of the *St. Louis Post Dispatch*, Nixon had a White House aide, Tom Huston, review the FBI files on the Chennault Affair.[67] He produced a very detailed report in late February 1970 that reached the desk of the president.

Sixteen months later, on June 17, 1971, Nixon ordered a break-in by White House operatives of the Brookings Institution. Huston incorrectly reported that the organization had a file on the bombing halt negotiations. Nixon told his aides on tape: "Goddamn it, get in and get those files. Blow the safe and get it."

When Kissinger asked why, believing it contained nothing of value, Nixon responded: "To blackmail him [Johnson]. Because he used the bombing halt for political people."

"The bombing halt file would really kill Johnson," Haldeman chimed in.

Kissinger replied there was nothing there, but the president refused to believe him. Over the next two weeks, he ordered the break in three more times, and its planning led to the creation of the Special Investigations Unit that became known as the "Plumbers," who won notoriety *exactly* one year later with a break in at the Democratic National Committee headquarters at the Watergate complex.[68]

With only a few exceptions, the Chennault Affair faded from public view after Nixon took office. Eventually, Watergate overshadowed any revelations, while Rostow protected the president's legacy after Johnson passed in 1973.

Yet, the affair highlighted challenges facing LBJ in late 1968, as the election and Vietnam siphoned the lion's share of his energy and time. The South Vietnamese clearly saw a weakened president, one who had staked his presidency on them. Yet, they felt Nixon would give them a better deal. Thieu clearly dragged his feet on going to Paris, clearly influenced by those in the Nixon campaign wanting to prevent a breakthrough. But, Johnson had little leverage by this point and few weapons to counter Thieu's intransigence.

But, the efforts by Johnson to manage the crisis show a president torn by his own principles regarding the presidency. While he showed no remorse in employing the intelligence services against US citizens, he maintained a belief that the office of the presidency must be protected as an institution. He could have been overtly partisan, something he avoided throughout most of the election cycle, and turned the tables on Nixon, whom he personally disliked and feared would dismantle his Great Society. But, he hesitated to even leak the story to the press, although he gave it to Humphrey, who also failed to use it.

Throughout, he remained cautious and patient, despite having aides push him to blow the whistle on the Nixon campaign. However, in this case, he likely made a huge error by not releasing the information before the election. Instead of preventing a scandal, it seemed to set the stage for a much larger one. Had Johnson lived past 1973, he might have lived to regret not at least reining in Nixon's proclivities to use all means necessary for political victories and saved the country from the devastating disaster of Watergate that certainly diminished the presidency.

But not long after the final reports of Chennault's activities arrived, LBJ prepared to ride off into the sunset while Democrats licked their wounds. Nixon prepared to victoriously march into the capitol after years of desiring to sit in the Oval Office. As 1968 neared its long and tortuous conclusion, the groundwork was laid for calamities in the years that followed.

CHAPTER 11

The Last Dance, January 1969

Sergeant Paul Glynn quietly tapped on the door of the president's bedroom.

"It's seven o'clock, Mr. President," he said softly.

"Come in," the president responded.

In walked Glynn accompanied by Sergeant Kenneth Gaddis. They had rarely appeared together throughout the previous five years, usually alternating days serving the president.

"I was surprised to see them together," LBJ noted, "but then I realized they had probably decided to make this gesture to mark the special significance of the day."[1]

LBJ understood: "The day was January 20, 1969 – the last morning I would wake up in this room, the last day I would live in this house. It was the day the mantle of the American Presidency would be shifted, in one of the great pageants of our democracy, from my shoulders to those of Richard Nixon."[2]

For more than two months, Johnson had moved toward this day. It was an end to his political career that spanned more than three decades. He achieved his goal of rising to the highest office in the land, but the dream extracted a heavy toll, particularly over his final year in office. A final surrender of power paralleled a welcome of the rush to end and return home and away from the madness of 1968. He was simultaneously melancholy about the past and excited about the future in Texas.

He maintained his routine, shuffling through reports from the night before, even in the final hours in office. LBJ observed: "Presidents come and go, but the Presidency goes on without interruption."[3]

Figure 10 President Johnson and the first lady as they prepare for a formal event just after the presidential election in 1968. (Courtesy of the LBJ Library)

Soon after waking, he picked up the phone and called Busby. Ignoring traditional greetings, the president asked: "Have you seen the *Post* this morning?"

"His tone was edged with the mixture of indignation he reserved for his daily encounters with the paper," Busby remembered. Barely awake he replied: "No sir. I haven't seen the papers."

"Well let me you read you the terrible things the *Post* is saying," LBJ responded.

Busby knew LBJ often practiced editing major newspapers in the morning, complaining about perceived slights.

As the president continued, Busby doubted the word "terrible" actually characterized the story. "As he read through the offending article, my suspicions were confirmed: He could find only an occasional adjective or verb to which he disagreed." In fact, as he listened, "Buzz" found most of the article "quite generous and kind," something the president even acknowledged, "I guess that's pretty good for the *Post.*"[4]

As the president wound down, Busby wondered aloud: "Where are you now?"

Offended by a perceived slight, LBJ grumbled: "Why, I'm still at the White House, of course." Then, he chuckled, "At least for now."

After complaining about the movers taking everything not nailed down, a subdued president observed, "You got me out of this town. Are you still planning to stay?"

"Yes, sir. I suppose we will be here for a long time," Busby replied.

"I'll be going back to Texas about three o'clock. You still don't want to go?" the president asked.

"No," responded his fellow Texan.

Then, the president queried: "What are your plans?"

"I have a lot of starting over to do, Mr. President. It will be a while before I know what I am going to do."

LBJ simply responded, "Yes. I guess all of us can say that."

They talked for a while about whether the president should jump into teaching at the newly established LBJ School at the University of Texas. Busby counseled: "You have a long time to go, Mr. President. I hope you won't be in a hurry to commit yourself to teaching or anything else."

Pleased, the president responded: "That's the way I feel too. When I get back to that ranch, I'm going to get up every morning and do just exactly what I've always wanted to do for forty years." Hesitating, he added: "Nothing."[5]

As the conversation ended, Busby told LBJ: "I hope that you find great happiness."

Wanting to avoid such sentiments, Johnson retreated and said, "Yes, uh, yes." He spoke quickly, "Well, like I said, if you ever change your mind about coming back to Texas, let me know."

The president concluded: "All right. That's about all, I guess. Well, see you again sometime."[6]

Such goodbyes had become commonplace over the last few weeks. At his last cabinet meeting, members praised his record. Russ Wiggins, new US Ambassador to the UN, told the president: "It is seldom that within the electoral span of a single administration do we plant and harvest. Usually the results are deferred until after the administration has been succeeded by others. We are real orchardists and not grain grower. Crop maturity is long deferred." Wiggins concluded however, "I feel confident ... that when the fruits of your policies are gathered in, Americans are going to say, 'How great the harvest has been.'"[7]

At the State of the Union on January 14, he entered the room to the sounds of William "Fishbait" Miller's announcement: "The Pres-ee-dent of the United States." A wave of applause swept over the room, lasting minutes, as the tall Texan made his way to the front. Once on the speaker's stand, he proudly absorbed and cherished the outpouring of emotion from friends and foes alike.

That night, LBJ relished outlining the many successes of his presidency. Christian observed: "fifty-one times during the forty-five-minute speech he was interrupted by applause."[8]

As he neared the completion, the president told the audience: "I hope it may be said, a hundred years from now, that by working together we helped to make our country more just, more just for all of its people, as well as to insure the blessings of liberty for all our posterity ... But I believe that at least it will be said that we tried."[9]

"He closed his speech book" and "then the shouts and cheers from both Democrats and Republicans erupted," Christian remembered. As the president slowly made his way out the door of the chamber, he shook dozens of hands as "the more sentimental Congressmen began to sing 'Auld Lang Syne'."[10]

While enjoying the adulation, he was simultaneously sad about the volume of goodbyes, especially on his last day. He called his long-time and devoted administrative assistant, Mary Rather, and quickly dictated two letters to her. After finishing, he asked her to have Jim Jones bring them over later for his signature.

Then, he asked a White House aide Jim DeVier to join him in the bedroom. There, on the big canopy bed, he spread out nine presidential proclamations supported by Secretary of the Interior Stewart Udall. He wanted LBJ to sign executive orders under the Antiquities Act that added seven million acres to the national park system.

LBJ hesitated. "They are just too big," he told Devries. "A President shouldn't take this much land without the approval of Congress."

So the two men laid out the eight proclamations on the bed. If he signed all, it would constitute more land than ever added at one time by executive order, building on the four million he had already designated.

Walking around the bed, he fretted over each, already having read each multiple times. Finally, after much thought, he selected four total-ing around 300,000 acres, including a new national monument of Marble Canyon in Arizona. "We'll settle on these,"[11] he told DeVier.

Even to the end, Johnson fretted about establishing a precedent that his successors might abuse. He genuinely respected the office of the presidency and wanted to protect its integrity, at least within his own opinions of what mattered. LBJ wanted to shield its prerogatives, but in this case, the former senator worried about overstepping his authority. While such matters often seemed to escape him in other situations, often he wrestled with the importance of his actions and the office.

With so much going on around him, LBJ stressed: "The hands of the clock seemed to be moving faster now."[12]

The same seemed true for Lady Bird, who awoke earlier than her husband, noting it was like "when I was a child and it was the day to go to the County Fair and I didn't want to miss a thing."[13] Unlike the president, who busily scurried about in the last few hours in the White House, she wanted to soak in everything.

For a few fleeting moments, LBJ and Lady Bird shared breakfast, talking while admiring the view out across the broad south lawn and to the ellipse to the Jefferson Memorial.[14]

Afterwards, she took a last stroll through the residence, partly looking for any personal objects left behind. However, mostly Lady Bird just wanted "to stand still and absorb the feeling of the Yellow Room and the Lincoln Sitting Room." She called someone to take down portraits of her and Lyndon and gave them to the curator. Then she headed to the Pineapple Bedroom to look once more at the guest book and the names of the myriad people who had shared time with the first family at the White House.[15]

Christian intercepted her at one point, and listened as she murmured: "I'm just saying goodbye to a wonderful, wonderful place."[16]

LBJ avoided such reflection and sentimentality and moved quickly around the offices, taking time to order Harry Middleton to prepare some Medal of Freedom citations while signing documents filling another dozen or so vacancies on national boards and councils. His time in office quickly disappeared.

LBJ was a creature of habit, visiting the barber for a quick trim, signing the letters brought by Mary Rather as he sat in the chair. He handed them to Jim Jones with the instructions: "Hold these two letters until later." However, the president added: "But make sure you bring them to my attention before we leave for the Capitol."

With movers sweeping through the residence and staffers emptying their offices, the president headed for his bedroom.

There he found Lady Bird putting on her peach and pink dress for the inauguration. She took time to put on an "elegant mink hat" that she described as "an indulgence ... how often will I wear it at Stonewall?"[17]

Entering, he found laid out on the bed his clothes: an Oxford gray club coat, striped trousers, four-in-hand tie, something suggested by Nixon.

At 10:15 a.m., Leonard Marks, the president's personal representative for inaugural arrangements entered and informed the first couple that Hubert and Muriel Humphrey were only minutes away.

As she prepared to leave the room, Lady Bird thought about all the "leave-takings or what-it-is" that had already "been lived through in a previous, quieter time … By now I was sort of anesthetized – in armor – and still I had the feeling of 'going to the Fair' and wanting to absorb and take in everything, remember it, but not feel it."[18]

The two exited the room and met Luci and Lynda. Entering the elevator, DeVier arrived with the documents on expanding federal lands that the president signed as the group descended to the ground floor of the Executive Mansion.

With little fanfare, they entered the Red Room, the space redecorated by Jackie Kennedy to reflect the American Empire style. The red silk wall contrasted the gold outlines of the frames of the portraits. Among these portraits included Gilbert Stuart's painting of Dolly Madison. In the middle of the room, the large French chandelier hung, while a blazing fire raged in the white porcelain-framed fireplace, warming those who just entered. The setting contrasted greatly with where they would be a few hours later.

Slowly, the party gathered, including new vice president Spiro Agnew and his wife. Small talk followed between the president, Humphrey, and others as they waited. Within a short time, word came of the Nixon family's impending arrival.

At 10:30 a.m., just as planned, Nixon and his entourage arrived, passing through the northwest gate and approaching the north portico. Lady Bird watched Pat emerge from the huge black limousine wearing a "rosy-red outfit, belted with touches of fur" followed by Tricia and Julie accompanied by her husband, David, "lanky and smiling that famous Eisenhower smile."[19]

Others joined him, including House Speaker John McCormack, senators Mike Mansfield and Everett Dirksen, along with Congressman Gerald Ford.[20]

The scene differed greatly than in 1953 when Eisenhower refused to enter the White House and waited for Truman in an idling car. When the president entered, they barely spoke to each other.[21]

Instead, when Richard and Pat arrived, LBJ greeted her with a kiss on the cheek and invited them inside for hot beverages. There was some awkwardness when they tried to enter the doors, neither side knowing the protocol of who should enter first. Lady Bird solved the issue quickly, grabbing Pat by the arm and saying, "Shall we go in?"[22]

Inside, Johnson, Nixon, and Humphrey struck up a conversation in an atmosphere LBJ described as "jovial and light-hearted."

In typical Johnson fashion, LBJ started with a tale about stopping once in Texas where he met a man and said: "Let me tell you a story."

Immediately, the man responded: "OK, but how long will it take?"

Using that as a jumping off point, LBJ said: "Well, Dick. I don't want to be like that fellow, but I am curious. How long will your inaugural address take?"

Nixon responded eighteen to twenty minutes.

Then the president-elect turned to Humphrey and told him with a smile, "Hubert, why don't you deliver the address for me."

The Minnesotan answered graciously, "Dick, I had planned to do that, but you sort of interfered. Since you're more familiar with the text than I am; I guess you ought to go ahead and deliver it as scheduled."[23]

LBJ and Nixon moved off into a corner to talk privately. Nixon emphasized, "he had a deep appreciation of the relationship that existed between President Eisenhower and me during my term. He said that he intended to maintain this kind of relationship with me and to improve it in any way he could."[24]

The conversation reflected the evolving relationship that existed between the two. The former vice president carefully nurtured it, even going so far as to send Billy Graham as his emissary in August, promising not to undermine Johnson in his remaining days in office.

Even after winning, when the two met, he deferred to LBJ and it paid dividends as the White House made every effort to ensure a smooth transition.

Not long after, Jones entered the room with several more official documents to sign. LBJ asked for the two letters he dictated earlier. "They were to my sons-in-law, Chuck Robb and Pat Nugent, who were both fighting in Vietnam. They were personal notes indicating the pride that Lady Bird and I had in both of them. Those two letters were the last documents I signed as President of the United States."[25]

Then, at 11:05, Marks announced, "It's time to get into the cars." LBJ and Nixon entered the first car while Lady Bird and Pat followed in another. As they departed, Lady Bird looked back at the façade of the White House. "There, glued to one of the windows, were the faces of John Fickland and Jerman ... And on the steps smiling and blowing kisses were many members of our staff. That was my last view as I drove away from the White House."[26]

As the presidential cavalcade turned onto Pennsylvania Avenue and traveled toward the Capitol, LBJ waved out the windows at the crowds gathering along the presidential parade route. Lady Bird noticed: "It was strange – there were very few people – a little knot here, a small group there."[27]

In the ride over, LBJ momentarily reflected: "I knew that I would be coming back occasionally, but I also knew that no matter how often I returned I was really saying good-by to the city that had been my home for so many years." He knew Washington "would remain for me the site of conflicting emotions. I had ridden its streets both in obscurity and in the spotlight of national attention." It was a foreign land compared to Texas, but it had an incalculable pull on LBJ.

LBJ and Nixon talked freely during the ride. LBJ complained about hearing how little Senator Edmund Muskie contributed to Humphrey's campaign. He snorted how the press "slobbered over Muskie" but highlighted how the senator only delivered Maine, while Agnew helped bring in five southern states.[28]

Once they reached the Capitol, everyone shuffled into the office of Senator Margaret Chase Smith, to await the state of the ceremony. LBJ and Nixon moved into an adjoining room, where they waited for the orders to exit into the cold January day.

Before LBJ stepped out, Lady Bird and Muriel walked down the steps to become "face to face with the great sea" of faces in the crowd. In the front row, she turned to view Lyndon entering. "He looked very tall and handsome and impressive, and very relaxed,"[29] she remembered. The president advanced as the band played one last time, "Hail the Chief," the sun peeking through the clouds as the chilly wind swept across the mall.

Then LBJ watched Nixon enter, standing at the top as a musical fanfare greeted him. His aide, H. R. Haldeman, remembered Nixon's face expressing the feeling "this was his time! He had arrived, he was in full command."[30] Another Nixon confidant, Arthur Burns, had a less positive view, watching him "closely as he walked down the steps of the Capitol. I could not detect a touch of humility in his demeanor or in his facial expression. This bothered me very much."[31]

LBJ admitted as he watched the ceremony that he took time to reflect "as I have done so many times in the last several years" on just "how inadequate any man is for the office of the American Presidency." He stressed, "the magnitude of the job dwarfs every man who aspires to it. Every man who occupies the position has to strain the utmost of his ability to fill it."[32]

He also thought about Vietnam. "I had fervently sought peace through every available channel and at every opportunity and could have done no more," he emphasized. He later told Lady Bird and Nixon that he could proudly say that he finished without "having had to haul down the flag, compromise my principles, or run out on our obligations, our commitments, and our men who were upholding those obligations and commitments in Vietnam."[33]

But, Vietnam had undermined his presidency and sabotaged his legacy. He had not cut and run, but as he left office, tens of thousands had died, billions had been spent, and the country had been ripped apart like no time since 1861. He sat there watching Nixon take over, when if he had made different decisions at many junctures along the way, he could have helped the country avoid the trauma. Even at this late point, he could not see the full ramifications of his choices, refusing to the end to admit any true error on his part.

In between the reflections, LBJ listened as Nixon called for people to "lower our voices ... We cannot learn from one another until we stop shouting at one another." At the end, he made a point (later put on his gravestone): "The greatest honor history can bestow is the title of peacemaker."[34] Both were sentiments that LBJ shared.

It was a short ceremony, Lady Bird observing: "It was low-keyed, restrained, grave ... None of the youthful ebullience, the poetic brilliance of the Kennedy Inauguration, nor the robust, roaring Jacksonian quality of ours."[35] She continued: "There was no high trumpet calls to action, and probably just as well. God knows there's plenty of striving in the last five, actually the last eight, years. Maybe the country is tired of striving – maybe we just want to hold still – absorb the deluges of change for a while."

As Nixon finished, LBJ admitted: "The long, hard effort was over now, and I was glad to see it end." He noted: "I had known sorrow and anger, frustration and disappointment, pain and dismay. But more than anything else, I had experienced a towering pride and pleasure at having had my chance to make my contribution to solving the problems of our time."[36]

On hearing Nixon conclude his oath of office with "so help me God," LBJ called them "welcome words." He thought to himself, "the nightmare of having to be the man who pressed the button to start World War III was passing."[37]

Johnson was ambivalent about the end of his term. Tired and having lost political momentum, especially in 1968 when he suffered a series of stinging defeats with the Fortas/Thornberry nomination and on gun control, he was happy to leave the contentious politics behind in D.C. However, he also worried about his legacy, particularly in civil rights and social programs, where he feared Republicans and conservative Democrats would work hard to undo the gains. But, by this point, there was little he could do other than hope for the best as his political power came crashing down, especially during the year he characterized as a continuous nightmare.

LBJ and Lady Bird filed out of the congested area and toward a black limo to join Lynda and Luci. Then, they sped away with a motorcycle escort while the Nixons entered their vehicle to head down Pennsylvania Avenue, just like the Johnson family had four years earlier.

While Johnson headed away for a lunch at the Clifford's home in Georgetown, Nixon received a dose of what LBJ had endured for years. As his armored limo headed up the parade route, protestors carried signs usually reserved for LBJ. "Nixon's the One ... the Number One War Criminal," while others burned small American flags.

Near 12th Street, the protestors threw bottles, beer cans, and pieces of garbage. The riot cops moved in, forcing the procession to stop.

Nixon became "angry that a group of protestors carrying a Vietcong flag had made us captives in our car." Incensed, he ordered the driver to open the sunroof. Suddenly, he rose, his upper body jutting out into the cold air, his arms raised in a V-for Victory sign.[38]

For the first time in a long time, there were no protestors awaiting LBJ. His family headed toward the Cliffords' home in northwest D.C., where Clark and Marny had arranged a final luncheon for the Johnsons. Lady Bird remembered approaching the home, fully expecting a media frenzy as information had leaked about the gathering.[39]

Instead, Lady Bird exclaimed: "It looked as if we had moved backward in time to some particularly homey campaign rally!" Instead of reporters, the Johnsons found the front lawn of the Cliffords' secluded home occupied by people, "little boys up the apple trees, babies in arms, high school and college youngsters carrying signs – 'WE'LL NEVER FORGET YOU, LBJ' ... 'LBJ, YOU WERE GOOD FOR THE U.S.A.'" Someone in the group unfurled a Texas flag while others waved a huge American flag as the former first family exited their limo.[40]

Waiting out front, Clark and Marny stood at the end of the sidewalk, marveling at the congregation of people. They watched LBJ and Lady Bird work the crowd, shaking hands and speaking briefly into microphones that were thrust into their faces. Somewhere along the line, Luci disappeared, reveling in no longer having secret service agents shadowing her every move.

LBJ entered the house immensely pleased, telling Clifford: "They didn't come to see the President, they came to see Lyndon Johnson."[41]

This was important to Johnson. It reflected a chance to bask in the sunshine of people who appreciated his efforts on their behalf. These were supporters who saw the enormous strides the country made in civil rights, social programs, infrastructure, and the environment. While Vietnam hung over that day's festivities much like the last year, this particular group only wanted to celebrate the positives and focus on the LBJ they knew and valued.

Immediately, Lady Bird stressed: "Inside that warm and welcoming house there awaited one of the most significant and dear parties we shall ever attend."[42]

Everyone who meant so much to the Johnsons, including the Rusks, Rostows, Humphrey, Jake and Beryl Pickle as well as senators Mike Monroney, Gale McGee, Birch Bayh, and Henry Jackson, were there.

"Only one thing marred my sheer delight . . . and that was that we had to leave no later than 3 to get to Austin before the Inaugural proceedings there got under way," Lady Bird lamented. "So time was our tyrant," but she added: "One of the blessings of the future may be that this tyrant will fade into the wings!"

At one point, she looked out on the front lawn, still full of people. One young man held up a sign, "LBJ IN '72." Lady Bird waved, and then the young man turned the sign around and it read: "LYN IN 2004."

As they moved through the house, LBJ and Lady Bird thanked everyone for coming and all that they had done during the past five years.

Then, several people disappeared upstairs with LBJ, who requested that Lady Bird join him. In a bedroom, LBJ bestowed the Medal of Freedom on Averell Harriman, Rostow, Rusk, Clifford, and Bill White, reading each citation, speaking in a low and restrained voice. Marny's eyes filled with tears as Lady Bird stressed: "White . . . (a) tough and seasoned man seemed close to tears." Choking up, he praised LBJ in a few words, the most memorable being "gallant."[43] LBJ observed: "For me, the ceremony was one of the most gratifying moments of that eventful day."[44]

This act reflected the magnanimous side of the president that appeared at various points of his life. There was no political gain in making the awards other than rewarding loyal public servants who he believed served him and the country quite well. Near the end of his presidency, he chose this route over becoming bitter and paranoid about Nixon and his actions in the last days of office.

After returning to the party, LBJ remembered it being a "carefree occasion, but there were unavoidable overtones of nostalgia," as "this was an assembly of old friends who had traveled roads both rough and smooth together for many years; and together we had helped to write a rather remarkable chapter in American history. These were people who had been with us in sunshine and sorrow."[45]

But soon, Lady Bird highlighted: "The hands of the clock prodded us on." She ate at the sumptuous banquet, taking time to help Luci lift Marny's treasures out of the reach of the rambunctious Lyn.

Then, the signal came: "Time to go!" Lady Bird hugged Marny and thanked her for the hospitality. As they exited, LBJ stopped on the porch and addressed the crowd standing in a light rain, telling them how much he loved Washington after thirty years, promising to return. Slowly, the two marched to the car as "God bless you, Mr. President" and "We'll miss you, Lyndon," rang out from the crowd.

As they left, Harriman yelled to Christian: "Tell the press that Marny Clifford regrets that she has but one lawn to give to her country."[46]

Within a short time, the Johnsons arrived at Andrews Airbase. There, a huge crowd of people lined the fence. Savoring the moment, LBJ walked past the military escorts toward his admirers. He shook hands just like on the campaign trail. Suddenly, a band began playing a series of songs including his favorites: "Ruffles and Flourishes" and the "Yellow Rose of Texas."

After a while, he finally returned to the plane, thinking: "Here along the last mile of the long campaign, I reached out to them for the last time, shaking hands along the fence, to say my own good-by."[47]

Lady Bird surveyed the crowd, and just as promised, the Cliffords and Rusks had sped over to say one final farewell. Others joined them, including the lone Republican congressman from Texas, George H. W. Bush, who paid his final respects to the Texas president.[48]

As he turned to take in the spectacle one more time, LBJ saw "faces in the crowd that I had known for almost forty years, men and women whose lives and careers spanned Lady Bird's and mine and who were part of the excitement of Washington when we were young." He saw staff members "who had worked with me throughout my public life, from the early congressional days of 1931 to the last days in the White House." He stressed: "They carried signs that spoke of their love and gratitude, gifts of the heart which I reciprocated in fullest measure."[49]

After soaking in everything, the former president and his family stood at attention for a military honor guard to fire a twenty-one-gun salute as the band played one last time, "Hail to the Chief."[50] Carrying Lyn up the steps of a Boeing 707, No. 26000, he stopped at the top and took one final opportunity to turn and wave to the well-wishers. Soon, "the doors closed, the motors revved, and we were airborne," Lady Bird remembered.[51] Clifford watching from the ground noted: "The plane circled Washington for one last look, then headed west – and home – to Texas."[52]

Then, the president staged his first major statement about retirement. After the doors shut, Johnson lighted a cigarette and proceeded to draw in several deep breaths.

Seeing this, Luci begged him to extinguish it, exclaiming: "How could you smoke now?"

Young Lyn picked up cues from his mother and pointed at it, motioning he should put it out.

"Luci," LBJ snorted, "take the child out of here."

When she hesitated, he roared: "Look, for fourteen years I've wanted to smoke when I wanted to smoke and for fourteen years I have I had a country to serve, children to raise, and a job to do. Now, the job is done, and the children are raised. It's my turn."

Luci retreated and the president enjoyed his cigarette.[53]

The small act reflected a larger reality of an end of sacrifices to the country. For years, he toiled as a public servant. To him, it was not about enjoying life and stopping those acts denied him as he sought to sustain his health to continue his duties. He craved cigarettes and rich foods and drink. The symbolism of his defiance was not lost on many people around him.

After the initial outburst, Lady Bird remembered: "It was a quiet flight down." Tired from a rush of activities over the past few weeks, and especially the tumult of the day, they sat quietly and reflectively.[54]

About 5:30, the plane touched down at Bergstrom Airbase just southeast of downtown Austin. It was a relatively warm January day, in the low 70s, as the Johnsons exited Air Force One for the final time.

Awaiting them were more than an estimated 10,000 supporters, who lined the fences and barricades carrying Texas flags and banners praising the Johnsons, and clapping and yelling for them. A huge sign hung above the Base Operations: "WELCOME HOME, MR. PRESIDENT AND FAMILY."

The festivities had a special flourish as the members of the University of Texas Longhorn Band, decked out in their bright Burnt Orange and white uniforms, began blasting out "The Eyes of Texas."

Figure 11 President Johnson walks with Lady Bird while holding his grandson Lyn, as they greet well-wishers at Bergstrom Air Base in Austin on Inauguration Day, 1969. (Courtesy of the LBJ Library)

At the bottom of the stairs, a slew of dignitaries awaited, including the young Lieutenant Governor Ben Barnes, complete in his dinner jacket as he prepared to make the rounds of inaugural balls. Others joined him, including UT Chancellor Harry Ransom and his wife Hazel as well as Austin Mayor Harry Akin, whose wife presented Lady Bird with a "beautiful bouquet of the first flowers of spring – iris, tulips, narcissus, violets."

LBJ stepped up to a microphone and gave a short speech encouraging the people in attendance to support President Nixon. "Let us try, to help our new leader, who after all is the only President we have. I hope that you will be as good to him as you have been to me." He admitted: "We have left a lot of unsolved problems on Mr. Nixon's desk, not because we wanted to but because the times in which we live required us to."[55]

He shared a few other ideas, asking his supporters and all Americans to "present a united front to the world that is indivisible," and concluded: "Whether we are Democrats or Republicans, Texans or New Yorkers, we love our country, or we ought to love it."

Then, he moved instinctively toward the fence line, grabbing hands with both of his, reveling in every moment. He returned, picked up Lyn, and along with Lynda and his granddaughter Lucinda he went over to meet the well-wishers. He continued for as long as he could, showing his appreciation to the fans as the evening faded and the day came closer to an end.

Finally, he joined Lady Bird, Lynda, and Lucinda to board the *Jetstar* that would carry them to the ranch. They said good-bye to Luci and Lyn, who headed for their own home. As they prepared to part, Lady Bird "looked over my shoulder and there was a silver crescent of a new moon, bright and clear and full of promise."[56]

The flight from Austin to the ranch took only a few minutes. The plane touched down on the long airstrip slicing through the center of the property, taxiing down to the hanger only a short distance from the main house.

In the darkness, they received a big surprise when more than five hundred local people greeted them, led by the ranch manager, Dale Malechek, as well as Father Wunibald Schnieder and Reverend Norman Truesdell from the local Catholic and Lutheran churches. Surveying the crowd, Lady Bird commented, "some ... had known Lyndon all his life and his father before him."

LBJ invited all into the hangar and gave a "long and glowing talk about how glad he was to be home." He found people he knew his whole life, "the preachers and the teachers, the farmers and the ranchers, the men and women I had known my whole life – from Stonewall, Hye, Johnson City, Albert, and Fredericksburg. They all looked as if they were glad to see us, and God knows we were glad to see them."[57]

The crowd finally dispersed and Johnson went into the house. "The fire was burning on the raised hearth in the living room, flickering on the familiar pictures and old books and the big comfortable chair," he recalled.[58]

It was refreshing to be home where people valued him, far away from the Georgetown elites who looked down on him and constantly criticized him in their newspapers and everyday life. These people had known him for many years. They recognized his shortcomings but also that he had made good and brought a lot of recognition to the Hill Country. No longer was he referred to as "Mr. President," but simply Lyndon.

After changing clothes, Lady Bird and Lyndon walked in the yard along the Perdenales River on that mild evening. The stars shone bright unlike the cold and overcast Washington D.C. they had just left. Earlier in the day, LBJ was president of the United States. But now, for the first time in thirty years, he was a rancher far from the seats of power.

As they walked back toward the house, he saw the luggage near the back door and under the carport piled in a "giant mound." He observed: "For the first time in five years there were no aides to carry the bags inside." Lady Bird started to laugh, telling her husband, "the coach has turned back into a pumpkin and the mice have all run away."[59]

Lady Bird went to bed early. As she fell asleep, a line of poetry kept coming into her head. "I seek to celebrate my glad release, the Tents of Silence and the Camp of Peace." But she noted, "And yet it's not quite the right exit line for me because I have loved almost every day of these five years."[60]

LBJ went outside one more time. He looked up at the clear Texas sky, and remembered surveying the skies for orbiting satellites in October 1957. "I thought of all that had happened in the years between. I remembered once again the story I had heard about one of the astronauts from the crew of Apollo 8, which a month ago had circled the moon only a few miles above the surface. Soon after his return to earth the astronaut had stepped into his backyard at home and had looked up at the moon. He had wondered if it really could be true that he had been there. Perhaps."

LBJ continued about talking to some friends and highlighting the story. "Perhaps, I told them, the time would come when I would look back at the majesty and the power and the splendor of the Presidency and find it hard to believe that I had actually been there."

However, he concluded, "on this night I knew I had been there. And I knew also that I had given it everything that was in me."[61]

Conclusion

Since his last day in office, Johnson had spent most of his time at the ranch working on his memoir and helping with the planning of his library that opened in May 1971. But, over time, he made fewer public appearances as his health deteriorated.

But on December 11, 1972, he was ready for a major one. However, an early winter storm gripped Central Texas. It was a cold, dreary day at the ranch as the fireplaces blazed throughout Stonewall keeping people warm while they hunkered down and stayed off the icy roads.

In the house, a struggle waged between LBJ and Lady Bird. He desperately wanted to travel to Austin to participate in a major conference on civil rights at his library. In contrast, his wife begged him to watch the events from the ranch. The recalcitrant Johnson firmly responded that he would travel to Austin to participate, come hell or high water.

He impatiently jumped in the car and began traversing the sixty-five miles over partially frozen roads to Austin, at one point taking the wheel, much to the great horror of Lady Bird. Already under the weather, he persevered until reaching the library. They entered the large, ten-story monument to his political legacy, just above the towering football stadium sandwiched between the campus and the highway.

For much of the day, LBJ listened backstage in the lower level Great Hall Auditorium as others talked about the struggles of the past decades, with a special emphasis on the 1960s.

Toward the end of the day, his turn came to talk. The audience watched him slowly amble across the stage toward the podium, his hair much longer and greyer than many remembered. This was not the man who towered above his colleagues and rivals, but one who looked frail and fragile.

To the amazement of many, even as he started, he pulled out a nitroglycerin tablet and slipped it under his tongue. One person observed, he did so "to ease the pain of his enlarged and broken heart."

LBJ surveyed the crowd. Up front were Vice President Hubert Humphrey and Justice Thurgood Marshall, not far from civil rights stalwarts Roy Wilkins and Dorothy Height. Reynaldo J. Garza, the first Mexican American on the federal bench, appointed by LBJ, sat nearby. Finally, he took great pride in seeing up front a young Barbara Jordan, the recently elected first African American congressperson in Texas since Reconstruction.

Then, he began talking about the struggles of the past and evoked with great clarity and force some of the battle cries from the civil rights movement of the past twenty years: "Let us continue!" and "We shall overcome!"

Instead of telling stories about passing laws, LBJ emphasized, "I [don't] want this symposium to spend two days talking about what we've done." Instead, he forcefully said: "The progress has been much too small. I'm kind of ashamed of myself that I had six years and couldn't do more. So let no one delude himself that his work is done. To be black or brown in a white society is not to stand on equal ground."

Finally, he concluded: "We've proved that great progress is possible. We know how much remains to be done. And if our efforts continue, and if our will is strong, and if our hearts are right, and if our courage remains our constant companion – then I am confident we shall overcome."

As LBJ left the podium, Congress of Racial Equality (CORE) director Roy Innis and Reverend Kendall Smith of the National Council of Churches began screaming that the symposium could not end unless attendees protested the attacks on civil rights by President Richard Nixon and the Republicans, including those on busing and weakening of enforcement of recent civil rights legislation.

Startled by the vehemence of the disruption, civil rights activist Clarence Mitchell stood between the protestors and Johnson, yelling he would shield him "from demagogues whether white or black."

But, it was hardly an attack on the former president and more about the current administration. So, LBJ wheeled around and moved back toward the microphone, obviously energized by the challenge. Without fanfare, he listened to the protests of Innis and Smith, but then responded.

He told a story about a judge and a town drunk who watched WWI veterans of the Bonus Army being driven out of Washington by federal troops.

The judge argued that "there is everything right – about a group saying, 'Mr. President, we would like you to set aside an hour to let us talk.'" But he warned: "You don't need to start off by saying he is terrible – because he doesn't think he's terrible. Start talking about how you believe that he wants to do what's right and how you believe this is right, and you'll be surprised how many who want to do what's right will try to help you."

As one person noted: "Here was the old Lyndon Johnson, still urging people of very different viewpoints 'to come reason together,' still recommending the balm of friendly persuasion as a vital part of his own special 'Johnson treatment.'"

Johnson continued: "While I can't provide much go-go at this stage of my life, I can provide a lot of hope and dreams and encouragement, and I'll see a few wormy cows now and then and contribute. Let's watch what's been done, and see it is preserved, but let's say we have just begun, and let's go on. Until every boy and girl born in this land, whatever state, whatever color, can stand on the same level ground, our job will not be done."[1]

As he left once more, LBJ received a rousing ovation from the audience. He temporarily basked in adulation and left satisfied and temporarily reinvigorated.

However, only a month later, on January 22, 1973, he rose and attended to some business before taking a nap. Around 3:45 p.m., Secret Service agents received a distress call and rushed over. The former president lay unconscious on his bedroom floor, so they began CPR. Ultimately, they flew him to San Antonio, but in mid-flight, the doctor declared him dead.

After a state funeral, where LBJ's body lay in the Capitol Rotunda, he returned home for burial at the ranch. On January 25th, Governor John Connally eulogized him, telling the gathered group at the ranch's cemetery under huge oak trees: "Along this stream and under these trees he loved, he will now rest. He first saw light here. He last felt life here. May he now find peace here."[2]

Thus ended one of the most colorful and influential political careers in American history, one spanning more than three decades. It covered some of the most significant points in US history, from the Great Depression through WWII and into the Cold War, culminating with the tumultuous latter half of the 1960s.

But in years of notable changes, few stood out like 1968. LBJ correctly appraised the country on leaving office: "There were deep divisions in the country, perhaps deeper than any we had experienced since the Civil War. They were divisions that could destroy us if they were not attended to and ultimately healed. But there were also divisions I felt powerless to correct."[3]

"So 1968 had really been a year of peaks as well as valleys."[4] At the Thanksgiving breakfast in late November, 1968, LBJ noted, "Americans looking back at 1968 may be more inclined to ask God's mercy and guidance than to offer him thanks for his blessings."[5]

The year 1968 was a series of crises, one after another, beginning with the seizure of the *Pueblo* and deteriorating further with the Tet Offensive and assassinations of MLK and RFK. The tumultuous battle over Fortas and Thornberry was followed by the Soviet invasion of Czechoslovakia and then riots in Chicago at the Democratic National Convention. The year ended with the divisive presidential election that insured a political calamity only a few years later. By any standard, it was one of the most difficult years in American history.

Despite the significant challenges, Johnson performed well during most of the crises. This included the *Pueblo* and Czechoslovakia as well as his sincere efforts to try to negotiate with the Soviets and even North Vietnam once he moved beyond responding to Tet. Often, he showed wisdom in considering multiple outcomes, patience in not acting impulsively, and forbearance in looking for diplomatic solutions over military ones.[6]

The president also generally exercised caution, patience, and fore-sight in dealing with the domestic disturbances of 1968, particularly the race riots that followed the assassination of Martin Luther King, Jr. He resisted calls from angry whites, including prominent congressmen and senators, to employ more force. Instead, he judiciously used troops to quell the violence. When employing force, he showed a propensity to think about the long-term ramifications and removed them as soon as possible.

Finally, on a different level, he often demonstrated empathy toward those involved in the crises. In the case of the rioters, unlike many others, he sympathized with their plight, something he instinctively understood and tried to address in the Great Society programs. While denouncing the violence, he clearly recognized the root causes rather than simply ascribing them to personal or cultural failures.

He also demonstrated great compassion, going counter to the common perception of him as a self-serving and crass individual. His interaction with the Kennedys after the assassination of Robert Kennedy showed him at his best. He went out of his way to assist the family during their tragedy, despite the bitter rivalry with RFK. It was a genuine expression of sym-pathy and concern, particularly toward Rose and Ethel.

Of course, his well-documented persona of being brash and some-times abusive also appeared clearly on display throughout 1968. The most apparent remained his treatment of his loyal vice president, Hubert Humphrey, who endured a series of insults as the Democratic standard front runner from the summer of 1968 forward. Often in their relation-ship, Johnson heaped ridicule on Humphrey, but in 1968, it intensified with the vice president's efforts to cement his role as leader of the Democratic Party. LBJ sabotaged him during much of the race, particu-larly at Chicago, where he let personal ambitions and the obsession with Vietnam destroy Humphrey's chances.

He also showed other character flaws in 1968. His relationship with Abe Fortas and the ethical lines both men crossed led to the dramatic showdown over the nomination of a chief justice. While driven by partisanship in an election year, Republican lawmakers working with vindictive southern Democrats undoubtedly had a point in challenging Johnson on what role Fortas played in the White House.

A blind spot existed not only relating to his relationship with Fortas but also the charges of cronyism resulting from choosing Homer Thornberry. Like other points in 1968, Johnson often experienced self-inflicted wounds.

How he interacted with people, including those closest to him, shows the complexity of the man who endured significant trials during 1968. The tumultuous year challenged leaders around the world, but especially the president of the United States. Many unexpected obstacles arose that ultimately drained the nation and brought about changes that continued into the next decade, many with very negative consequences, such as Watergate.

What also emerges from the story of Johnson and 1968 was something readily apparent in the two years leading into the nightmare year: the centrality of Vietnam. The bloody conflict in Southeast Asia received the lion's share of the president's attention, especially after 1965. By 1967, it had hobbled him despite the public relations effort during the year to try to rally the American people to support his policies. A Johnson adviser, Eric Goldman, noted, "the ebullient leader given to moments of testiness and rage was now, day after day, bitter, truculent, peevish – and suspicious of the fundamental good sense and integrity of anyone who did not endorse the Vietnam War."[7]

But, he could not seem to escape the quagmire, despite pushing the San Antonio Formula in September 1967 that sought negotiations but with significant requirements that Hanoi invariably looked likely to reject, at least through the aftermath of the Tet Offensive. One journalist noted that in his years of covering politics that "almost nobody ever admits being wrong about anything – and the wronger they were, the less willing they are to concede error."[8]

This was certainly on display regarding Johnson and Vietnam, especially through March 31, 1968, but also beyond at a number of junctures where negotiations and a search for a different path such as those proposed by his political opponents caused Johnson to lash out at people, including King, Kennedy, Eugene McCarthy, and Humphrey. The war handicapped him, clearly led to his decision not to seek reelection, and handicapped his political efforts throughout the year. Its centrality in American political life in 1968 cannot be underestimated.

Vietnam, along with the conservative backlash developing since 1965 over civil rights and the expansion of government programs, ensured Johnson encountered significant barriers in 1968. His legislative and foreign policy efforts that year clearly demonstrated the diminution of his power and that of other liberal policymakers after the heady years of 1964 and 1965. Johnson and his allies won few major successes outside of Fair Housing. Like other points in US history during the progressive era and New Deal, fatigue set in regarding reform and wars undermined the reformist zeal. The year 1968 marked a watershed in the postwar efforts to create a society envisioned by Franklin Roosevelt and his aco-lytes including Johnson and marked the rise of a conservative backlash that has dominated for many years, including the election in 2016.

Thus, even fifty years later, the echoes of 1968 reverberate loudly in America, as one person has noted: "History may not repeat itself but it does rhyme." At the time of this writing in spring 2017, the country has witnessed ongoing political battles resulting from the ascendancy of Johnson, ranging from attacks on health care and civil rights to the environment and education. The administration of President Donald Trump appears to want to dismantle not only the programs of its prede-cessor, but especially those of Johnson.

But it goes beyond the political battles to the echoes of 1968, with racial tensions that have spilled over in places like Ferguson, Missouri, and the ongoing struggle to overcome racial disparities in many sectors of American society. The country appears primed for heightened ten-sions and confrontations, but this time with many more angles beyond the traditional ones and extending to other racial sectors, including Latinos and especially immigrants.

The foreign policy challenges even sound remarkably similar. The North Koreans remain a thorn in the side of the United States, this time with threats related to the use of missiles and nuclear weapons. Beyond that, much like the Chennault Affair, a foreign government likely played a role in shaping the outcome of a presidential election with the possible collusion of one of the campaigns. For all that seemed to change, much remains eerily similar on many levels of America and the world fifty years later.

In the final analysis, 1968 was a heartbreaking year for the president and the country. Goldman added: "No one who worked in Lyndon Johnson's White House can fail to have been moved by the dedication, the abilities and the force he brought to the Presidency of the United States." But, while he dealt well with many of the challenges of 1968, the fact remains that the country clearly slipped off the tracks and headed toward a nadir during the 1970s.

Goldman finally concluded: "It was just as difficult not to recall the lines from one of his copybook poems, John Greenleaf Whittier's Maud Muller: 'For of all sad words of tongue or pen, The saddest are these: It might have been.' The story of Lyndon Johnson's Presidency is a story of tragedy in the ancient haunting sense of the word, the strong man overwhelmed by forces, from within and without."[9]

Those words would likely not have been written in 1965 or 1966. However, by the end of the nightmare year of 1968, they appeared extremely appropriate. The effects were significant for Johnson and his dreams as well as those of many Americans. Understanding the tumultuous year and the responses of Johnson provides Americans insights into what has transpired and how tragic years like that one shaped our current political discourse, often for the worse.

Glossary of Participants

Ball, George – US Ambassador to the United Nations between June
and September of 1968. Ball led the committee that investigated the
capture of the *U.S.S. Pueblo*.

Bunker, Ellsworth – hawkish US Ambassador to South Vietnam in 1968.

Busby, Horace – one-time speechwriter and long-time confidant of President Johnson. He helped write some of Johnson's most memorable
speeches, including the March 31 section on the president's decision
not to seek reelection.

Califano Jr., Joseph A. (Joe) – served as President Johnson's Special
Assistant. Califano was the chief domestic affairs aide and researched
policy initiatives, developed legislation, and coordinated the communication efforts of the executive branch.

Carpenter, Liz – long-time confidant and press secretary for Lady
Bird Johnson who sometimes contributed to writing the president's
speeches.

Christian, George – White House Press Secretary from 1967 until the
inauguration of President Richard Nixon in January 1969.

Christopher, Warren – US Deputy Attorney General and prominent
advisor on issues including the race riots and the Chicago Convention.

Clark, Ramsey – US Attorney General between 1967 and 1969. Clark was
a strong advocate for civil rights and often clashed with many in the
White House over his legal interpretations.

Clifford, Clark – succeeded Robert McNamara as Secretary of Defense
in early 1968 and was a prominent presidential advisor throughout
the remainder of Johnson's term, often siding with the doves in the
Pentagon on Vietnam.

Connally, John – Texas Governor and long-time confidant of President Johnson. He would serve as the Secretary of the Treasury under President Nixon.

Daley, Richard – close confidant of Johnson and mayor of Chicago during the tumultuous 1968 Democratic National Convention.

Fehmer, Marie – long-time administrative assistant to the president.

Fortas, Abe – nominated and confirmed to the US Supreme Court in 1965. In 1968, President Johnson nominated Fortas to the position of Chief Justice, but Fortas failed to be confirmed by the Senate and ultimately resigned from the bench in 1969.

Fowler, Henry – served as Secretary of the Treasury and tackled issues such as inflation, often siding with deficit hawks in their efforts to cut social spending.

Goldberg, Arthur – US Ambassador to the United Nations who resigned his post in June 1968 over the direction of the Vietnam War.

Helms, Richard – Director of the Central Intelligence Agency in 1968.

Humphrey, Hubert – loyal Vice President to Johnson and 1968 Democratic Presidential Candidate.

Jones, James Robert "Jim" – influential chief of staff under Johnson in 1968 and later US congressman and US Ambassador to Mexico.

Katzenbach, Nicholas – served as Undersecretary of State in 1968 under Johnson and supported negotiations during the *Pueblo* incident and worked on several other issues during 1968.

Kennedy, Robert – served as his older brother's (JFK) Attorney General and was later elected as a Senator for New York. Kennedy was Johnson's long-time political rival and was assassinated after winning the California presidential primary race in 1968.

Krim, Arthur – close friend and advisor to Johnson.

Manatos, Mike – important legislative assistant in the White House in 1968.

McCarthy, Eugene – Democratic Senator from Minnesota and 1968 Presidential candidate whose candidacy helped push Johnson to reconsider his reelection bid.

McNamara, Robert – Secretary of Defense until early 1968 when he became president of the World Bank.

McPherson, Harry – White House special counsel and Johnson's speech-writer in 1968 known for his willingness to challenge the president on many issues.

Middleton, Harry – staff assistant and speechwriter for Johnson. He would later serve as the director of the Lyndon Baines Johnson Presidential Library and Museum.

Murphy, Patrick – Washington, D.C. Director of Public Safety and key player during the riots following the assassination of MLK.

Reedy, George – long-time confidant to Johnson and former White House Press Secretary who returned as a special assistant in 1968.

Roche, John – special advisor and speechwriter.

Rostow, Walt – long-time National Security Advisor and close advisor on foreign policy who demonstrated a strong commitment to US involvement in Vietnam and proved hawkish on many issues related to the Soviet Union.

Rusk, Dean – Secretary of State, 1961 and 1969, and loyal Johnson supporter. He supported hawkish positions on Vietnam but pushed for negotiations with the Soviets in 1968 until their invasion of Czechoslovakia.

Temple, Larry – served as White House Counsel between 1967 and 1969 and advised on issues such as the Fortas nomination and use of force during the riots in 1968.

Thompson, Llewellyn "Tommy" – US Ambassador to the Soviet Union.

Thornberry, Homer – was nominated to the Fifth Circuit Court of Appeals by Johnson in 1965. In 1968, Johnson nominated Thornberry to the Supreme Court, but his nomination was quietly dismissed after Abe Fortas' failed confirmation as Chief Justice.

Vance, Cyrus – US Deputy Secretary of State. Vance managed the *U.S.S. Pueblo* incident from South Korea and served on the peace commission meeting in Paris in 1968.

Watson, Marvin – served as White House Appointments Secretary until early 1968 and Postmaster General under Johnson and was instrumental in the passage of Great Society programs and close confidant to the president on matters regarding elections.

Westmoreland, William – US Commander in South Vietnam who transitioned out of command after Tet: subsequently replaced by General Creighton Abrams.

Wheeler, Earle – Chairman of the Joint Chiefs of Staff and leading advocate for increasing the number of US troops in Vietnam in 1968.

Notes

INTRODUCTION

1. James U. Cross, *Around the World with LBJ: My Wild Ride as Air Force One Pilot, White House Aide, and Personal Confidant* (Austin: University of Texas Press, 2008), 134–135.
2. Cross, *Around the World with LBJ*, 154.
3. Lyndon B. Johnson, *"Remarks to Service Personnel and Award of Distinguished Service Medal and Medal of Freedom to Military and Civilian Leaders, Cam Ranh Bay, Vietnam,"* 23 December 1967, *Public Papers of the President of the United States: Lyndon B. Johnson* (Washington, D.C.: Government Printing Office, 1968), 1185.
4. Lady Bird Johnson, *A White House Diary* (New York: Holt, Rinehart and Winston, 1970), 606.
5. Robert Mann, *A Grand Delusion: America's Descent into Vietnam* (New York: Basic Books, 2001), 442.
6. Nicholas deB. Katzenbach, *Some of It Was Fun: Working with RFK and LBJ* (New York: W. W. Norton, 2008), 255.
7. Kathleen Hall Jamieson, *Packaging the Presidency: A History and Criticism of Presidential Campaign Advertising* 2nd edition (New York: Oxford University Press, 1996), 221.
8. Joseph A. Fry, *Debating Vietnam: Fulbright, Stennis, and Their Senate Hearings* (Lanham, MD: Rowman & Littlefield, 2006), 139.
9. Robert Dallek, *Flawed Giant: Lyndon Johnson and His Times, 1961–1973* (New York: Oxford University Press, 1998), 491.
10. *U.S. News and World Report*, 2 January 1967, 22.
11. *Newsweek*, 20 March 1967, 25.
12. Various materials, 1964–1968, White House Famous Names, Box 8, LBJ Library.
13. Randall Woods, *Prisoners of Hope: Lyndon B. Johnson, the Great Society, and the Limits of Liberalism* (New York: Basic Books, 2016), 313.
14. Woods, *Prisoners of Hope*, 313–314.
15. Woods, *Prisoners of Hope*, 314–315.
16. Lyndon Baines Johnson, *The Vantage Point: Perspectives of the Presidency, 1963–1969* (New York: Holt, Rinehart and Winston, 1972), 533.
17. Clark Clifford with Richard Holbrooke, *Counsel to the President: A Memoir* (New York: Random House, 1991), 461.

18. Richard Rovere, "Freedom: Who Needs It," *The Atlantic Monthly* (May 1968): 39.

19. Harris Poll, *The Nation*, 30 December 1968, 708.

20. *New York Times*, 10 February 1968.

21. Jules Witcover, *The Year the Dream Died: Revisiting 1968 in America* (New York: Grand Central Publishing, 1998); David Farber, *The Age of Great Dreams: America in the 1960s* (New York: Hill & Wang, 1994).

22. Robert Dallek, *Lone Star Rising: Lyndon Johnson and His Times, 1908–1960* (New York: Oxford University Press, 1991) and *Flawed Giant: Lyndon B. Johnson and His Times, 1961–1973* (New York: Oxford University Press, 1998); Randall B. Woods, *LBJ: Architect of American Ambition* (New York: Free Press, 2006); Robert A. Caro, *The Path to Power* (New York: Vintage Books, 1990), *Means of Ascent* (New York: Vintage Books, 1991); *Master of the Senate* (New York: Vintage Books, 2003); *The Passage of Power* (New York: Vintage Books, 2013).

23. Mitchell B. Lerner, *The Pueblo Incident: A Spy Ship and the Failure of American Foreign Policy* (Lawrence: University Press of Kansas, 2002); Clay Risen, *A Nation on Fire: America in the Wake of the King Assassination* (New York: Wiley, 2009).

24. Phone interview by the author with Joseph Califano, Jr., 15 February 2017.

25. Irving Bernstein, *Guns or Butter: The Presidency of Lyndon Johnson* (New York: Oxford University Press, 1996), 19.

26. "What a Year," *Time* (30 August 1968).

CHAPTER 1: A NATION ON THE BRINK

1. Lady Bird Johnson, *A White House Diary* (New York: Holt, Rinehart and Winston, 1970), 616.

2. Horace W. Busby, *The Thirty-First of March: An Intimate Portrait of Lyndon Johnson's Final Days in Office* (New York: Farrar, Straus and Giroux, 2005), 173.

3. Busby, *The Thirty-First of March*, 173.

4. National Educational Television Network, Broadcast Transcript of the "State of the Union/68," 17 January 1968, p. 12, Papers of Lyndon Baines Johnson, President, 1963–1969, Speeches, Box 151, LBJ Library.

5. National Educational Television Network, Broadcast Transcript of the "State of the Union/68," 17 January 1968, p. 12, Papers of Lyndon Baines Johnson, President, 1963–1969, Speeches, Box 151, LBJ Library.

6. Lyndon Johnson notes, State of Union file, 8 December 1967, Statements of Lyndon Baines Johnson, January 7, 1968–January 17, 1968, Box 260, LBJ Library.

7. Joseph A. Califano, Jr., *The Triumph and Tragedy of Lyndon Johnson: The White House Years* (New York: Touchstone, 1991), 253.

8. National Educational Television Network, Broadcast Transcript of the "State of the Union/68," 17 January 1968, p. 12, Papers of Lyndon Baines Johnson, President, 1963–1969, Speeches, Box 151, LBJ Library.

9. Califano, Jr., *The Triumph and Tragedy of Lyndon Johnson*, 255.

10. Califano, Jr., *The Triumph and Tragedy of Lyndon Johnson*, 253–254.

11. Robert Dallek, *Flawed Giant: Lyndon Johnson and His Times, 1961–1973* (New York: Oxford University Press, 1998), 515.

12. Herbert Y. Schandler, *Lyndon Johnson and Vietnam: The Unmaking of a President* (Princeton: Princeton University Press, 1977), 130.

13. George Reedy, *Lyndon Johnson: A Memoir* (New York: Andrews and McMeel, 1982), 150.

14. Robert E. Kintner to George Christian, 16 January 1968, Statements of Lyndon Baines Johnson, January 7, 1968–January 17, 1968, Box 260, LBJ Library.

15. George Reedy to Johnson, 15 January 1968, Statements of Lyndon Baines Johnson, January 7, 1968–January 17, 1968, Box 260, LBJ Library. Others weighed in on foreign relations, especially Vietnam. Rusk stressed on January 12, "I believe it important that the State of the Union be consistent with the San Antonio formula. It went as far as anyone can reasonably and fairly go in the search for a peaceful settlement." He liked the emphasis: "Our war aim is peace" and stressed he wanted a focus on "a reliable peace must be our central purpose." Dean Rusk to Harry McPherson, 12 January 1968, Statements of Lyndon Baines Johnson, January 7, 1968–January 17, 1968, Box 260, LBJ Library; Rusk to Johnson, 12 January 1968, Statements of Lyndon Baines Johnson, January 7, 1968–January 17, 1968, Box 260, LBJ Library.

16. Walt Rostow to Johnson, 14 January 1968, Statements of Lyndon Baines Johnson, January 7, 1968–January 17, 1968, Box 260, LBJ Library.

17. Dean Acheson to Walt Rostow, 19 December 1967, Statements of Lyndon Baines Johnson, January 7, 1968–January 17, 1968, Box 260, LBJ Library.

18. "Formulating Presidential Program Is a Long Process," *Congressional Quarterly*, 24 January 1968, 1–3.

19. Busby, *The Thirty-First of March*, 173.

20. The president in January 21 (Advance Gallup Poll) had a 51 percent to 39 percent lead over Nixon with 10 percent undecided (Nixon had lost 10 points since November). Against Rockefeller, it was: 46 percent Johnson, 40 percent Rockefeller, and 14 percent undecided. The latter lost 14 points since November. He led by 20 points over Romney and Reagan. Panzer to Johnson, 19 January 1968, Papers of LBJ, President, 1963–1969, EX PL 2 8/23/67–9/18/67, Box 88, LBJ Library.

21. LBJ went on for a while, raving about "this war. This goddam war," but simultaneously talked about how the polls showed that most Democrats approved of his conduct in waging it and bragged, "I've got the nomination. Somebody may try, but they can't take it away. I've got my votes already." Panzer to Johnson, 19 January 1968, Papers of LBJ, President, 1963–1969, EX PL 2 8/23/67–9/18/67, Box 88, LBJ Library.

22. Busby, *The Thirty-First of March*, 180.

23. Johnson, *White House Diary*, 615.

24. Califano, Jr., *The Triumph and Tragedy of Lyndon Johnson*, 255.

25. Memorandum from Joe Califano to Johnson, 17 January 1968, Statements of Lyndon Baines Johnson, January 7, 1968–January 17, 1968, Box 260, LBJ Library.

26. Johnson, *White House Diary*, 616.

27. Liz Carpenter to Johnson, 16 January 1968, Statements of Lyndon Baines Johnson, January 7, 1968–January 17, 1968, Box 260, LBJ Library.

28. Johnson, *White House Diary*, 616.

29. Johnson, *White House Diary*, 616.

30. President Lyndon B. Johnson Papers, Daily Diary, 17 January 1968, LBJ Library.

31. President Lyndon B. Johnson Papers, Daily Diary, 17 January 1968, LBJ Library.

32. President Lyndon B. Johnson Papers, Daily Diary, 17 January 1968, LBJ Library.

33. Johnson, *White House Diary*, 617.

34. Johnson, *White House Diary*, 617.

35. Johnson, *White House Diary*, 618.

36. Lewis Gould, *1968: The Election That Changed America* 2nd edition (Chicago: Ivan R. Dee, 2010), 32.

37. Johnson, *White House Diary*, 618.

38. National Educational Television Network, Broadcast Transcript of the "State of the Union/68," 17 January 1968, p. 17, Papers of Lyndon Baines Johnson, President, 1963–1969, Speeches, Box 151, LBJ Library.

39. Johnson, *White House Diary*, 619.

40. Califano, Jr., *The Triumph and Tragedy of Lyndon Johnson*, 257.

41. Califano, Jr., *The Triumph and Tragedy of Lyndon Johnson*, 256.

42. *Washington Post*, 28 January 1968.

43. *Washington Post*, 28 January 1968.

44. Johnson, *White House Diary*, 619.

45. McPherson to Moynihan, 23 January 1968, Statements of Lyndon Baines Johnson, January 7, 1968–January 17, 1968, Box 260, LBJ Library.

46. Lyndon B. Johnson, "Annual Message to the Congress on the State of the Union," 17 January 1968, *Public Papers of the President of the United States: Lyndon B. Johnson*, volume 1 (Washington, D.C.: U.S. Government Printing Office, 1970), 33.

47. Busby, *The Thirty-First of March*, 180.

48. Johnson, *White House Diary*, 619.

49. John Connally (with Mickey Herskowitz), *In History's Shadow: An American Odyssey* (New York: Hyperion, 1993), 202–203.

50. Watching closely, Lady Bird noted "somewhere in the speech the teleprompter failed. I could tell, though, I am not sure that many people in the audience could. I could see him leafing through three or four pages of text in front of him while he interpolated – I thought it was gracefully done. A time or two he added a few adjectives that I would have left off. I liked the spare bones better." Johnson, *White House Diary*, 619.

51. Johnson, *White House Diary*, 619.

52. National Educational Television Network, Broadcast Transcript of the "State of the Union/68," 17 January 1968, p. 25, Papers of Lyndon Baines Johnson, President, 1963–1969, Speeches, Box 151, LBJ Library.

53. National Educational Television Network, Broadcast Transcript of the "State of the Union/68," 17 January 1968, p. 27, Papers of Lyndon Baines Johnson, President, 1963–1969, Speeches, Box 151, LBJ Library.

54. Johnson, *White House Diary*, 619–620. The panel included Schlesinger, William F. Buckley, Walter Heller, Milton Friedman, Moyers, Reischauer, Moynihan, Stokes, and James Kilpatrick.
55. Johnson, *White House Diary*, 620.
56. Johnson, *White House Diary*, 620.
57. Irwin and Debi Unger, *LBJ: A Life* (New York: John Wiley & Sons, 1999), 445.
58. Fred Panzer to Johnson, 1 February 1968, Papers of Lyndon B. Johnson, President, 1963–1969, Speeches, Box 151, LBJ Library.
59. *Washington Post*, 28 January 1968.

CHAPTER 2: THOSE DIRTY BASTARDS, ARE THEY TRYING TO EMBARRASS US?
THE *PUEBLO* INCIDENT, JANUARY–DECEMBER 1968

1. Daniel P. Bolger, *Scenes from an Unfinished War: Low-Intensity Conflict in Korea, 1966–1969* (Fort Leavenworth, KS: U.S. Army Command and General Staff College, 1991), 62–65.
2. "The Economy: Jobs for 500,000," *Time* 91:5 (2 February 1968): 21.
3. Henry F. Graff, *The Tuesday Cabinet: Deliberation and Decision on Peace and War under Lyndon B. Johnson* (Englewood Cliffs, NJ, 1970).
4. Notes of the President's Tuesday National Security Lunch, 23 January 1968, Tom Johnson's Notes of Meetings, Box 2, LBJ Library.
5. "Notes of Meeting," 23 January 1968, *Foreign Relations of the United States, 1964–1968* 29:1, Part 1, Korea, Document 213 (Washington, D.C.: Government Printing Office, 2000), 461.
6. Johnson, Lyndon Baines Johnson, *The Vantage Point: Perspectives of the Presidency, 1963–1969* (New York: Holt, Rinehart and Winston, 1972), 535.
7. "Notes of Meeting," 23 January 1968, *Foreign Relations of the United States, 1964–1968* 29:1, Part 1, Korea, Document 213 (Washington, D.C.: Government Printing Office, 2000), 462.
8. *The Vantage Point*, 534.
9. Mitchell Lerner, "'Mostly Propaganda in Nature:' Kim Il Sung, the Juche Ideology, and the Second Korean War," North Korea International Documentation Project, Woodrow Wilson Center, 7 July 2011, www.wilsoncenter.org/publication/mostly-propaganda-nature-kim-il-sung-the-juche-ideology-and-the-second-korean-war.
10. Notes of Meeting," 24 January 1968, *Foreign Relations of the United States, 1964–1968*, 29:1, Part 1, Korea, Document 213 (Washington, D.C.: Government Printing Office, 2000), 476–481.
11. Robert David Johnson, *Congress and the Cold War* (New York: Cambridge University Press, 2006), 141.
12. *Congressional Record*, 23 January 1968 14:1 (Washington, DC: Government Printing Office, 1968), 679.
13. *Washington Post*, 27 January 1968. Earlier, he had told a reporter that the United States should do anything "including declaring war if necessary." *New York Times*, 24 January 1968.

14. *Chicago Tribune*, 28 January 1968.

15. Johnson, *The Vantage Point*, 536.

16. M. K. Nawaz, "The 'Pueblo' Affair and International Law," *The Indian Journal of International Law* 15 (1975): 497.

17. *Chicago Tribune*, 7 February 1968.

18. Notes of President's Meeting with the National Security Council, 24 January 1968, *Foreign Relations of the United States, 1964–1968*, 29:1, Part 1, Korea, Document 213 (Washington, D.C.: Government Printing Office, 2000), 477–481.

19. Johnson, *The Vantage Point*, 534.

20. Johnson, *The Vantage Point*, 535.

21. Lady Bird Johnson, *A White House Diary*, 25 January 1968 (New York: Holt, Rinehart and Winston, 1970), 625.

22. Notes of the President's Breakfast Meeting, 25 January 1968, Tom Johnson's Notes of Meetings, Box 2, LBJ Library. Johnson wrote a note to Kosygin: "I am urging your most serious personal attention to the irrational action of North Korean authorities in seizing the USS Pueblo in international waters." Telegram from Johnson to Kosygin, 25 January 1968, Tom Johnson's Notes of Meetings, Box 2, LBJ Library.

23. Christian, *The President Steps Down*, 139.

24. Notes of Meeting, 25 January 1968, *Foreign Relations of the United States, 1964–1968*, 29:1, Part 1, Korea, Document 213 (Washington, D.C.: Government Printing Office, 2000), 514–519.

25. Johnson, *The Vantage Point*, 535.

26. David Halberstam, *The Best and the Brightest* (New York: Penguin, 1972).

27. Notes of Meeting, 25 January 1968, *Foreign Relations of the United States, 1964–1968*, 29:1, Part 1, Korea, Document 213, 514–519. Frustrations abounded across the government. Chief of Naval Operations Thomas Moorer complained, "The North Koreans have made their own rules and they are new rules." "In Pueblo's Wake," *Time* (2 February 1968): 9.

28. Mitchell Lerner, *The Pueblo Incident: A Spy Ship and the Failure of American Foreign Policy* (Lawrence: University Press of Kansas, 2002), 127–128; Damon Kasberg, "Dyess Airpark Holds Airman's Tale," Air Force Combat Command, 15 November 2012, www.acc.af .mil/news/story.asp?id=123326256 [accessed 27 July 2015].

29. Johnson, *The Vantage Point*, 536.

30. "In Pueblo's Wake," 15.

31. George Ball, *The Past Has Another Pattern: Memoirs* (New York: W. W. Norton, 1982), 436.

32. Ball, *The Past Has Another Pattern*, 436.

33. Notes of the President's Meeting with Senator Dirksen and Congressman Ford, 30 January 1968, Tom Johnson's Notes of Meetings, Box 2, LBJ Library.

34. "Notes of a Meeting," 31 January 1968, *Foreign Relations of the United States, 1964–1968*, Volume VI, Vietnam, January-August 1968, Document 39. "Notes of the President's Breakfast Meeting with Congressional Leaders and Policy Advisors," 31 January 1968, Tom Johnson's Notes of Meeting, Box 2, LBJ Library.

35. *Newsweek*, 5 February 1968, 17.

36. Lerner, *The Pueblo Incident*, 143.

37. Rostow to LBJ, 27 January 1968, NSF, country file, Asia and the Pacific, Korea-*Pueblo* Incident, Box 257, LBJ Library.

38. Press Conference Remarks, 3 February 1968, NSC Histories, *Pueblo* Crisis, 1968, boxes 31–33, Vol. 13, public statements, tabs A-C.

39. Notes of the President's Meeting with the Democratic Congressional Leadership, 6 February 1968, Tom Johnson's Notes of Meetings, Box 2, LBJ Library.

40. Johnson, *A White House Diary*, 8 February 1968, 631.

41. Notes of Meeting," 10 February 1968, *Foreign Relations of the United States, 1964–1968*, Volume VI, Vietnam, January-August 1968, document 65.

42. Notes of the President's Meeting with Cyrus Vance, 15 February 1968, Tom Johnson's Notes of Meetings, Box 2, LBJ Library; Johnson, *The Vantage Point*, 388–389.

43. Notes of the President's Meeting with Cyrus Vance, 15 February 1968, Tom Johnson's Notes of Meetings, Box 2, LBJ Library; Johnson, *The Vantage Point*, 388–389.

44. "In Pueblo's Wake," 14.

45. Goldberg to LBJ, 22 February 1968, NA 2, 1967–1969, Central Files, POL 33–36, Box 2255, 2/21/68 Folder.

46. Clark Clifford (with Richard Holbrooke), *Counsel to the President: A Memoir* (New York: Random House, 1991), 466.

47. Johnson, *The Vantage Point*, 532–533.

48. Johnson, *The Vantage Point*, 536–537.

49. George Christian, *The President Steps Down: A Personal Memoir of the Transfer of Power* (New York: The Macmillan Company, 1970), 140.

50. Lerner, *The Pueblo Incident*, 199–200.

51. *Congressional Record*, 22 July 1968, vol. 114, pt. 14 (Washington, D.C.: Government Printing Office, 1969), 18098.

52. Christian, *The President Steps Down*, 138. The tragedies with North Korea continued immediately with LBJ's successor. On April 14, 1969, the North Koreans shot down an EC-121 reconnaissance plane in the Sea of Japan as it performed intelligence-collecting more than seventy miles from the coastline. All thirty-one people on board died. The Nixon administration protested, made a short show of force, and resumed flights a week later, although with more precautions. Some of the same people who criticized LBJ now praised Nixon for showing restraint.

53. *New York Times*, 14 August 1968.

54. Problems also resulted when pictures of eight members of the crew appeared with them extending their middle fingers to their captors. Not understanding the sign, the North Koreans failed to censor them. *Time* magazine carried the photo on October 18. Underneath, it read, "The North Koreans are having a hard time proving to the world that the captive crewmen of the U.S.S. *Pueblo* are a contrite and cooperative lot." *Time*, 18 October 1968, 38.

55. Lerner, *The Pueblo Incident*, 209.

56. Lerner, *The Pueblo Incident*, 209.

57. Jack Cheevers, *Act of War: Lyndon Johnson, North Korea, and the Capture of the Spy Ship Pueblo* (New York: NAL Caliber, 2013), 260.

58. Christian, *The President Steps Down*, 140.

59. Lerner, *The Pueblo Incident*, 211.

60. Lerner, *The Pueblo Incident*, 219.

61. *Newsweek*, 6 January 1969, 9.

62. New York Times, 24 December 1968, 22.

63. Richard Homan to LBJ, 23 December 1968, NSF, Defense, ND 19/CO 151, Box 205, LBJ Library. Not everyone agreed, as a Republican senator from Colorado, Gordon Allot, stressed: "If we intended to admit before the whole world that we were wrong, and then deny that we were wrong, and then to deny that our apology was valid, did we have to wait eleven months to do so." *Congressional Record*, 10 January 1969, 1:115, p. 432.

64. Johnson, *The Vantage Point*, 552.

65. Christian, *The President Steps Down*, 138.

66. Christian, *The President Steps Down*, 140.

67. Richard A. Mobley, *Flash Point North Korea: The Pueblo and EC-121 Crises* (Annapolis: Naval Institute Press, 2003), 98–115.

CHAPTER 3: TET

1. Memorandum from the Joint Chiefs of Staff to President Johnson, 29 January 1968, *FRUS, 1964–1968*, Document 30, 69–70.

2. Notes of Meeting, 30 January 1968, *FRUS, 1964–1968*, document 36, 79–82. The conversation drifted to how to retaliate and how to prevent such actions in the capitol. General Wheeler noted, "this is about as tough to stop as it to protect against an individual mugging in Washington, D.C." McNamara chimed in, "We need to keep General Loan in charge of the Saigon police. He should not be removed as some of our people in the State Department are suggesting." CIA Director Helms added, "I agree completely." As the meeting transitioned to another topic, McNamara emphasized, "the answer to the mortar attacks is success at Khesanh."

3. Don Oberdorfer, *Tet: The Turning Point in the Vietnam War* (Baltimore: Johns Hopkins University, 2001), 121.

4. Douglas Brinkley, *Cronkite* (New York: HarperCollins, 2012), 367.

5. Telephone Conversation between Lyndon Johnson and Robert McNamara, Presidential Telephone Conversations, 31 January 1968, Tape F68.02, PNO 1, LBJ Library.

6. For more on the topic, reference: Joseph A. Fry, *Debating Vietnam: Fulbright, Stennis, and Their Senate Hearings* (Lanham, MD: Rowman and Littlefield, 2006); Robert David Johnson, *Congress and the Cold War* (New York: Cambridge University Press, 2005).

7. "Notes of a Meeting," 31 January 1968, *FRUS, 1964–1968*, Document 39, 86–88.

8. White House Daily Diary, 31 January 1968, LBJ Library.

9. Oberdorfer, *Tet*, 162; White House Daily Diary, 31 January 1968, LBJ Library. Later, LBJ acknowledged about Tet and his optimistic reports: "This is not to imply that Tet was

not a shock, in one degree or another, to all of us. We knew that a show of strength was coming; it was more massive than we anticipated." Johnson, *The Vantage Point*, 384. Katzenbach wrote: "Supporters of the war did their best to paint such a picture (of a U.S. military victory) in the days and weeks following Tet. But even if true, it was irrelevant. The massive attacks on the heels of upbeat progress reports effectively destroyed the public's confidence in the administration and the president's leadership." Nicholas deB. Katzenbach, *Some of It Was Fun: Working with RFK and LBJ* (New York: W. W. Norton, 2008), 273.

10. Lyndon Johnson, "Remarks of the Presidential Prayer Breakfast," 1 February 1968, *Public Papers of the Presidents of the United States, Lyndon Johnson January 1-June 30, 1968* (Washington, D.C.: Government Publishing Office, 43.

11. Robert Dallek, *Flawed Giant: Lyndon Johnson and His Times, 1961–1973* (New York: Oxford University Press, 1998), 504.

12. Arthur J. Dommen, *The Indochinese Experience of the French and Americans: Nationalism and Communism in Cambodia, Laos, and Vietnam* (Bloomington: Indiana University Press, 2001), 672; Oberdorfer, *Tet*, 164–165.

13. Harry McPherson, *A Political Education* (Boston: Little, Brown and Company, 1972), 424.

14. Emmett S. Redford and Richard T. McCulley, *White House Operations: The Johnson Presidency* (Austin: University of Texas Press, 1986), 72. Interview by the author with Larry Temple, 29 June 2016, Austin, Texas.

15. Clifford, *Counsel to the President*, 485.

16. Karnow, *Vietnam*, 548. He added: "I watched the invasion of the American embassy compound, and the terrible sight of General Loan killing the Vietcong captive. You got a sense of the awfulness, the endlessness, of the war – and, though it sounds naïve, the unethical quality of the war in which a prisoner is shot point blank range."

17. Johnson, *The Vantage Point*, 384.

18. Notes of Meeting, 6 February 1968, *FRUS, 1964–1968*, document 58, 135–137.

19. Notes of Meeting, 6 February 1968, *FRUS, 1964–1968*, document 58, 135–137.

20. Notes of the President's Meeting with the Democratic Congressional Leadership, 6 February 1968, Tom Johnson's Notes of Meetings, Box 2, LBJ Library. Wheeler chimed in about giving a good briefing to the senator, but Rostow summed it up best. "If the war goes well, the American people are with us. If the war goes badly they are against us ... I think the men in uniform now have the burden in determining how much support or lack of support we get." Later in the day, Byrd called to apologize for his criticism of the president at the morning meeting. Notes of the President's Tuesday Luncheon Meeting, 6 February 1968, Tom Johnson's Notes of Meetings, Box 2, LBJ Library.

21. Dallek, *Flawed Giant*, 505.

22. Peter Braestrup, *Big Story: How the American Press and Television Reported and Interpreted the Crisis of Tet 1968 in Vietnam and Washington* (Boulder, CO: Westview Press, 1977), 685.

23. Johnson, *White House Diary* 7 February 1968, 629.

24. "Notes of President's Meeting with the National Security Council," 7 February 1968, Tom Johnson's Notes of Meetings, Box 2, LBJ Library.

25. Clark Clifford with Richard Holbrooke, *Counsel to the President: A Memoir* (New York: Random House, 1991), 477.

26. George Reedy, *Lyndon Johnson: A Memoir* (New York: Andrews and McMeel, 1982), 150.

27. Johnson, *A White House Diary*, 8 February 1968, 631.

28. Notes of Meeting, 9 February 1968, *FRUS, 1964–1968*, document 64, 158–168. At one point, the president even asked Rusk, "Dean, should we have more than the Tonkin Gulf resolution in going into this? Should we ask for a declaration of war?" Rusk simply responded, "I do not recommend a declaration of war" arguing that "it might be a direct challenge to Moscow and Peking, in a way we have never challenged them before. There would be very severe international effects."

29. Lyndon B. Johnson, *Public Papers of the Presidents of the United States: Lyndon B. Johnson, 1968–69*, 12 February 1968, Book 1 (Washington, D.C.: Government Printing Office, 1970), 218–219.

30. Notes of Meeting, 12 February 1968, *FRUS, 1964–1968*, document 70, 188–96. Beyond the troop levels, the JCS also placed pressure on the president to extend their bombing targets in Hanoi and Haiphong harbor. Some pushed back. When queried, McNamara noted: "As I have said before, the military value is small. The risk is very high. The chances for civilian casualties are very high." The president tabled the matter. Notes of Meeting, 13 February 1968, *FRUS, 1964–1968*, document 74, 206–210.

31. Johnson, *The Vantage Point*, 387–388.

32. Clifford, *Counsel to the President*, 479.

33. Johnson, *My Brother Lyndon*, 210.

34. Walter LaFeber, *The Deadly Bet: LBJ, Vietnam, and the 1968 Election* (Lanham, MD: Rowman and Littlefield, 2005), 42–43.

35. Jeff Shesol, *Mutual Contempt: Lyndon Johnson, Robert Kennedy, and the Feud That Defined a Decade* (New York: W. W. Norton, 1997), 413.

36. Thurston Clarke, *The Last Campaign: Robert F. Kennedy and 82 Days That Inspired America* (New York: Henry Holt, 2008), 35–36.

37. Clarke, *The Last Campaign*, 34. He also questioned the administration's assertions of victory, particularly since mass uprisings never materialized. "How ironic it is, that we should claim a victory because a people whom we have given sixteen thousand [American] lives, billions of dollars, and almost a decade to defend, did not rise in arms against us." Palermo, *In His Own Right*, 102.

38. Dean Rusk (as told to Richard Rusk), *As I Saw It* (New York: W. W. North & Company, 1990), 417.

39. Karnow, *Vietnam*, 548.

40. Thomas W. Zeiler, *Dean Rusk: Defending the American Mission Abroad* (Wilmington, DE: Scholarly Resources, 2000), 183.

41. Rusk, *As I Saw It*, 477.

42. Karnow, *Vietnam*, 548.

43. Clifford, *Counsel to the President*, 485.

44. Joseph A. Califano, Jr., *The Triumph and Tragedy of Lyndon Johnson: The White House Years* (New York: Touchstone, 1991), 263.

45. Califano, *The Triumph and Tragedy of Lyndon Johnson*, 264.
46. Johnson, *The Vantage Point*, 390. From the notes, LBJ reached several conclusions on potential paths. "Accept the Wheeler-Westmoreland proposal [at] an expenditure of an additional $10 billion in fiscal 1969 . . . combine the military increase with a new peace initiative . . . maintain the status quo on troop commitments and change our strategy protecting only 'essential' areas and reducing offensive operations in unpopulated areas." Johnson, *The Vantage Point*, 389–390.
47. Notes of Meeting, 28 February 1968, *FRUS, 1964–1968*, document 91, 267–75.
48. Rusk, *As I Saw It*, 418. LBJ had earlier even moaned to the JCS, "bomb, bomb, bomb, that's all you know." Herring, *America's Longest War*, 225.
49. Harold P. Ford, *CIA and the Vietnam Policymakers: Three Episodes, 1962–1968* (Ann Arbor: University of Michigan Library, 1998), 125. Wheeler also told the president, "in short, it [disaster] was a very near thing." Chester J. Pach, Jr., "Tet on TV: U.S. Nightly News Reporting and Presidential Policy Making," in Caroline Fink, Philipp Gassert, and Detlef Junker, *1968: The World Transformed* (New York: Cambridge University Press, 1998), 56.
50. Memorandum for the Record (Rostow to Johnson), 29 February 1968, *FRUS, 1964–1968*, document 93, 279–281. The hawks, especially Rostow, supported Wheeler. In mid-March, he told LBJ: "If we lose our heads at this critical moment and listen to the extremists, we might" lose all of the region to "aggression . . . open the way to a new phase of Communist expansion . . . and bring us closer to a Third World War." LaFeber, *The Deadly Bet*, 60.
51. LaFeber, *The Deadly Bet*, 60–61.
52. Johnson, *The Vantage Point*, 393; Clifford, *Counsel to the President*, 489.
53. Soon, LBJ's top advisers added one: "What probable Communist reaction could we expect to each of the possible alternative courses of action?" Johnson, *The Vantage Point*, 394.
54. Johnson, *The Vantage Point*, 395.
55. Brinkley, *Cronkite*, 377–378.
56. Brinkley, *Cronkite*, 377–378.
57. Mark K. Updegrove, *Indomitable Will: LBJ in the Presidency* (New York: Crown Publishers, 2002), 261. There was some debate as some quoted LBJ as "If I've lost Cronkite, I've lost Middle America" or "If I've lost Cronkite, I've lost the war." Brinkley, *Cronkite*, 380. Others responded negatively to Cronkite's editorial. Rusk complained, "I was very disgusted with the media, particularly CBS and Walter Cronkite." Westmoreland added, "I think they deceived the American people." He even took on CBS later in a court case over libel regarding a documentary, "The Uncounted Enemy: A Vietnam Deception." Brinkley, *Cronkite*, 379.
58. John Prados, *Vietnam: The History of an Unwinnable War, 1945–1975* (Lawrence: University Press of Kansas, 2009), 247. Clifford's doubts dated to 1965 when he counseled against the massive buildup. In addition, during the summer of 1967, he traveled to Australia, the Philippines, and other allied nations at the request of the president. On returning, he remembered being "puzzled, troubled, concerned" and believed,

"our assessment of the danger to the stability of Southeast Asia and the Western Pacific was exaggerated." Karnow, *Vietnam*, 552. McNamara noted his fatigue with "requests from the Wheelers of the world" and complained the military had "no plan to win the war." LaFeber, *The Deadly Bet*, 52.

59. Clifford, *Counsel to the President*, 475.

60. Clifford, *Counsel to the President*, 476.

61. Karnow, *Vietnam*, 554.

62. George Herring, *America's Longest War: The United States and Vietnam, 1950–1975* 5th edition (New York: McGraw-Hill, 2014), 245.

63. Karnow, *Vietnam*, 554.

64. Karnow, *Vietnam*, 554.

65. There were many economic problems plaguing the country, including a new gold crisis, more imbalance in payments, and fear of inflation in the winter of 1968.

66. The paragraphs on the Clifford Report exist in the Notes of Meeting, 4 March 1968, *FRUS, 1964–1968*, document 104, 316–327. Rusk stressed that a bombing halt could take place with little military risk because of the upcoming rainy season, although he opposed a full bombing halt as "we owed it to our men in uniform not to allow the North Vietnamese a free ride down the Ho Chi Minh Trail." He hoped that "limiting our bombing to areas around the demilitarized zone (DMZ) and to tactical air support was a major initiative, which I hoped we might parlay into talks with Hanoi." Rusk, *As I Saw It*, 479. "I knew Rusk never raised this kind of matter without considerable thought," the president noted. Johnson, *The Vantage Point*, 398.

67. Johnson, *The Vantage Point*, 398–399.

68. Johnson, *The Vantage Point*, 398.

69. Johnson, *The Vantage Point*, 400. Rusk also wanted the bombing halt to "put additional responsibility on Hanoi for not seeking peace." When queried about how long the bombing halt would last, Rusk responded, "my guess is that a bombing pause would last about three days. It would not hold up if they attacked Khe Sanh or the cities. If there is no response from Hanoi by the time the bad weather has ended, we could resume the bombing. We would not have lost much militarily, and we might regain the public initiative." Clifford, *Counsel to the President*, 496–497.

70. Johnson, *The Vantage Point*, 402.

71. *New York Times*, 10 March 1968.

72. Johnson, *A White House Diary*, 10 March 1968, 637.

73. Johnson, *A White House Diary*, 10 March 1968, 637.

74. LBJ speculated "the story had come from after comparing its content and tone with some of the more pessimistic assessments compiled in previous weeks at lower levels in the government, especially by Pentagon officials." He added, "it was obvious that the sources for the story did not know or understand what was going on in my mind, and they were not party to my dealings with my senior advisers; nor did they understand the decision-making process." He thought that political motives underlay the release only two days before the New Hampshire primary. He felt that "this story, and others like

that would inevitably follow, would create controversy and solve nothing. Such reports would ... give Hanoi an impression of increased divisiveness in our country. The fact was that I had firmly decided against sending anything approaching 206,000 additional men to Vietnam." Johnson, *The Vantage Point*, 402.

75. Clifford, *Counsel to the President*, 501. Even weeks later, LBJ fumed about the betrayal. In a telephone conversation with Russell, Johnson complained that McNamara's whiz kids "practically want us to surrender." He personally named Enthoven, Steadman, and Warnke, and complained bitterly about Nitze refusing to testify on Capitol Hill in defense of the Military Assistance Program. Russell called for their replacement, but LBJ highlighted that Clifford shielded them to help with the transition and Johnson admitted there were good people "but it is a question of just how fast you disrupt them until he can kind of get his feet on the ground and know who is who and what Department they are running." Telephone conversation between Johnson and Russell, 22 March 1968, Tape F6803.02, PNO 8.

76. Johnson, *The Vantage Point*, 403–404.

77. Johnson, *The Vantage Point*, 403–404.

78. He added, "I believed that no American who heard the hearings could have failed to understand better why we were engaged in Southeast Asia and what we hoped to see develop there." He cited the positive flow of mail (two to one) in favor of Rusk and the administration's policies in the time that followed. Johnson, *The Vantage Point*, 404.

79. Terry H. Anderson, *The Sixties* (New York: Longman, 1999), 188.

80. Shesol, *Mutual Contempt*, 417.

81. Jonathan Darman, *Landslide: LBJ and Ronald Reagan at the Dawn of a New America* (New York: Random House, 2014), 353.

82. *New Hampshire Union Leader*, 3 May 2011.

83. The White House watched Bobby carefully through polling and kept extensive files on RFK, including Marvin Watson. For example, see folders in: Papers of Lyndon Johnson, President 1963–1969, Office Files of White House Aides, Marvin Watson, Box 25, LBJ Library.

84. Shesol, *Mutual Contempt*, 418.

85. Shesol, *Mutual Contempt*, 418–419.

86. Not long after the New Hampshire results, Bill Moyers traveled with Arthur Schlesinger, Jr. to meet with RFK at the "21" restaurant. On the way, he described LBJ as "impene-trable" and living inside a "paranoid" bubble. He stressed that "four more years of Johnson would be ruinous for the country." He then emphasized Johnson "flees from confrontations. He is willing to take on people like Goldwater and Nixon, to whom he feels superior. But he does not like confrontations when he does not feel superior." Shesol, *Mutual Contempt*, 418.

87. Clifford, *Counsel to the President*, 503. Clifford submitted a six-page memorandum of the meeting to the White House afterward. Clark Clifford, "Memorandum of Conference with Senator Robert Kennedy and Theodore C. Sorenson," 14 March 1968, White House Famous Names, Box 8, LBJ Library.

88. Clifford, *Counsel to the President*, 503–504.

89. Clifford, *Counsel to the President*, 504–505.

90. Clifford, *Counsel to the President*, 504–505.

91. Notes of Senator Robert F. Kennedy's Press Conference, 16 March 1968, White House Famous Names, Box 8, LBJ Library.

92. Clifford, *Counsel to the President*, 505.

93. Johnson, *A White House Diary*, 17 March 1968, 641.

94. Robert Dallek, *Flawed Giant*, 510.

95. Memorandum for the Record, 18 March 1968, *Foreign Relations of the United States, 1964–1968*, Volume VI, Vietnam, January-August 1968, document 140.

96. Memorandum for the Record, 18 March 1968, *Foreign Relations of the United States, 1964–1968*, Volume VI, Vietnam, January-August 1968, document 140.

97. Clifford, *Counsel to the President*, 508.

98. Bui Diem, *In the Jaws of History* (Boston, MA: Houghton-Miflin, 1987), 225.

99. Telephone Conversation between Johnson and Clifford, 20 March 1968, Tape F6805.02, PNO 5, LBJ Library.

100. Telephone Conversation between Johnson and Clifford, 20 March 1968, Tape F6805.02, PNO 5, LBJ Library.

101. Notes of Meeting, 20 March 1968, *Foreign Relations of the United States, 1964–1968*, Volume VI, Vietnam, January-August 1968, document 147.

102. John Acacia, *Clark Clifford: The Wise Man of Washington* (Lexington: University Press of Kentucky, 2009), 262.

103. Acacia, *Clark Clifford*, 262.

104. Clifford, *Counsel to the President*, 513.

105. Clifford, *Counsel to the President*, 513.

106. Clifford, *Counsel to the President*, 514.

107. Notes of Meeting, 26 March 1968, *Foreign Relations of the United States, 1964–1968*, Volume VI, Vietnam, January-August 1968, document 156. In the meeting, LBJ complained bitterly that no one outside of the military seemed to be giving a positive appraisal and that in the Pentagon "it is the civilians that are cutting our guts out." He already received reports from Fortas and Rostow about the previous night, where he noted, "Carter [sic] and DePuy weren't up to par last night." He lamented "our fiscal situation is abominable . . . We are not getting the tax bill. The deficit could be over 30. If it does, the interest rate will raise." He continued, "the country is demoralized. You must know about it," directing most of his focus to Abrams who had been in Vietnam for a long time. He complained, "Nitze says he would resign if we sent extra troops. What we have been doing has got us in a mess." Then, in a strange turn, LBJ said: "I would give Westmoreland 206,000 men if he said he needed them and if we could get them." Wheeler simply responded: "They will settle for the 13,500." The meeting ended with more griping about how bad things were, including taxes and the economy and how congressional hearings continued to wound the administration.

108. Notes of Meeting, 26 March 1968, *Foreign Relations of the United States, 1964–1968*, Volume VI, Vietnam, January-August 1968, document 158.

109. Randall Woods, *LBJ: Architect of American Ambition* (New York: Free Press, 2006), 834. Acheson wrote afterward, "the gold crisis had dampened expansionist ideas ... the town is in an atmosphere of crisis." LaFeber, *The Deadly Bet*, 57.

110. Notes of Meeting, 26 March 1968, *Foreign Relations of the United States, 1964–1968*, Volume VI, Vietnam, January-August 1968, document 158.

111. Only a few dissented as Bradley suggested, "we should send only support troops." Taylor protested strongly: "I am dismayed. The picture I get is a very different from that you have. Let's not concede the home front; let's do something about it." Notes of Meeting, 26 March 1968, *Foreign Relations of the United States, 1964–1968*, Volume VI, Vietnam, January-August 1968, document 158.

112. Clifford, *Counsel to the President*, 518.

113. Notes of Meeting, 26 March 1968, *Foreign Relations of the United States, 1964–1968*, Volume VI, Vietnam, January-August 1968, document 158.

114. Woods, *Architect of American Ambition*, 834. He also ordered DePuy and Carver to the White House to give him the same briefing, although Habib escaped the tortuous rendition by being in Ohio. The president announced they passed. Clifford, *Counsel to the President*, 518.

115. Johnson, *The Vantage Point*, 385.

CHAPTER 4: AS A RESULT, I WILL NOT SEEK REELECTION

1. Jan Jarboe Russell, *Lady Bird: A Biography of Mrs. Johnson* (New York: Scribner, 1999), 300.

2. Lady Bird Johnson, *A White House Diary* (New York: Holt, Rinehart, and Winston, 1970), 642.

3. Lyndon Baines Johnson, *The Vantage Point: Perspectives of the Presidency, 1963–1969* (New York: Holt, Rinehart and Winston, 1971), 431.

4. Russell, *Lady Bird*, 300.

5. Johnson, *A White House Diary*, 642.

6. Michael H. Hunt, *Lyndon Johnson's War: America's Cold War Crusade in Vietnam, 1945–1968* (New York: Hill and Wang, 2011).

7. Horace W. Busby, *The Thirty-First of March: An Intimate Portrait of Lyndon Johnson's Final Days in Office* (New York: Farrar, Straus and Giroux, 2005), 188.

8. Busby, *The Thirty-First of March*, 188–189.

9. Busby, *The Thirty-First of March*, 189–190.

10. Busby, *The Thirty-First of March*, 189.

11. Busby, *The Thirty-First of March*, 190.

12. Busby, *The Thirty-First of March*, 190–191.

13. Busby, *The Thirty-First of March*, 191.

14. Busby, *The Thirty-First of March*, 191–192, 194.

15. Busby, *The Thirty-First of March*, 195.

16. Busby, *The Thirty-First of March*, 196.

17. Busby, *The Thirty-First of March*, 196.

18. Busby, *The Thirty-First of March*, 181.

19. Johnson, *The Vantage Point*, 431–432.

20. Johnson, *The Vantage Point*, 425.

21. Johnson also noted: "And I remembered Grandmother Johnson," he often noted, "who had had a stroke and stayed in a wheelchair throughout my childhood, unable even to move her hands or to speak so that she could be understood." Johnson, *The Vantage Point*, 425.

22. Johnson, *The Vantage Point*, 426–427.

23. Jack Valenti argued, "It was the Vietnam War that cut the arteries of the LBJ Administration." Jack Valenti, *A Very Human President* (New York: W.W. Norton & Company, 1975), 367.

24. Johnson, *The Vantage Point*, 426–427.

25. Frank E. Vandiver, *Shadows of Vietnam: Lyndon Johnson's War* (College Station: Texas A&M Press, 1997), 331.

26. A. J. Langguth, *Our Vietnam: The War, 1954–1975* (New York: Simon and Schuster, 2000), 494.

27. Doris Kearns Goodwin, *Lyndon Johnson and the American Dream* (New York: St. Martin's Press, 1976), 338.

28. Jim Jones, "Behind L.B.J.'s Decision Not to Run in '68," *New York Times*, 16 April 1988.

29. Johnson, *The Vantage Point*, 432.

30. Johnson, *The Vantage Point*, 432.

31. Johnson, *The Vantage Point*, 432.

32. Johnson, *The Vantage Point*, 432.

33. Jim Jones, "Behind L.B.J.'s Decision Not to Run in '68," *New York Times*, 16 April 1988.

34. Johnson, *The Vantage Point*, 432.

35. Walter LaFeber, *The Deadly Bet: LBJ, Vietnam, and the 1968 Election* (Lanham, MD: Rowman & Littlefield, 2005), 62.

36. Busby, *The Thirty-First of March*, 205.

37. Busby, *The Thirty-First of March*, 204.

38. Busby, *The Thirty-First of March*, 204.

39. Busby, *The Thirty-First of March*, 206–207.

40. Busby, *The Thirty-First of March*, 207.

41. Russell, *Lady Bird*, 300–301.

42. Johnson, *A White House Diary*, 643.

43. White House Diary, 31 March 1968, p. 3, Lyndon B. Johnson Library, Austin, Texas [hereafter LBJ Library].

44. Johnson, *A White House Diary*, 643.

45. Johnson, *A White House Diary*, 643.

46. Busby, *The Thirty-First of March*, 209.

47. Johnson, *A White House Diary*, 643.

48. Busby, *The Thirty-First of March*, 211.

49. Busby, *The Thirty-First of March*, 207.

50. Busby, *The Thirty-First of March*, 212.

51. Busby, *The Thirty-First of March*, 212.
52. Busby, *The Thirty-First of March*, 213.
53. Busby, *The Thirty-First of March*, 214.
54. Christian to Johnson, 31 March 1968, Papers of Lyndon Johnson, The President's Appointment File [Diary Backup], 3/27/68-4/3/68, Box 94, LBJ Library.
55. Busby, *The Thirty-First of March*, 214–215.
56. Johnson, *A White House Diary*, 644.
57. Johnson, *A White House Diary*, 643.
58. Johnson, *A White House Diary*, 644–645.
59. Busby, *The Thirty-First of March*, 216.
60. Johnson, *A White House Diary*, 644.
61. Johnson, *A White House Diary*, 644.
62. Walt W. Rostow, "Memorandum of Record," *Foreign Relations of the United States,* January-August 1968, Vietnam, Volume VI, (Washington D.C.: Government Printing Office, 2002), 492.
63. Rostow, "Memorandum of Record," 492.
64. Rostow, "Memorandum of Record," 493.
65. Anatoly Dobrynin, *In Confidence: Moscow's Ambassador to America's Six Cold War Presidents, 1962–1986* (New York: Times Books, 1995), 171; Rostow, "Memorandum of Record," 493.
66. Not long after, Dobrynin exited a meeting with Rostow. As he exited, he came on the president once more. LBJ pulled him aside and told him under the strictest of confidence that he intended not to run for reelection, noting he was the first foreigner to hear the news and that only a few others knew including Lady Bird. "I want to show them that I have no obsessive lust for power, as many believe. I want to spend the rest of my time serving the country, not the party." Dobrynin noted that LBJ "spoke with difficulty and could hardly hide his emotions." Dobrynin, *In Confidence*, 172.
67. Dobrynin, *In Confidence*, 172.
68. Busby, *The Thirty-First of March*, 221.
69. Busby, *The Thirty-First of March*, 222.
70. Busby, *The Thirty-First of March*, 223.
71. Busby, *The Thirty-First of March*, 224.
72. Busby, *The Thirty-First of March*, 224.
73. Busby, *The Thirty-First of March*, 225.
74. Clark Clifford (with Richard Holbrooke), *Counsel to the President: A Memoir* (New York: Random House, 1991), 523.
75. Johnson, *A White House Diary*, 645.
76. Clifford, *Counsel to the President: A Memoir*, 523.
77. Clifford, *Counsel to the President*, 524–525.
78. Marvin Watson, *Chief of Staff: Lyndon Johnson and His Presidency* (New York: Thomas Dunne, 2004), 284.
79. Johnson, *The Vantage Point*, 424.
80. Watson, *Chief of Staff*, 284.

81. Johnson, *The Vantage Point*, 434.
82. Johnson, *A White House Diary*, 645.
83. Johnson, *The Vantage Point*, 434.
84. Johnson, *A White House Diary*, 645.
85. Russell, *Lady Bird*, 300.
86. Lyndon B. Johnson, "The President's Address to the Nation Announcing Steps to Limit the War in Vietnam and Reporting His Decision Not to Seek Reelection," 31 March 1968, *Public Papers of the President of the United States, 1968–1969*, Book 1 (January 1-June 30, 1968), (Washington, D.C.: United States Government Printing Office, 1970), 469.
87. Johnson, *A White House Diary*, 646.
88. Johnson, "The President's Address to the Nation Announcing Steps to Limit the War in Vietnam and Reporting His Decision Not to Seek Reelection," 470–471.
89. Johnson, "The President's Address to the Nation Announcing Steps to Limit the War in Vietnam and Reporting His Decision Not to Seek Reelection," 473.
90. Johnson, "The President's Address to the Nation Announcing Steps to Limit the War in Vietnam and Reporting His Decision Not to Seek Reelection," 473.
91. Russell, *Lady Bird*, 301.
92. Johnson, "The President's Address to the Nation Announcing Steps to Limit the War in Vietnam and Reporting His Decision Not to Seek Reelection," 476.
93. Johnson, "The President's Address to the Nation Announcing Steps to Limit the War in Vietnam and Reporting His Decision Not to Seek Reelection," 476.
94. Johnson, "The President's Address to the Nation Announcing Steps to Limit the War in Vietnam and Reporting His Decision Not to Seek Reelection," 476.
95. Johnson, *A White House Diary*, 645–646.
96. Johnson, *A White House Diary*, 646.
97. From the President's Daily Diary. As cited in *Foreign Relations of the United States, January-August 1968, Vietnam, Volume VI*, (Washington D.C.: Government Printing Office, 2002), 495.
98. Johnson, *A White House Diary*, 646.
99. Johnson, *A White House Diary*, 644.
100. Lyndon B. Johnson, "The President's News Conference of March 31, 1968," 31 March 1968, *Public Papers of the President of the United States, 1968–1969*, Book 1 (January 1-June 30, 1968), (Washington, D.C.: United States Government Printing Office, 1970), 476.
101. Frank Cormier, *LBJ: The Way He Was* (Garden City, NY: Doubleday & Company, 1977), 266.
102. Johnson, "The President's News Conference of March 31, 1968," 479. The *Washington Post* editorial board stressed about the speech that LBJ "made a personal sacrifice in the name of national unity that entitled him to a very special place in the annals of American history ... The President last night put unity ahead of his own advancement and his own pride." As cited in Joseph A. Califano, Jr., *The Triumph & Tragedy of Lyndon Johnson: The White House Years* (New York: Simon & Schuster, 1991), 270.

103. (President's Daily Diary). *Foreign Relations of the United States,* January-August 1968, Vietnam, Volume VI, (Washington D.C.: Government Printing Office, 2002), 495.

104. Johnson, *A White House Diary,* 644.

105. Sam Houston Johnson to LBJ, 1 April 1968, Family Correspondence, Box 2, LBJ Library; Sam Houston Johnson, *My Brother Lyndon* (New York: Cowles Book Company, 1970), 249–250.

106. *Washington Post,* 1 April 1968.

107. *New York Times,* 1 April 1968.

108. Robert Dallek, *Flawed Giant: Lyndon Johnson and His Times, 1961–1973* (New York: Oxford University Press, 1998), 530.

109. Woods, *LBJ,* 837.

110. Theodore H. White, *The Making of the President: 1968* (New York: Harper, 1969), 145.

CHAPTER 5: THE DAYS THE EARTH STOOD STILL

1. Joseph A. Califano, Jr., *The Triumph and Tragedy of Lyndon Johnson: The White House Years* (New York: Touchstone, 1991), 273.

2. Horace Busby, *The Thirty-First of March: An Intimate Portrait of Lyndon Johnson's Final Days in Office* (New York: Farrar, Straus and Giroux, 2005), 230.

3. Lady Bird Johnson, *A White House Diary* (New York: Holt, Rinehart and Winston, 1970), 647.

4. Lyndon Baines Johnson, *Vantage Point: Perspectives of the Presidency, 1963–1969* (New York: Holt, Rinehart and Winston, 1971), 173.

5. At the last minute, he asked to bring Lyn, joking "we should take him – or else he will be raised half Baptist and a half Catholic." However, the tired child stayed on Air Force One because they thought it would be hard for him to sit through a two-hour service. Daily Diary, 4 April 1968, White House Files, LBJ Library.

6. Johnson, *Vantage Point,* 173–174.

7. Clay Risen, *A Nation on Fire: America in the Wake of the King Assassination* (New York: John Wiley & Sons, 2009), 30.

8. "Notes of Meeting," *Foreign Relations of the United States, 1964–1968,* Volume VI, Vietnam, January-August 1968, document 181; Johnson, *Vantage Point,* 174.

9. Johnson, *Vantage Point,* 174.

10. Wolfgang Mieder, *"Making A Way Out of No Way": Martin Luther King's Sermonic Proverbial Rhetoric* (New York: Peter Lang Publishing, 2010), 346.

11. Hoover to Clark, 20 February 1968, Personal Papers of Ramsey Clark, Box 67, LBJ Library.

12. At one point, the CIA even reported Soviet plans to invade South Carolina or Georgia to spark a massive uprising by African Americans against the United States. It cited "credible sources" that uncovered the plan. LBJ acknowledged that some plan might have existed in some Soviet leaders' minds, especially after Cuba, but "I think it's a ridiculous report. It will never happen. I know that the world is a dangerous place, but

in this instance whoever prepared this report should be put out to pasture." W. Marvin Watson and Sherwin Markman, *Chief of Staff: Lyndon Johnson and His Presidency* (New York: Thomas Dunne Books, 2004), 211.

13. Nick Kotz, *Judgment Days: Lyndon Baines Johnson, Martin Luther King, Jr., and the Laws That Changed America* (Boston: Houghton-Miflin, 2005), 414–415.

14. Johnson, *Vantage Point*, 174.

15. Johnson, *Vantage Point*, 174.

16. Johnson, *Vantage Point*, 173.

17. Califano, *The Triumph and Tragedy of Lyndon Johnson*, 274.

18. "Statement by the President on the Assassination of Dr. Martin Luther King, Jr.," 4 April 1968, The American Presidency Project, www.presidency.ucsb.edu/ws/?pid= 28781 [accessed 29 September 2015].

19. Califano, *The Triumph and Tragedy of Lyndon Johnson*, 275.

20. Busby, *The Thirty-First of March*, 236.

21. *Washington Evening Star*, 5 April 1968.

22. Kyle Longley, *Grunts: The American Combat Soldier in Vietnam* (Armonk, NY: M. E. Sharpe, 2008), 129.

23. Johnson, *Vantage Point*, 175–176.

24. Risen, *A Nation on Fire*, 67.

25. Daily Diary, 4 April 1968, White House Central Files, LBJ Library, 15.

26. Johnson, *A White House Diary*, 648.

27. Busby, *The Thirty-First of March*, 237.

28. Califano, Jr., *The Triumph and Tragedy of Lyndon Johnson*, 275.

29. Busby, *The Thirty-First of March*, 237.

30. Busby, *The Thirty-First of March*, 237.

31. Busby, *The Thirty-First of March*, 237.

32. Busby, *The Thirty-First of March*, 238.

33. Lyndon Johnson, Daily Diary, 5 April 1968, White House Central Files, LBJ Library.

34. Busby, *The Thirty-First of March*, 238.

35. Risen, *A Nation on Fire*, 88.

36. Busby, *The Thirty-First of March*, 238.

37. Johnson, *Vantage Point*, 176.

38. Michael W. Flamm, *Law and Order: Street Crime, Civil Unrest, and the Crisis of Liberalism in the 1960s* (New York: Columbia University Press, 2005), 145.

39. Califano, *The Triumph and Tragedy of Lyndon Johnson*, 276.

40. Risen, *A Nation on Fire*, 89.

41. Warren Christopher, *Chances of a Lifetime: A Memoir* (New York: Scribner, 2001), 57.

42. *New York Times*, 6 April 1968.

43. Lyndon B. Johnson, *Public Papers of the President of the United States, 1968–1969* volume 1 (Washington: Government Printing Office, 1970), 179–180.

44. Busby, *The Thirty-First of March*, 239.

45. Busby, *The Thirty-First of March*, 239.

46. Busby, *The Thirty-First of March*, 241.

47. Busby, *The Thirty-First of March*, 241.
48. Califano, *The Triumph and Tragedy of Lyndon Johnson*, 279.
49. Interview by the author with Larry Temple, June 29, 2016, Austin, Texas.
50. Busby, *The Thirty-First of March*, 241.
51. Christopher, *Chances of a Lifetime*, 58–59.
52. Risen, *A Nation on Fire*, 127.
53. Flamm, *Law and Order*, 146.
54. Risen, *A Nation on Fire*, 133.
55. Risen, *A Nation on Fire*, 135–136.
56. Califano, *The Triumph and Tragedy of Lyndon Johnson*, 279.
57. Califano, *The Triumph and Tragedy of Lyndon Johnson*, 280.
58. Daily Diary, 5 April 1968, White House Central Files, LBJ Library.
59. Califano, *The Triumph and Tragedy of Lyndon Johnson*, 280–281.
60. FBI Office in Atlanta to Hoover, 8 April 1968, Papers of Lyndon Johnson, President, 1963–1969, Confidential Files, Box 14; Ronald C. Towns, Special Agent in Charge Atlanta to Assistant Director Kelley, 8 April 1968, Papers of Lyndon Johnson, President, 1963–1969, Confidential Files, Box 14, LBJ Library. Barefoot Sanders wrote Jim Jones: "Congressman John Davis of Georgia called me yesterday to urge that the President not go to Atlanta for the King funeral. Davis reported that a preacher friend of his - - who is a fundamentalist, Ku Kluxer-type - - called Davis to say that the President's life would be in danger in Atlanta. Davis did not identify the man who gave him this information and says that he absolutely cannot do that. But he is certain that the information was given to him in good faith and so gives it some credence." Barefoot Sanders to Jim Jones, 8 April 1968, Papers of Lyndon Johnson, White House Central Files (WHCF) GEN FE, Box 5, LBJ Library.
61. Sam Houston Johnson, *My Brother Lyndon* (New York: Cowles Books, 1969), 257.
62. *Washington Post*, 6 April 1968.
63. Califano, *The Triumph and Tragedy of Lyndon Johnson*, 281.
64. Harry McPherson, *A Political Education* (Boston: Little, Brown and Company, 1972), 367.
65. McPherson, *A Political Education*, 369.
66. *Wall Street Journal*, 8 April 1968.
67. William Westmoreland, *A Soldier Reports* (New York: Doubleday & Company, 1976), 362.
68. Woods, *LBJ*, 839.
69. Risen, *A Nation on Fire*, 165.
70. Lyndon B. Johnson to Shapiro, 6 April 1968, *Public Papers of the Presidents of the United States*, Book 1, January 1-June 30, 1968 (Washington, D.C.: Government Printing Office, 1970), 479.
71. Christopher, *Chances of a Lifetime*, 59–60.
72. Christopher, *Chances of a Lifetime*, 59–60.
73. Califano, *The Triumph and Tragedy of Lyndon Johnson*, 281.
74. Risen, *A Nation on Fire*, 186.
75. Califano, *The Triumph and Tragedy of Lyndon Johnson*, 281.
76. Lyndon Johnson, Daily Diary, 7 April 1968, White House Central Files, LBJ Library.

77. Lyndon B. Johnson, "Telegram to the Governor of Maryland in Response to His Request for Federal Troops in Baltimore," 7 April 1968, *Public Papers of the Presidents of the United States*, Book 1, January 1-June 30, 1968 (Washington, D.C.: Government Printing Office, 1970), 498.

78. Lyndon Johnson, Daily Diary, 7 April 1968, White House Central Files, LBJ Library.

79. Kotz, *Judgment Days*, 418.

80. Risen, *A Nation on Fire*, 25. Congressman Emmanuel Celler noted after five years of LBJ, "I don't think there was any president that could have driven – I used that word advisedly – driven the Congress as hard as he did." Robert Mann, *The Walls of Jericho: Lyndon Johnson, Hubert Humphrey, Richard Russell, and the Struggle for Civil Rights* (New York: Harcourt, Brace & Company, 1996), 482.

81. Busby, *The Thirty-First of March*, 243.

82. Charles M. Lamb, *Housing Segregation in Suburban America since 1960: Presidential and Judicial Politics* (New York: Cambridge University Press, 2005), 33.

83. Woods, *LBJ*, 840.

84. Mann, *The Walls of Jericho*, 481.

85. Lamb, *Housing Segregation in Suburban America since 1960*, 481.

86. Johnson, *Vantage Point*, 177–178.

87. Johnson, *Vantage Point*, 177.

88. Johnson, *Vantage Point*, 177.

89. Leah Wright Rigueur, *The Loneliness of the Black Republican: Pragmatic Politics and the Pursuit of Power* (Princeton: Princeton University Press, 2015), 129.

90. Kotz, *Judgment Days*, 417.

91. Lyndon B. Johnson, "Letter to the Speaker of the House Urging Enactment of the Fair Housing Bill," 5 April 1968, *Public Papers of the Presidents of the United States*, Book 1, January 1-June 30, 1968 (Washington, D.C.: Government Printing Office, 1970), 496–497.

92. Kotz, *Judgment Days*, 418.

93. Mann, *The Walls of Jericho*, 482.

94. Kotz, *Judgment Days*, 419.

95. Rebecca Burns, *Burial For King: Martin Luther King Jr.'s Funeral and the Week That Transformed Atlanta and Rocked the Nation* (New York: Scribner, 2011), 143.

96. Burns, *Burial For King*, 148–149.

97. The night before, he traveled to Camp David and the Aspen Lodge to meet with Ambassador Ellsworth. Exhausted, he fell asleep in a chair in the living room and napped for a good long time while people moved about quietly and talked in hushed voices. Lyndon Johnson, Daily Diary, 8 April 1968, White House Central Files, LBJ Library.

98. Burns, *Burial For King*, 159.

99. Kotz, *Judgment Days*, 419–420.

100. Kotz, *Judgment Days*, 420.

101. Kotz, *Judgment Days*, 420.

102. Lyndon B. Johnson, "The President's New Conference of April 10, 1968," 10 April 1968, *Public Papers of the Presidents of the United States*, Book 1, January 1-June 30, 1968, 504.

103. Lyndon B. Johnson, "Broadcast Statement by the President Following the Passage of the Civil Rights Act," 10 April 1968, *Public Papers of the Presidents of the United States*, Book 1, January 1-June 30, 1968, 507.

104. Lyndon B. Johnson, "Broadcast Statement by the President Following the Passage of the Civil Rights Act," 10 April 1968, *Public Papers of the Presidents of the United States*, Book 1, January 1-June 30, 1968, 507.

105. Lyndon B. Johnson, "Remarks on Signing the Civil Rights Act (April 11, 1968)," Miller Center, University of Virginia, Charlottesville, Virginia, http://millercenter.org/president/speeches/speech-4036.

106. Johnson, *Vantage Point*, 178.

107. Flamm, *Law and Order*, 145.

CHAPTER 6: HE HATED HIM, BUT HE LOVED HIM

1. Lady Bird Johnson, *A White House Diary* (New York: Holt, Rinehart and Winston, 1970), 680.

2. Johnson, *A White House Diary*, 680.

3. Johnson, *A White House Diary*, 680.

4. *Washington Daily News*, 6 June 1968.

5. *Washington Daily News*, 6 June 1968.

6. The night after the March 31 speech, LBJ received a telegram from RFK. "First of all, let me say that I fervently hope that your new efforts for peace in Vietnam will succeed. Your decision regarding the presidency subordinates self to country and is truly magnanimous. I respectfully and earnestly request an opportunity to visit with you as soon as possible to discuss how we might work together in the interest of national unity during the coming months." Kennedy to Johnson, 1 April 1968, Papers of LBJ, President, 1963–1969, White House Central File, Name File, Kennedy, Robert F., Box 98, LBJ Library.

7. Regarding the planned meeting with RFK, Cater proposed: "Rather than honoring Bobby Kennedy's request for a private get-together, you could ask both McCarthy and Kennedy to join you and your Cabinet for a discussion of ways to unify the country. At such a Cabinet Meeting . . . you might simply call on each one to present his views . . . and then ask each of your Cabinet Members, including the Vice President, to give his views." Cater to Johnson, 1 April 1968, Papers of LBJ, President, 1963–1969, White House Central File, Name File, Kennedy, Robert F., Box 98, LBJ Library.

8. Daily Diary, 3 April 1968, Papers of LBJ, LBJ Library.

9. Memorandum of Meeting, 3 April 1968, White House Famous Names, File Kennedy, Robert F. 1968 Campaign, Box 8, LBJ Library.

10. Memorandum of Meeting, 3 April 1968, White House Famous Names, File Kennedy, Robert F. 1968 Campaign, Box 8, LBJ Library.

11. Lyndon Baines Johnson, *Vantage Point: Perspectives of the Presidency, 1963–1969* (New York: Holt, Rinehart and Winston, 1971), 541–542.

12. Charles Murphy to Johnson, 4 April 1968, Papers of Lyndon Johnson, President's Appointment File [Diary Backup], 3/27/68-4/3/68. LBJ Library. In late April, Sorenson called Murphy and asked for a briefing for Senator Kennedy on foreign policy and defense matters. He also asked on whether administration officials "would be able to indicate their support of candidates" as discussed in the earlier meeting between LBJ and RFK. He said yes, although Sorenson pressed on the matter of Cabinet worrying, "different standards might be applied when people came out for Humphrey than when they came out for Kennedy." Sorenson to Murphy, 28 April 1968, Papers of LBJ, President, 1963–1969, White House Central File, Name File, Kennedy, Robert F., Box 98, LBJ Library.

13. David Milne, *America's Rasputin: Walt Rostow and the Vietnam War* (New York: Hill and Wang, 2008), 221.

14. Joseph A. Califano, Jr., *The Triumph and Tragedy of Lyndon Johnson: The White House Years* (New York: Touchstone, 1991), 302.

15. Johnson to Rose Kennedy, 5 June 1968, Papers of LBJ, President, 1963–1969, White House Central File, Name File, Kennedy, Robert F., Box 98, LBJ Library.

16. Johnson to Kennedy, 6 June 1968, Papers of LBJ, President, 1963–1969, White House Central File, Name File, Kennedy, Robert F., Box 98, LBJ Library.

17. Memorandum for the Record by Tom Johnson, 5 June 1968, Papers of LBJ, President, 1963–1969, White House Central File, Name File, Kennedy, Robert F., Box 98, LBJ Library.

18. Memorandum from Manatos to Johnson, 5 June 1968, Papers of LBJ, President, 1963–1969, White House Central File, Name File, Kennedy, Robert F., Box 98, LBJ Library.

19. Reedy to Johnson, 5 June 1968, White House Famous Names, Box 8, LBJ Library.

20. Califano to Johnson, 5 June 1968, White House Famous Names, Box 8, LBJ Library. There was a killing of three white Marines and a white woman in Georgetown by three African Americans from San Jose who claimed to be there to participate with the Poor People's Campaign but had no registration or interaction. Califano to Johnson, 5 June 1968, White House Famous Names, Box 8, LBJ Library.

21. Califano to Johnson, 5 June 1968, White House Famous Names, Box 8, LBJ Library.

22. Califano, Jr., *The Triumph and Tragedy of Lyndon Johnson*, 299.

23. Eric Sevareid, "CBS News Special Report," 5 June 1968, Papers of Lyndon Johnson, Office Files of Harry McPherson, Box 21, LBJ Library.

24. Clinton Hill to the White House, 5 June 1968, White House Famous Names, Box 8, LBJ Library.

25. Lyndon Johnson, "Statement of the President on the Shooting of Senator Robert F. Kennedy," 5 June 1968, Papers of Lyndon Johnson, President, 1963–1969, WHCF, GEN JL, Box 33, LBJ Library. Jack Valenti complained that the June 5 speech emphasized the "sickness" of society, and admitted being troubled by "a theme that

recurred in the body of the speech, the notion that our society is disfigured, that we are sick and violent and that this assassination somehow was a mirror of that infliction."

Matt Nimetz acknowledged understanding "how Jack got that impression," but stressed the statement by the president: "It would be just as wrong, and just as self-deceptive, to conclude from this act that our country itself is sick, that it has lost its balance, that it has lost its sense of direction, even its common decency." He emphasized, "This passage is a clear statement against the 'sickness of America' thesis, which blames the deaths on the American people." Nimetz to Califano, 17 June 1968, Papers of Lyndon Johnson, President, 1963–1969, WHCF, GEN JL, Box 33, LBJ Library.

26. Califano, Jr., *The Triumph and Tragedy of Lyndon Johnson*, 300–301.

27. Califano, Jr., *The Triumph and Tragedy of Lyndon Johnson*, 301.

28. Lyndon Johnson, White House Daily Diary, 6 June 1968, The Papers of Lyndon Johnson, LBJ Library.

29. Unnamed file and author, 7 June 1968, White House Famous Names, Box 8, LBJ Library.

30. Gaither to Califano, 5 June 1968, Office Files of White House Aides, Gaither, Box 17, LBJ Library.

31. Califano to Johnson, 7 June 1968, White House Famous Names, Box 8, LBJ Library.

32. FBI to Clark, The Personal Papers of Ramsey Clark, Box 123, LBJ Library.

33. Phone call between Johnson and Ted Kennedy, 6 June 1968, Lyndon B. Johnson Presidential Recordings, Tape: WH6806.01, Conversation, 13113, Miller Center, University of Virginia, Charlottesville, VA.

34. Lyndon B. Johnson, "Statement by the President on the Death of Senator Kennedy," 6 June 1968, *Public Papers of the President, 1968–69*, volume 1 (Washington: Government Printing Office, 1970), 693.

35. Califano, Jr., *The Triumph and Tragedy of Lyndon Johnson*, 301.

36. Gail Sheehy, "Ethel Kennedy and the Arithmetic of Life and Death," *New York Times Magazine* (17 June 1968): 30.

37. Randall Woods, *Prisoners of Hope: Lyndon B. Johnson, the Great Society, and the Limits of Liberalism* (New York: Basic Books, 2016), 376.

38. Samuel C. Patterson and Keith R. Eakins, "Congress and Gun Control," in John W. Bruce and Clyde Wilcox, eds., *The Changing Politics of Gun Control* (Lanham, MD: Rowman and Littlefield, 1998), 50.

39. For years, the NRA and its vocal supporters had undercut gun control. LBJ's plan included a ban on mail order that he called "murder by mail order" and supported ending the practice after Lee Harvey Oswald purchased his rifle from reading the NRA magazine, *American Rifleman*. He also wanted to create a national registration of all guns and licensing of all owners. In the days after the shooting, he renewed pressure on members of the Senate Judiciary Committee to move the gun control bill to the Senate floor. *Washington Post*, 16 December 2012.

40. Lyndon B. Johnson, "Letter to the President of the Senate and to the Speaker of the House Urging Passage of an Effective Gun Control Law," 6 June 1968, *Public Papers of the President, 1968–69*, volume 1, 694–695.
41. *Washington Post*, 16 December 2012.
42. Johnson, *A White House Diary*, 682.
43. Johnson, *A White House Diary*, 682.
44. Rufus W. Youngblood: *My Life with Five Presidents* (New York: Simon and Schuster, 1973), 227.
45. *New York Times*, 7 June 1968.
46. Califano, Jr., *The Triumph and Tragedy of Lyndon Johnson*, 298.
47. *New York Times*, 7 June 1968.
48. Johnson, *A White House Diary*, 683.
49. *New York Times*, 7 June 1968.
50. *Washington Post*, 8 June 1968.
51. *New York Times*, 7 June 1968.
52. Johnson, *A White House Diary*, 683.
53. Johnson, *A White House Diary*, 684.
54. Johnson, *A White House Diary*, 684.
55. *New York Times*, 7 June 1968.
56. Johnson, *A White House Diary*, 685.
57. Johnson, *A White House Diary*, 684–685.
58. Johnson, *A White House Diary*, 685.
59. Johnson, *A White House Diary*, 685.
60. Johnson, *A White House Diary*, 685.
61. Califano, Jr., *The Triumph and Tragedy of Lyndon Johnson*, 303.
62. Califano, Jr., *The Triumph and Tragedy of Lyndon Johnson*, 303.
63. Johnson, *A White House Diary*, 686.
64. Johnson, *A White House Diary*, 686.
65. Johnson, *A White House Diary*, 686–687.
66. Bob Fleming, "President's Funeral Participation," White House Famous Names, Box 8, LBJ Library.
67. Califano, Jr., *The Triumph and Tragedy of Lyndon Johnson*, 303.
68. Jackie Kennedy to Lyndon and Lady Bird Johnson, 22 June 1968, Papers of Lyndon Johnson, White House Central Files (WHCF) GEN FE, Box 5, LBJ Library.
69. LBJ to Ethel Kennedy, 19 June 1968, 22 June 1968, Papers of Lyndon Johnson, WHCF, GEN FE, Box 5, LBJ Library. She had written in four handwritten pages: "You and Mrs. Johnson have done so much to help my family and me in the past days. You were both so kind and generous and I shall always remember with deep gratitude your warm and immediate assistance. I especially want you to know, Mr. President, how much you lightened our burden by making the airplanes available to us – Air Force One – and the others, and by having permission to land at LaGuardia. The hard work of your staff on the tickets and invitations to the Mass was invaluable ... We shall always be grateful to you ... for honoring Bobby by attending his funeral, by meeting

the train in Washington and by accompanying us to Arlington." Ethel Kennedy to LBJ, no date given, Papers of Lyndon Johnson, White House Central Files (WHCF) GEN FE, Box 5, LBJ Library.

70. Lyndon B. Johnson, "Remark and Statement Upon Signing Order Establishing the national Commission on the Causes and Prevention of Violence," 6 June 1968, *Public Papers of the President, 1968–69*, volume 1, 697–699.

71. Woods, *Prisoners of Hope*, 377.

72. Woods, *Prisoners of Hope*, 376.

73. Califano, Jr., *The Triumph and Tragedy of Lyndon Johnson*, 305.

74. Califano, Jr., *The Triumph and Tragedy of Lyndon Johnson*, 307.

75. Califano, Jr., *The Triumph and Tragedy of Lyndon Johnson*, 307.

76. Califano, Jr., *The Triumph and Tragedy of Lyndon Johnson*, 307.

77. Irwin Unger and Debi Unger, *LBJ: A Life* (New York: John Wiley & Sons, 1999), 470.

78. Draft for "Signing Statement on Omnibus Crime Control and Safe Streets Act of 1968, H.R. 5037," 15 June 1968, Personal Papers of Warren Christopher, Box 2, LBJ Library.

79. Lyndon Johnson, Press Conference No. 132 of the President of the United States, 24 October 1968, Personal Papers of Warren Christopher, Box 2, LBJ Library.

80. *Washington Post*, 16 December 2012.

CHAPTER 7: THE BIG STUMBLE

1. Warren highlighted that his good health and his fifty years of public service, including his time on the Supreme Court, were "satisfying in every respect." He concluded: "When I entered the public service, 150 million of our 200 million people were not yet born. I, therefore, conceive it to be my duty to give way to someone who will have more years ahead of him to cope with the problems which will come to the Court." Lyndon Johnson, "Press Conference No. 128 of the President of the United States," 26 June 1968, Papers of Lyndon Johnson, Files Pertaining to Abe Fortas and Homer Thornberry, Box 1, LBJ Library.

2. Ed Cray, *Chief Justice: A Biography of Earl Warren* (New York: Simon and Schuster, 1997), 210.

3. Joseph A. Califano, Jr., *The Triumph and Tragedy of Lyndon Johnson: The White House Years* (New York: Touchstone, 1991), 308.

4. Califano, Jr., *The Triumph and Tragedy of Lyndon Johnson*, 308–309.

5. Clark Clifford, *Counsel to the President: A Memoir* (New York: Random House, 1991), 555.

6. Clifford, *Counsel to the President*, 556.

7. Manatos to Johnson, 25 June 1968, Papers of Lyndon Johnson, Fort, T, Box 195, LBJ Library.

8. Lyndon Baines Johnson, *The Vantage Point: Perspectives of the Presidency, 1963–1969* (New York: Holt, Rinehart and Winston, 1971), 547.

9. Lyndon Johnson, "Press Conference No. 128 of the President of the United States," 26 June 1968, Papers of Lyndon Johnson, Files Pertaining to Abe Fortas and Homer Thornberry, Box 1, LBJ Library.

10. Robert Griffin, "Reports of Chief Justice Warren's Resignation," 21 June 1968, *Congressional Record—Senate*, S7499–7500.

11. *Rocky Mountain News*, 28 June 1968.

12. *Chicago Sun-Times*, 15 August 1968.

13. Manatos to Johnson, 25 June 1968, Papers of Lyndon Johnson, Files Pertaining to Abe Fortas and Homer Thornberry, Box 1, LBJ Library.

14. Califano, Jr., *The Triumph and Tragedy of Lyndon Johnson*, 309. On the other hand, Nelson Rockefeller defended the choices and criticized Nixon and other Republicans for their challenge. He called Fortas "an outstanding appointment – he's a brilliant lawyer." *Rocky Mountain News*, 28 June 1968.

15. Califano, Jr., *The Triumph and Tragedy of Lyndon Johnson*, 310.

16. Califano, Jr., *The Triumph and Tragedy of Lyndon Johnson*, 308.

17. Califano, Jr., *The Triumph and Tragedy of Lyndon Johnson*, 310.

18. Sanders to Johnson, 28 June 1968, Papers of Lyndon Johnson, Files Pertaining to Abe Fortas and Homer Thornberry, Box 1, LBJ Library.

19. Califano, Jr., *The Triumph and Tragedy of Lyndon Johnson*, 310.

20. Califano, Jr., *The Triumph and Tragedy of Lyndon Johnson*, 311.

21. Robert Dallek, *Flawed Giant: Lyndon Johnson and His Times, 1961–1973* (New York: Oxford University Press, 1998), 558.

22. Califano to Johnson, 29 June 1968, Papers of Lyndon Johnson, Files Pertaining to Abe Fortas and Homer Thornberry, Box 1, LBJ Library.

23. The White House also sought help from prominent New York lawyer Ed Weisl to influence prominent newspaper magnate Sam Newhouse. Johnson wanted the *New Orleans Times Picayune* to write editorials to pressure Louisiana's senators, including Russell Long. Califano to Johnson, 29 June 1968, Papers of Lyndon Johnson, Files Pertaining to Abe Fortas and Homer Thornberry, Box 1, LBJ Library.

24. Dallek, *Flawed Giant*, 558.

25. Dallek, *Flawed Giant*, 558.

26. Califano to Johnson, 29 June 1968, Papers of Lyndon Johnson, Files Pertaining to Abe Fortas and Homer Thornberry, Box 1, LBJ Library.

27. Sanders to Clark, 27 June 1968, Papers of Lyndon Johnson, Files Pertaining to Abe Fortas and Homer Thornberry, Box 1, LBJ Library.

28. Califano, Jr., *The Triumph and Tragedy of Lyndon Johnson*, 311.

29. Califano, Jr., *The Triumph and Tragedy of Lyndon Johnson*, 310.

30. Califano, Jr., *The Triumph and Tragedy of Lyndon Johnson*, 311.

31. Goldstein to Jones, 2 July 1968, Papers of Lyndon Johnson, Fort, T, Box 195, LBJ Library. LBJ helped maintain Dirksen's support by promising to support a Subversive Activities Control Board, something he used to curry favor with some conservatives. Dallek, *Flawed Giant*, 560.

32. *New York Post*, 3 July 1968.

33. The White House sought information on the actions and criticisms of its opponents. Warren Christopher, in particular, gathered information, including a list of judges nominated by presidents after March 31 during their last year in office. A few days

later, he reported, "we have now confirmed a clear precedent for the retirement of a Supreme Court Justice effective upon the qualification of his successor. On July 9, 1902, Justice Horace Gray, who was succeeded on the Court by Justice Oliver Wendell Holmes, Jr., sent his resignation to the President 'to take effect upon the appointment and qualifying of my successor.'" Christopher to Temple, 2 July 1968, Papers of Lyndon Johnson, Files Pertaining to Abe Fortas and Homer Thornberry, Box 2, LBJ Library.

34. Robert A. Caro, *The Passage of Power: The Years of Lyndon Johnson* (New York: Vintage Books, 2012), 285–294.

35. Dallek, *Flawed Giant*, 559.

36. Dallek, *Flawed Giant*, 562.

37. Califano, Jr., *The Triumph and Tragedy of Lyndon Johnson*, 314.

38. Johnson, *The Vantage Point*, 546.

39. Califano, Jr., *The Triumph and Tragedy of Lyndon Johnson*, 315. Vicky McCammon captured the essence of the relationship according to Califano. "I don't think [Johnson] really felt that just because Abe Fortas was on the Supreme Court that he and Abe Fortas should divorce themselves from each other. He really didn't believe that that was necessary. He honestly didn't. He tried to be careful, because he didn't want to be criticized ... he really tried not to ask Abe Fortas about a lot of things, but in the end result he really needed his judgment on it. I think it was hard for him to make huge, important decisions domestically without his counsel. It's sort of hard to get a new lawyer in the middle of your biggest trial."

40. Califano, Jr., *The Triumph and Tragedy of Lyndon Johnson*, 315.

41. Lyndon Johnson, 22 May 1968, Papers of Lyndon Johnson, Office Files of White House Aides, Larry Temple, Box 1, LBJ Library. On March 30, the *Atlanta Constitution* wrote an article that highlighted the president of the Chatham Council on Human Relations, who called Lawrence a "segregationist with extreme views." The editorial board highlighted Lawrence's opposition to the judge who ordered the desegregation in Little Rock and stressed "it is high time that a more rigorous selection be instituted for the federal bench. It is not good enough just to be some senator's friend." *Atlanta Constitution*, 30 March 1968.

42. Johnson, *The Vantage Point*, 545–546.

43. Gilbert C. Fite, *Richard B. Russell, Jr.: Senator from Georgia* (Chapel Hill: University of North Carolina Press, 1991), 480.

44. Russell to Johnson, Papers of Lyndon Johnson, Office Files of White House Aides, Larry Temple, Box 1, LBJ Library.

45. Russell to Johnson, Papers of Lyndon Johnson, Office Files of White House Aides, Larry Temple, Box 1, LBJ Library.

46. Johnson to Russell, Papers of Lyndon Johnson, Office Files of White House Aides, Larry Temple, Box 1, LBJ Library. During discussions over the letter, McPherson wrote the president. "After all Russell has gone through to get his man appointed, this has the quality of a back-of-the-hand slap. To him it would probably read, 'If you still want this bum at that time, I'll appoint him.'" McPherson to Johnson, Papers of Lyndon Johnson, Office Files of White House Aides, Larry Temple, Box 1, LBJ Library.

47. Califano, Jr., *The Triumph and Tragedy of Lyndon Johnson*, 313.

48. Dallek, *Flawed Giant*, 561.

49. Dallek, *Flawed Giant*, 561.

50. *Great Falls Tribune*, 11 October 1968.

51. Bruce Allen Murphy, *Fortas: The Rise and Ruin of a Supreme Court Justice* (New York: William Morrow and Company, 1988), 358–359. Later, a Newsweek reporter, Sam Shaffer, uncovered the secret deal and asked the president for a response. Johnson whipped out his vote count and insisted: "Sam Shaffer is wrong. I have the votes for confirmation. Here they are." Also, in an oral history, Griffin said it was a phone call. It appears the meeting occurred, but there may have been subsequent phone calls.

52. Goldstein to Jones, 2 July 1968, Papers of Lyndon Johnson, Fort, T, Box 195, LBJ Library.

53. Califano, Jr., *The Triumph and Tragedy of Lyndon Johnson*, 311.

54. Califano, Jr., *The Triumph and Tragedy of Lyndon Johnson*, 312.

55. Laura Kalman, *Abe Fortas: A Biography* (New Haven, CT: Yale University Press, 1990), 336.

56. Kyle Longley, *Senator Albert Gore, Sr.: Tennessee Maverick* (Baton Rouge: Louisiana State University, 2004), 212.

57. Kalman, *Abe Fortas*, 337.

58. Clearly, the Republicans and southern Democrats hoped to embarrass Fortas and the president with their selection of speakers led by Kent Courtney, national chairman of the Conservative Society of America, Marx Lewis, chairman of the Council Against Communist Subversion, W. B. Hicks, Jr., executive secretary of the Liberty Lobby and James J. Clancy, an attorney for the executive board, for the National Organization, Citizens for Decent Literature. "Nominations of Abe Fortas and Homer Thornberry," Hearings Before the Committee on the Judiciary, United States Senate, 90th Congress, 2nd Session, July 11–23, 1968 (Washington, D.C.: Government Printing Office, 1968), 1–365.

59. Kalman, *Abe Fortas*, 337–340.

60. Califano, Jr., *The Triumph and Tragedy of Lyndon Johnson*, 314.

61. Kalman, *Abe Fortas*, 339–340.

62. Manatos to Johnson, 16 July 1968, Papers of Lyndon Johnson, Files Pertaining to Abe Fortas and Homer Thornberry, Box 2, LBJ Library.

63. Johnson, *The Vantage Point*, 546.

64. Manatos to Johnson, 25 July 1968, Papers of Lyndon Johnson, Files Pertaining to Abe Fortas and Homer Thornberry, Box 2, LBJ Library.

65. Jack Bass and Marilyn W. Thompson, *Strom: The Complicated Personal and Political Life of Strom Thurmond* (New York: PublicAffairs, 2005), 206.

66. Califano, Jr., *The Triumph and Tragedy of Lyndon Johnson*, 314.

67. Manatos to Johnson, 29 July 1968, Papers of Lyndon Johnson, Fortas, Box 196, LBJ Library.

68. Lyndon Johnson, Press Conference #129 of the President of the United States, 31 July 1968, Files Pertaining to Abe Fortas and Homer Thornberry, Box 3, LBJ Library.

69. *Washington Post*, 3 August 1968. About this same time, Sam Shaffer of *Newsweek* notified Califano that Fortas would not be confirmed and that forty-three hard votes existed against cloture. He told Califano the pornography issue had devastated the nomination and that mail ran heavily against Fortas. "Some southern senators, he tells me, have discovered they can placate the Jewish vote by promising to work for arms for Israel and therefore they are not worried about opposition to Fortas." Califano to Christopher, 5 August 1968, Personal Papers of Warren Christopher, Box 14, LBJ Library. Not everyone agreed. An editorial in the *Jewish Week Weekly* in early August noted: "We do not suggest than any Senator who is opposed to confirming Fortas need defend himself against suspicion of anti-Semitism. We do decidedly suggest that anyone who filibusters against a decision, as if it were a holy cause to stop Justice Abe Fortas despite the wishes of the majority of the Senate, is suspiciously motivated." *Jewish Week Weekly*, 1 August 1968.
70. *Washington Post*, 12 August 1968.
71. Califano, Jr., *The Triumph and Tragedy of Lyndon Johnson*, 316.
72. Califano, Jr., *The Triumph and Tragedy of Lyndon Johnson*, 316.
73. Johnson, *The Vantage Point*, 547.
74. Johnson, *The Vantage Point*, 547.
75. Interview of Larry Temple by Joe B. Frantz, 11 August 1970, Oral History Collection, Johnson Library, 2.
76. Califano, Jr., *The Triumph and Tragedy of Lyndon Johnson*, 317.
77. Califano, Jr., *The Triumph and Tragedy of Lyndon Johnson*, 317.
78. Dallek, *Flawed Giant*, 563.
79. Randall Woods, *LBJ: Architect of American Ambition* (New York: Free Press, 2006), 853.
80. Califano, Jr., *The Triumph and Tragedy of Lyndon Johnson*, 317.
81. Califano, Jr., *The Triumph and Tragedy of Lyndon Johnson*, 317–318.
82. Califano, Jr., *The Triumph and Tragedy of Lyndon Johnson*, 318.
83. Califano, Jr., *The Triumph and Tragedy of Lyndon Johnson*, 318.
84. Manatos to Johnson, 16 September 1968, Files Pertaining to Abe Fortas and Homer Thornberry, Box 3, LBJ Library. Senator Cooper said about the American University affair, "My fourth cousin, Paul Porter, should have used better judgment." He added, Senator Dirksen is "throwing a lot of sand in everybody's eyes and no doubt he would like to come out as the savior of the nomination after awhile." McPherson to Manatos, 20 September 1968, Files Pertaining to Abe Fortas and Homer Thornberry, Box 3, LBJ Library.
85. For a good study on the matter, reference: Kevin M. Kruse, *One Nation under God: How Corporate America Invented Christian America* (New York: Basic Books, 2015).
86. Russell to Johnson, 26 September 1968, Files Pertaining to Abe Fortas and Homer Thornberry, Box 3, LBJ Library.
87. In the end, he said: "I appreciate the confidence in my qualifications which led you to nominate me as Chief Justice. I wish particularly to thank my colleagues at the bar and law schools for their support, and to express my appreciation to those members of the United States Senate who have supported me." Fortas to Johnson, 1 October 1968, Papers of Lyndon Johnson, Fortas, Box 196, LBJ Library.

88. "I urge all involved with and concerned about our Constitution and its form of government to pledge now that this shall be no precedent, that the Senate hereafter will act by majority will and never fail to address itself to the issues which it has the Constitutional duty to answer." Lyndon Johnson, "Statement by the President," 2 October 1968, Papers of Lyndon Johnson, Office Files of the White House Aides, John Macy, Box 190, LBJ Library.

89. One commentator noted: "Another strand in the tangled skein is Justice Fortas' activity as presidential adviser. There is precedent for it – Brandeis and Frankfurter – but that does not make it right." A writer noted that when Fortas told the committee that he was there to merely "sum up the arguments on the one side, the considerations on the other side" that even strong supporter Hart lamented "I confess I think all of us, as citizens, had the notion that contact between Presidents and Justices of the Court would be social only. In general … he [Fortas] has formed part of the Court's dominant majority. Hence he is regarded representative of it. The Senate would discredit itself if he were denied confirmation by a filibuster, with no floor vote on the nomination itself. The entire episode is deplorable, particularly so if the nomination fails." Alexander M. Bickel, "Fortas, Johnson and the Senate: Voting the Court Up or Down," *The New Republic*, 28 September 1968, 22.

90. Office of the White House Press Secretary, "Statement by the President," 10 October 1968, Files Pertaining to Abe Fortas and Homer Thornberry, Box 3, LBJ Library.

91. Dallek, *Flawed Giant*, 564.

92. Lady Bird Johnson, *A White House Diary* (New York: Holt, Rinehart and Winston, 1970), 712–713.

93. Johnson, *A White House Diary*, 713.

94. Johnson, *The Vantage Point*, 547.

CHAPTER 8: THE TANKS ARE ROLLING

1. Lyndon B. Johnson, "Remarks in Detroit at the Annual Convention of the Veterans of Foreign Wars," 19 August 1968, *Public Papers of the President, 1968*, volume 2 (Washington, D.C.: Government Printing Office).

2. Lady Bird Johnson, *A White House Diary* (New York: Holt, Rinehart and Winston, 1970), 703.

3. Johnson, *A White House Diary*, 704.

4. Mark Kramer, "The Prague Spring and the Soviet Invasion," in Günter Bischof, Stefan Kamer, and Peter Ruggenthaler, eds., *The Prague Spring and the Warsaw Pact Invasion of Czechoslovakia in 1968* (Lanham, MD: Rowman & Littlefield, 2010), 53.

5. Thomas Alan Schwartz, *Lyndon Johnson and Europe: In the Shadow of Vietnam* (Cambridge, MA: Harvard University Press, 2003), 214; Mitchell B. Lerner, "Trying to Find the Guy Who Invited Them: Lyndon B. Johnson, Bridge Building and the End of the Prague Spring," *Diplomatic History* (January 2008): 77–103.

6. Robert Dallek, *Lone Star Rising: Lyndon Johnson and His Times, 1908–1960* (New York: Oxford University Press, 1991), 507.

7. Clifford, *Counsel to the President*, 559.

8. Clifford, *Counsel to the President*, 559.

9. Clifford, *Counsel to the President*, 560.

10. Clifford, *Counsel to the President*, 561.

11. Anatoly Dobrynin, *In Confidence: Moscow's Ambassador to America's Six Cold War Presidents* (1962–1986) (New York: Times Books, 1995), 179–180.

12. Lyndon B. Johnson, *Vantage Point: Perspectives of the Presidency, 1963–1969* (New York: Holt, Rinehart, and Winston, 1971), 487–488.

13. Summary of Meeting, 20 August 1968, *Foreign Relations of the United States, 1964–1968*, volume XVII Eastern Europe (Washington, D.C.: Government Printing Office, 1996), 236.

14. Summary of Meeting, 20 August 1968, *Foreign Relations of the United States, 1964–1968*, volume XVII Eastern Europe (Washington, D.C.: Government Printing Office, 1996), 236.

15. Dobrynin, *In Confidence*, 180.

16. Dobrynin, *In Confidence*, 180.

17. Dobrynin, *In Confidence*, 180.

18. Summary of Meeting, 20 August 1968, *Foreign Relations of the United States, 1964–1968*, volume XVII Eastern Europe (Washington, D.C.: Government Printing Office, 1996), 240–241.

19. *Washington Post*, 23 August 1968.

20. Johnson, *A White House Diary*, 704.

21. Notes of Emergency Meeting of the National Security Council, 20 August 1968, *Foreign Relations of the United States, 1964–1968*, volume XVII Eastern Europe (Washington: Government Printing Office, 1996), 243, also, Notes of Emergency Meeting of the National Security Council, 20 August 1968, Papers of Lyndon Johnson, National Security File, NSC Meeting File, Box 2, LBJ Library.

22. Notes of Emergency Meeting of the National Security Council, 20 August 1968, *Foreign Relations of the United States, 1964–1968*, volume XVII Eastern Europe (Washington, D.C.: Government Printing Office, 1996), 244.

23. Notes of Emergency Meeting of the National Security Council, 20 August 1968, *Foreign Relations of the United States, 1964–1968*, volume XVII Eastern Europe (Washington, D.C.: Government Printing Office, 1996), 245.

24. Dean Rusk (as told to Richard Rusk), *As I Saw It* (New York: W. W. Norton, 1990), 351.

25. George W. Ball, *The Past Has Another Pattern: Memoirs* (New York: W. W. Norton, 1982), 440.

26. Johnson, *Vantage Point*, 487.

27. Johnson, *Vantage Point*, 487.

28. Johnson, *A White House Diary*, 704.

29. Clifford, *Counsel to the President*, 561.

30. *Washington Post*, 21 August 1968; *New York Times*, 21 August 1968.

31. Lyndon B. Johnson, "Statement by the President Calling on the Warsaw Pact Allies to Withdraw From Czechoslovakia," 21 August 1968, *Public Papers of the Presidents of the United States: Lyndon B. Johnson, 1968–69* Book II (Washington, D.C.: U.S. Government Printing Office, 1970), 456.

32. Ball, *The Past Has Another Pattern*, 440.

33. Ball, *The Past Has Another Pattern*, 441.

34. Ball, *The Past Has Another Pattern*, 441.

35. *New York Times*, 22 August 1968.

36. Ball, *The Past Has Another Pattern*, 441.

37. Ball, *The Past Has Another Pattern*, 442–443.

38. Memorandum from the Department of State Executive Secretary Read to Rostow, 23 August 1968, *Foreign Relations of the United States, 1964–1968*, volume XVII Eastern Europe (Washington, D.C.: Government Printing Office, 1996), 252.

39. Ball, *The Past Has Another Pattern*, 442–443.

40. Clifford, *Counsel to the President*, 561.

41. Clifford, *Counsel to the President*, 561.

42. For example, reference: Oleg Kalugin, *The First Directorate: My 32 Years in Intelligence and Espionage against the West* (New York: St. Martin's Press, 1994), 105–111.

43. Dean Rusk, "Cabinet Report on Czechoslovakia and Vietnam," 22 August 1968, *Weekly Compilation of Presidential Documents* (Washington, D.C.: Government Printing Office, 1996), 1265. Rusk concluded "Those who try to confuse it . . . are undertaking an enormous burden and among other things, an enormous disservice to the clarity which is important if we are to have peace in the world."

44. *New York Times*, 22 August 1968.

45. *New York Times*, 22 August 1968.

46. *New York Times*, 22 August 1968.

47. Notes of Cabinet Meeting, 22 August 1968, *Foreign Relations of the United States, 1964–1968*, volume XVII, Eastern Europe (Washington, D.C.: Government Printing Office, 1996), 249.

48. *Washington Post*, 23 August 1968.

49. Gunter Bischof, "'No Action': The Johnson Administration and the Warsaw Pact Invasion of Czechoslovakia in August 1968," in Gunter Bischof, Stefan Karner, and Peter Ruggenthaler, eds., *The Prague Spring and the Warsaw Pact Invasion of Czechoslovakia in 1968* (Lanham, MD: Rowman and Littlefield Publishers, 2010), 220.

50. Nicholas deB. Katzenbach, *Some of It was Fun: Work with RFK and LBJ* (New York: W. W. Norton, 2008), 289.

51. Schwartz, *Lyndon Johnson and Europe*, 216. Sitting in the Cabinet Room, the group listened as CIA Director opened the meeting by highlighting, "Rumanians were in a state of considerable apprehension" that the Soviets would continue their pattern in their country. Then, Rusk highlighted, "highly mobilized charged world reaction" against the Soviet invasion, noting, "in the very nature of their system, the Soviet Union pays special attention to propaganda aspects."

52. Summary of Meeting, 23 August 1968, *Foreign Relations of the United States, 1964–1968*, volume XVII, Eastern Europe (Washington, D.C.: Government Printing Office, 1996), 250–252.

53. Summary Notes of the 590th Meeting of the National Security Council, 4 September 1968, *Foreign Relations of the United States, 1964–1968*, volume XVII, Eastern Europe (Washington: Government Printing Office, 1996), 274–277. Also, Summary Notes of

the 590th Meeting of the National Security Council, 4 September 1968, Lyndon Johnson Papers, National Security File, NSC Meeting File, Box 2, LBJ Library.

54. Schwartz, *Lyndon Johnson and Europe*, 216.

55. Rusk, then told Dobrynin how the United States had been interested in "better relations and better understanding between our two countries," but the invasion opened the president "to strong criticisms for his efforts in building better relations with the Soviet Union." Memorandum of Conversation, 23 August 1968, *Foreign Relations of the United States, 1964–1968*, volume XVII, Eastern Europe (Washington, D.C.: Government Printing Office, 1996), 254.

56. Memorandum of Conversation, 23 August 1968, *Foreign Relations of the United States, 1964–1968*, volume XVII, Eastern Europe (Washington, D.C.: Government Printing Office, 1996), 254.

57. *New York Times*, 31 August 1968.

58. Summary Notes of the 590th Meeting of the National Security Council, 4 September 1968, *Foreign Relations of the United States, 1964–1968*, volume XVII, Eastern Europe (Washington, D.C.: Government Printing Office, 1996), 278.

59. Rostow to Johnson, 4 September 1968, Papers of Lyndon Johnson, National Security File, NSC Meetings File, Box 2, LBJ Library.

60. Summary Notes of 590th NSC Meeting, 4 September 1968, Papers of Lyndon Johnson, National Security File, NSC Meetings File, Box 2, LBJ Library.

61. John Prados, "Prague Spring and SALT: Arms Limitation Setbacks in 1968," in H. W. Brands, ed., *The Foreign Policies of Lyndon Johnson: Beyond Vietnam* (College Station: Texas A&M Press, 1999), 19–36.

62. Robert Dallek, *Flawed Giant: Lyndon Johnson and His Times, 1961–1975* (New York: Oxford University Press, 1998), 555–556.

63. Ella Ackerman and Tracey German, "From Soviet Bloc to Democratic Security Building," in Graeme P. Herd and Jennifer D. P. Moroney, eds., *Security Dynamics in the Former Soviet Bloc* (New York: Routledge, 2003), 5; Johan Galtung, "A Structural Theory of Imperialism," in Peter J. Cain and Mark Harrison, eds., *Imperialism: Critical Concepts in Historical Studies* vol II (New York: Routledge, 2001), 104.

64. Johnson, *The Vantage Point*, 490.

65. George Christian, *The President Steps Down: A Personal Memoir of the Transfer of Power* (New York: The Macmillan Company, 1970), 145.

66. *New York Times*, 4 August 1969.

67. Christian, *The President Steps Down*, 145.

68. Dobrynin, *In Confidence*, 186–187.

69. Johnson, *Vantage Point*, 489–490.

CHAPTER 9: THE PERFECT DISASTER

1. Pierre Salinger, *P.S.: A Memoir* (New York: St. Martin's Press, 1995), 197–198.

2. Justin A. Nelson, "Drafting Lyndon Johnson: The President's Secret Role in the 1968 Democratic Convention," *Presidential Studies Quarterly* 30:4 (December 2000): 694.

3. He added the man "showed me some things, some plans, and presented the President's actions as just a paternal interest in the small details of the convention – not the overall policy direction." Tom Johnson to Lyndon Johnson, 20 May 1968, Papers of Lyndon B. Johnson, President, 1963–1969, EX PL1, 10/1/67-6/30/68, Box 79, LBJ Library.

4. Tom Johnson to Lyndon Johnson, 20 May 1968, Papers of Lyndon B. Johnson, President, 1963–1969, EX PL1, 10/1/67-6/30/68, Box 79, LBJ Library.

5. Temple to Johnson, 20 May 1968, Papers of Lyndon B. Johnson, President, 1963–1969, EX PL1, 10/1/67-6/30/68, Box 79, LBJ Library.

6. Drew Pearson outlined the inside story of the president making sure Hale Boggs, not Edmund Muskie (whom Humphrey wanted), took the position of chair of the Platform Committee. "Boggs is highly competent but HHH wanted Muskie in the spot in order to let the convention have a look at him as a vice presidential possibility. The President's man got the job." Tom Johnson to Johnson, 2 September 1968, Papers of Lyndon B. Johnson, President 1963–1969, EX PL1, 10/1/67-6/30/68, Box 79, LBJ Library.

7. Joseph A. Califano, Jr., *The Triumph and Tragedy of Lyndon Johnson: The White House Years* (New York: Touchstone, 1991), 319.

8. Nelson, "Drafting Lyndon Johnson," 696. The DNC paid for the cost of production, $125,000.

9. Reedy to Johnson, 24 July 1968, Papers of LBJ, President, 1963–1969, EX PL, 7/1/68-8/31/68, Box 90, LBJ Library.

10. Califano, *The Triumph and Tragedy of Lyndon Johnson*, 319.

11. Panzer to Johnson, Papers of LBJ, President, 1963–1969, EX PL, 7/1/68-8/31/68, Box 90, LBJ Library.

12. John Criswell to Jim Jones, 9 August 1968, Papers of Lyndon Johnson, Confidential File, Box 77, LBJ Library.

13. John Criswell to Jim Jones, 9 August 1968, Papers of Lyndon Johnson, Confidential File, Box 77, LBJ Library.

14. Robert Schulzinger, *A Time for War: The United States and Vietnam, 1941–1975* (New York: Oxford University Press, 1997), 267–269.

15. Dallek, *Flawed Giant*, 571. It even led Johnson to assert that Nixon "may prove more responsible than the Democrats" on Vietnam.

16. Early reports to the president showed Humphrey's loyalty on the matter. Jones wrote on August 21 in relation to the discussion of Vietnam within the Platform Committee: "The Vice President has not varied one inch from what he discussed with the President at the Ranch. However, I will tell him about this call and we will see if we can't control our people a little better." Jones to Johnson, 21 August 1968, Papers of LBJ, President, 1963–1969, GEN PL/Wagner, Robert, 11/22/63-1/13/64, Box 25, LBJ Library.

17. Hubert Humphrey, *The Education of a Public Man: My Life and Politics* (Minneapolis: University of Minnesota Press, 1991), 290–291.

18. Humphrey, *The Education of a Public Man*, 291.

19. Theodore H. White, *The Making of the President 1968* (New York: Harper Perennial, 1969), 317.

20. Phone interview by the author with Joseph Califano, 15 February 2017; phone interview by the author with Jim Jones, 13 February 2017.

21. Marvin Watson (with Sherwin Markman), *Chief of Staff: Lyndon Johnson and His Presidency* (New York: St. Martin's Press, 2004), 296.

22. Humphrey, *The Education of a Public Man*, 292.

23. Watson, *Chief of Staff*, 299.

24. Jules Witcover, *The Year the Dream Died: Revisiting 1968 in America* (New York: Warner Books, 1997), 315. O'Brien acknowledged "I took that for the bluff that it was . . . but it underscored the uncertainty of Humphrey's position as he struggled for the presidential nomination that had eluded him since 1960."

25. Witcover, *The Year the Dream Died*, 315.

26. Tom Johnson to Johnson, 2 September 1968, Papers of Lyndon B. Johnson, President, 1963–1969, EX PL1, 10/1/67-6/30/68, Box 79, LBJ Library.

27. Humphrey, *The Education of a Public Man*, 292.

28. Jones to Johnson, 24 August 1968, Papers of LBJ, President, 1963–1969, GEN PL/ Wagner, Robert, 11/22/63-1/13/64, Box 25, LBJ Library.

29. Jones to Johnson, 24 August 1968, Papers of LBJ, President, 1963–1969, GEN PL/ Wagner, Robert, 11/22/63-1/13/64, Box 25, LBJ Library.

30. Witcover, *The Year the Dream Died*, 322.

31. John Connally (with Mickey Herskowitz), *In History's Shadow: An American Odyssey* (New York: Hyperion, 1993), 203.

32. Watson, *Chief of Staff*, 298.

33. Watson, *Chief of Staff*, 299.

34. Matusow, *The Unraveling of America*, 417.

35. Irwin Unger and Debi Unger, *LBJ: A Life* (New York: John Wiley & Sons, 1999), 481.

36. Nelson, "Drafting Lyndon Johnson," 699.

37. Witcover, *The Year the Dream Died*, 328.

38. Nelson, "Drafting Lyndon Johnson," 701. In another case, after a meeting on Czechoslovakia only days before the convention, LBJ pulled aside Humphrey and blasted him, questioning his presidential mettle, calling him too soft on foreign policy and cowing too often to the McCarthy people on Vietnam. He also zeroed in on testing the patience of Johnson, Connally, and other southerners on the unit rule. White, *The Making of the President, 1968*, 326.

39. Another group of thirteen operative named the Taxonist Corps Toilers joined Watson and Connally in sounding out the delegates over drafting Johnson. John Ben Shepherd, a Johnson loyalist, led the group. Nelson, "Drafting Lyndon Johnson," 703–705.

40. Ibid., 320.

41. Allen J. Matusow, *The Unraveling of America: A History of Liberalism in the 1960s* (New York: Harper & Row, 1984), 418.

42. Nelson, "Drafting Lyndon Johnson," 707.

43. Lady Bird Johnson, *A White House Diary* (New York: Holt, Rinehart and Winston, 1970), 705.

44. Califano, *The Triumph and Tragedy of Lyndon Johnson*, 319.

45. Califano to Johnson, 26 August 1968, Papers of Lyndon B. Johnson, President, 1963–1969, EX PL1, 10/1/67-6/30/68, Box 79, LBJ Library.

46. Califano, *The Triumph and Tragedy of Lyndon Johnson*, 319.

47. Nelson, "Drafting Lyndon Johnson," 710.

48. Califano, *The Triumph and Tragedy of Lyndon Johnson*, 321.

49. Johnson, *A White House Diary*, 705.

50. Johnson, *A White House Diary*, 705.

51. Johnson, *A White House Diary*, 705.

52. Telephone conversation between Lyndon Johnson and Everett Dirksen, 27 August 1968, *Foreign Relations of the United States, 1964–1968*: Vietnam, January-August 1968 (Washington, D.C.: U.S. Government Printing Office, 2002), 981.

53. Connally, *In History's Shadow*, 203.

54. Watson, *Chief of Staff*, 300–301.

55. Witcover, *The Year the Dream Died*, 328.

56. Nelson, "Drafting Lyndon Johnson," 708.

57. Califano, *The Triumph and Tragedy of Lyndon Johnson*, 321.

58. Daily Diary, 27 August 1968, Papers of LBJ, LBJ Library.

59. Nelson, "Drafting Lyndon Johnson," 709.

60. Johnson, *A White House Diary*, 705.

61. Johnson, *A White House Diary*, 706.

62. Johnson, *A White House Diary*, 706.

63. Johnson, *A White House Diary*, 706.

64. Johnson, *A White House Diary*, 706.

65. Johnson, *A White House Diary*, 706.

66. Johnson, *A White House Diary*, 706.

67. Witcover, *The Year the Dream Died*, 328.

68. Johnson, *A White House Diary*, 705.

69. Witcover, *The Year the Dream Died*, 315.

70. Daily Diary, 28 August 1968, Papers of LBJ, LBJ Library.

71. Witcover, *The Year the Dream Died*, 332.

72. Salinger, *P.S.: A Memoir*, 204.

73. Witcover, *The Year the Dream Died*, 332.

74. Kyle Longley, *Senator Albert Gore, Sr.: Tennessee Maverick* (Baton Rouge: Louisiana State University Press, 2004), 214.

75. Witcover, *The Year the Dream Died*, 333.

76. Tom Johnson to Johnson, 2 September 1968, Papers of Lyndon B. Johnson, President, 1963–1969, EX PL1, 10/1/67-6/30/68, Box 79, LBJ Library.

77. Clark Clifford (with Richard Holbrooke), *Counsel to the President: A Memoir* (New York: Random House, 1991), 565.

78. Witcover, *The Year the Dream Died*, 333.

79. Witcover, *The Year the Dream Died*, 333.

80. Matusow, *The Unraveling of America*, 420.

81. Matusow, *The Unraveling of America*, 420.

82. Watson, *Chief of Staff*, 301.

83. Witcover, *The Year the Dream Died*, 336.

84. Maurice Isserman and Michael Kazin, *America Divided: The Civil War of the 1960s* 5th edition (New York: Oxford University Press, 2015), 231.

85. Matusow, *The Unraveling of America*, 421.

86. Nelson, "Drafting Lyndon Johnson," 710.

87. Califano, *The Triumph and Tragedy of Lyndon Johnson*, 321.

88. Irving Bernstein, *Guns or Butter: The Presidency of Lyndon Johnson* (New York: Oxford University Press, 1996), 515.

89. Watson, *Chief of Staff*, 300.

90. Daily Diary, 29 August 1968, Papers of LBJ, LBJ Library.

91. White, *The Making of the President, 1968*, 358.

92. Witcover, *The Year the Dream Died*, 341.

93. White, *The Making of the President, 1968*, 358–359.

94. Witcover, *The Year the Dream Died*, 342.

95. White, *The Making of the President, 1968*, 358–359.

96. Johnson, *A White House Diary*, 706.

97. "The violence in Chicago was one of the greatest political assets Nixon had," he added as "the extremists made it impossible for us to carry states like Oklahoma, Kentucky, and Tennessee, which should have been Humphrey states." Lyndon B. Johnson, *The Vantage Point: Perspectives of the Presidency, 1963–1969* (New York: Holt, Rinehart and Winston, 1971), 543, 549.

98. Bernstein, *Guns or Butter*, 515.

CHAPTER 10: IS THIS TREASON?

1. "Notes of Meetings," 29 October 1968, *Foreign Relations of the United States, 1964–1968*, Volume VII, Vietnam, September 1968–January 1969 (Washington, D.C.: Government Printing Office, 2003), 399–407.

2. "Notes of Meetings," 29 October 1968, *Foreign Relations of the United States, 1964–1968*, Volume VII, Vietnam, September 1968–January 1969 (Washington, D.C.: Government Printing Office, 2003), 412.

3. Jules Witcover, *The Year the Dream Died: Revisiting 1968 in America* (New York: Warner Books, 1997), 411–412.

4. "Notes of Meetings," 29 October 1968, *Foreign Relations of the United States, 1964–1968*, Volume VII, Vietnam, September 1968–January 1969 (Washington, D.C.: Government Printing Office, 2003), 412.

5. Witcover, *The Year the Dream Died*, 413.

6. For a very good work on Chennault and her background and efforts, reference: Catherine Forslund, *Anna Chennault: Informal Diplomacy and Asian Relations* (Lanham, MD: Rowman and Littlefield, 2002).

7. William Safire, *Before the Fall: An Inside View of the Pre-Watergate White House* (New York: Doubleday & Company, 1975), 89.

8. Witcover, *The Year the Dream Died*, 286.

9. Witcover, *The Year the Dream Died*, 312.

10. As a result, Rusk encouraged the embassy to inform Thieu and Prime Minister Huong that they encourage their "ministers refrain from commenting on the progress of the electoral campaign in the United States." Rusk to Embassy, 29 August 1968, Anna Chennault Record, Individual Reviewed Folders from Various Collections, Folder 2 of 2, LBJ Library.

11. Whitney Shoemaker (assistant to the president) to Allen Johnson, 15 November 1968, Papers of the President, 1963–1968, GEN PL 8/16/67-, Box 4, LBJ Library.

12. White, *The Making of the President 1968*, 440–441.

13. *New York Times*, 31 December 1968.

14. Witcover, *The Year the Dream Died*, 398.

15. Christian to Johnson, 25 October 1968, Papers of Lyndon B. Johnson, President, 1963–1969, EX PL/Humphrey, Hubert H./Pro, Box 26, LBJ Library.

16. Bryce N. Harlow, Oral History by Michael L. Gillette, Tape 2, 6 May 1979, 58, LBJ Library. Some have questioned the assertion of Harlow, noting that he did not know the person and instead relied on someone who knew another guy. Ken Hughes, *Chasing Shadows: The Nixon Tapes, the Chennault Affair, and the Origins of Watergate* (Charlottesville: University of Virginia Press, 2015).

17. Stephen Ambrose, *Nixon: The Triumph of a Politician, 1962–1972*, volume 2, (New York: Touchstone Books, 1987), 209.

18. Ambrose, *Nixon*, 210.

19. Ambrose, *Nixon*, 209.

20. Peniel E. Joseph, *Stokley: A Life* (New York: Basic, 2014), 234.

21. Notes of Meeting, 31 October 1968, *Foreign Relations of the United States, 1964–1968*, Volume VII, Vietnam, September 1968–January 1969 (Washington, D.C.: Government Printing Office, 2003), 467–468.

22. Nguyen Tien Hung and Jerrold L. Schecter, *The Palace File* (New York: Harper and Row, 1986), 23–24.

23. Carl Solberg, *Hubert Humphrey: A Biography* (New York: W.W. Norton, 1984), 393.

24. Witcover, *The Year the Dream Died*, 408.

25. Witcover, *The Year the Dream Died*, 409.

26. Rostow to Johnson, 30 October 1968, Anna Chennault Record, Individual Reviewed Folders from Various Collections, Folder 1 of 2, LBJ Library.

27. Rostow to Johnson, 30 October 1968, 31 October 1968, Anna Chennault Record, Individual Reviewed Folders from Various Collections, Folder 1 of 2, LBJ Library.

28. Witcover, *The Year the Dream Died*, 410.

29. Telephone Conversation between Johnson, Humphrey, Nixon, Wallace, 31 October 1968, *Foreign Relations of the United States, 1964–1968*, Volume VII, Vietnam, September 1968–January 1969 (Washington, D.C.: Government Printing Office, 2003), 477.

30. Solberg, *Hubert Humphrey*, 395.

31. Telephone Conversation Between Johnson and Humphrey, 31 October 1968, *Foreign Relations of the United States, 1964–1968*, Volume VII, Vietnam, September 1968–January 1969 (Washington, D.C.: Government Printing Office, 2003), 486.
32. Solberg, *Hubert Humphrey*, 394.
33. Solberg, *Hubert Humphrey*, 394.
34. "Editorial Note," *Foreign Relations of the United States, 1964–1968*, Volume VII, Vietnam, September 1968–January 1969 (Washington, D.C.: Government Printing Office, 2003), 493.
35. Rostow to Johnson, 1 November 1968, Rostow to Johnson, 4 November 1968, Anna Chennault Record, Individual Reviewed Folders from Various Collections, Folder 1 of 2, LBJ Library.
36. Telephone conversation between Johnson and Rowe, 1 November 1968, *Foreign Relations of the United States, 1964–1968*, Volume VII, Vietnam, September 1968–January 1969 (Washington, D.C.: Government Printing Office, 2003), 507.
37. George Herring, *America's Longest War: The United States and Vietnam* 5th edition (New York: McGraw-Hill, 2014), 271.
38. Jones to Johnson, 2 November 1968, National Security File, Country File, Vietnam, Memos to the President/Bombing Halt Decision, Vol. IV [2 of 3], LBJ Library. Also, *Foreign Relations of the United States, 1964–1968*, Volume VII, Vietnam, September 1968–January 1969 (Washington, D.C.: Government Printing Office, 2003), 525.
39. "Editorial Note," *Foreign Relations of the United States, 1964–1968*, Volume VII, Vietnam, September 1968–January 1969 (Washington, D.C.: Government Printing Office, 2003), 523.
40. Telephone conversation between Johnson and Dirksen, 2 November 1968, *Foreign Relations of the United States, 1964–1968*, Volume VII, Vietnam, September 1968–January 1969 (Washington, D.C.: Government Printing Office, 2003), 524.
41. Bryce N. Harlow, Oral History by Michael L. Gillette, Tape 2, 6 May 1979, 56, LBJ Library.
42. Telephone Conversation between Johnson and Smathers, 3 November 1968, *Foreign Relations of the United States, 1964–1968*, Volume VII, Vietnam, September 1968–January 1969 (Washington, D.C.: Government Printing Office, 2003), 536.
43. Telephone Conversation between Johnson and Smathers, 3 November 1968, *Foreign Relations of the United States, 1964–1968*, Volume VII, Vietnam, September 1968–January 1969 (Washington, D.C.: Government Printing Office, 2003), 537.
44. Tape F6811.01 PNO 7 Telephone Conversation between Johnson and Nixon, 3 November 1968, *Foreign Relations of the United States, 1964–1968*, Volume VII, Vietnam, September 1968–January 1969 (Washington, D.C.: Government Printing Office, 2003), 539.
45. *New York Times*, 4 November 1968.
46. Tape F6811.01 PNO 7 Telephone Conversation between Johnson and Nixon, 3 November 1968, *Foreign Relations of the United States, 1964–1968*, Volume VII, Vietnam, September 1968–January 1969 (Washington, D.C.: Government Printing Office, 2003), 539–540.

47. Tape F6811.01 PNO 7 Telephone Conversation between Johnson and Nixon, 3 November 1968, *Foreign Relations of the United States, 1964–1968*, Volume VII, Vietnam, September 1968–January 1969 (Washington, D.C.: Government Printing Office, 2003), 543–544.

48. As Johnson considered his next step, on November 4, a White House aide wrote about the Nixon campaign: "The object of the exercise was to nullify the political impact of the President's decision by making it dubious. They think that goal has been achieved. They think the political effect of the bombing halt has been reduced by 25%–33%."

   "The damage was done via Thieu in Saigon, through low level Americans."

   "They think the damage has been done ... Thieu, in their judgment, will continue his present line until it becomes impossible." Unknown source of memorandum, 4 November 1968, Anna Chennault Record, Individual Reviewed Folders from Various Collections, Folder 1 of 2, LBJ Library.

49. Hung and Schecter, *The Palace File*, 23–24.

50. Hung and Schecter, *The Palace File*, 23–24. Chennault, *The Education of Anna* as quoted by Seymour Hersh, *The Price of Power*, 21.

51. Robert Parry, "The Almost Scoop on Nixon's Treason," Consortiumnews.com, 7 June 2012, Anna Chennault Folder, Individual Reviewed Folders from Various Collections, Folder 1 of 2, LBJ Library. Also, reference: Beverly Deepe Keever, *Death Zones and Darling Spies: Seven Years of Vietnam War Reporting* (Lincoln: University of Nebraska Press, 2013).

52. Rusk remembered: "Late in the campaign, perhaps nervous about the prospects of a settlement, some Nixon backers reportedly encouraged Thieu to hold out in the talks."

   "I never had any evidence that Richard Nixon himself was involved, but rumors abounded that Spiro Agnew and Anna Chennault had contacted the South Vietnamese. I never got to the bottom of it, but because the evidence was so sketchy, I did tell Lyndon Johnson that I didn't think he should go public with this." Dean Rusk (as told to Richard Rusk), *As I Saw It* (New York: W. W. North & Company, 1990), 488.

53. Rostow to Johnson, 4 November 1968, Anna Chennault Record, Individual Reviewed Folders from Various Collections, Folder 1 of 2, LBJ Library; Robert Parry, "The Almost Scoop on Nixon's Treason," Consortiumnews.com, 7 June 2012, Anna Chennault Folder, Individual Reviewed Folders from Various Collections, Folder 1 of 2, LBJ Library. Rusk would emphasize: "We get information like this every day, some of it very damaging to American political figures. We have always taken the view that with respect to such sources there is no public 'right to know.' Such information is collected simply for the purposes of national security."

54. Rostow sent another cable to Johnson at the ranch. "Saville Davis volunteered that his own newspaper would certainly not print the story in the form in which it was filed; but they might print a story which said Thieu, on his own, decided to hold out until after the election. Incidentally, the story as filed is stated to be based on Vietnamese sources, and not U.S., in Saigon." Rostow to Johnson, 4 November 1968, Anna Chennault Record, Individual Reviewed Folders from Various Collections, Folder 1 of 2, LBJ Library.

55. *Washington Evening Star*, 18 November 1968.

56. *Chicago Daily News*, 15 November 1968. In response, an observer emphasized: "To many American officials here it is offensive that the government for which Johnson literally gave up the Presidency and sacrificed his political career should treat him in this way."

57. Hoover to Bromley Smith, 7 November 1968, Anna Chennault Record, Individual Reviewed Folders from Various Collections, Folder 2 of 2, LBJ Library.

58. Rostow to Johnson, 8 November 1968, Anna Chennault Record, Individual Reviewed Folders from Various Collections, Folder 1 of 2, LBJ Library.

59. Tom Hutson to Nixon, 25 February 1970, White House Central Files, Nixon Library, p. 7.

60. Tom Hutson to Nixon, 25 February 1970, White House Central Files, Nixon Library, p. 7.

61. Rostow to Johnson, 12 November 1968, Anna Chennault Record, Individual Reviewed Folders from Various Collections, Folder 1 of 2, LBJ Library.

62. Smith to Johnson, 27 November 1968, Anna Chennault Record, Individual Reviewed Folders from Various Collections, Folder 1 of 2, LBJ Library.

63. Rostow to Johnson, 10 December 1968, Anna Chennault Record, Individual Reviewed Folders from Various Collections, Folder 1 of 2, LBJ Library.

64. "If he believes the material it contains should not be opened for research, I would wish him empowered to re-close the file for another fifty years when the procedure outlined above should be repeated." Rostow to Middleton, 26 June 1973, Anna Chennault Record, Individual Reviewed Folders from Various Collections, Folder 1 of 2, LBJ Library.

65. Safire, *Before the Fall*, 88.

66. Bryce N. Harlow, Oral History by Michael L. Gillette, Tape 2, 6 May 1979, 56, LBJ Library.

67. *Boston Globe*, 6 January 1969; Memo of Phone Conversation between Rostow and Tom Ottend, 3 January 1969, Anna Chennault Record, Individual Reviewed Folders From Various Collections, Folder 1 of 2, LBJ Library.

68. Hughes, *Chasing Shadows*, 1–3.

CHAPTER 11: THE LAST DANCE, JANUARY 1969

1. Lyndon B. Johnson, *The Vantage Point: Perspectives of the Presidency, 1963–1969* (New York: Holt, Rinehart and Winston, 1971), 561.

2. Johnson, *The Vantage Point*, 561.

3. Johnson, *The Vantage Point*, 561.

4. Horace Busby, *The Thirty-First of March: An Intimate Portrait of Lyndon Johnson's Final Days in Office* (New York: Farrar, Straus and Giroux, 2005), 244–245.

5. At one point, LBJ joked about returning home. "But I want to go back, like Ponce de Leon, to the Fountain." George Christian, *The President Steps Down: A Personal Memoir of the Transfer of Power* (New York: Macmillan Company, 1970), 256

6. For the entire conversation, reference: Busby, *The Thirty-First of March*, 244–249.

7. Johnson, *The Vantage Point*, 561.

8. Christian, *The President Steps Down*, 271; Erwin Duggan, "State of the Union Draft," 30 October 1968, President, 1963–1969, Speeches, Box 151, LBJ Library.

9. Lady Bird Johnson, *A White House Diary* (New York: Holt, Rinehart and Winston, 1970), 767–778.

10. Christian, The President Steps Down, 271.

11. Johnson, *The Vantage Point*, 562–563.

12. Johnson, *The Vantage Point*, 563.

13. Johnson, *A White House Diary*, 775.

14. Johnson, *Vantage Point*, 564.

15. Johnson, *A White House Diary*, 775.

16. Christian, *The President Steps Down, 275.*

17. Johnson, *A White House Diary*, 776.

18. Johnson, *A White House Diary*, 776.

19. Johnson, *A White House Diary*, 776.

20. Johnson, *Vantage Point*, 562–563.

21. Stephen E. Ambrose, *Nixon: The Triumph of a Politician, 1962–1972* volume II (New York: Simon and Schuster, 1987), 243.

22. Johnson, *A White House Diary*, 775–776.

23. Johnson, *Vantage Point*, 564.

24. Johnson, *Vantage Point*, 564.

25. Johnson, *Vantage Point*, 564.

26. Johnson, *A White House Diary*, 777.

27. Johnson, *A White House Diary*, 777.

28. Ambrose, *Nixon*, 243.

29. Johnson, *A White House Diary*, 778.

30. H. R. Haldeman, *The Haldeman Diaries: Inside the Nixon White House* (New York: G. P. Putnam's Sons, 1994), 18.

31. Henry Kissinger added that Nixon's "jaw jutted defiantly and yet he seemed uncertain, as if unsure that he was really there" and added that Nixon's pants legs were "as always, a trifle short." Evan Thomas, *Being Nixon: A Man Divided* (New York: Random House, 2016), 195–96.

32. Johnson, *Vantage Point*, 566–567.

33. Johnson, *Vantage Point*, 566–567.

34. Thomas, *Being Nixon*, 196.

35. Johnson, *A White House Diary*, 778.

36. Johnson, *Vantage Point*, 567.

37. Johnson, *Vantage Point*, 566.

38. Thomas, *Being Nixon*, 196.

39. Johnson, *A White House Diary*, 779.

40. Johnson, *A White House Diary*, 779.

41. Clark Clifford, *Counsel to the President: A Memoir* (New York: Random House, 1991), 606.

42. Johnson, *A White House Diary*, 779.

43. Johnson, *A White House Diary*, 780.

44. Johnson, *Vantage Point*, 567.

45. Johnson, *Vantage Point*, 567.

46. Clark Clifford, *Counsel to the President*, 607.

47. Johnson, *Vantage Point*, 568.

48. Clifford, *Counsel to the President*, 607.

49. Johnson, *Vantage Point*, 567–568.

50. Christian, *The President Steps Down*, 276.

51. Johnson, *A White House Diary*, 781.

52. Clifford, *Counsel to the President*, 607.

53. Jan Jarboe Russell, *Lady Bird: A Biography of Mrs. Johnson* (New York: Scribner, 1999), 304–305.

54. Johnson, *A White House Diary*, 781–782.

55. Johnson, *Vantage Point*, 568.

56. Johnson, *A White House Diary*, 782.

57. Johnson, *Vantage Point*, 568.

58. Johnson, *A White House Diary*, 782.

59. Johnson, *Vantage Point*, 568.

60. Johnson, *A White House Diary*, 783.

61. Johnson, *Vantage Point*, 568.

CONCLUSION

1. The entire story is contained in Nick Kotz, *Judgment Days: Lyndon Baines Johnson, Martin Luther King, Jr., and the Laws That Changed America* (Boston, MA: Houghton Mifflin, 2005), 423–425.

2. John Connally (with Mickey Herskowitz), *In History's Shadow: An American Odyssey* (New York: Hyperion, 1993), 215.

3. Johnson, *The Vantage Point*, 553.

4. Johnson, *The Vantage Point*, 552.

5. Lyndon Johnson, "Proclamation 3881, Thanksgiving Day, 1968," *Public Papers of the President: Lyndon B. Johnson, 1968–69*, 15 November 1968, volume 2, (Washington, D.C.: Government Printing Office, 1970), 1129.

6. Mitchell B. Lerner, *The Pueblo Incident: A Spy Ship and the Failure of American Foreign Policy* (Lawrence: University of Kansas Press, 2002), 237.

7. Eric Goldman, *The Tragedy of Lyndon Johnson* (New York: Knopf, 1969), 590–593.

8. *New York Times*, 1 May 2017.

9. Goldman, *The Tragedy of Lyndon Johnson*, 530.

Bibliography

INTERVIEWS BY THE AUTHOR

Temple, Larry, June 29, 2016, Austin, TX.

TELEPHONE INTERVIEWS BY THE AUTHOR

Califano, Joe, February 15, 2017.

Jones, Jim, February 13, 2017.

MEMOIRS

Ball, George W. *The Past Has Another Pattern: Memoirs.* New York: W.W. Norton, 1982.

Bui, Diem, and David Chanoff. *In the Jaws of History.* Boston: Houghton Mifflin, 1987.

Chennault, Anna. *The Education of Anna.* New York: Times, 1980.

Christian, George. *The President Steps Down: A Personal Memoir of the Transfer of Power.* New York: Macmillan Company, 1970.

Christopher, Warren. *Chances of a Lifetime: A Memoir.* New York: Scribner, 2001.

Clifford, Clark M., and Richard C. Holbrooke. *Counsel to the President: A Memoir.* New York: Random House, 1991.

Cormier, Frank. *LBJ: The Way He Was.* Garden City, NY: Doubleday & Company, 1977.

Cross, James U. *Around the World with LBJ: My Wild Ride as Air Force One Pilot, White House Aide, and Personal Confidant.* Austin: University of Texas Press, 2008.

Dobrynin, Anatoly. *In Confidence: Moscow's Ambassador to America's Six Cold War Presidents, 1962–1986.* New York: Times Books, 1995.

Haldeman, H. R. *The Haldeman Diaries: Inside the Nixon White House.* New York: G.P. Putnam's sons, 1994.

Humphrey, Hubert H., and Norman Sherman. *The Education of a Public Man: My Life and Politics.* Minneapolis: University of Minnesota Press, 1991.

Johnson, Lady Bird. *A White House Diary.* New York: Holt, Rinehart and Winston, 1970.

Johnson, Lyndon B. *The Vantage Point: Perspectives of the Presidency, 1963–1969.* New York: Holt, Rinehart and Winston, 1972.

Johnson, Sam Houston. *My Brother, Lyndon.* New York: Cowles Book, 1970.

Kalugin, Oleg. *The First Directorate: My 32 Years in Intelligence and Espoinage Against the West.* New York: St. Martin's Press, 1994.

Katzenbach, Nicholas. *Some of It Was Fun: Working with RFK and LBJ.* New York: W.W. Norton, 2008.

Keever, Beverly Deepe. *Death Zones and Darling Spies: Seven Years of Vietnam War Reporting.* Lincoln: University of Nebraska Press, 2013.

McPherson, Harry. *A Political Education.* Boston: Little, Brown and company, 1972.

Reedy, George E. *Lyndon B. Johnson, A Memoir.* New York: Andrews and McMeel, 1982.

Rusk, Dean. *As I Saw it: A Secretary of State's Memoirs.* New York: W. W. North & Company, 1990.

Safire, William. *Before the Fall: An Inside View of the Pre-Watergate White House.* New York: Doubleday & Company, 1975.

Salinger, Pierre. *P.S. A memoir.* New York: St. Martin's Press, 1995.

Valenti, Jack. *A Very Human President.* New York: W.W. Norton & Sons, 1975.

Watson, W. Marvin, and Sherwin Markman. *Chief of Staff: Lyndon Johnson and His Presidency.* New York: Thomas Dunne Books, 2004.

Westmoreland, William C. *A Soldier Reports.* Garden City, NY: Doubleday & Company, 1976.

Youngblood, Rufus W. *20 Years in the Secret Service; My Life with Five Presidents.* New York: Simon and Schuster, 1973.

ORAL HISTORY COLLECTIONS

Lyndon B. Johnson Library, Oral History Collection. Austin, TX
    Bryce N. Harlow, Interviewed by Michael L. Gillette, 6 May 1979
    Larry Temple, interviewed by Joe. B. Frantz, 11 August 1970.

GOVERNMENT DOCUMENTS

"Editorial Note." In *Foreign Relations of the United States, 1964–1968*, Vol VII. Washington, D.C.: Government Printing Office, 2003.

Johnson, Lyndon B. "Annual Message to the Congress on the State of the Union, 17 January 1968." In *Public Papers of the President of the United States: Lyndon B. Johnson, 1968.* Vol 1. Washington, D.C.: U.S. Government Printing Office, 1970.

Johnson, Lyndon B. "Broadcast Statement by the President Following the Passage of the Civil Rights Act, 10 April 1968." In *Public Papers of the Presidents of the United States, January-June 1968.* Washington, D.C.: Government Printing Office, 1970.

Johnson, Lyndon B. "Letter to the President of the Senate and to the Speaker of the House Urging Passage of an Effective Gun Control Law, 6 June 1968." In *Public Papers of the President, 1968–69.* Vol 1. Washington D.C.: Government Printing Office, 1970.

Johnson, Lyndon B. "Letter to the Speaker of the House Urging Enactment of the Fair Housing Bill, 5 April 1968." In *Public Papers of the Presidents of the United States, January-June 1968.* Washington, D.C. Government Printing Office, 1970.

Johnson, Lyndon B. "Lyndon B. Johnson to Shapiro, 6 April 1968." In *Public Papers of the President, January-June 1968.* Washington, D.C.: Government Printing Office, 1970.

Johnson, Lyndon B. "President's Daily Diary." In *Foreign Relations of the United States, 1964–1968,* Vol VI. Washington, D.C.: Government Printing Office, 2002.

Johnson, Lyndon B. "Proclamation 3881, Thanksgiving Day, 15 November 1968." In *Public Papers of the President: Lyndon B. Johnson, 1968–69.* Vol 2. Washington, D.C.: Government Printing Office, 1970.

Johnson, Lyndon B. "Remark and Statement upon Signing Order Establishing the National Commission on the Causes and Prevention of Violence, 6 June 1968." In *Public Papers of the President, 1968–69.* Vol 1. Washington D.C.: Government Printing Office, 1970.

Johnson, Lyndon B. "Remarks in Detroit at the Annual Convention of the Veterans of Foreign Wars, 19 August 1968." In *Public Papers of the President: Lyndon B. Johnson, 1968.* Vol 2. Washington, D.C.: Government Printing Offices, 1970.

Johnson, Lyndon B. "Remarks of the Presidential Prayer Breakfast, 1 February 1968." In *Public Papers of the Presidents of the United States: Lyndon B. Johnson, 1968.* Washington, D.C.: Government Publishing Office, 1970.

Johnson, Lyndon B. "Remarks on Signing the Civil Rights Act, 11 April 1968." Miller Center. Accessed April 15, 2016. http://millercenter.org/president/speeches/speech-4036.

Johnson, Lyndon B. "Remarks to Service Personnel and Award of Distinguished Service Medal and Medal of Freedom to Military and Civilian Leaders, Cam Ranh Bay, Vietnam, 23 December 1967." In *Public Papers of the President of the United States: Lyndon B. Johnson.* Washington, D.C.: Government Printing Office, 1968.

Johnson, Lyndon B. "Statement by the President Calling on the Warsaw Pact Allies to Withdraw From Czechoslovakia, 21 August 1968." In *Public Papers of the Presidents of the United States: Lyndon B. Johnson, 1968–69.* Vol 2. Washington, D.C.: U.S. Government Printing Office, 1970.

Johnson, Lyndon B. "Statement by the President on the Assassination of Dr. Martin Luther King, Jr." *The American Presidency Project.* (4 April 1968). Accessed September 29 2015., www.presidency.ucsb.edu/ws/?pid=28781

Johnson, Lyndon B. "Statement by the President on the Death of Senator Kennedy, 6 June 1968." In *Public Papers of the President, 1968–69.* Vol 1. Washington, D.C.: Government Printing Office, 1970.

Johnson, Lyndon B. "Telegram to the Governor of Maryland in Response to His Request for Federal Troops in Baltimore, 7 April 1968." In *Public Papers of the Presidents of the United States, January-June 1968.* Washington, D.C.: Government Printing Office, 1970.

Johnson, Lyndon B. "The President's Address to the Nation Announcing Steps to Limit the War in Vietnam and Reporting His Decision Not to Seek Reelection, 31 March 1968." In *Public Papers of the President of the United States: Lyndon B. Johnson, 1968.* Washington, D.C.: United States Government Printing Office, 1970.

Johnson, Lyndon B. "The President's New Conference of April 10, 1968, 10 April 1968." In *Public Papers of the Presidents of the United States, January-June 1968.* Washington, D.C.: Government Printing Office, 1970.

Johnson, Lyndon B. "The President's News Conference of March 31, 1968, 31 March 1968." In *Public Papers of the President of the United States, 1968.* Washington, D.C.: United States Government Printing Office, 1970.

Johnson, Lyndon B. *Public Papers of the Presidents of the United States: Lyndon B. Johnson, 1968–69.* Vol 1. Washington, D.C.: Government Printing Office, 1970.

Joint Chiefs of Staff. "Memorandum to President Johnson, 29 January 1968." In *Foreign Relations of the United States, 1964–1968.* Washington, D.C.: Government Printing Office, 2000.

Jones, Jim. "Jones to Johnson, 2 November 1968." *In Foreign Relations of the United States, 1964–1968,* Vol VII. Washington, D.C.: Government Printing Office, 2003.

Kasberg, Damon. "Dyess Airpark Holds Airman's Tale." *Air Force Combat Command.* (2012). Accessed July 27, 2015. www.acc.af.mil/news/story.asp?id=123326256

Lerner, Mitchell. "'Mostly Propaganda in Nature:' Kim Il Sung, the Juche Ideology, and the Second Korean War." *North Korea International Documentation Project.* Woodrow Wilson Center, July 7, 2011, www.wilsoncenter.org/publication/mostly-propaganda-nature-kim-il-sung-the-juche-ideology-and-the-second-korean-war.

Lyndon B. Johnson Library. Austin, TX.

Anna Chennault Record
Confidential Files
Family Correspondence
Files Pertaining to Abe Fortas and Homer Thornberry
National Security Council Histories
National Security Files
Office Files of White House Aides
Oral History Collection
Papers of Lyndon B. Johnson
Papers of the President
Personal Papers of Ramsey Clark
Personal Papers of Warren Christopher
President's Appointment File
Presidential Telephone Conversations
Speeches
Statements of Lyndon B. Johnson
Tom Johnson's Notes of Meetings
White House Central Files
White House Daily Diaries
White House Famous Names

"Memorandum for the Record, 18 March 1968." In *Foreign Relations of the United States, 1964–1968.* Vol VI. Washington, D.C.: Government Printing Office, 2002.

"Memorandum of Conversation, 23 August 1968." In *Foreign Relations of the United States, 1964–1968,* Vol XVII. Washington D.C.: Government Printing Office, 1996.

"Notes of Cabinet Meeting, 22 August 1968." In *Foreign Relations of the United States, 1964–1968,* Vol XVII. Washington D.C.: Government Printing Office, 1996.

"Notes of Emergency Meeting of the National Security Council, 20 August 1968." In *Foreign Relations of the United States, 1964–1968,* Vol XVII. Washington D.C.: Government Printing Office, 1996.

"Notes of Meeting, 10 February 1968." In *Foreign Relations of the United States, 1964–1968*. Washington, D.C.: Government Printing Office, 2000.

"Notes of Meeting, 12 February 1968." In *Foreign Relations of the United States, 1964–1968*. Washington, D.C.: Government Printing Office, 2000.

"Notes of Meeting, 13 February 1968." In *Foreign Relations of the United States, 1964–1968*. Washington, D.C.: Government Printing Office, 2000.

"Notes of Meeting, 20 March 1968." In *Foreign Relations of the United States, 1964–1968*, Vol VI, Washington, D.C.: Government Printing Office, 2002.

"Notes of Meeting, 23 January 1968." In *Foreign Relations of the United States, 1964–1968*. Washington, D.C.: Government Printing Office, 2000.

"Notes of Meeting, 24 January 1968." In *Foreign Relations of the United States, 1964–1968*. Washington, D.C.: Government Printing Office, 2000.

"Notes of Meeting, 25 January 1968." In *Foreign Relations of the United States, 1964–1968*. Washington, D.C.: Government Printing Office, 2000.

"Notes of Meeting, 26 March 1968." In *Foreign Relations of the United States, 1964–1968*, Vol VI, Washington, D.C.: Government Printing Office, 2002.

"Notes of Meeting, 28 February 1968." In *Foreign Relations of the United States, 1964–1968*. Washington, D.C.: Government Printing Office, 2000.

"Notes of Meeting, 30 January 1968." In *Foreign Relations of the United States, 1964–1968*. Washington, D.C.: Government Printing Office, 2000.

"Notes of Meeting, 31 January 1968." In *Foreign Relations of the United States, 1964–1968*. Washington, D.C.: Government Printing Office, 2000.

"Notes of Meeting, 4 March 1968." In *Foreign Relations of the United States, 1964–1968*. Washington, D.C.: Government Printing Office, 2000.

"Notes of Meeting, 6 February 1968." In *Foreign Relations of the United States, 1964–1968*. Washington, D.C.: Government Printing Office, 2000.

"Notes of Meeting, 9 February 1968." In *Foreign Relations of the United States, 1964–1968*. Washington, D.C.: Government Printing Office, 2000.

"Notes of Meetings, 1968." In *Foreign Relations of the United States, 1964–1968*, Vol VI, Washington, D.C.: Government Printing Office, 2002.

"Notes of Meetings, 29 October 1968." In *Foreign Relations of the United States, 1964–1968*, Vol VII, Vietnam, September 1968-January 1969. Washington, D.C.: Government Printing Office, 2003.

Reed,."Memorandum from the Department of State Executive Secretary Read to Rostow, 23 August 1968." In *Foreign Relations of the United States, 1964–1968*, Vol XVII. Washington D.C.: Government Printing Office, 1996.

Richard Nixon Library. Yorba Linda, CA

White House Central Files

Rostow, Walt W. "Memorandum for the Record, 29 February 1968." In *Foreign Relations of the United States, January-August 1968*, Vol VI. Washington D.C.: Government Printing Office, 2002.

Rusk, Dean. "Cabinet Report on Czechoslovakia and Vietnam, 22 August 1968." In *Weekly Compilation of Presidential Documents*. Washington, D.C.: Government Printing Office, 1996.

Griffin, Robert, Senator. "Reports of Chief Justice Warren's Resignation." *Congressional Record* (21 June 1968). S7499–7500.

"Summary Notes of the 590th Meeting of the National Security Council, 4 September 1968." In *Foreign Relations of the United States, 1964–1968*, Vol XVII. Washington D.C.: Government Printing Office, 1996.

"Summary of Meeting, 20 August 1968." In *Foreign Relations of the United States, 1964–1968*. Vol XVII. Washington D.C.: Government Printing Office, 1996.

"Summary of Meeting, 23 August 1968." In *Foreign Relations of the United States, 1964–1968*, Vol XVII. Washington D.C.: Government Printing Office, 1996.

"Telephone conversation Between Johnson and Dirksen, 2 November 1968." In *Foreign Relations of the United States, 1964–1968*, Vol VII. Washington, D.C.: Government Printing Office, 2003.

"Telephone Conversation between Johnson and Everett Dirksen, 27 August 1968." In *Foreign Relations of the United States, 1964–1968*. Washington, D.C.: Government Printing Office, 2002.

"Telephone Conversation Between Johnson and Humphrey, 31 October 1968." In *Foreign Relations of the United States, 1964–1968*, Vol VII. Washington, D.C.: Government Printing Office, 2003.

"Telephone Conversation between Johnson and Nixon, 3 November 1968." In *Foreign Relations of the United States, 1964–1968*, Vol VII. Washington, D.C.: Government Printing Office, 2003.

"Telephone conversation between Johnson and Rowe, 1 November 1968." In *Foreign Relations of the United States, 1964–1968*, Vol VII. Washington, D.C.: Government Printing Office, 2003.

"Telephone Conversation between Johnson and Smathers, 3 November 1968." In *Foreign Relations of the United States, 1964–1968*, Vol VII. Washington, D.C.: Government Printing Office, 2003.

"Telephone Conversation between Johnson, Humphrey, Nixon, Wallace, 31 October 1968." In *Foreign Relations of the United States, 1964–1968*, Vol VII. Washington, D.C.: Government Printing Office, 2003.

University of Virginia, Miller Center. Charlottesville, VA

Lyndon B. Johnson Presidential Recordings
Presidential Speeches

U.S. Congress. *Congressional Record*, 10 January 1969, 1:115, p. 432. Washington, D.C.: Government Printing Office, 1969.

U.S. Congress. *Congressional Record*, 23 January 1968. 14:1. Washington, D.C.: Government Printing Office, 1968: 679.

U.S. Congress. *Congressional Record*, 22 July 1968, vol. 114, pt. 14. Washington, D.C.: Government Printing Office, 1968: 18098.

U.S. Congress. Senate. Committee on the Judiciary. "Nominations of Abe Fortas and Homer Thornberry." 90th Cong., 2nd Sess., July 11 and July 23, 1968. Washington, D.C.: Government Printing Office, 1968.

BOOKS

Acacia, John. *Clark Clifford: The Wise Man of Washington*. Lexington, KY: University Press of Kentucky, 2009.

Ambrose, Stephen E. *Nixon: The Triumph of a Politician, 1962–1972*, Vol 2. New York: Touchstone Books, 1987.

Anderson, Terry H. *The Sixties*. New York: Longman, 1999.

Bass, Jack, and Marilyn W. Thompson. *Strom: The Complicated Personal and Political Life of Strom Thurmond*. New York: Public Affairs, 2005.

Bernstein, Irving. *Guns or Butter: The Presidency of Lyndon Johnson*. New York: Oxford University Press, 1996.

Bischof, Günter, Stefan Kamer, and Peter Ruggenthaler, eds., *The Prague Spring and the Warsaw Pact Invasion of Czechoslovakia in 1968*. Lanham, MD: Rowman & Littlefield, 2010.

Bolger, Daniel P. *Scenes from an Unfinished War: Low Intensity Conflict in Korea: 1966–1969*. Fort Leavenworth, KS: U.S. Army Command and General Staff College, 1991.

Braestrup, Peter. *Big Story: How the American Press and Television Reported and Interpreted the Crisis of Tet 1968 in Vietnam and Washington*. Boulder, CO: West-view, 1977.

Brands, H. W. *The Foreign Policies of Lyndon Johnson: Beyond Vietnam*. College Station, TX: Texas A & M University Press, 1999.

Brinkley, Douglas. *Cronkite*. New York: HarperCollins, 2012.

Bruce, John W., and Clyde Wilcox. *The Changing Politics of Gun Control*. Lanham, MD: Rowman & Littlefield, 1998.

Burns, Rebecca. *Burial for a King: Martin Luther King Jr.'s Funeral and the Week That Transformed Atlanta and Rocked the Nation*. New York: Scribner, 2011.

Busby, Horace W. *The Thirty-first of March: An Intimate Portrait of Lyndon Johnson's Final Days in Office*. New York: Farrar, Straus and Giroux, 2005.

Cain, Peter J., and Mark Harrison. *Imperialism: Critical Concepts in Historical Studies*, Vol 2. New York: Routledge, 2001.

Califano, Joseph A. *The Triumph & Tragedy of Lyndon Johnson: The White House Years*. New York: Touchstone, 1991.

Caro, Robert A. *Master of the Senate*. New York: Vintage Books, 2003.

Caro, Robert A. *Means of Ascent*. New York: Vintage Books, 1991.

Caro, Robert A. *The Passage of Power: The Years of Lyndon Johnson*. New York: Vintage Books, 2012.

Caro, Robert A. *The Path to Power*. New York: Vintage Books, 1990.

Cheevers, Jack. *Act of War: Lyndon Johnson, North Korea, and the Capture of the Spy Ship Pueblo*. New York: NAL Caliber, 2013.

Clarke, Thurston. *The Last Campaign: Robert F. Kennedy and 82 Days That Inspired America*. New York: Henry Holt, 2008.

Connally, John Bowden, and Mickey Herskowitz. *In History's Shadow: An American Odyssey*. New York: Hyperion, 1993.

Cray, Ed. *Chief Justice: A Biography of Earl Warren*. New York: Simon & Schuster, 1997.

Crespino, Joseph. *Strom Thurmond's America*. New York: Hill and Wang, 2012.

Dallek, Robert, and Lawrence Freedman. *Flawed Giant: Lyndon Johnson and His times, 1961–1973*. New York: Oxford University Press, 1998.

Dallek, Robert. *Lone Star Rising: Lyndon Johnson and His Times, 1908–1960*. New York: Oxford University Press, 1991.

Darman, Jonathan. *Landslide: LBJ and Ronald Reagan at the Dawn of a New America*. New York: Random House, 2014.

Dommen, Arthur J. *The Indochinese Experience of the French and the Americans: Nationalism and Communism in Cambodia, Laos, and Vietnam*. Bloomington: Indiana University Press, 2001.

Farber, David. *The Age of Great Dreams: America in the 1960s*. New York: Hill & Wang, 1994.

Fink, Carole, Philipp Gassert, and Detlef Junker. *1968, the World Transformed*. New York: Cambridge University Press, 1998.

Fite, Gilbert C. *Richard B. Russell, Jr.: Senator from Georgia*. Chapel Hill: University of North Carolina Press, 1991.

Flamm, Michael W. *Law and Order: Street Crime, Civil Unrest, and the Crisis of Liberalism in the 1960s*. New York: Columbia University Press, 2005.

Ford, Harold P. *CIA and the Vietnam Policymakers: Three Episodes, 1962–1968*. Ann Arbor: University of Michigan Library, 1998.

Forslund, Catherine. *Anna Chennault: Informal Diplomacy and Asian Relations.* Lanham, MD: Rowman and Littlefield, 2002.

Fry, Joseph A. *Debating Vietnam: Fulbright, Stennis, and Their Senate Hearings.* Lanham, MD: Rowman & Littlefield, 2006.

Gilbert, Ben W. *Ten Blocks from the White House: Anatomy of the Washington Riots of 1968.* New York: F.A. Praeger, 1968.

Goldman, Eric F. *The Tragedy of Lyndon Johnson.* New York: Alfred A. Knopf, 1969.

Goodwin, Doris Kearns. *Lyndon Johnson and the American Dream.* New York: St. Martin's Press, 1976.

Gould, Lewis L. *1968: The Election That Changed America.* Chicago: Ivan R. Dee, 2010.

Graff, Henry F. *The Tuesday Cabinet; Deliberation and Decision on Peace and War under Lyndon B. Johnson.* Englewood Cliffs, NJ: Prentice-Hall, 1970.

Halberstam, David. *The Best and the Brightest.* New York: Penguin, 1972.

Herd, Graeme P., and Jennifer D. P. Moroney. *Security Dynamics in the Former Soviet Bloc.* New York: Routledge, 2003.

Herring, George C. *America's Longest War: The United States and Vietnam, 1950–1975.* 5th edn. New York: McGraw-Hill, 2014.

Hersh, Seymour M. *The Price of Power: Kissinger in the Nixon White House.* New York: Summit, 1983.

Hughes, Ken. *Chasing Shadows: The Nixon Tapes, the Chennault Affair, and the Origins of Watergate.* Charlottesville: University of Virginia Press, 2014.

Hunt, Michael H. *Lyndon Johnson's War: America's Cold War Crusade in Vietnam, 1945–1968.* New York: Hill and Wang, 2011.

Isserman, Maurice, and Michael Kazin. *America Divided: The Civil War of the 1960s.* New York: Oxford University Press, 2015.

Jamieson, Kathleen Hall. *Packaging the Presidency: A History and Criticism of Presidential Campaign Advertising.* New York: Oxford University Press, 1996.

Johnson, Robert D. *Congress and the Cold War.* New York: Cambridge University Press, 2006.

Joseph, Peniel E. *Stokley: A Life.* New York: Basic, 2014.

Kalman, Laura. *Abe Fortas: A Biography.* New Haven, CT: Yale University Press, 1990.

Karnow, Stanley. *Vietnam, a History.* New York: Viking, 1983.

Kotz, Nick. *Judgment Days: Lyndon Baines Johnson, Martin Luther King, Jr., and the Laws That Changed America.* Boston: Houghton Mifflin, 2005.

Kruse, Kevin M. *One Nation Under God: How Corporate America Invented Christian America.* New York: Basic Books, 2015.

LaFeber, Walter. *The Deadly Bet: LBJ, Vietnam, and the 1968 Election*. Lanham, MD: Rowman & Littlefield, 2005.

Lamb, Charles M. *Housing Segregation in Suburban America since 1960: Presidential and Judicial Politics*. New York: Cambridge University Press, 2005.

Langguth, A. J. *Our Vietnam: The War, 1954–1975*. New York: Simon & Schuster, 2000.

Lerner, Mitchell B. *The Pueblo Incident: A Spy Ship and the Failure of American Foreign Policy*. Lawrence: University Press of Kansas, 2002.

Longley, Kyle. *Grunts: The American Combat Soldier in Vietnam*. Armonk, NY: M.E. Sharpe, 2008.

Longley, Kyle. *Senator Albert Gore, Sr.: Tennessee Maverick*. Baton Rouge: Louisiana State University Press, 2004.

Mann, Robert. *A Grand Delusion: America's Descent into Vietnam*. New York: Basic Books, 2001.

Mann, Robert. *The Walls of Jericho: Lyndon Johnson, Hubert Humphrey, Richard Russell, and the Struggle for Civil Rights*. New York: Harcourt Brace & Company, 1996.

Matusow, Allen J. *The Unraveling of America: A History of Liberalism in the 1960s*. New York: Harper & Row, 1984.

Mieder, Wolfgang. *"Making a Way out of No Way": Martin Luther King's Sermonic Proverbial Rhetoric*. New York: Peter Lang, 2010.

Milne, David. *America's Rasputin: Walt Rostow and the Vietnam War*. New York: Hill and Wang, 2008.

Mobley, Richard A. *Flash Point North Korea: The Pueblo and EC-121 Crises*. Annapolis, MD: Naval Institute Press, 2003.

Murphy, Bruce Allen. *Fortas: The Rise and Ruin of a Supreme Court Justice*. New York: William Morrow & Company, 1988.

Nguyen, Gregory Tien Hung, and Jerrold L. Schecter. *The Palace File*. New York: Harper & Row, 1986.

Oberdorfer, Don. *Tet!: The Turning Point in the Vietnam War*. Baltimore, MD: Johns Hopkins University Press, 2001.

Palermo, Joseph A. *In His Own Right: The Political Odyssey of Senator Robert F. Kennedy*. New York: Columbia University Press, 2002.

Prados, John. *Vietnam: The History of an Unwinnable War, 1945–1975*. Lawrence: University Press of Kansas, 2009.

Redford, Emmette S., and Richard T. McCulley. *White House Operations: The Johnson Presidency*. Austin: University of Texas Press, 1986.

Reedy, George E. *Lyndon B. Johnson: A Memoir*. New York: Andrews and McMeel, 1982.

Rigueur, Leah W. *The Loneliness of the Black Republican: Pragmatic Politics and the Pursuit of Power*. Princeton, NJ: Princeton University Press, 2015.

Risen, Clay. *A Nation on Fire: America in the Wake of the King Assassination*. New York: John Wiley & Sons, 2009.

Russell, Jan Jarboe. *Lady Bird: A Biography of Mrs. Johnson*. New York: Scribner, 1999.

Schandler, Herbert Y. *Lyndon Johnson and Vietnam: The Unmaking of a President*. Princeton, NJ: Princeton University Press, 1977.

Schmitz, David F. *The Tet Offensive: Politics, War, and Public Opinion*. Lanham, MD: Rowman & Littlefield, 2005.

Schulzinger, Robert D. *A Time for War: The United States and Vietnam, 1941–1975*. New York: Oxford University Press, 1997.

Schwartz, Thomas Alan. *Lyndon Johnson and Europe: In the Shadow of Vietnam*. Cambridge, MA: Harvard University Press, 2003.

Shesol, Jeff. *Mutual Contempt: Lyndon Johnson, Robert Kennedy, and the Feud That Defined a Decade*. New York: W.W. Norton, 1997.

Solberg, Carl. *Hubert Humphrey: A Biography*. New York: W.W. Norton, 1984.

Thomas, Evan. *Being Nixon: A Man Divided*. New York: Random House, 2016.

Unger, Irwin, and Debi Unger. *LBJ: A Life*. New York: John Wiley & Sons, 1999.

Updegrove, Mark K. *Indomitable Will: LBJ in the Presidency*. New York: Crown, 2002.

Vandiver, Frank Everson. *Shadows of Vietnam: Lyndon Johnson's War*. College Station: Texas A & M University Press, 1997.

White, Theodore H. *The Making of the President: 1968*. New York: Harper Perennial, 1969.

Willbanks, James H. *The Tet Offensive: A Concise History*. New York: Columbia University Press, 2008.

Witcover, Jules. *The Year the Dream Died: Revisiting 1968 in America*. New York: Warner Books, 1997.

Woods, Randall B. *LBJ: Architect of American Ambition*. New York: Free Press, 2006.

Woods, Randall Bennett. *Prisoners of Hope: Lyndon B. Johnson, the Great Society, and the Limits of Liberalism*. New York: Basic Books, 2016.

Zeiler, Thomas W. *Dean Rusk: Defending the American Mission Abroad*. Wilmington, DE: Scholarly Resources, 2000.

ARTICLES AND ESSAYS

Bickel, Alexander M. "Fortas, Johnson and the Senate: Voting the Court Up or Down." *The New Republic*, 28 September 1968.

"Formulating Presidential Program Is a Long Process," *Congressional Quarterly*, 24 January 1968, 1–3.

"In Pueblo's Wake." *Time*. February 2, 1968.

Jones, Jim. "Behind L.B.J.'s Decision Not to Run in '68." *New York Times*. 16 April 1988.

Lerner, Mitchell B. "Trying to Find the Guy Who Invited Them: Lyndon B. Johnson, Bridge Building and the End of the Prague Spring." *Diplomatic History* (January 2008): 77–103.

Nawaz, M. K. "The 'Pueblo' Affair and International Law." *The Indian Journal of International Law* (1975): 497.

Nelson, Justin A. "Drafting Lyndon Johnson: The President's Secret Role in the 1968 Democratic Convention." *Presidential Studies Quarterly* (December 2000): 694.

Parry, Robert. "The Almost Scoop on Nixon's Treason." *Consortiumnews.com*, 7 June 2012.

Rovere, Richard. "Freedom: Who Needs It." *The Atlantic Monthly*. May 1968.

Sheehy, Gail. "Ethel Kennedy and the Arithmetic of Life and Death," *New York Times Magazine*. 17 June 1968.

"The Economy: Jobs for 500,000," *Time*. February 2, 1968.

"The North Koreans are having a hard time proving to the world that the captive crewmen of the U.S.S. Pueblo are a contrite and cooperative lot." Photo. *Time*. October 18, 1968.

"What a Year." *Time*. August 20, 1968.

NEWSPAPERS

Atlanta Constitution
Boston Globe
Chicago Daily News
Chicago Sun-Times
Chicago Tribune
Great Falls Tribune
Jewish Week Weekly
New Hampshire Union Leader
New York Post
New York Times
Newsweek
Rocky Mountain News

The Nation
The New Republic
U.S. News and World Report
Wall Street Journal
Washington Daily News
Washington Evening Star
Washington Post

Index

Abernathy, Ralph, 108
ABM. *See* Anti-Ballistic Missile Treaty
Abrams, Creighton, 232, 286
academic leaders, 11
acceptance speech, of Humphrey, H., 229–230
Acheson, Dean, 16, 81–82
Ackerly, Gardner, 124
African-Americans, 27, 111, 305–306
    broken promises to, 116
    discrimination against, 117
    housing prices and, 130
    Marines killed by, 310
    rioting of, 88
    violence and, 119
    violence denounced and, 114–115
Agnew, Spiro, 128, 239, 242, 252
Aiken, George, 77–78
Air Force One, 270
aircraft, 38–39
airpower, 80–81
Akin, Harry, 270–271
Albert, Carl, 223, 227
Alexander, Cliff, 113
Allen, Dick, 234
Allot, Gordon, 294
American University Law School, 180, 317
Anderson, George, 43–44
Anderson, John, 133
annual production, 25
Anti-Ballistic Missile Treaty (ABM), 185–186
anti-crime bill, 11–12, 27
anti-poverty measures, 105
Antiquities Act, 260
anti-riot programs, 11–12
anti-Semitism, 167
anti-war platform, 224

anti-war protestors, 3, 21–22, 71–72, 223
Arlington Cemetery, 154
armed protection, 36
arms control, 187
Army of the Republic of Vietnam (ARVN), 2
arson, 118–119
ARVN. *See* Army of the Republic of Vietnam
assassinations, 277
    of Kennedy, R., 137, 144–145
    of King, M. L., 108–110
Au Ngoc Ho, 235
Austin, Paul, 166

Baker, Bobby, 168
balance budget, 27
Ball, George, 81, 191, 194–195, 283
    Malik's bitter debate with, 195
    USS Pueblo capture investigated by, 43–44
Barnes, Ben, 270–271
Baygan, Lee, 21
Bernstein, Leonard, 150–151
Bible Belt, 180–181
Bill of Economic Rights, 124
B'nai B'rith, 168
Boggs, Hale, 46, 207
bombing, 67–69, 71, 80
bombing halt, 81–82, 243
    Abrams reluctance of, 232
    Hanoi demanding, 235–236
    political motive of, 237, 328
    Rusk and risks of, 297–298
    Soviet ambassador suggesting, 96–97
    Vietnam War with considered, 74, 80, 232
    Westmoreland's warning on, 213–214
Bookbinder, Hyman, 167
Bork, Robert, 183–184

Bradley, Omar, 81
Branch, Ben, 108
Brezhnev, Leonid, 196
Brezhnev Doctrine, 202–203
Bridge of No-Return, 53
Brody, David, 167
Brooke, Edward, 166
Brown, H. Rap, 114
Brown v. Board, 136
Bryant, Anita, 223
Bucher, Lloyd, 38, 53
Bucher, Rose, 50–51
Buckley, William F., 29
Bui Diem, 78–79, 235, 249, 251
Bundy, McGeorge, 82
Bundy, William, 79–80, 241
Bunker, Ellsworth, 133, 283
burial site, of Kennedy, Robert, 145, 153
Burns, Arthur, 265
Busby, Horace, 91, 112–113, 283
  arguments not swerving, 93–94
  information leak and, 206
  Johnson, Lyndon, and, 17–19, 111,
    258–259
  president addresses written by, 85–86
  reelection speech by, 86–87, 91, 94–95, 97
  State of Union observations of, 10, 28
Bush, George H. W., 269
Byrd, Harry, 46, 166
Byrd, Robert, 60, 123, 164

Cabinet Meeting, 198, 309, 320
Califano, Joe, 7–8, 11–12, 283
  academic leaders met by, 11
  Fortas, A., civil rights programs and,
    177–178
  Fortas, A., comments of, 168–169, 171,
    174
  Fortas, A., not being confirmed from,
    178, 317
  Johnson, Lyndon, comments of, 140
  Johnson, Lyndon, convention role and,
    207
  Johnson, Lyndon, meeting with, 122–123
  Johnson, Lyndon, silence comments of,
    154
  Kennedy, Robert, burial site briefing by,
    145
  Kennedy, Rose, comments of, 153
  pessimistic moods and, 67–68
  political fight campaign and, 165

State of Union watched by, 24
Texas schoolteacher story and, 173
Vietnam leadership concerns and, 13
Carmichael, Stokley, 114, 122–123, 237
Caro, Robert, 5–6
Carpenter, Liz, 7–8, 19–20, 283
Carswell, G. Harrold, 183–184
Carter, Doug, 101
Carver, George, 81
Catholic Archbishop, 106
Ceausescu, Nicolae, 199–200
Celler, Emmanuel, 308
Chamberlain, Wilt, 132
character flaws, 278–279
Chatham Council on Human Relations,
  315
Chennault, Anna, 234
  Agnew managing activities of, 252
  Diem contacted by, 251
  Humphrey, H., and activities of, 241
  surveillance of, 239
  SVG activities with, 252, 328
  Thieu meeting with, 235–236
  White House monitoring, 241–242
Chennault, Claire, 234
Chennault Affair, 6, 252, 328–329
  Johnson, Lyndon, personality and, 7
  Republican Party and, 234
  Watergate overshadowing, 254–255
Chiang Kai-Shek, 239
Chicago, 126
  Christopher sent to, 126
  Democratic convention disaster in,
    226–227, 231
  federal troops in, 126, 216
  Johnson, Lyndon, possible visit to, 209
  Johnson, Lyndon, speech planned for,
    218
  Johnson, Lyndon, viewing destruction in,
    127–128
  Nixon, R., and violence in, 325
  protestors in, 216
Chief Justices, 7, 158–159, 161–162,
  181–182
China Lobby, 240, 242, 245–246
Christian, George, 28–29, 94, 144, 283
  gunboat diplomacy and, 53–54
  Johnson, Lyndon, comments of, 71–72
  reelection speech and, 86–87
  USS Pueblo comments of, 40
Christian Science Monitor report, 249

Christopher, Warren, 115–116, 120–121, 141, 283
  in Chicago, 126
  White House information gathered by, 314–315
Church, Frank, 39, 56–57
citizens, 5–6, 60
civil rights, 4, 105, 112, 177–178
  bill signing on, 135
  conference on, 274–276
  conservative opposition on, 136
  economic programs and, 125
  movement, 110, 116
  speech after meeting on, 113
  violence and, 117, 124
Clancy, James, 175
Clark, Mark, 43–44
Clark, Ramsey, 108, 122, 145, 283–284
  great friendships destroyed by, 171
  Republican senators contacted by, 166–167
  wiretapping opposed by, 157
Clifford, Clark, 5, 98, 112–113, 283–284
  airpower comment of, 80–81
  decision comments of, 98–99
  Johnson, Lady Bird, and gathering at home of, 267–268
  Kennedy, Robert, and, 78
  leaks investigation by, 74–75
  Nixon, R., story comments of, 249
  presidential nomination and, 77–78
  as Secretary of Defense, 32–33
  South Korea comments by, 47
  Southeast Asia stability comment of, 297–298
  Supreme Court nomination and, 161–162
  task force led by, 70, 72
Clifford, Marny, 98, 267–268
Cohen, Wilbur, 101
Cohen, William, 166
"Cold War Knighthood," 81
Colmer, William, 133
Communism, 58, 72, 240
confirmation votes, 316
Congress (U.S.), 27, 129
  conservative forces in, 158
  Constitutional duty of, 318
  gun trafficking laws in, 143–144, 147
  Johnson, Lyndon, and, 122–123, 308
  leaders of, 46, 115–116, 123

obstructionism in, 125
  speech preparations to, 124
  USS Pueblo and, 44–46
Congress of Racial Equality (CORE), 275–276
Connally, John, 21, 94, 214–215, 228, 276
conservative opposition, 136
conservative shift, 158, 162
constitutional crisis, 241–242
constitutional duty, of Congress, 318
Cook, Terence James, 106, 144
Cooper, Sherman, 77–78
CORE. *See* Congress of Racial Equality
Cormier, Frank, 58
crime rates, 26
crisis management, 57, 110–111, 197, 199, 277–278
Criswell, John, 207, 209
Cronkite, Walter, 71–72
cronyism, 161, 164, 173–174, 183
Cross, James, 1
Czechoslovakia
  cabinet meeting discussing, 198
  conspiracy against, 188–190
  European problems and, 202
  invasion verbal protests and, 198
  Johnson, Lyndon, challenge of, 204
  Nixon, R., told of invasion of, 193
  Prague Spring in, 186–187, 192
  refugees from, 201–202
  Soviet invasion of, 191, 193–194, 320
  summit meeting postponed due to, 202–203
  U.S. military intervention unlikely in, 198
  Warsaw Pact invasion of, 188

Daley, Richard, 98–99, 102–103, 122–123, 283–284
  Johnson, Lyndon, possible Chicago visit and, 209
  National Guard sent in by, 126
  Ribicoff angering, 226–227
Dallek, Robert, 5–6
darker side, of Johnson, Lyndon, 231
Davis, Savelle, 249, 328
death, of Johnson, Lyndon, 276
debates, 94–95, 180, 195, 218
decision-making method, 87
declaration of war, 296
Deepe, Beverly, 248
DeLoach, Cartha "Deke," 239

Demilitarized Zone (DMZ), 235–236
Democratic National Convention, 7, 191,
    199–200, 205, 206, 217, 218, 222, 230,
    277, 284
  anti-war compared to status quo
    platforms at, 224
  debates unfolding in, 218
  Democratic party disaster at, 226–227, 231
  draft Johnson movement and, 219–221
  Johnson, Lyndon, not attending, 221
  Johnson, Lyndon, role in, 207, 221, 231
  Nixon, R., win and, 209
  nomination process at, 227–228
  party unity disappeared at, 225
  Vietnam platform battle at, 223–226
  White House shaping, 207
Democratic Party, 97, 205
  convention disaster for, 226–227, 231
  Johnson, Lyndon, not seeking reelection
    and, 205–206
  party unity disappeared of, 225
  platform of, 211–213
  Vietnam damaging, 213
democratic successes, 23
DePuy, William, 81
DeVier, Jim, 260
Dien Bien Phu, 55
Dillon, Douglas, 82
DiMaggio, Joe, 32
diplomatic mission, 47–48
diplomatic solutions, 67
Dirksen, Everett, 130–131, 142, 165, 199
  court nominations comment of, 168
  Nixon, R., campaign review of, 243
  pornography debate and, 180
  USS Pueblo and, 44–45
dirty movies issue, 180
discrimination, 117
DMZ. See Demilitarized Zone
Dobrynin, Anatoly, 96–97, 139–140,
    188–190, 303
Dominican Republic, 196
Douglas, Helen Gahagan, 236
Douglas, Paul, 130, 179
Draft Johnson movement, 205, 209,
    214–215, 219–221
Draft Teddy Kennedy movement, 223
Druid Hill Park, 128
Dubček, Alexander, 186
Dulles, John Foster, 186–187
Dutch fishing vessel, 52

Eastland, James, 162–163, 177–178
Ebenezer Baptist Church, 132
economy, 25–26, 125
Edelman, Peter, 66
Eisenhower, Milton, 142
Eisenhower Commission, 158
Ellington, Buford, 111, 228
Ellsworth, Bunker, 61–62, 233–234
Elsey, George, 186–187
emotional trance, 151–152
enemy casualties, 62
enemy collusion, 237, 243–244, 250, 253
English, Ron, 132
eulogy, 149–150
Europe, 202
Evans, Rowland, 24–25, 27
Evers, Charles, 141
Executive Branch, 168, 318
"The Eyes of Texas," 270–271

fair housing, 133, 168–169
Fair Housing Act, 129–132, 135, 280
  political legacy and, 105–106
  positive from tragedy with, 7–8
Farber, David, 5–6
Fauntroy, Walter, 112, 114, 116
federal lands, 262
federal troops, 114
  in Chicago, 126, 216
  race riots and, 4–5
  states requesting, 128
  in Washington, D.C., 119–122
Fehmer, Marie, 94, 112–113, 283–284
filibuster opposition, 178–179
financial costs, 73
Finch, Robert, 245–246
First Amendment rights, 131, 176
First Tet Offensive, 6
Fonda, Henry, 132
food shortages, 35
Ford, Gerald, 21, 44–45, 131–132, 199
Ford, Henry III, 166
foreign policy, 23, 187, 265, 280
Fort Bragg, 64–65
Fortas, Abe, 28–29, 79–80, 283–284
  analyses of, 173
  Califano commenting on, 168–169, 171,
    174
  Chief Justice nomination of, 7
  civil rights programs and, 177–178
  confirmation unlikely for, 178, 317

dirty movies issue of, 180
Eastland objecting to, 163, 177
embarrassment hope for, 316
Goldberg replaced by, 160
Griffin doubting independence of, 175
Johnson, Lady Bird, dinner invitation to,
    182
Johnson, Lyndon, character flaws and,
    278–279
Johnson, Lyndon, lobbying for, 166–167
Johnson, Lyndon, relationship with,
    168–169, 315
McPherson finding picture of, 167
nomination discussed of, 161–162
nomination issue of, 158–159
nomination process failure of, 183
nomination withdrawal requested by,
    181–182
political fight for, 165–166
presidents contact with, 318
as president's lawyer, 173
as progressive, 175
Russell supporting, 170
Russell voting against, 180–181
seminar teaching payment received by,
    180
Senate confirmation and, 164
Senate Judiciary Committee questioning,
    173–174
support gratitude of, 317
Thurmond chastising, 176
as tormented man, 179
Fortas, Carol, 182–183
Fowler, Henry, 12, 73, 283–284
Franklin, Aretha, 217
fraternal solicitude, 195
Fulbright, J. William, 37, 56–57, 199
funeral, 144–145
    of Johnson, Lyndon, 277
    Kennedy, Robert, arrangements for, 146,
        312–313
    Kennedy, Robert, procession for, 148–150
    of Kennedy, Robert, 149–151, 153–154
    of King, M. L., 123, 133, 307

Gaddis, Kenneth, 85
Gaither, Jim, 144–145
Gallup, George, 5–6
Gallup Poll, 289
Gardner, John, 114
Garza, Reynaldo J., 275

Geneva agreements, 71
Geneva meeting, 203
ghettos, 126
Gideon, Clarence, 164
Ginsberg, David, 211–213
Glynn, Paul, 17–18, 85
Goldberg, Arthur, 3, 38–39, 41, 106
    Fortas, A., replacing, 160
    North Korean discussions and, 49
Goldman, Eric, 279, 281
Goldstein, Ernest, 167
Goodwin, Dick, 205
Gore, Albert, Sr., 57, 104, 173–174, 225
government violence, 107
Graham, Billy, 152
Grand Park, 226
Great Society programs, 12, 125, 278
    crisis of expectation, 13
    guests benefiting from, 22–23
    spending cuts and, 28
Griffin, Robert, 164, 172–175, 182
Gun Control Act (1968), 157
gun control laws, 27, 142, 156–158
    Johnson, Lyndon, seeking, 146–147
    Kennedy, Robert, honored with, 142, 156
    Kennedy, Robert, speech on, 146
    violence and, 147
gun crime, 142
gun trafficking laws, 143–144, 147
gunboat diplomacy, 53–54

Habib, Philip, 81
Haddad, Norman, 127
"Hail to the Chief," 269
Haines, Ralph E., 120–121
Haldeman, John, 244, 253, 264
Halleck, Charles, 132
Halperin, Morton, 72
handguns, cheap, 157
Harlow, Bryce, 244
Harper, John, 166–167
Harriman, Averell, 96, 139–140
Hart, Phil, 174
Hatcher, Richard, 115
Hatfield, Mark, 166–167
Hayden, Carl, 45
Haynsworth, Clement, 183–184
heart attack, 20
Height, Dorothy, 114, 275
Helms, Richard, 32–33, 45, 187, 283–284
Heuvel, William vanden, 227

Hickenlooper, Bourke, 21, 199
Higbee, USS, 43
Higginbotham, Leon, 112, 144, 166
highlight film, 208
Hodges, Duane, 53
Hoffman, Abbie, 216
Holt, Harold, 1
Homan, Richard, 294
Hoover, J. Edgar, 88, 108
Horner, Jack, 41
hostages, 6
  release sought for, 34, 49–52
  return of, 53
House Rules Committee, 133
housing prices, 130
human dignity, 114
humanitarian crisis, 201–202
Humphrey, Hubert, 7, 275, 284
  acceptance speech of, 229–230
  Chennault, A., activities and, 241
  compromising position and, 210–211
  as drained and empty, 152
  Johnson, Lyndon, criticism of, 323
  Johnson, Lyndon, disloyalty charge
    against, 211, 215–216, 322
  Johnson, Lyndon, holding back, 215
  Johnson, Lyndon, meeting with, 90
  Johnson, Lyndon, platform dissatisfaction
    and, 212–213
  Johnson, Lyndon, surrendering
    presidency and, 90
  Johnson, Lyndon, undercutting, 231, 278
  memorial service attendance of, 116–118
  nomination won by, 227–228
  poll gap being reduced by, 236
  position splitting party of, 226
  presidential candidacy of, 91, 323
  promising platform supported by,
    211–212
  USS Pueblo comments of, 51
  Vice President selection by, 228, 322
  Vietnam position of, 212, 215
  White House gathering with, 262
  White House humiliating, 215
Humphrey, Muriel, 152, 264
Huston, Tom, 253

inflation, 13
information sources, 249, 251
Innis, Roy, 275–276
insecurities, 20

Jackson, Mahalia, 132
Jacobsen, Jake, 213–214
Javits, Jacob, 104, 166–167
Jay, John, 168–169
Jenner, Albert, 162
joblessness, 26
Jobs Corps, 22–23
Joel, Lawrence, 22–23
Johnson, Harold, 120
Johnson, Lady Bird
  Clifford, C., home gathering and,
    267–268
  comments to, 19
  convention excitement and, 218
  crime and violence comments of, 27
  daughters emotional of, 95
  day suspended in unreality from, 147–148
  diet change forced by, 20
  emotional trance comment of, 151–152
  final draft reading comments of, 20
  Fortas, A., dinner invitation worries of,
    182
  gloomy day statement of, 74
  Greek tragedy and, 148–150
  Johnson, Lyndon, changing mind worries
    of, 93–94
  Johnson, Lyndon, reelection decision
    and, 93
  Kennedy, Robert, assassination and, 137
  line of poetry remembered by, 273
  prayers for president and, 40
  reelection speech suggestions of, 99
  reelection statement observations of,
    28–29
  relief felt by, 101
  Rusk testimony recalled by, 190
  Russian Ambassador meeting and, 96
  speech optimism of, 30–31
  State of Union address comments of, 10,
    21–22
  State of Union optimism of, 30–31
  teleprompter failure noticed by, 290
  Thornberry comments of, 161
  three-ring circus comment of, 223
  USS Pueblo pressures mounting and,
    38–39
  Vietnam trip and, 1–3
  Vietnam worries stated by, 74–75
  White House departure of, 264
  White House goodbyes of, 261
Johnson, Lyndon Baines. *See specific topics*

Johnson, Sam, 28–29
Johnson, Sam Houston, 50
Johnson, Tom, 108, 169, 205–206
Jones, Jim, 106, 152, 213–214, 260, 284
Jones, Solomon, 108
Jordan, Barbara, 275

Katzenbach, Nicholas, 49, 67–68, 145, 237, 284
    invasion verbal protests comments of, 198
    mass attacks destroying confidence and, 294–295
    Vietnam issue comments of, 3
Kearns, Doris, 223–224
Kennedy, Ethel, 150–151, 155, 312–313
Kennedy, Jackie, 106, 113, 132, 149–150
    Johnson, Lyndon, thank you note from, 154
    Red Room decorated by, 262
Kennedy, John F., 17–18, 149
Kennedy, Robert, 66, 76–77, 92, 284
    assassination of, 137, 144–145
    burial site of, 145, 153
    as chief political revival, 3
    Clifford, R., and, 78
    funeral arrangements for, 146, 312–313
    funeral of, 149–151, 153–154
    funeral procession of, 148–150
    gun control honoring, 142, 156
    gun control speech of, 146
    Johnson, Lady Bird, and assassination of, 137
    Johnson, Lyndon, compassion and, 140, 150–151, 154, 278, 312–313
    Johnson, Lyndon, feud with, 149
    Johnson, Lyndon, meeting with, 138–139
    Johnson, Lyndon, nomination after, 205–206
    Johnson, Lyndon, reelection and, 89
    Johnson, Lyndon, telegram from, 309
    legacy of what-might-have-been, 144
    memorial film played about, 229
    as presidential candidate, 78
    Vietnam used by, 83
    Vietnam War policy reevaluation and, 77–78
    White House keeping files on, 4
Kennedy, Rose, 140, 153–154
Kennedy, Ted, 140, 146, 149–150, 208, 223
Kerner Commission, 119
Khan, Ayub, 2

Khe Sanh, 55, 69
Khrushchev, Nikita, 191
Kilpatrick, Carroll, 58
Kim Il-Sung, 35, 52
    MAC meetings agreement of, 46, 48
    U.S. apology demanded by, 48, 51–52
King, Coretta, 109–110, 113
King, Martin Luther, Jr., 4, 278
    assassination of, 108–110
    civil rights movement of, 110, 116
    funeral service of, 123, 133, 307
    Johnson, T., and shooting of, 108
    legislation honoring, 130–131
    in Lorraine Hotel, 107
    memorial service for, 113, 116–118, 132
    national television mourning of, 117
    racial tensions over, 111
    Tuck claiming violence following, 134
King, Martin Luther, Sr., 115
Kissinger, Henry, 236, 253
Klein, Herbert, 250
Korean Military Armistice Commission (MAC), 33–34, 45–46, 48
Kosygin, Alexi, 39, 49, 185–186, 196
Kreeger, David Lloyd, 167
Krim, Arthur, 85–86, 93, 98, 112–113, 178–179, 284
Ku Klux Klan, 112, 123
Kung, Louis, 235–236
Kuter, Laurence, 43–44

lame duck president, 178, 182
Lattimore, Owen, 164
law enforcement, 27
lawlessness, 142–143
Lawrence, Alexander, 170–171, 315
leaks, 19–20, 43–44, 74–75, 206
legislation, 134–135, 157
    King, M. L., honored with, 130–131
    McPherson on bad, 156
legislative agenda, 8
Leonard, Eleanor, 51
Leonard, James, 51
Lerner, Mitch, 6
Levinson, Larry, 14, 144–145, 208
Lincoln Park, 217
Loan (General) killing, 295
Lockheed Air Service, 1
Lodge, Henry Cabot, 81
Loeb, Harry, 113
Logan Act, 237–238

Long, Russell, 164
looting, 118–119

MAC. *See* Korean Military Armistice
    Commission
MacArthur, Douglas, 152–153
mail order sales, 157
Mailer, Norman, 226–227
Malechek, Dale, 272
Malik, Yakov, 194–195
Manatos, Mike, 140, 162–163, 175, 284
manpower programs, 26
Mansfield, Mike, 21, 46, 77–78, 142
    Nixon, R., campaign review of, 243
    pornography debate and, 180
Mao Zedong, 186
Marines, killing of, 310
Marks, Leonard, 101, 261
Marshall, Thurgood, 112, 160, 275
McCammon, Vicky, 315
McCarthy, Abigail, 102–103
McCarthy, Eugene, 10, 66, 75–76, 284
McClellan, John, 163, 175
McCormack, John, 114, 131–132, 152
McCormack, Thomas, 21
McCulloch, William, 131–132
McGill, Ralph, 169
McGovern, George, 3, 196–197
McGrory, Mary, 111
McNair, Robert, 228
McNamara, Robert, 32–33, 35–36, 145, 284
    aircraft called up by, 39
    extended bombing targets comment of,
    296
    North Korean ships and, 42
    troop increase plan and, 63–65, 67–68
    Vietnam War comments of, 56–57
McPherson, Harry, 14, 27, 144, 284
    bad legislation comment of, 156
    Fortas, A., picture found by, 167
    Johnson, Lyndon, highlight film and, 208
    Johnson, Lyndon, letter from, 315
    pessimistic moods and, 67–68
    public funds and programs from, 125
    Tet Offensive influencing, 59
Meany, George, 99, 211–212
Medal of Freedom, 261, 268
media, 297–299
    leaks to, 19–20, 43–44, 74–75
    Nixon campaign's interference and, 248
Medicare, 12

memorial film, for Kennedy, Robert, 229
memorial service, for King, M. L., 113,
    116–118, 132
mental illness, 156
Mexican American communities, 129
Middleton, Harry, 252, 261, 285
midterm elections, 130
military action, 43, 53–54, 191
Military Assistance Program, 299
military resources, 33–34, 41, 45, 67–68
military victory, 61–63, 81
Milk Producers Association convention, 200
Miller, William "Fishbait," 23, 259
Mills, Wilbur, 12, 28
mistakes, not admitting, 13–14, 62, 279
Mitchell, Clarence, Jr., 114, 135, 275–276
Mitchell, John, 235
Model Cities, 27
Monroney, Mike, 137–138
morale issue, 95
Morse, Wayne, 56–57, 179
mortar attacks, 55–56
Moyers, Bill, 29, 299
Moynihan, Patrick, 27, 29
Mundt, Karl, 252
Murphy, Charles, 138–139, 211, 310
Murphy, Patrick, 119, 285
Murphy, Robert D., 203
Muskie, Edmund, 207, 229, 264

National Commission on the Causes and
    Prevention of Violence, 155
National Educational Television (NET),
    22–23
National Guard, 88, 121, 126, 141
national park system, 260
National Rifle Association (NRA), 147, 158,
    311
national security advisors, 32–33, 35–36,
    326
NATO Treaty, 199–200
negotiated settlement, 16
negotiating skills, 34–35
NET. *See* National Educational Television
New York Times, 149–150, 193–194
Newhouse, Sam, 314
Nguyen Cao Ky, 79, 238
Nguyen Hoan, 252
Nguyen Ngoc Loan, 59
Nguyen Tien Hung, 238
Nguyen Van Kieu, 238

Nguyen Van Thieu, 2, 79, 210, 233, 238
 Chennault, A., meeting with, 235–236
 independence exerted by, 242
Nimetz, Matt, 310–311
Nixon, Pat, 262–263
Nixon, Richard, 5–6, 50–51
 anger exploited by, 125
 Burns not detecting humility in, 265
 campaign review and, 243
 character lacking of, 236
 Chicago violence benefiting, 325
 Christian Science Monitor report and, 249
 Clifford, C., comments on story about,
   249
 Communists negotiations and, 240
 Czech invasion conveyed to, 193
 Democratic Convention win and, 209
 enemy collusion and, 237, 243–244, 250,
   253
 filibuster opposition sought from,
   178–179
 Johnson, Lyndon, discussion with,
   245–247, 263
 Johnson, Lyndon, encouraging support
   of, 270–271
 Johnson, Lyndon, entering race and, 209
 Johnson, Lyndon, frustrated by, 233
 Johnson, Lyndon, not exposing, 252
 Logan Act against, 237–238
 media and campaign interference of, 248
 North Korea restraint of, 293
 peace process undermined by, 234,
   238–239, 242, 244, 248
 presidential election won by, 250
 protestors angering, 266
 Rostow, W., exposing activity of, 251
 Soviet invasion exploited by, 197
 Supreme Court appointments and, 164
 SVG receiving communications from,
   245
 treasonous activities and, 239
 U.S. overextended statement of, 36
 Vietnam strategy of, 233–234
 Vietnams better treatment from, 235
nomination process, 183, 227–228
Non-Proliferation Treaty (NPT), 185–186
North Korea, 31
 aggression of, 38
 captives of, 293
 Goldberg and continuing discussions
   with, 49

information lacking on, 35–36
McNamara and ships of, 42
MIG-21 incident of, 53–54
military action considered against, 43,
   53–54
Nixon, R., restraint toward, 293
Smith comments on, 46
spying charges from, 49
strengthening position against, 38
U.S. threats from, 280
USS Pueblo near, 32, 35
White House castigated by, 45
North Vietnamese, 71
 negotiation willingness of, 105, 210
 peace talk agreement of, 238–239
 respecting DMZ promise of, 235–236
 Tet Offensive launched by, 55–56
Novak, Robert, 24–25, 27
NPT. *See* Non-Proliferation Treaty
NRA. *See* National Rifle Association
nuclear weapons, 185–186
Nugent, Luci, 87, 89, 93, 97–98, 105–106
 birthday party with, 221–222
 emotional reaction of, 95
 Johnson, Lyndon, roaring at, 269
 longest wake ever comments of,
   230–231
 reelection bid and, 21
 speech reaction of, 101
Nugent, Pat, 87, 92, 263

OAS. *See* Organization of American States
oath of office ceremony, 265–266
O'Boyle, Patrick, 113
O'Brien, Larry, 211–212
office of presidency, 260
official funeral, 144–145
open housing, 131
Organization of American States (OAS),
   196–197
Oswald, Lee Harvey, 156, 311
Ottend, Tom, 253

Pak Chung Kuk, 46, 48, 53
Palm Sunday Mass, 127
paranoid bubble, 299
Paris Peace talks, 210, 219–220, 238–239,
   245–246, 248
 Nixon, R., undermining, 234, 238–239,
   242, 244, 248
 Vietnam and goal in, 24, 96, 100

Park Chung-hee, 2, 32
  commitments demanded by, 50
  South Korea in Vietnam and, 50
  U.S. squeezed by, 35
Parole Authority of the Immigration and
    Nationality Act, 201–202
patience, of Johnson, Lyndon, 7–8, 53–54
Paul VI (pope), 2
peace with honor, 79–80
peacemaker, 265
Pearson, Drew, 226, 322
Peck, Gregory, 208
pessimistic moods, 67–68, 71–72
Pickle, Jake, 131–132, 220–221
Pigasus, 216
policy decision, 69–70
politics, 6–7, 256, 277
  bombing halt and, 237, 328
  Fair Housing Act and legacy in, 105–106
  Fortas, A., fight in, 165–166
polls, 30, 104–105, 289
Poor People's March, 107, 141, 310
pornography, 175, 180–181, 317
Porter, Paul, 179–180, 317
poverty, 129, 141
Prague Spring, 186–187, 192
"Precious Lord, Take My Hand," 116, 132
prerepudiated document, 52
president, 173–174, 256
  address by, 85–86
  Clifford, C., and nomination of, 77–78
  Fortas, A., contact with, 318
  Fortas, A., lawyer of, 173
  Johnson, Lyndon, giving all to, 273
  Johnson, Lyndon, story of tragedy as, 281
  lame duck, 178, 182
  legacy of, 89–90, 265
  oath of office ceremony for, 265–266
  power diminution of, 8, 82–83
  power limits of, 7, 34
  prayers for, 40
  speech canceled by, 108
  White House transition of, 262–264
presidential candidate
  Humphrey, H., as, 91, 323
  Kennedy, Robert, as, 78
  Secret Service for, 137–138
presidential election (1968)
  Nixon, R., winning, 250
  State of Union significance to, 10–11
  SVG influence on, 250

presidential prayer breakfast, 58–59
press conference, 103, 109–110
progressive principles, 25
protestors, 216, 220, 226, 266
psychological victory, 58–59
public funds and programs, 125
public opinion, 75, 82, 105
Pueblo, USS (intelligence ship), 6, 32, 35,
    43–44
  armed protection of, 36
  cautious reaction to, 37
  Christian's comments on, 40
  Congress and, 44–46
  crisis manufactured with, 34
  daily meetings on, 41
  Dirksen and, 44–45
  heavy toll on president of, 49
  Helms and diversion of, 45
  hostage release sought of, 34, 49–52
  hostages returned of, 53
  Humphrey, H., comments on, 51
  Johnson, Lady Bird, and pressures from,
    38–39
  national television explanation of, 44
  options dealing with, 32–33, 40–43
  outside territorial waters, 37
  response to, 37
  Soviet Union complicity of, 42
  suicide mission sinking, 43
  U.S. imperialism and, 48
  U.S. position on, 53

racism, 4–5, 111, 115–117
Randolph, Jennings, 213–214
Ransom, Harry, 270–271
Rather, Mary, 260–261
Ray, James Earl, 151
Red Room, 262
Reedy, George, 13–14, 16, 62, 141, 285
  Sutherland visiting, 208
reelection, 89
  Busby editing speech for, 86–87, 91,
    94–95, 97
  Democratic party and, 205–206
  final decision devised for, 93–94
  Johnson, Lady Bird, and decision on, 93
  Johnson, Lady Bird, speech suggestions
    on, 99
  Johnson, Lyndon, not seeking, 16–19,
    87–89, 91, 98–100, 182, 205–206
  Nugent, Luci, and, 21

speech, 86–87, 99–104
statement, 28–29
Reid, Charlotte, 50–51
Reischauer, Edwin, 29
"Report from Vietnam," 71
Republican Convention, 208–209
Republican Party, 234, 316
Republican senators, 166–167
Reston, James, 22–23
retaliation, 47, 50
retirement, 88
Ribicoff, Abraham, 226–227
rioting, 11–12
    of African-Americans, 88
    deadly force lacking on, 123
    preventing, 115
    process of law and, 135–136
    race, 4–5
    understanding causes of, 129
    in Washington, D.C., 112–113, 118–122
Risen, Clay, 6
Rivers, Mendell, 36, 57, 199
Robb, Chuck, 28–29, 65, 263
Robb, Lynda Johnson, 21, 58, 105–106, 269
    birthday party with, 221–222
    emotional reaction of, 95
    pregnant and weary, 84
    speech reaction of, 101
Roche, Chuck, 140
Roche, John, 14, 59, 285
Romania, 200–202
Romney, George, 4
Roosevelt, Franklin, 17–18, 280
Rostow, Elspeth, 98
Rostow, Eugene, 239
Rostow, Walt W., 16, 32–33, 98, 295
    Acheson comments to, 81
    Captain's confession statement of, 38
    decision comments of, 98–99
    Dobrynin meeting with, 188–190
    hard line taken by, 42
    if war goes well comment of, 295
    information sources comment of, 249
    Johnson, Lyndon, and Dobrynin
        meeting, 303
    military victory sought by, 60–63
    Nixon, R., activity exposure and, 251
    Saigon mortar attacks and, 55–56
    securing deal challenge to, 46
    ship seizure comment of, 38–39
    Wheeler supported by, 297

Rovere, Richard, 5
Rowan, Carl, 88
Rowe, Jim, 89, 241–242
Rubin, Jerry, 216
"Ruffles and Flourishes," 269
Rusk, Dean, 32–33, 67, 191, 285
    bombing halt risks from, 297–298
    bombing intensification and, 67–68
    declaration of war comment of, 296
    Diem stern warning from, 79
    Johnson, Lady Bird, recalling testimony
        of, 190
    State of Union address and, 289
Russell, Richard, 23, 161, 163, 166–167
    controversy of, 172
    defection of, 172–173
    Fortas, A., supported by, 170
    Fortas, A., vote and, 180–181
    Johnson, Lyndon, communications cut
        with, 171
    Lawrence nomination and, 170
    Military Assistance Program and, 299
    Thornberry supported by, 170
Russian ambassador, 96–97
Rustin, Bayard, 112
Ryan, William Fitts, 133

Sachs, Alexander, 233
Safe Streets Act, 27, 146–147, 156, 158
Safire, William, 253
Saigon, mortar attacks on, 55–56
Salinger, Pierre, 205
San Antonio Formula
    negotiations built off, 70
    for Vietnam War, 13–14, 24, 56, 69–70,
        210, 279
Sanders, Harold "Barefoot", 131–132
Scali, John, 67
Schlesinger, Arthur, Jr., 29
Schnieder, Wunibald, 272
SCLC. See Southern Christian Leadership
    Conference
Scott, Hugh, 166
Secret Service, 23, 137–138, 144, 149
Secretary of Defense, 32–33
Security Council, 194–195
seminar teaching payment, 180
Senate confirmation, 164, 171, 181–182
Senate Judiciary Committee, 173–174
separation of powers, 169, 175
settlement, negotiated, 16

Sevareid, Eric, 142, 152
Shaffer, Sam, 316–317
Shapiro, Samuel, 126
Sherman, Norman, 241
ship seizure, 38–39
Shriver, Sargent, 94
Sidney, Hugh, 41, 58, 131–132
Sirhan, Sirhan Bishara, 145
sixtieth birthday, 219–224
Smathers, George, 244–246
Smith, Bromley, 252
Smith, John, 46
Smith, Kendall, 275–276
Smith, Margaret Chase, 45, 57, 264
Smith, Merriman, 205–206
Smith, Stephen, 208
social divisions, 277
social justice, 135
social programs, 27
socialism, 186, 202–203
society sickness, 310–311
socio-economic change, 129
soldiers morale, 101
Sorenson, Ted, 76, 211
South Carolina, 305–306
South Korea, 38–39, 47, 50
South Vietnam
    acting in interest of, 234
    increased effort sought from, 63
    independence sought by, 55–56
    leadership inadequate in, 81
    Nixon, R., promising better treatment to,
        235
    Paris Peace talks boycott by, 245–246, 248
    peace process undermined and, 248
    U.S. extrication from, 78–79
    U.S. reliance of, 79
South Vietnamese Government (SVG),
        13–14, 100
    Chennault, A., activities with, 252, 328
    democratic successes in, 23
    Nixon, R., and communications to, 245
    optimism about, 24
    U.S. presidential election influence of,
        250
    U.S. troops influencing, 72
Southeast Asia stability, 297–299
Southern Christian Leadership Conference
    (SCLC), 112
southern Democrats, 166–167, 172, 177, 316
Southwest Texas State College, 214–215

Soviet Union, 96–97
    Czech invasion by, 191, 193–194, 320
    invasion opposition against, 192, 195
    Johnson, Lyndon, criticism and, 196
    Johnson, Lyndon, double-crossed by, 195
    Johnson, Lyndon, playing on fears of, 96
    Nixon, R., exploiting invasion by, 197
    Rusk worrying about response of, 191
    South Carolina invasion plans of,
        305–306
    U.S. condemnation of, 195
    U.S. relations with, 321
    U.S. Romania warnings to, 200–201
    U.S. tensions with, 185–186
    USS Pueblo and complicity of, 42
    Wheeler and military strength of, 199
"Soviets Enter Czechoslovakia," 193–194
speech, 30–31, 146
    Busby's reelection, 86–87, 91, 94–95, 97
    civil rights meeting and, 113
    Congress and preparations of, 124
    Humphrey, H., acceptance, 229–230
    Johnson, Lyndon, personal sacrifices in,
        304
    Johnson, Lyndon, planning Chicago, 218
    Nixon, R., support encouraged in,
        270–271
    Nugent, L., reaction to, 101
    president canceling, 108
    racism and discrimination in, 117
    reelection, 86–87, 99–104
spending cuts, 28
spying charges, 49
St. Francis of Assisi, 229
St. Louis Post Dispatch, 253
St. Patrick's Cathedral, 148–150
state funeral, 144–145
State of the Union address, 6, 11, 19, 98–99
    Busby's observations of, 10, 28
    Califano watching, 24
    early drafts of, 14
    economic issues in, 25–26
    evaluations of, 30–31
    final draft reading of, 20, 23
    Johnson, Lady Bird, comments on, 10,
        21–22
    Johnson, Lady Bird, optimism of, 30–31
    Johnson, Lyndon, successes outlined in,
        259
    observations on, 10
    polls on, 30

presidential election significance of, 10–11
reelection statement and, 28–29
Rostow, W., recommendations on, 16
Rusk and, 289
Secret Service agents and, 23
Vietnam discussion in, 23
violence and unrest in, 26–27
Stennis, John, 57
Stevenson, Coke, 160
Stokes, Carl, 29
"Stop the War," 225
strategic missiles, 190
Stuart, Gilbert, 262
suicide mission, 43
Sullivan, Leon, 114–115
summit meeting, 202–203
Supreme Court
appointments, 164
businessmen with cases in, 180
decisions from, 168–169
Executive Branch separation with, 168, 318
nominations, 161–162, 168
as politicized, 183–184
Senate confirmation failure for, 181–182
Warren serving on, 313
Sutherland, Jack, 208
SVG. See South Vietnamese Government

"Take My Hand, Precious Lord," 116, 132
Talmadge, Herman, 166
task force, 70, 72
tax surcharge, 27
Taxonist Corps Toilers, 323
Taylor, Maxwell, 81, 152–153
Teachers Corps, 22–23
teleprompter failure, 290
television, 44, 117
Temple, Larry, 59, 120, 161, 179, 285
information leak investigated by, 206
Tennery, B. J., 180
territorial waters, 37
Tet Offensive, 6, 46, 71, 277, 279
characterization of, 63–64
complete failure characterization of, 58–59
crisis of confidence on, 75
desperate attack of, 57–58
differing opinions on, 61–62
illusions of war and, 104

McPherson influenced by, 59
North Vietnamese launching, 55–56
pessimism from, 71–72
problems caused by, 66
show of strength in, 294–295
Texas schoolteacher story, 173
Thayer, Walter, 178–179
Thompson, Tommy, 190, 201, 203, 285
Thornberry, Homer, 166–167, 285
Chief Justice nomination of, 7
convention watched by, 222
Johnson, Lady Bird, comments on, 161
Johnson, Lyndon, character flaws and, 278–279
nomination discussed of, 161–162
nomination process failure of, 183
Russell supporting, 170
Senate confirmation and, 164
Thurmond, Strom, 36, 125, 135–136, 176–177
Tito, Josip, 199–200
Tower, John, 239, 251
treason, 237, 239
troops
costs of increase in, 69
increase in, 63–65, 67–68
SVG and U.S., 72
Westmoreland's allotment of, 74
Wheeler and plan for increase in, 63–65, 67–70
Truesdell, Norman, 272
Trump, Donald, 280
Truxton, USS, 43
Tuck, William, 134
Turner Joy (ship), 38–39
Tydings, Joseph, 147–148, 156

U Thant, 71, 106
Union Station, 152–153
United Nations, 192
United Nations Charter, 194–195
United States (U.S.)
annual production of, 25
conservative shift in, 158, 162
crime rates in, 26
Czech refugees to, 201–202
foreign policy of, 23
Kim Il-Sung demand on, 48, 51–52
military intervention unlikely by, 198
Nixon stating overextension of, 36
North Korean threats to, 280

United States (U.S.) (cont.)
  Park squeezing, 35
  political and social divisions in, 277
  power limits of, 8, 186–187
  problems facing, 11
  South Vietnam extrication of, 78–79
  South Vietnam's reliance on, 79
  Soviet aggression condemnation from,
    195
  Soviet relations with, 321
  Soviet Union tensions with, 185–186
  Soviet Union warnings from, 200–201
  SVG and troops of, 72
  SVG influence on presidential election
    of, 250
  USS Pueblo and imperialism of, 48
  USS Pueblo position of, 53
  Vietnam War killing soldiers of, 65
  violence in, 121, 128

Valenti, Jack, 2–3, 310–311
Valera, Eamon de, 151
Van Dyk, Ted, 241
Vance, Cyrus, 47–48, 122–123, 238–239,
  285–286
Vice President selection, 228, 322
Viet Cong, 210, 295
Vietnam trip, 1–3
Vietnam War, 3
  anti-war protestors and, 3
  bombing effectiveness in, 69, 80
  bombing halt considered in, 74, 80, 232
  Califano and leadership concerns on, 13
  citizens feelings toward, 60
  Communist conspiracy and, 33–34
  as corrosive topic, 24–25
  crisis of confidence on, 56, 74–75
  Democratic Convention platform on,
    223–226
  Democratic Party damaged by, 213
  desperate attack in, 57–58
  enemy casualties reported by, 62
  extended bombing targets in, 296
  feedback wanted on, 87
  financial costs of, 73
  growing criticism of, 73–74
  Humphrey, H., position on, 212, 215
  independent commission on, 76
  isolation and resentment caused by, 8
  Johnson, Lady Bird, and worries about,
    74–75

Johnson, Lyndon, tortured by, 3, 60–61,
  82–83, 88, 234, 265, 279
Kennedy, Robert, and policy reevaluation
  of, 77–78
Kennedy, Robert, using, 83
McNamara's comments on, 56–57
military resources diverted from, 33–34,
  41, 45
mood swings over, 59
negotiated settlement and, 16
Nixon, R., strategy on, 233–234
peace as goal in, 24, 96, 100
pessimism toward, 71–72
polls showing approval and, 289
potential paths of, 297
public opinion about, 75, 82
reelection speech including, 100
Rostow, W., comment on, 295
San Antonio Formula for, 13–14, 24, 56,
  69–70, 210, 279
shifting opinions about, 67
soldiers morale and, 101
with South Korea, 50
State of Union discussion on, 23
Tet Offensive destroying illusions about,
  104
U.S. soldiers killed in, 65
Valenti comments on, 3
Westmoreland's version of, 71, 126
withdrawal with honor from, 89–90
violence, 26–27, 155
  African-American leaders denouncing,
    114–115
  African-Americans and, 119
  civil rights and, 117, 124
  crisis management of, 110–111
  government purveyor of, 107
  gun control and, 147
  King, M. L., followed by, 134
  lawlessness and, 142–143
  neutralizing, 110
  Nixon, R., and Chicago, 325
  political, 6–7
  protestor warnings on, 220
  in State of Union address, 26–27
  in U.S., 121, 128
Vo Nguyen Gap, 79
Voting Rights Act (1965), 4

Wallace, George, 125
War on Poverty, 5

Warnke, Paul, 72
Warren, Earl, 160, 313
Warren Commission, 142
Warsaw Pact allies, 188, 191, 194–195
Washington, D.C., 112–113, 118–122
Washington, Walter, 114, 121, 141
Washington Post, 104, 193–194, 304
Watergate, 254–255
Watson, Marvin, 24–25, 86, 98, 108, 285–286
  interview of, 217
  protestor violence warnings of, 220
"We Shall Overcome," 116
Weaver, Robert, 116–118
Weiler, Mary, 5
Weisl, Ed, 314
Westmoreland, William, 55, 67–68, 285–286
  bombing halt warning from, 213–214
  enemy casualties reported by, 62
  morale issue and, 95
  troop allotment request of, 74
  urgent messages from, 64
  Vietnam War version from, 71, 126
Wheeler, Earle, 32–33, 45, 55, 285–286
  military victory sought by, 61–63
  no military action comment of, 191
  optimistic appraisal from, 82
  Rostow, W., supporting, 297
  Soviet military strength comment of, 199
  troop increase plan and, 63–65, 67–70
White, Theodore, 226–227, 241
White, William, 3, 28–29, 230
White House, 4, 34, 314
  Chennault, A., monitored by, 241–242
  Christopher gathering information for, 314–315
  Democratic Convention shaped by, 207
  final farewells and, 269
  Humphrey, H., humiliated by, 215

Humphrey, H., with gathering at, 262
Johnson, Lady Bird, departure from, 264
Johnson, Lady Bird, goodbyes to, 261
Johnson, Lyndon, and shackles of, 92
  leaks feared from, 19–20
  North Korea castigation of, 45
  presidential transition gathering at, 262–264
white society, 115–116
white vigilantes, 128
Whitman, Charles, 156
Whittier, John Greenleaf, 281
Wicker, Tom, 88
Wiggins, Russ, 259
Wilkins, Roy, 275
Wilson, Harold, 46, 62–63
Wilson, Woodrow, 87–88
wiretapping, 157
Wise Men (advisory group), 80–83
Witcover, Jules, 5–6
withdrawal with honor, 89–90
Woodruff, Robert, 108
Woods, Randall, 5–6
Woods, Rose Mary, 235–236
Woodward, Gilbert, 52–53
World War III fears, 40, 64–65
Wright, John, 43

X File, 252, 329

Yastrzemski, Carl, 32
"Yellow Rose of Texas," 269
Young, Andrew, 108
Young, Whitney, 178–179
Youngblood, Rufus, 147–148

Zablocki, Clement J., 199